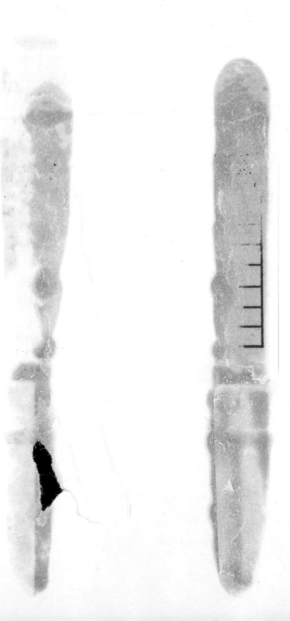

THE
YALE REVIEW
ANTHOLOGY

THE
YALE REVIEW
ANTHOLOGY

Edited with an Introduction by

WILBUR CROSS *and* HELEN MACAFEE

Essay Index Reprint Series

 BOOKS FOR LIBRARIES PRESS
FREEPORT, NEW YORK

INTERNATIONAL STANDARD BOOK NUMBER:

0-8369-2098-8

LIBRARY OF CONGRESS CATALOG CARD NUMBER:

72-128336

PRINTED IN THE UNITED STATES OF AMERICA

INTRODUCTION

I N one of his many fine poems which "The Yale Review" has published, Robert Frost gave an old phrase a new birth, as his way is, by writing of "outer" and "inner weather." We have been tempted to borrow his words and use them for a purpose of our own—to describe our idea of a magazine. Let us say, then, that a magazine as we think of it is a kind of weather report, aiming to record both outer and inner weather: the world around us and the world within. This might seem to be enough of a task, but actually the magazine of liberal intentions has more to do than that. It has to interpret as well as record, proposing a direction for action and thought. In so far as contributors and editors perform their work well, each issue analyzes the interrelations of the main pressure areas, high or low, public or private; and each relates, in the light of its principles, the time we feel slipping through our fingers to time gone and time to come.

It has been said that in the editing which all of us do to our memories we are apt to forget the fair weather and to dwell on the storms. So in New England we still talk of the blizzard of 1888 when March comes round—not to mention the hurricane of 1938, in the unforgettable September of that year, the month of Munich. But the generation which came of age about 1911— when "The Yale Review" first appeared in its present form— can hardly be blamed if it has been preoccupied with disasters, especially what we may call "unnatural" as opposed to "natural" disasters. Despite some famous lashings of wind and rain, man has outdone nature in trouble-making these last three decades. Fine breathing spells in human affairs have been few, and brief as dreams.

For this reason, most of the authors who have written for us on public life have had to take a grave tone. As it happened, the leading article in our first issue, for Autumn, 1911—an article by William Graham Sumner entitled "War"—was a startling forecast of the troubles we have since gone through. Looking ahead, Sumner wrote: "There is only one thing rationally to be expected, and that is a frightful effusion of blood in revolution and war during the century now opening."

Just as most of us remember the storms rather than the sunny days, so we are all apt to call to mind our right prophecies rather than our wrong ones. Of course, not all the assertions on world affairs in succeeding pages of "The Yale Review" have been so amply—and for the world so bitterly—borne out as Professor Sumner's. But readers, we feel sure, will pardon us if we do not try to recall here the errors of commission or omission made in our now large company of contributions, particularly as we believe they will agree with us that the company as a whole has stood up remarkably well under the fierce and rapid fire of events. Like other editors, we are more likely to be engrossed in the future than the past, and when we ourselves think of old errors, it is chiefly to consider how we can guard against going wrong again. Aside from the authors themselves, only their editors can appreciate to the full the difficulties of analyzing and interpreting the great issues of the day, which must be discussed, because of the urgency of decision upon them, even though the archives that might disclose the complete truth are still sealed. We should like to cite for gallantry the long line of our writers who have striven skilfully and generously to give shape and substance to the vague or deceptive features of the outer weather in which we have lived. Many of them, it seems, have written better than they knew. To judge from the numerous requests received for the right of reprinting, years after a first appearance in some cases, articles that were directed towards a particular crisis have often proved to be hardy perennials.

Yet a good many articles on current questions, no matter how broadly conceived, are bound sooner or later to lose their hold— because their subjects subside or pass into a new phase. We have, therefore, chosen for this anthology of our longer prose contributions fewer of the able articles on public questions than of contributions in other kinds. Among the latter it has been hard to keep the list down to a feasible length because of the number that seemed to call for reprinting. Old friends of the magazine will miss—as we do ourselves—not a few old favorites. Nevertheless, we hope that this selection, within its limits, will appear to symbolize fairly the work we have published. Furthermore, we hope that it will at least suggest major characteristics of the generation which "The Yale Review" has spanned—its wide range of intellectual effort and its vitality of literary expression, which has found new forms or new uses for the general article, the critical essay, and the short story. Some of the pieces here reprinted were published long ago—as, for example, Walter Lippmann's youthful essay, "Second-Best Statesmen," from our Summer, 1922, issue; or, from an earlier issue, Professor Beers's delightful recollections of Emerson, which gave us a sense of being in the apostolic succession. As we have lately re-read these and the other selections, it seems to us that they still keep their prime freshness and vigor.

Soon after "The Yale Review" assumed its present form and its subtitle, "A National Quarterly," an English critic remarked that to be exact the magazine should style itself "A Cosmopolitan Quarterly." It is true that we welcomed then, and we welcome now, collaborators from other countries than our own. This, too, despite problems of translation involved—which are, as all who have anything to do with them know, a peculiar weariness to the flesh. We are glad to publish again here, with the American essays and short stories, work that speaks for the great cultural traditions of England and Germany, Russia and France.

In these times of mortal division, the outer weather may not look propitious for such future reunions of different members of the human family. The more reason, then, why humanists (among whom we count ourselves) should strive with all their wisdom and strength towards a world in which men of good will and sound mind, whatever their race or walk of life, may yet work together in freedom and at peace. If that effort is made on a grand scale—we believe and shall continue to believe—it will be possible once again to say happily, as Emily Dickinson said in lines printed in "The Yale Review" relating to the inner weather:

> Somehow myself survived the night
> And entered with the day.

To our poets, book critics, and other contributors whose work could not be included here, as well as to the authors represented, we should like to acknowledge our esteem and gratitude. As we have reminded them many times in these last thirty years, "The Yale Review" is mainly what they have made it. We wish especially to thank the authors whose contributions appear in this anthology, and their literary executors, agents, and publishers in various cases, for their courtesy in allowing us a second use of their good things—good things of many kinds, from those that would lighten a dull hour with laughter to those that open the mind to humanity's deepest concerns.

HELEN MACAFEE
WILBUR CROSS

ACKNOWLEDGMENTS

IN addition to the authors, the following friends of "The Yale Review" have helped to make this anthology possible by granting permission to reprint, and their coöperation is gratefully acknowledged: The Clarendon Press for *Greek Ideals in Modern Civilization* by Sir Richard Livingstone from "Greek Ideals and Modern Life"; Columbia University and Harcourt, Brace & Company for *Law and Literature* by Benjamin Cardozo from "Law and Literature"; Coward-McCann, Inc., for *Queens of France* by Thornton Wilder from "The Long Christmas Dinner and Other Plays in One Act"; Doubleday, Doran & Company, Inc., and the executors of the Hugh Walpole Estate for *The Whistle* by Hugh Walpole from "All Souls' Night" (1933); Duell, Sloan & Pearce, Inc., for *Country Full of Swedes* by Erskine Caldwell from "Jackpot"; Harcourt, Brace & Company for *How Should One Read a Book?* by Virginia Woolf from "The Second Common Reader" (1932); Harper & Brothers for *Ports of Call* by H. M. Tomlinson from "Pipe All Hands!" and *Uniqueness of Man* by Julian Huxley from "Man Stands Alone"; Alfred A. Knopf, Inc., for *Broomsticks* by Walter de la Mare from "Broomsticks and Other Tales," *Disillusion* by Thomas Mann from "Stories of Three Decades," and *The Greatest Love Story in the World* by Clarence Day, Jr., from "After All," where it is called *The Sequel to Ibsen's "A Doll's House"*; Longmans, Green & Company, for *Montaigne* by André Gide from "The Living Thoughts of Montaigne"; The Macmillan Company for *Patterns of Success* by John Hodgdon Bradley from "Patterns of Survival," and *Second-Best Statesmen* by Walter Lippmann from "Men of Destiny"; Oxford University Press (New York) for *The Power of the Written Word* by Stephen Vincent Benét from "A Summons to the Free" in the series, *America in a World at War;* Stanford University Press for *The American Writers and the New World* by Archibald MacLeish; The Viking Press, Inc., for *The Egg Tree* by James Still from "River of Earth" (1940).

CONTENTS

IMAGINATIVE LITERATURE

ESSAYS AND SKETCHES

HOW SHOULD ONE READ A BOOK?

By VIRGINIA WOOLF

AT this late hour of the world's history, books are to be found in almost every room in the house —in the nursery, in the drawing room, in the dining room, in the kitchen. But in some houses they have become such a company that they have to be accommodated with a room of their own—a reading room, a library, a study. Let us imagine that we are now in such a room; that it is a sunny room, with windows opening on a garden, so that we can hear the trees rustling, the gardener talking, the donkey braying, the old women gossiping at the pump—and all the ordinary processes of life pursuing the casual irregular way which they have pursued these many hundreds of years. As casually, as persistently, books have been coming together on the shelves. Novels, poems, histories, memoirs, dictionaries, maps, directories; black letter books and brand new books; books in French and Greek and Latin; of all shapes and sizes and values, bought for purposes of research, bought to amuse a railway journey, bought by miscellaneous beings, of one temperament and another, serious and frivolous, men of action and men of letters.

Now, one may well ask oneself, strolling into such a room as this, how am I to read these books? What is the right way to set about it? They are so many and so various. My appetite is so fitful and so capricious. What am I to do to get the utmost possible pleasure out of them? And is it pleasure, or profit, or what is it that I should seek? I will lay before you some of the thoughts that have come to me on such an occasion as this. But you will notice the note of interrogation at the end of my title. One may think about reading as much as one chooses, but no one is going to lay down laws about it. Here in this room, if nowhere else, we breathe the air of freedom. Here simple and learned, man and woman are alike. For though reading seems so simple—a mere matter of knowing the alphabet—it is indeed so difficult that it is doubtful whether anybody knows anything about it. Paris is the capital of France; King John signed the Magna Charta; those are facts; those can be taught; but how are we to teach people so to read "Paradise Lost" as to see that it is a great poem, or "Tess of the D'Urbervilles" so as to see that it is a good novel? How are we to learn the art of reading for ourselves? Without attempting to lay down laws upon a subject that has not been legalized, I will make a few suggestions, which may serve to show you how not to read, or to stimulate you to think out better methods of your own.

And directly we begin to ask how should one read a book we are faced by the fact that books differ; there are poems, novels, biographies on the book shelf there; each differs from the other as a tiger differs from a tortoise, a tortoise from an elephant. Our attitude must always be changing, it is clear. From different books we must ask different qualities. Simple as this sounds, people are always behaving as if all books were of the same species— as if there were only tortoises or nothing but tigers. It makes them furious to find a novelist bringing Queen Victoria to the throne six months before her time; they will praise a poet enthusiastically for teaching them that a violet has four petals and a daisy almost invariably ten. You will save a great deal of time and temper better kept for worthier objects if you will try to make out before you begin to read what qualities you expect of a novelist, what of a poet, what of a biographer. The tortoise is bald and shiny; the tiger has a thick coat of yellow fur. So books too differ: one has its fur, the other has its baldness.

Yes; but for all that the problem is not so simple in a library as at the Zoölogical Gardens. Books have a great deal in common; they are always overflowing their boundaries; they are always breeding new species from unexpected matches among themselves. It is difficult to know how to approach them, to which species each belongs. But if we remember, as we turn to the bookcase, that each of these books was written by a pen which, consciously or unconsciously, tried to trace out a design, avoiding this, accepting that, adventuring the other; if we try to follow the writer in his experiment from the first word to the last, without imposing our design upon him, then we shall have a good chance of getting hold of the right end of the string.

To read a book well, one should read it as if one were writing it. Begin not by sitting on the bench among the judges but by standing in the dock with the criminal. Be his fellow worker, become his accomplice. Even, if you wish merely to read books, begin by writing them. For this certainly is true: one cannot write the most ordinary little story, attempt to describe the simplest event—meeting a beggar, shall we say, in the street—without coming up against difficulties that the greatest of novelists have had to face. In order that we may realize, however briefly and crudely, the main divisions into which novelists group themselves, let us imagine how differently Defoe, Jane Austen, and Thomas Hardy would describe the same incident—this meeting a beggar in the street. Defoe is a master of narrative. His prime effort will be to reduce the beggar's story to perfect order and simplicity. This happened first, that next, the other thing third. He will put in nothing, however attractive, that will tire the reader unnecessarily, or divert his attention from what he wishes him to know. He will also make us believe, since he is a master, not of romance or of comedy, but of narrative, that everything that happened is true. He will be extremely precise therefore. This happened, as he tells us on the first pages of "Robinson Crusoe," on the first of September. More subtly and artfully, he will hypnotize us into a state of belief by dropping out casually some little unnecessary fact—for instance, "my father called me one morning into his chamber, where he was confined by the gout." His father's gout is not necessary to the story, but it is necessary to the truth of the story, for it is thus that anybody who is speaking the truth adds some small irrelevant detail without thinking. Further, he will choose a type of sentence which is flowing but not too full, exact but not epigrammatic. His aim will be to present the thing itself without distortion from his own angle of vision. He will meet the subject face to face, foursquare, without turning aside for a moment to point out that this was tragic, or that beautiful; and his aim is perfectly achieved.

But let us not for a moment confuse it with Jane Austen's aim. Had she met a beggar woman, no doubt she would have been interested in the beggar's story. But she would have seen at once that for her purposes the whole incident must be transformed. Streets and the open air and adventures mean nothing to her, artistically. It is character that interests her. She would at once make the beggar into a comfortable elderly man of the upper middle classes, seated by his fireside at his ease. Then, instead of plunging into the story vigorously and veraciously, she will write a few paragraphs of accurate and artfully seasoned introduction, summing up the circumstances and sketching the character of the gentleman she wishes us to know. "Matrimony as the origin of change was always disagreeable" to Mr. Woodhouse, she says. Almost immediately, she thinks it well to let us see that her words are corroborated by Mr. Woodhouse himself. We hear him talking. "Poor Miss Taylor—I wish she were here again. What a pity it is that Mr. Weston ever thought of her." And when Mr. Woodhouse has talked enough to reveal himself from the inside, she then thinks it time to let us see him through his daughter's eyes. "You got Hannah that good place. Nobody thought of Hannah till you mentioned her." Thus she shows us Emma flattering him and humoring him. Finally then, we have Mr. Woodhouse's character seen from three different points of view at once; as he sees himself; as his daughter sees him; and as he is seen by the marvellous eye of that invisible lady Jane Austen herself. All three meet in one, and thus we can pass round her characters free, apparently, from any guidance but our own.

Now let Thomas Hardy choose the same theme—a beggar met in the street—and at once two great changes will be visible. The street will be transformed into a vast and sombre heath; the man or woman will take on some of the size and indistinctness of a statue. Further, the relations of this human being will not be towards other people, but towards the heath, towards man as law-giver, towards those powers which are in control of man's destiny. Once more our perspective will be completely changed. All the qualities which were admirable in "Robinson Crusoe," admirable in "Emma," will be neglected or absent. The direct literal statement of Defoe is gone. There is none of the clear, exact brilliance of Jane Austen. Indeed, if we come to Hardy from one of these great writers we shall exclaim at first that he is "melodramatic" or "unreal" compared with them. But we should bethink us that there are at least two sides to the human soul; the light side and the dark side. In company, the light side of the mind is exposed; in solitude, the dark. Both are equally real, equally important. But a novelist will always tend to expose one rather than the other; and Hardy, who is a novelist of the dark side, will contrive that no clear, steady light falls upon his people's faces, that they are not closely observed in drawing rooms, that they come in contact with moors, sheep, the sky and the stars, and in their solitude are directly at the mercy of the gods. If Jane Austen's characters are real in the drawing room, they would not exist at all upon the top of Stonehenge. Feeble and clumsy in drawing rooms, Hardy's people are large-limbed and vigorous out of doors. To achieve his purpose Hardy is neither literal and four-square like Defoe, nor deft and pointed like Jane Austen. He is cumbrous, involved, metaphorical. Where Jane Austen describes manners, he describes nature. Where she is matter of fact, he is romantic and poetical. As both are great artists, each is careful to observe the laws of his own perspective, and will not be found confusing us (as so many lesser writers do) by introducing two different kinds of reality into the same book.

Yet it is very difficult not to wish them less scrupulous. Frequent are the complaints that Jane Austen is too prosaic, Thomas Hardy too melodramatic. And we have to remind ourselves that it is necessary to approach every writer differently in order to get from him all he can give us. We have to remember that it is one of the qualities of greatness that it brings heaven and earth and human nature into conformity with its own vision. It is by reason of this masterliness of theirs, this uncompromising idiosyncrasy, that greater writers often require us to make heroic efforts in order to read them rightly. They bend us and break us. To go from Jane Austen to Hardy, from Peacock to Trollope, from Scott to Meredith, from Richardson to Kipling, is to be wrenched and distorted, thrown this way and then that. Besides, everyone is born with a natural bias of his own in one direction rather than in another. He instinctively accepts Hardy's vision rather than Jane Austen's, and, reading with the current and not against it, is carried on easily and swiftly by the impetus of his own bent to the heart of his author's genius. But then Jane Austen is repulsive to him. He can scarcely stagger through the desert of her novels.

Sometimes this natural antagonism is too great to be overcome, but trial is always worth making. For these difficult and inaccessible books, with all their preliminary harshness, often yield the richest fruits in the end, and so curiously is the brain compounded that while tracts of literature repel at one season, they are appetizing and essential at another.

If, then, this is true—that books are of very different types, and that to read them rightly we have to bend our imaginations powerfully, first one way, then another—it is clear that reading is one of the most arduous and exhausting of occupations. Often the pages fly before us and we seem, so keen is our interest, to be living and not even holding the volume in our hands. But the more exciting the book, the more danger we run of over-reading. The symptoms are familiar. Suddenly the book becomes dull as ditchwater and heavy as lead. We yawn and stretch and cannot attend. The highest flights of Shakespeare and Milton become intolerable. And we say to ourselves—is Keats a fool or am I?— a painful question, a question, moreover, that need not be asked if we realized how great a part the art of not reading plays in the art of reading. To be able to read books without reading them, to skip and saunter, to suspend judgment, to lounge and loaf down the alleys and bye-streets of letters is the best way of rejuvenating one's own creative power. All biographies and memoirs, all the hybrid books which are largely made up of facts, serve to restore to us the power of reading real books—that is to say, works of pure imagination. That they serve also to impart knowledge and to improve the mind is true and important, but if we are considering how to read books for pleasure, not how to provide an adequate pension for one's widow, this other property of theirs is even more valuable and important. But here again one should know what one is after. One is after rest, and fun, and oddity, and some stimulus to one's own jaded creative power.

One has left one's bare and angular tower and is strolling along the street looking in at the open windows. After solitude and concentration, the open air, the sight of other people absorbed in innumerable activities, comes upon us with an indescribable fascination.

The windows of the houses are open; the blinds are drawn up. One can see the whole household without their knowing that they are being seen. One can see them sitting round the dinner table, talking, reading, playing games. Sometimes they seem to be quarrelling—but what about? Or they are laughing—but what is the joke? Down in the basement the cook is reading a newspaper aloud, while the housemaid is making a piece of toast; in comes the kitchen maid and they all start talking at the same moment—but what are they saying? Upstairs a girl is dressing to go to a party. But where is she going? There is an old lady sitting at her bedroom window with some kind of wool work in her hand and a fine green parrot in a cage beside her. And what is she thinking? All this life has somehow come together; there is a reason for it; a coherency in it, could one but seize it. The biographer answers the innumerable questions which we ask as we stand outside on the pavement looking in at the open window. Indeed there is nothing more interesting than to pick one's way about among these vast depositories of facts, to make up the lives of men and women, to create their complex minds and households from the extraordinary abundance and litter and confusion of matter which lies strewn about. A thimble, a skull, a pair of scissors, a sheaf of sonnets, are given us, and we have to create, to combine, to put these incongruous things together. There is, too, a quality in facts, an emotion which comes from knowing that men and women actually did and suffered these things, which only the greatest novelists can surpass. Captain Scott, starving and freezing to death in the snow, affects us as deeply as any made-up story of adventure by Conrad or Defoe; but it affects us differently. The biography differs from the novel. To ask a biographer to give us the same kind of pleasure that we get from a novelist is to misuse and misread him. Directly he says "John Jones was born at five-thirty in the morning of August 13, 1862," he has committed himself, focussed his lens upon fact, and if he then begins to romance, the perspective becomes blurred, we grow suspicious, and our faith in his integrity as a writer is destroyed. In the same way fact destroys fiction. If Thackeray, for example, had quoted an actual newspaper account of the Battle of Waterloo in "Vanity Fair," the whole fabric of his story would have been destroyed, as a stone destroys a bubble.

But it is undoubted that these hybrid books, these warehouses and depositories of facts, play a great part in resting the brain and restoring its zest of imagination. The work of building up a life for oneself from skulls, thimbles, scissors, and sonnets stimulates our interest in creation and rouses our wish to see the work beautifully and powerfully done by a Flaubert or a Tolstoi. Moreover, however interesting facts may be, they are an inferior form of fiction, and gradually we become impatient of their weakness and diffuseness, of their compromises and evasions, of the slovenly sentences which they make for themselves, and are eager to revive ourselves with the greater intensity and truth of fiction.

It is necessary to have in hand an immense reserve of imaginative energy in order to attack the steeps of poetry. Here are none of those gradual introductions, those resemblances to the familiar world of daily life with which the novelist entices us into his world of imagination. All is violent, opposite, unrelated. But various causes, such as bad books, the worry of carrying on life efficiently, the intermittent but powerful shocks dealt us by beauty, and the incalculable impulses of our own minds and bodies frequently put us into that state of mind in which poetry is a necessity. The sight of a crocus in a garden will suddenly bring to mind all the spring days that have ever been. One then desires the general, not the particular; the whole, not the detail; to turn uppermost the dark side of the mind; to be in contact with silence, solitude, and all men and women and not this particular Richard, or that particular Anne. Metaphors are then more expressive than plain statements.

Thus in order to read poetry rightly, one must be in a rash, an extreme, a generous state of mind in which many of the supports and comforts of literature are done without. Its power of

make-believe, its representative power, is dispensed with in favor
of its extremities and extravagances. The representation is often
at a very far remove from the thing represented, so that we have
to use all our energies of mind to grasp the relation between, for
example, the song of a nightingale and the images and ideas
which that song stirs in the mind. Thus reading poetry often
seems a state of rhapsody in which rhyme and metre and sound
stir the mind as wine and dance stir the body, and we read on,
understanding with the senses, not with the intellect, in a state
of intoxication. Yet all this intoxication and intensity of delight
depend upon the exactitude and truth of the image, on its being
the counterpart of the reality within. Remote and extravagant as
some of Shakespeare's images seem, far-fetched and ethereal as
some of Keats's, at the moment of reading they seem the cap
and culmination of the thought; its final expression. But it is useless to labor the matter in cold blood. Anyone who has read a
poem with pleasure will remember the sudden conviction, the
sudden recollection (for it seems sometimes as if we were about
to say, or had in some previous existence already said, what
Shakespeare is actually now saying), which accompany the reading of poetry, and give it its exaltation and intensity. But such
reading is attended, whether consciously or unconsciously, with
the utmost stretch and vigilance of the faculties, of the reason no
less than of the imagination. We are always verifying the poet's
statements, making a flying comparison, to the best of our powers,
between the beauty he makes outside and the beauty we are
aware of within. For the humblest among us is endowed with the
power of comparison. The simplest (provided he loves reading) has that already within him to which he makes what is
given him—by poet or novelist—correspond.

    With that saying, of course, the cat is out of the bag. For this
admission that we can compare, discriminate, brings us to this
further point. Reading is not merely sympathizing and understanding; it is also criticizing and judging. Hitherto our endeavor has been to read books as a writer writes them. We have
been trying to understand, to appreciate, to interpret, to sym-
pathize. But now, when the book is finished, the reader must
leave the dock and mount the bench. He must cease to be the

friend; he must become the judge. And this is no mere figure of speech. The mind seems ("seems," for all is obscure that takes place in the mind) to go through two processes in reading. One might be called the actual reading; the other the after reading. During the actual reading, when we hold the book in our hands, there are incessant distractions and interruptions. New impressions are always completing or cancelling the old. One's judgment is suspended, for one does not know what is coming next. Surprise, admiration, boredom, interest, succeed each other in such quick succession that when, at last, the end is reached, one is for the most part in a state of complete bewilderment. Is it good? or bad? What kind of book is it? How good a book is it? The friction of reading and the emotion of reading beat up too much dust to let us find clear answers to these questions. If we are asked our opinion, we cannot give it. Parts of the book seem to have sunk away, others to be starting out in undue prominence. Then perhaps it is better to take up some different pursuit—to walk, to talk, to dig, to listen to music. The book upon which we have spent so much time and thought fades entirely out of sight. But suddenly, as one is picking a snail from a rose, tying a shoe, perhaps, doing something distant and different, the whole book floats to the top of the mind complete. Some process seems to have been finished without one's being aware of it. The different details which have accumulated in reading assemble themselves in their proper places. The book takes on a definite shape; it becomes a castle, a cowshed, a gothic ruin, as the case may be. Now one can think of the book as a whole, and the book as a whole is different, and gives one a different emotion, from the book received currently in several different parts. Its symmetry and proportion, its confusion and distortion can cause great delight or great disgust apart from the pleasure given by each detail as it is separately realized. Holding this complete shape in mind it now becomes necessary to arrive at some opinion of the book's merits, for though it is possible to receive the greatest pleasure and excitement from the first process, the actual reading—though this is of the utmost importance, it is not so profound or so lasting as the pleasure we get when the second process—the after reading—is finished, and we hold the book clear, secure, and (to the best of our powers) complete in our minds.

But how, we may ask, are we to decide any of these questions—is it good, or is it bad?—how good is it, how bad is it? Not much help can be looked for from outside. Critics abound; criticisms pullulate; but minds differ too much to admit of close correspondence in matters of detail, and nothing is more disastrous than to crush one's own foot into another person's shoe. When we want to decide a particular case, we can best help ourselves, not by reading criticism, but by realizing our own impression as acutely as possible and referring this to the judgments which we have gradually formulated in the past. There they hang in the wardrobe of our mind—the shapes of the books we have read, as we hung them up and put them away when we had done with them. If we have just read "Clarissa Harlowe," for example, let us see how it shows up against the shape of "Anna Karenina." At once the outlines of the two books are cut out against each other as a house with its chimneys bristling and its gables sloping is cut out against a harvest moon. At once Richardson's qualities—his verbosity, his obliqueness—are contrasted with Tolstoi's brevity and directness. And what is the reason of this difference in their approach? And how does our emotion at different crises of the two books compare? And what must we attribute to the eighteenth century, and what to Russia and the translator? But the questions which suggest themselves are innumerable. They ramify infinitely, and many of them are apparently irrelevant. Yet it is by asking them and pursuing the answers as far as we can go that we arrive at our standard of values, and decide in the end that the book we have just read is of this kind or of that, has merit in that degree or in this. And it is now, when we have kept closely to our own impression, for-mulated independently our own judgment, that we can most profitably help ourselves to the judgments of the great critics —Dryden, Johnson, and the rest. It is when we can best defend our own opinions that we get most from theirs.

So, then—to sum up the different points we have reached in this essay—have we found any answer to our question, how should we read a book? Clearly, no answer that will do for everyone; but perhaps a few suggestions. In the first place, a good reader will give the writer the benefit of every doubt; the help of all his imagination; will follow as closely, interpret as intelligently as he can. In the next place, he will judge with the utmost severity. Every book, he will remember, has the right to be judged by the best of its kind. He will be adventurous, broad in his choice, true to his own instincts, yet ready to consider those of other people. This is an outline which can be filled in at taste and at leisure, but to read something after this fashion is to be a reader whom writers respect. It is by the means of such readers that masterpieces are helped into the world.

If the moralists ask us how we can justify our love of reading, we can make use of some such excuse as this. But if we are honest, we know that no such excuse is needed. It is true that we get nothing whatsoever except pleasure from reading; it is true that the wisest of us is unable to say what that pleasure may be. But that pleasure—mysterious, unknown, useless as it is—is enough. That pleasure is so curious, so complex, so immensely fertilizing to the mind of anyone who enjoys it, and so wide in its effects, that it would not be in the least surprising to discover, on the day of judgment when secrets are revealed and the obscure is made plain, that the reason why we have grown from pigs to men and women, and come out from our caves, and dropped our bows and arrows, and sat round the fire and talked and drunk and made merry and given to the poor and helped the sick and made pavements and houses and erected some sort of shelter and society on the waste of the world, is nothing but this: we have loved reading.

THE AMERICAN LANGUAGE

By H. L. MENCKEN

THE first Englishman to notice an Americanism sneered at it aloofly, thus setting a fashion that many of his countrymen have been following ever since. He was one Francis Moore, a ruffian who came out to Georgia with Oglethorpe in 1735, and the word that upset him was *bluff,* in the sense of "a cliff or headland with a broad precipitous face." He did not deign to argue against it; he simply dismissed it as "barbarous," apparently assuming that all Englishmen of decent instincts would agree with him. For nearly a century they seem to have done so, and *bluff* lingered sadly below the salt. When it was printed at all in Great Britain it was set off by sanitary quotation marks, or accompanied by other hints of deprecation, as *rubberneck, hot spot* and *nerts* are accompanied to-day. But then, in 1830, the eminent Sir Charles Lyell used it shamelessly in the first volume of his monumental "Principles of Geology," and from that day to this it has been a perfectly respectable if somewhat unfamiliar word in England, with a place in every dictionary.

Its history is the history of almost countless other Americanisms. They have been edging their way into English since early colonial times, and, for more than a century past, in constantly increasing volume, but I can't recall one that didn't have to run a gantlet of opposition in the motherland, at times verging upon the frantic. After the Revolution, that opposition took on the proportions of a holy war. Never an American book came out that the English reviewers did not belabor its vocabulary violently. The brunt of the attack, of course, had to be borne by the poetasters of the era—for example, Joel Barlow, whose "Columbiad" (1807) loosed a really terrifying geyser of abuse. But even the most serious writers got their share—among them,

Jefferson, John Marshall, Noah Webster, and John Quincy Adams. Jefferson's crime was that he had invented the verb *to belittle*. It was, one may argue plausibly, a very logical, useful, and perhaps even nifty word, and seventy-five years later the prissy Anthony Trollope was employing it without apology. But when Jefferson ventured to use it in his "Notes on Virginia" (1787) "The London Review" tossed and raged in a manner befitting the discovery of a brace of duelling pistols beneath the cope of the Archbishop of Canterbury, and for several years following its dudgeon was supported virtuously by most of the other reviews. "What an expression!" roared the "London." "It may be an elegant one in Virginia, but for our part, all we can do is to *guess* at its meaning. For shame, Mr. Jefferson! Freely, good sir, will we forgive all your attacks, impotent as they are illiberal, upon our national character; but for the future spare—O spare, we beseech you, our mother-tongue!"

The underscoring of *guess* was a fling in passing at another foul Americanism. It was the belief of most Englishmen then, as it is to-day, that the use of the verb in the sense of *to suppose* or *assume* originated in this country. It is actually to be found, in that meaning precisely, in "Measure For Measure" and "Henry VI"; nay, in Chaucer, Wycliffe, and Gower. But such historical considerations have never daunted the more ardent preservers of the King's English. When a word acquires an American flavor it becomes anathema to them, even though it may go back to Boadicea. *To advocate* offers an instructive example. It appeared in English in the dark backward and abysm of time, but during the eighteenth century it seems to have dropped out of general use, though Burke used it. Towards the end of the century it came into vogue in this country, and soon it made its way back to the land of its birth. It was received with all the honors proper to an invasion of Asiatic cholera. The reviews denounced it as loutish, "Gothic," and against God, and lumped it with *to compromit* and *to happify* as proof that civilization was impossible in America, and would be so forevermore. Even Benjamin Franklin, returning from England in 1789, was alarmed into begging Noah Webster to "reprobate" it, along with *to notice, to progress,* and *to oppose.* There is no record of Noah's reply, but it is most unlikely that he did any reprobating, for when he began to make dictionaries he included all four verbs, and they have been listed in every considerable dictionary published since, whether in this country or in England.

The leader of the heroic struggle to keep Americanisms out of Britain, in its early stages, was the celebrated William Gifford, editor of "The Quarterly Review." Gifford was a killer in general practice, and his savage assaults on Wordsworth, Shelley, and Keats are still unpleasantly remembered. He was the first magazine editor in history to make the trade pay, and when he died in 1828 he left £25,000 and was buried in Westminster Abbey. One of his major specialties was the villainousness of everything American, from politics to table manners and from theology to speechways. Among the allegations that he either made himself or permitted his contributors to make were these: (a) that the Americans employed naked colored women to wait upon them at table, (b) that they kidnapped Scotsmen, Irishmen, Hollanders, and Welshmen and sold them into slavery, and (c) that they were planning to repudiate the English language altogether, and adopt Hebrew in its place. This last charge, as it flew from tongue to tongue, acquired variorum readings. One of them made the new American language an Indian dialect, another made it Greek, and a third was to the effect that the people of Britain would be forced to acquire Greek, thus leaving English to the wicked will of the barbaric Yankees. It all sounds idiotic to-day, but in 1814 it was taken quite seriously by many Englishmen. Gifford was a tyrannical editor and so vastly enjoyed slashing his contributors' copy that Southey once denounced him as "a butcherly review-gelder." But anything that was against the damyankee passed his eye unscathed, and he piled up accusations in a manner so shameless that "The North American Review" was moved to protest that if the tirade went on it would "turn into bitterness the last drops of good-will towards England that exist in the United States."

In the early Twenties of that century there was some amelioration, and when Gifford retired from the "Quarterly" in 1824, voices that were almost conciliatory began to be heard. They heaped praises on Niagara Falls, found something to commend in Cooper's "Spy," and even had kind words for the speed and luxuriousness of American canalboats. But my most diligent researches have failed to unearth anything complimentary to the American language. It continued to be treated as a grotesque and immoral gibberish, full of uncouth terms and at war with all the canons of English. Every British traveller who came to these shores between the War of 1812 and the Civil War had something to say about the neologisms his ears and eyes encountered on his tour, and nearly all were constrained to deplore them. Captain Basil Hall, who was here in 1827 and 1828, went about in a palpitating daze, confounded and outraged by the signs on American places of business. *Clothing Store* he interpreted after long thought, and *Flour and Feed Store* after prayer and soul-searching, but what on earth was a *Leather and Finding Store?* Captain Thomas Hamilton, who followed five years later, found it impossible to penetrate to "the precise import" of *Dry-Goods Store*, and when he encountered an establishment offering *Hollow Ware, Spiders, and Fire-Dogs* he gave up in despair.

Hall was not one to take it lying down. He decided to call upon Noah Webster, whose American Dictionary of the English Language had just come out, to find out what the Yankees meant by using the mother tongue so cruelly. Webster shocked him by arguing stoutly that "his countrymen had not only a right to adopt new words, but were obliged to modify the language to suit the novelty of the circumstances, geographical and political, in which they were placed." The great lexicographer "who taught millions to spell but not one to sin" went on to observe judicially that it was "quite impossible to stop the progress of language—it is like the course of the Mississippi, the motion of which, at times, is scarcely perceptible; yet even then it possesses a momentum quite irresistible. Words and expressions will be forced into use in spite of all the exertions of all the writers in the world."

"But surely," persisted Hall, "such innovations are to be deprecated?"

"I don't think that," replied old Noah. "If a word becomes universally current in America, where English is spoken, why should it not take its station in the language?"

"Because," declared Hall with magnificent pertinacity, "there are words enough already."

This heroic dogma is still heard in England, where even native novelties are commonly opposed violently, and not infrequently strangled at birth. There seems to be, in the modern Englishman, very little of that ecstasy in word-making which so prodigiously engrossed his Elizabethan forebears. Shakespeare alone probably put more new words into circulation than all the English writers since Carlyle, and they were much better ones. The ideal over there to-day is not picturesque and exhilarating utterance, but correct and reassuring utterance, and one of its inevitable fruits is that bow-wow jargon which Sir Arthur Quiller-Couch describes in "On the Art of Writing" as "the medium through which boards of government, county councils, syndicates, committees, commercial firms, express the processes as well as the conclusions of their thought, and so voice the reason of their being." It is, at its worst, at least in accord with what are taken to be the principles of English grammar, and at its best it shows excellent manners and even a kind of mellifluous elegance; indeed, the English, taking one with another, may be said to write much better than we do—at all events by the standards of the schoolmaster. But what they write is seldom animated by anything properly describable as bounce. It lacks novelty, variety, audacity. There is little juice in it. The reader confronted by it is treated politely and lulled pleasantly, but he seldom enjoys the enchantment of surprise. That diligent search for new and racy locutions which occupied so much of the work day of Walt Whitman and William Dean Howells alike, and is practised so assiduously by scores of saucy Andersons and Hemingways, Sandburgs and Saroyans to-day, is carried on across the ocean by only a few extravagant eccentrics, virtually all of whom —for example, James Joyce and Ezra Pound—are non- and even anti-Englishmen. The hundred-per-cent English writers, save when they stoop to conscious wickedness, seldom depart very far from the jargon of Quiller-Couch. It is by no means a monopoly of the classes he named, nor is it reserved for solemn occasions. I find it also in my favorite English weekly, the "News of the World," which is devoted principally to sports, the theatres, and the more scabrous varieties of crime, and is probably a far better mirror of England than the "Times." When the "News of the World" reports the downfall of a rural dean or a raid on a Mayfair night club, the thing is done in a style so tight and brittle that nothing to match it is discoverable in this country, at least outside the pages of "The Homiletic Review." "When we want to freshen our speech," Mrs. Virginia Woolf was lately saying, "we borrow from American—*poppycock, rambunctious, flip-flop, booster, good mixer*. All the expressive, ugly, vigorous slang which creeps into use among us, first in talk, later in writing, comes from across the Atlantic."

But whether slang or something better, it always encounters opposition—sometimes merely sullen, but at other times extremely violent. At more or less regular intervals, war upon the invasion is declared formally, and there ensues a long uproar, with the papers full of choleric letters to the editor. One such sharpening of activity was loosed early in 1933, when the chief constable of Wallasey, a suburb of Liverpool, reported in alarm that his policemen were being called *cops* by the tougher youngsters of the place, and otherwise insulted with blasphemies picked up from American movies. "*Oh-yeahs*," he said, "are frequent in answer to charges, and we are promised *shoots-up in the burg* [*sic*] and threatened to be *bumped off*." Half the amateur publicists who took a hand in the discussion which followed, advocated using the cat on the offenders, and the other half demanded that American movies be barred from England as intolerable public menaces, like cattle infected with foot-and-mouth disease. As usual, the debate ended in philological futilities. Was *oh yeah* actually English, even bad English, insane English? Or was it only an American borrowing from one of the dialects of the savage Red Indians, or maybe from Polish, Pennsylvania Dutch, Gullah, Yiddish, or some other such godless and anti-British lingo? No matter! *Oh yeah* continues to flourish from the Lizard to Unst, and with it *cop* flourishes too. The latter, in fact, has swept upward from the level of bad boys baiting constables to that of bishops following their transcendental occasions. Even before the chief constable of Wallasey sounded his cry of "Wolf!" a right reverend father in God had been charged before the Farnham (Surrey) magistrates with applying *speed-cop* on a public road to a member of the *mobile police*. Overhauled in his car, so the testimony went, he had demanded, "Are you a *speed-cop?*" His Lordship denied with some heat that he had used the term, or anything else so unseemly, but the magistrates apparently concluded that he must have let it slip, for they took a serious view of his very modest adventure in speeding, fined him £10, and suspended his driving license for three months. I give his name and dignities as a warning to lesser evildoers. He was the Right Reverend Cyril Henry Gelding-Bird, D.D. (Oxon.), Assistant Bishop of Guildford and Archdeacon of Dorking, and a man previously unknown to the police.

Whenever an Americanism comes publicly into question in England, there are efforts to track down its etymology, and sometimes the theories offered are extremely bizarre. In January, 1935, for example, the London "Morning Post" opened its columns to a furious and fantastic discussion of the verb-phrase, *to get his goat*. I content myself with one of the explanations: "Among the Negroes in Harlem it is the custom for each household to keep a goat to act as general scavenger. Occasionally one man will steal another's goat, and the household débris then accumulates to the general annoyance." The truth is that *to get his goat* seems to be of French origin, and in the form of *prendre sa chèvre*, philological genealogists have traced it back to the year 1585. But whatever is strange and upsetting is put down, in England, to the hellish ingenuity of Americans—save, of course, when genuine Americanisms are claimed as really English. This last happens often enough to give what may be called a cockeyed aspect to the perennial pother. In 1934 even the learned Dr. C. T. Onions, one of the editors of the great Oxford Dictionary, succumbed to the madness by offering to find in the dictionary any alleged Americanism that a reporter for the London "Evening News" could name. The reporter began discreetly with *fresh* (in the sense of *saucy*), *to figure* (in the sense of *to believe* or *conclude*), and *to grill* (in the sense of *to question*), and Dr. Onions duly found them all. But when the reporter proceeded to *bunkum*, the learned editor had to forget conveniently that its progenitor was the thoroughly American *buncombe*, when *rake-off* followed he had to admit that the earliest example in the dictionary was from an American work, and when *boloney* and *nerts* were hurled at him he blew up with a bang.

Here, of course, Dr. Onions and his interlocutor ended on the level of slang, but there is no telling where they would be if they could be translated to the year 2036. *Boloney*, like *to belittle*, has the imprimatur of an eminent tribune of the people, and is quite as respectable, philologically speaking, as *buncombe*, *gerrymander*, *pork barrel*, *filibuster*, *carpetbagger*, *gag rule*, or *on the fence*. All these came into American from the argot of politics, and got only frowns from the schoolmarm, but they are all quite sound American to-day, and most of them have gone into English. As for *nerts*, it seems to be but one more member of an endless dynasty of euphemisms, beginning with *zounds* and coming down to *son-of-a-gun*, *gee*, and *darn*. *Darn*, like *nerts*, is an Americanism, and Dr. Louise Pound has demonstrated that it descends from *eternal*, which first turned into *tarnal* and then lost its tail and borrowed the head of *damn*. I have heard a bishop use it freely in private discourse, with a waggish sprinkling of actual *damns*. *Son-of-a-gun* is now so feeble and harmless that the Italians in America use it as a satirical designation for native Americans, who seem to them to fall far behind the Italian talent for profanity and objurgation. It is, I believe, a just criticism. Some time ago I was engaged by a magazine to do an article on American and English swearwords. After two or three attempts I had to give it up, for I found that neither branch of our ancient Frisian tongue could show anything worthy of serious consideration. The antinomians of England stick to two or three banal obscenities, one of which, *bloody*, is obscene only formally, and we Americans seldom get beyond variations of *hell* and *damn*. A single Neapolitan boatman could swear down the whole population of Anglo-Saxondom.

Bloody is perfectly innocuous in the United States, and it may be innocuous in England also on some near to-morrow—or even more disreputable than it is to-day. There is no predicting the social career of words. Dr. Leonard Bloomfield says that even "our word *whore,* cognate with the Latin *carus* (dear), must have been at one time a polite substitute for some term now lost." Prophecy fails just as dismally when propriety does not come into question. Shakespeare's numerous attempts to introduce new words, some of them his own inventions and others borrowed from the slang of the Bankside, failed almost as often as they succeeded. He found ready takers for *courtship, lonely, sportive, multitudinous, hubbub* and *bump,* but his audiences would have none of *definement,* in the sense of description, or of *citizen* as an adjective, and both seem strange and uncouth to us to-day, though all the others are as familiar and as decorous as *cat* or *rat.* When John Marston used *strenuous* in 1599 it was attacked by Ben Jonson as barbarous, but a dozen years later it had got into Chapman's Homer, and by 1670 it was being used by Milton. It remained perfectly respectable until 1900, when Theodore Roosevelt announced the Strenuous Life. Both the idea and the term struck the American fancy, and in a little while the latter passed into slang, and was worn so threadbare that all persons of careful speech sickened of it. To this day it carries a faintly ridiculous connotation, and is seldom used seriously. But by 1975 it may be restored to the dignity of *psychopath* or *homoousian.* No one can say yes with any confidence, and no one can say no. "Even the greatest purist," observes Robert Lynd, "does not object to the inclusion of *bogus* in a literary English vocabulary, though a hundred years ago it was an American slang word meaning an apparatus for coining false money. *Carpetbagger* and *bunkum* are other American slang words that have naturalized themselves in English speech, and *mob* is an example of English slang that was once as vulgar as *photo.*"

Three Americanisms borrowed by English to one Briticism come into American! The true score, I suspect, is even more favorable to the Yankee as word-maker. Down to 1820, according to Sir William Craigie, the trans-Atlantic trade in neologisms ran mainly westward, but then it began to shift, and to-day it is very heavily eastward. It would be difficult to recall a dozen British inventions that have entered the common American vocabulary since the World War, but the number of Americanisms taken into English must run to hundreds, and perhaps even to thousands. The American movie and talkie, of course, have been responsible for the introduction of many of them, but there is something beyond that, and something more fundamental. They are adopted in England simply because England has nothing to offer in competition with them—that is, nothing so apt or pungent, nothing so good. His Lordship of Guildford did not apply *speed-cop* to that *mobile policeman* as a voluntary act of subversion, born of a desire to shock and insult the realm; he let it slip for the single reason that it was an irresistibly apposite and satisfying term. And so with all the other Americanisms that challenge and consume their British congeners. They win fairly on palpable points and by every rule of the game. Confronted by the same novelty, whether in object or in situation, the Americans always manage to fetch up a name for it that not only describes it but also illuminates it, whereas the English, since the Elizabethan stimulant oozed out of them, have been content merely to catalogue it. There was a brilliant exemplification of the two approaches in the early days of railways. The English, having to name the wedge-shaped fender that was put in front of the first locomotives, called it a *plough*, which was almost exactly what it was, but the Americans gave it the bold and racy appellation of *cowcatcher*. For the casting which guides the wheels from one rail to another the English coined the depressingly obvious name of *crossing-plate;* the Americans, setting their imaginations free, called it a *frog*. The same sharp contrast appears every time there is a call for a new word to-day. The American *movie* is obviously much better than the English *cinema;* it is even better English. So is *radio* better than *wireless,* though it may be Latin, and *job-holder* better than *public servant,* though it is surely literal enough, and *shock absorber* vastly better than *anti-bounce clip,* and *highball* than *whisky and soda,* and *bouncer* than *chucker-out,* and *chain store* than *multiple shop,* and *string bean* than *French bean,* and *union suit* than *combination.* Confronting the immensely American *rubberneck,* Dr. J. Y. T. Greig of Newcastle could only exclaim "one of the best words ever coined!" And in the face of *lounge lizard,* Horace Annesley Vachell fell silent like Sir Isaac Newton on the seashore, overwhelmed by the solemn grandeur of the linguistic universe.

One finds in current American all the characters and tendencies that marked the rich English of Shakespeare's time—an eager borrowing of neologisms from other languages, a bold and often very ingenious use of metaphor, and a fine disdain of the barricades separating the parts of speech. The making of new words is not carried on only, or even principally, to fill gaps in the vocabulary; indeed, one may well agree with Captain Hall that "there are words enough already." It is carried on because there survives in the American something that seems to have faded out of the Englishman: an innocent joy in word-making for its own sake, a voluptuous delight in the vigor and elasticity of the language. The search for the *mot juste* is an enterprise that is altogether too pedantic for him; he much prefers to solve his problem by non-Euclidian devices. *Hoosegow* was certainly not necessary when it appeared, for we already had a large repertory of synonyms for *jail*. But when the word precipitated itself from the Spanish *juzgado* somewhere along the Rio Grande it won quick currency, and in a little while it was on the march through the country, and soon or late, I suppose, it will produce its inevitable clipped forms, *hoose* and *gow*, and its attendant adjective and verb. *Corral*, which entered by the same route in the Forties of the last century, had hatched a verb before the Civil War, and that verb, according to Webster's New International (1934), now has four separate and distinct meanings. *Bummer*, coming in from the German, is now clipped to *bum*, and is not only noun, verb, and adjective but also adverb. *Buncombe*, borrowed by the English as *bunkum*, has bred *bunco* and *bunk* at home, both of which rove the parts of speech in a loose and easy way, and the last of which has issue in the harsh verb *to debunk*, still under heavy fire in England.

The impact of such lawless novelties upon the more staid English of the motherland is terrific. The more they are denounced as heathen and outlandish, the quicker they get into circulation. Nor do they prosper only on the level of the vulgate, and among careless speakers. There are constant complaints in the English newspapers about their appearance in the parliamentary debates, and even in discourses from the sacred desk, and they begin to show themselves also in *belles-lettres*, despite the English dislike of new ways of writing. Their progress, in fact, is so widespread and so insidious that they often pop up in the diatribes that revile them; the Englishman, conquered at last, can no longer protest against Americanisms without using them. Moreover, they are now supported actively by a definitely pro-American party of writers and scholars, and though it is still small in numbers, at least compared to the patriot band, it shows some distinguished names. The late Robert Bridges, Poet Laureate, was an active member of it, and among its other adherents are Wyndham Lewis, Edward Shanks, Richard Aldington, and Sir John Foster Fraser. Sir William Craigie, perhaps the first of living lexicographers, is so greatly interested in the American form of English that he has spent the years since 1925 in a scientific examination of it, and will presently begin the publication of an elaborate dictionary. If only because of the greater weight of the population behind it, it seems destined to usurp the natural leadership of British English, and to determine the general course of the language hereafter. But its chief advantage in this struggle is really not the numerical one, but the fact that its daring experiments and iconoclasms lie in the grand tradition of English, and are signs of its incurable normalcy and abounding vigor.

How far it will move away from the theorizing of grammarians and the policing of schoolmarms remains to be seen. They still make valiant efforts to curb its wayward spirit, but with gradually diminishing success. When, a few years ago, the late Sterling A. Leonard of the University of Wisconsin submitted a long series of their admonitions to a committee of educated Americans, including many philologians, he found that opinion was against them on that high level almost as decidedly as it was on lower ones. His judges favored scores of forms that the school grammars and popular handbooks of usage still condemn. Since then a more direct attack upon the conservative position has been made by Dr. Robert C. Pooley of the same university. He shows that some of the rules laid down with most assurance by pedants have no support in either history or logic, and are constantly violated by writers of unquestionable authority. There have even been rumblings of revolt in the conservative camp. The late George Philip Krapp of Columbia, who was surely anything but a radical, was of the opinion that English would undergo profound changes in the United States, and that many of them would be of such a character that its very grammatical structure would be shaken. Dr. George O. Curme of Northwestern University is another eminent grammarian who warns his colleagues that the rules they cherish have no genuine authority, and must be overhauled from time to time. Once they steel themselves to that sacrifice of their professional dignity, he says, "it will give a thrill to English-speaking students to discover that the English language does not belong to the schoolteacher but belongs to them, and that its future destiny will soon rest entirely in their hands."

Dr. Curme is always careful to think and speak of American as no more than a variation of English. But it must be obvious that, in late years, the tail has begun a vigorous wagging of the dog. "The facts that we ought to realize," says Edward Shanks to his fellow Britons, "and that we ignore when we talk loftily about Americanisms, are that America is making a formidable contribution to the development of our language, and that all our attempts to reject that contribution will in the long run be vain."

A PILGRIM IN CONCORD

By HENRY A. BEERS

THE Concord School of Philosophy opened its first session in the summer of 1879. The dust of late July lay velvet soft and velvet deep on all the highways; or, stirred by the passing wheel, rose in slow clouds, not unemblematic of the transcendental haze which filled the mental atmosphere thereabout.

Of those who had made Concord one of the homes of the soul, Hawthorne and Thoreau had been dead many years—I saw their graves in Sleepy Hollow;—and Margaret Fuller had perished long ago by shipwreck on Fire Island Beach. But Alcott was still alive and garrulous; and Ellery Channing—Thoreau's biographer—was alive. Above all, the sage of Concord, "the friend and aider of those who would live in the spirit," still walked his ancient haunts; his mind in many ways yet unimpaired, though sadly troubled by aphasia, or the failure of verbal memory. It was an instance of pathetic irony that in his lecture on "Memory," delivered in the Town Hall, he was prompted constantly by his daughter.

It seemed an inappropriate manner of arrival—the Fitchburg Railroad. One should have dropped down upon the sacred spot by parachute; or, at worst, have come on foot, with staff and scrip, along the Lexington pike, reversing the fleeing steps of the British regulars on that April day, when the embattled farmers made their famous stand. But I remembered that Thoreau, whose Walden solitude was disturbed by gangs of Irish laborers laying the tracks of this same Fitchburg Railroad, consoled himself with the reflection that hospitable nature made the intruder a part of herself. The embankment runs along one end of the pond, and the hermit only said:

It fills a few hollows
And makes banks for the swallows,
And sets the sand a-blowing
And the black-berries growing.

Afterwards I witnessed, and participated in, a more radical
profanation of these crystal waters, when two hundred of the
dirtiest children in Boston, South-enders, were brought down
by train on a fresh-air-fund picnic and washed in the lake just in
front of the spot where Thoreau's cabin stood, after having been
duly swung in the swings, teetered on the see-saws, and fed with
a sandwich, a slice of cake, a pint of peanuts, and a lemonade
apiece, by a committee of charitable ladies—one of whom was
Miss Louisa Alcott, certainly a high authority on "Little
Women" and "Little Men."

Miss Alcott I had encountered on the evening of my first day
in Concord, when I rang the door bell of the Alcott residence
and asked if the seer was within. I fancied that there was a trace
of acerbity in the manner of the tall lady who answered my ring,
and told me abruptly that Mr. Alcott was not at home, and that
I would probably find him at Mr. Sanborn's farther up the street.
Perspiring philosophers with dusters and grip-sacks had been
arriving all day and applying at the Alcott house for addresses
of boarding houses and for instructions of all kinds; and Miss
Louisa's patience may well have been tried. She did not take
much stock in the School anyway. Her father was supremely
happy. One of the dreams of his life was realized, and endless
talk and soul-communion were in prospect. But his daughter's
view of philosophy was tinged with irony, as was not unnatural
in a high-spirited woman who had borne the burden of the
family's support, and had even worked out in domestic service,
while her unworldly parent was transcendentalizing about the
country, holding conversation classes in western towns, from
which after prolonged absences he sometimes brought home a
dollar, and sometimes only himself. "Philosophy can bake no
bread, but it can give us God, freedom, and immortality" read
the motto—from Novalis—on the cover of the "Journal of
Speculative Philosophy," published at Concord in those years,
under the editorship of Mr. William T. Harris; but bread must

be baked, for even philosophers must eat, and an occasional impatience of the merely ideal may be forgiven in the over-worked practician.

On Mr. Frank Sanborn's wide, shady verandah, I found Mr. Alcott, a most quaint and venerable figure, large in frame and countenance, with beautiful, flowing white hair. He moved slowly, and spoke deliberately in a rich voice. His face had a look of mild and innocent solemnity, and he reminded me altogether of a large benignant sheep or other ruminating animal. He was benevolently interested when I introduced myself as the first fruits of the stranger and added that I was from Connecticut. He himself was a native of the little hill town of Wolcott, not many miles from New Haven, and in youth had travelled through the South as a Yankee pedlar. "Connecticut gave him birth," says Thoreau; "he peddled first her wares, afterwards, he declares, his brains."

Mr. Sanborn was the secretary of the School, and with him I enrolled myself as a pupil and paid the very modest fee which admitted me to its symposia. Mr. Sanborn is well known through his contributions to Concord history and biography. He was for years one of the literary staff of "The Springfield Republican," active in many reform movements, and an efficient member of the American Social Science Association. Almost from his house John Brown started on his Harper's Ferry raid, and people in Concord still dwell upon the exciting incident of Mr. Sanborn's arrest in 1860 as an accessory before the fact. The United States deputy marshal with his myrmidons drove out from Boston in a hack. They lured the unsuspecting abolitionist outside his door, on some pretext or other, clapped the handcuffs on him, and tried to get him into the hack. But their victim, planting his long legs one on each side of the carriage door, resisted sturdily, and his neighbors assaulted the officers with hue and cry. The town rose upon them. Judge Hoar hastily issued a habeas corpus returnable before the Massachusetts Supreme Court, and the baffled minions of the slave power went back to Boston.

The School assembled in the Orchard House, formerly the residence of Mr. Alcott, on the Lexington road. Next door was the Wayside, Hawthorne's home for a number of years, a cottage overshadowed by the steep hillside that rose behind it, thick with hemlocks and larches. On the ridge of this hill was Hawthorne's "out door study," a foot path worn by his own feet, as he paced back and forth among the trees and thought out the plots of his romances. In 1879 the Wayside was tenanted by George Lathrop, who had married Hawthorne's daughter, Rose. He had already published his "Study of Hawthorne" and a volume of poems, "Rose and Rooftree." His novel, "An Echo of Passion," was yet to come, a book which unites something of modern realism with a delicately symbolic art akin to Hawthorne's own.

A bust of Plato presided over the exercises of the School, and "Plato-Skimpole"—as Mr. Alcott was once nick-named—made the opening address. I remember how impressively he quoted Milton's lines:

> How charming is divine philosophy!
> Not harsh and crabbed, as dull fools suppose,
> But musical as is Apollo's lute.

Our *pièce de résistance* was the course of lectures in which Mr. Harris expounded Hegel. But there were many other lecturers. Mrs. Edna Cheney talked to us about art; though all that I recall of her conversation is the fact that she pronounced *always, olways*, and I wondered if that was the regular Boston pronunciation. Dr. Jones, the self-taught Platonist of Jacksonville, Illinois, interpreted Plato. Quite a throng of his disciples, mostly women, had followed him from Illinois and swelled the numbers of the Summer School. Once Professor Benjamin Peirce, the great Harvard mathematician, came over from Cambridge, and read us one of his Lowell Institute lectures, on the Ideality of Mathematics. He had a most distinguished presence and an eye, as was said, of black fire. The Harvard undergraduates of my time used to call him Benny Peirce; and on the fly leaves of their mathematical text books they would write, "Who steals my Peirce steals trash." Colonel T. W. Higginson read a single lecture on American literature, from which I carried away for future use a delightful story about an excellent Boston merchant who, being asked at a Goethe birthday dinner to make a few remarks, said that he "guessed that Go-ethe was the N. P. Willis of Germany."

Colonel Higginson's lecture was to me a green oasis in the arid desert of metaphysics, but it was regarded by earnest truth-seekers in the class as quite irrelevant to the purposes of the course. The lecturer himself confided to me at the close of the session a suspicion that his audience cared more for philosophy than for literature. Once or twice Mr. Emerson visited the School, taking no part in its proceedings, but sitting patiently through the hour, and wearing what a newspaper reporter described as his "wise smile." After the lecture for the session was ended, the subject was thrown open to discussion and there was an opportunity to ask questions. Most of us were shy to speak out in that presence, feeling ourselves in a state of pupilage. Usually there would be a silence of several minutes, as at a Quaker meeting waiting for the spirit to move; and then Mr. Alcott would announce in his solemn, musical tones "I have a thought"; and after a weighty pause, proceed to some Orphic utterance. Alcott, indeed, was what might be called the leader on the floor; and he was ably seconded by Miss Elizabeth Peabody, the sister of Nathaniel Hawthorne's wife. Miss Peabody was well known as the introducer of the German kindergarten, and for her life-long zeal in behalf of all kinds of philanthropies and reforms. Henry James was accused of having caricatured her in his novel "The Bostonians," in the figure of the dear, visionary, vaguely benevolent old lady who is perpetually engaged in promoting "causes," attending conventions, carrying on correspondence, forming committees, drawing up resolutions, and the like; and who has so many "causes" on hand at once that she gets them all mixed up and cannot remember which of her friends are spiritualists and which of them are concerned in woman's rights movements, temperance agitations, and universal peace associations. Mr. James denied that he meant Miss Peabody, whom he had never met or known. If so, he certainly divined the type. In her later years, Miss Peabody was nick-named "the grandmother of Boston."

I have to acknowledge, to my shame, that I was often a truant to the discussions of the School, which met three hours in the morning and three in the afternoon. The weather was hot and the air in the Orchard House was drowsy. There were many outside attractions, and more and more I was tempted to leave the philosophers to reason high—

> Of providence, foreknowledge, will, and fate—
> Fixed fate, free will, foreknowledge absolute—

while I wandered off through the woods for a bath in Walden, some one and a half miles away, through whose transparent waters the pebbles on the bottom could be plainly seen at a depth of thirty feet. Sometimes I went farther afield to White Pond, described by Thoreau, or Baker Farm, sung by Ellery Channing. A pleasant young fellow at Miss Emma Barrett's boarding house, who had no philosophy, but was a great hand at picnics and boating and black-berrying parties, paddled me up the Assabeth, or North Branch, in his canoe, and drove me over to Longfellow's Wayside Inn at Sudbury. And so it happens that, when I look back at my fortnight at Concord, what I think of is not so much the murmurous auditorium of the Orchard House, as the row of colossal sycamores along the village sidewalk that led us thither, whose smooth, mottled trunks in the moonlight resembled a range of Egyptian temple columns. Or I haunt again at twilight the grounds of the Old Manse, where Hawthorne wrote his "Mosses," and the grassy lane beside it leading down to the site of the rude bridge and the first battle-field of the Revolution. Here were the headstones of the two British soldiers, buried where they fell; here the Concord monument erected in 1836:

> On this green bank, by this soft stream
>> We set to-day a votive stone:
> That memory may their deed redeem
>> When, like our sires, our sons are gone.

In the field across the river was the spirited statue of the minuteman, designed by young Daniel Chester French, a Concord boy who has since distinguished himself as a sculptor in wider fields and more imposing works.

The social life of Concord, judging from such glimpses as could be had of it, was peculiar. It was the life of a village community, marked by the friendly simplicity of country neighbors, but marked also by unusual intellectual distinction and an addiction to "the things of the mind." The town was not at all provincial, or what the Germans call *kleinstädtisch:*—cosmopolitan, rather, as lying on the highway of thought. It gave one a thrill, for example, to meet Mr. Emerson coming from the Post Office with his mail, like any ordinary citizen. The petty constraint, the narrow standards of conduct which are sometimes the bane of village life were almost unknown. Transcendental freedom of speculation, all manner of heterodoxies, and the individual queernesses of those whom the world calls "cranks," had produced a general tolerance. Thus it was said, that the only reason why services were held in the Unitarian Church on Sunday was because Judge Hoar didn't quite like to play whist on that day. Many of the Concord houses have gardens bordering upon the river; and I was interested to notice that the boats moored at the bank had painted on their sterns plant names or bird names taken from the Concord poems—such as "The Rhodora," "The Veery," "The Linnæa," and "The Wood Thrush." Many a summer hour I spent with Edward Hoar in his skiff, rowing, or sailing, or floating up and down on this soft Concord stream— Musketaquit, or "grass-ground river"—moving through miles of meadow, fringed with willows and button bushes, with a current so languid, said Hawthorne, that the eye cannot detect which way it flows. Sometimes we sailed as far as Fair Haven Bay, whose "dark and sober billows," "when the wind blows freshly on a raw March day," Thoreau thought as fine as anything on Lake Huron or the northwest coast. Nor were we, I hope, altogether unperceiving of that other river which Emerson detected flowing underneath the Concord—

> Thy summer voice, Musketaquit,
>   Repeats the music of the rain,
> But sweeter rivers pulsing flit
>   Through thee as though through Concord plain. . . .
>
> I see the inundation sweet,
>   I hear the spending of the stream,

Through years, through men, through nature fleet,
Through love and thought, through power and dream.

Edward Hoar had been Thoreau's companion in one of his
visits to the Maine woods. He knew the flora and fauna of
Concord as well as his friend the poet-naturalist. He had a
large experience of the world, had run a ranch in New Mexico
and an orange plantation in Sicily. He was not so well known
to the public as his brothers, Rockwood Hoar, Attorney General in Grant's Cabinet, and the late Senator George Frisbie
Hoar, of Worcester; but I am persuaded that he was just as
good company; and, then, neither of these distinguished gentlemen would have wasted whole afternoons in eating the lotus
along the quiet reaches of the Musketaquit with a stripling
philosopher.

The appetite for discussion not being fully satisfied by the
stated meetings of the School in the Orchard House, the hospitable Concord folks opened their houses for informal symposia in the evenings. I was privileged to make one of a company that gathered in Emerson's library. The subject for the
evening was Shakespeare, and Emerson read, by request, that
mysterious little poem "The Phœnix and the Turtle," attributed to Shakespeare on rather doubtful evidence, but included
for some reason in Emerson's volume of favorite selections,
"Parnassus." He began by saying that he would not himself
have chosen this particular piece, but as it had been chosen for
him he would read it. And this he did, with that clean-cut,
refined enunciation and subtle distribution of emphasis which
made the charm of his delivery as a lyceum lecturer. When he
came to the couplet,

Truth may seem, but cannot be,
Beauty brag, but 'tis not she,

I thought that I detected an idealistic implication in the lines
which accounted for their presence in "Parnassus."

That shy recluse, Ellery Channing, most eccentric of the
transcendentalists, was not to be found at the School or the
evening symposia. He had married a sister of Margaret Fuller,

but for years he had lived alone and done for himself, and his oddities had increased upon him with the years. I had read and liked many of his poems—those poems so savagely cut up by Poe, when first published in 1843—and my expressed interest in these foundlings of the Muse gave me the opportunity to meet the author of "A Poet's Hope" at one hospitable table where he was accustomed to sup on a stated evening every week.

The Concord Summer School of Philosophy went on for ten successive years, but I never managed to attend another session. A friend from New Haven, who was there for a few days in 1880, brought back the news that a certain young lady who was just beginning the study of Hegel the year before, had now got up to the second intention, and hoped in time to attain the sixth. I never got far enough in Mr. Harris's lectures to discover what Hegelian intentions were; but my friend spoke of them as if they were something like degrees in Masonry. In 1905 I visited Concord for the first and only time in twenty-six years. There is a good deal of philosophy in Wordsworth's Yarrow poems—

> For when we're there, although 'tis fair,
> 'Twill be another Yarrow!—

and I have heard it suggested that he might well have added to his trilogy, a fourth member, "Yarrow Unrevisited." There is a loss, though Concord bears the strain better than most places, I think. As we go on in life the world gets full of ghosts, and at the capital of transcendentalism I was peculiarly conscious of the haunting of these spiritual presences. Since I had been there before, Emerson and Alcott and Ellery Channing and my courteous host and companion, Edward Hoar, and my kind old landlady Miss Barrett—who had also been Emerson's landlady and indeed everybody's landlady in Concord, and whom her youngest boarders addressed affectionately as Emma —all these and many more had joined the sleepers in Sleepy Hollow. The town itself has suffered comparatively few changes. True there is a trolley line through the main street— oddly called "The Milldam," and in Walden wood I met an automobile not far from the cairn, or stone pile, which marks the site of Thoreau's cabin. But the woods themselves were intact and the limpid waters of the pond had not been tapped to furnish power for any electric light company. The Old Manse looked much the same, and so did the Wayside and the Orchard House. Not a tree was missing from the mystic ring of tall pines in front of Emerson's house at the fork of the Cambridge and Lexington roads. On the central square the ancient tavern was gone where I had lodged on the night of my arrival and where my host, a practical philosopher—everyone in Concord had his philosophy,—took a gloomy view of the local potentialities of the hotel business. He said there was nothing doing—some milk and asparagus were raised for the Boston market, but the inhabitants were mostly literary people. "I suppose," he added, "we've got the smartest literary man in the country living right here." "You mean Mr. Emerson," I suggested. "Yes, sir, and a gentleman too."

"And Alcott?" I ventured.

"Oh, Alcott! The best thing he ever did was his daughters."

This inn was gone, but the still more ancient one across the square remains, the tavern where Major Pitcairn dined on the day of the Lexington fight, and from whose windows or door steps he is alleged by the history books to have cried to a group of embattled farmers "Disperse, ye Yankee rebels."

Concord is well preserved. Still there are subtle indications of the flight of time. For one thing, the literary pilgrimage business has increased, partly no doubt because trolleys, automobiles, and bicycles have made the town more accessible; but also because our literature is a generation older than it was in 1879. The study of American authors has been systematically introduced into the public schools. The men who made Concord famous are dead, but their habitat has become increasingly classic ground as they themselves have receded into a dignified, historic past. At any rate, the trail of the excursionist—the "cheap tripper," as he is called in England,—is over it all. Basket parties had evidently eaten many a luncheon on the first battle-field of the Revolution, and notices were posted about, asking the public not to deface the trees, and instructing them where to put their paper wrappers and *fragmenta regalia*. I could imagine Boston schoolma'ams pointing out to their classes, the minuteman, the monument, and other objects of interest, and calling for names and dates. The shores of Walden were trampled and worn in spots. There were spring-boards there for diving, and traces of the picnicker were everywhere. Trespassers were warned away from the grounds of the Old Manse and similar historic spots, by signs of "Private Property."

Concord has grown more self-conscious under the pressure of all this publicity and resort. Tablets and inscriptions have been put up at points of interest. As I was reading one of these on the square, I was approached by a man who handed me a business card with photographs of the monument, the Wayside, the four-hundred-year-old oak, with information to the effect that Mr. ———— would furnish guides and livery teams about the town and to places as far distant as Walden Pond and Sudbury Inn. Thus poetry becomes an asset, and transcendentalism is exploited after the poet and the philosopher are dead. It took Emerson eleven years to sell five hundred copies of "Nature," and Thoreau's books came back upon his hands as unsalable and were piled up in the attic like cord wood. I was impressed anew with the tameness of the Concord landscape. There is nothing salient about it: it is the average mean of New England nature. Berkshire is incomparably more beautiful. And yet those flat meadows and low hills and slow streams are dear to the imagination, since genius has looked upon them and made them its own. "The eye," said Emerson, "is the first circle: the horizon the second."

And the Concord books—how do they bear the test of re-visitation? To me, at least, they have—even some of the second-rate papers in the "Dial" have—now nearly fifty years since I read them first, that freshness which is the mark of immortality.

> No ray is dimmed, no atom worn:
> My oldest force is good as new;
> And the fresh rose on yonder thorn
> Gives back the bending heavens in dew.

I think I do not mistake, and confer upon them the youth which
was then mine. No, the morning light had touched their fore-
heads: the youthfulness was in *them.*

Lately I saw a newspaper item about one of the thirty thousand literary pilgrims who are said to visit Concord annually.
Calling upon Mr. Sanborn, he asked him which of the Concord
authors he thought would last longest. The answer, somewhat
to his surprise, was "Thoreau." I do not know whether this
report is authentic; but supposing it true, it is not inexplicable.
I will confess that, of recent years, I find myself reading Thoreau more and Emerson less. "Walden" seems to me more of
a book than Emerson ever wrote. Emerson's was incomparably
the larger nature, the more liberal and gracious soul. His, too,
was the seminal mind; though Lowell was unfair to the disciple, when he described him as a pistillate blossom fertilized
by the Emersonian pollen. For Thoreau had an originality of
his own—a flavor as individual as the tang of the bog cran-
berry, or the wild apples which he loved. One secure advantage he possesses in the concreteness of his subject matter. The
master, with his abstract habit of mind and his view of the
merely phenomenal character of the objects of sense, took up
a somewhat incurious attitude towards details, not thinking it
worth while to "examine too microscopically the universal tab-
let." The disciple, though he professed that the other world
was all his art, had a sharp eye for this. Emerson was Nature's
lover, but Thoreau was her scholar. Emerson's method was in-
tuition, while Thoreau's was observation. He worked harder
than Emerson and knew more,—that is, within certain defined
limits. Thus he read the Greek poets in the original. Emerson,
in whom there was a spice of indolence—due, say his biographers, to feeble health in early life, and the need of going
slow,—read them in translations and excused himself on the
ground that he liked to be beholden to the great English language.

Compare Hawthorne's description, in the "Mosses," of a day
spent on the Assabeth with Ellery Channing, with any chapter
in Thoreau's "Week." Moonlight and high noon! The great

romancer gives a dreamy, poetic version of the river landscape, musically phrased, pictorially composed, dissolved in atmosphere—a lovely piece of literary art, with the soft blur of a mezzotint engraving, say, from the designs by Turner in Rogers's "Italy." Thoreau, equally imaginative in his way, writes like a botanist, naturalist, surveyor, and local antiquary; and in a pungent, practical, business-like style—a style, as was said of Dante, in which words are things. Yet which of these was the true transcendentalist?

Matthew Arnold's discourse on Emerson was received with strong dissent in Boston, where it was delivered, and in Concord, where it was read with indignation. The critic seemed to be taking away, one after another, our venerated master's claims as a poet, a man of letters, and a philosopher. What! Gray a great poet, and Emerson not! Addison a great writer, and Emerson not! Surely there are heights and depths in Emerson, an inspiring power, an originality and force of thought which are neither in Gray nor in Addison. And how can these denials be consistent with the sentence near the end of the discourse, pronouncing Emerson's essays the most important work done in English prose during the nineteenth century—more important than Carlyle's? A truly enormous concession this; how to reconcile it with those preceding blasphemies?

Let not the lightning strike me if I say that I think Arnold was right—as he usually was right in a question of taste or critical discernment. For Emerson was essentially a prophet and theosophist, and not a man of letters, or creative artist. He could not have written a song or a story or a play. Arnold complains of his want of concreteness. The essay was his chosen medium, well-nigh the least concrete, the least literary of forms. And it was not even the personal essay, like Elia's, that he practised, but an abstract variety, a lyceum lecture, a moralizing discourse or sermon. For the clerical virus was strong in Emerson, and it was not for nothing that he was descended from eight generations of preachers. His concern was primarily with religion and ethics, not with the tragedy and comedy of personal lives, this motley face of things, *das bunte Menschenleben*. Anecdotes and testimonies abound to illustrate this. See

him on his travels in Europe, least picturesque of tourists, hastening with almost comic precipitation past galleries, cathedrals,
ancient ruins, Swiss alps, Como lakes, Rhine castles, Venetian
lagoons, costumed peasants, "the great sinful streets of Naples"
—and of Paris,—and all manner and description of local color
and historic associations; hastening to meet and talk with "a
few minds"—Landor, Wordsworth, Carlyle. Here he was in
line, indeed, with his great friend, impatiently waving aside
the art patter, with which Sterling filled his letters from Italy.
"Among the windy gospels," complains Carlyle, "addressed to
our poor Century there are few louder than this of Art. . . .
It is a subject on which earnest men . . . had better . . .
'perambulate their picture-gallery with little or no speech.' "
"Emerson has never in his life," affirms Mr. John Jay Chapman, "felt the normal appeal of any painting, or any sculpture,
or any architecture, or any music. These things, of which he
does not know the meaning in real life, he yet uses, and uses
constantly, as symbols to convey ethical truths. The result is
that his books are full of blind places, like the notes which will
not strike on a sick piano." The biographers tell us that he had
no ear for music and could not distinguish one tune from another; did not care for pictures nor for garden flowers; could
see nothing in Dante's poetry nor in Shelley's, nor in Hawthorne's romances, nor the novels of Dickens and Jane Austen.
Edgar Poe was to him "the jingle man." Poe, of course, had no
"message."

I read, a number of years ago, some impressions of Concord
by Roger Riordan, the poet and art critic. I cannot now put my
hand, for purposes of quotation, upon the title of the periodical
in which these appeared; but I remember that the writer was
greatly amused, as well as somewhat provoked, by his inability
to get any of the philosophers with whom he sought interviews
to take an æsthetic view of any poem, or painting, or other art
product. They would talk of its "message" or its "ethical content"; but as to questions of technique or beauty, they gently
put them oneside as unworthy to engage the attention of earnest
souls.

At the symposium which I have mentioned in Emerson's

library, was present a young philosopher who had had the advantage of reading—perhaps in proof sheets—a book about Shakespeare by Mr. Denton J. Snider. He was questioned by some of the guests as to the character of the work, but modestly declined to essay a description of it in the presence of such eminent persons; venturing only to say that it "gave the ethical view of Shakespeare," information which was received by the company with silent but manifest approval.

Yet, after all, what does it matter whether Emerson was singly any one of those things which Matthew Arnold says he was not—great poet, great writer, great philosophical thinker? These are matters of classification and definition. We know well enough the rare combination of qualities which made him our Emerson. Let us leave it there. Even as a formal verse-writer, when he does emerge from his cloud of encumbrances, it is in some supernal phrase such as only the great poets have the secret of:

> Music pours on mortals its beautiful disdain;

or

> Have I a lover who is noble and free?
> I would he were nobler than to love me.

PORTS OF CALL

By H. M. TOMLINSON

OUR steamer was bound for more ports in the Mediterranean, with power to add to their number, than I could remember when asked where we were going. Some of the ports I had never heard of, though later I found I had often made out bills of lading for them when a youth; they had been re-christened—if you can call it that—after the Great War.

When we put out from Liverpool our steamer, the *Zircon*, was two feet above her marks, for this was a recent voyage, and more war, and threats of still more, had frightened cargo away from her. Her lightness had one advantage. She is a very small ship, and her buoyancy kept most of the seas off her deck when an Atlantic depression met us. Instead of being swept, after she was clear of the lee of Ireland, she only became as giddy as a balloon. The rollers threatening on her starboard bow merely made her delirious. The men staggering towards the forecastle with their grub vanished in spray. Watching a fireman descend to the foredeck with his dinner, you gave a glance to windward, and speculated whether he would get it under cover before the next flight of spindrift washed the steam out of it.

The smells of a cargo ship, the sounds of wind and waters, and her movements, have an odd effect on an old voyager, off once more after a long spell ashore; they seem more of the past than the present. He has floated off into limbo. What he hears are but echoes in the hollow of eternity. He has escaped from time. He could believe that nothing has changed at sea. Here he is, continuing a voyage begun in a year he has forgotten. On the bridge at midnight the bell on the ship's head answers the bridge, while the dim foremast-head rakes the stars; and then the shadows arrive which are the relief for the middle

watch. He doubts those shadows. Are they not old messmates?
"South 30 West it is, sir!"

That bass voice of the unseen fellow who has just taken the
wheel was familiar, doubtless, on *Argo*.

Still, apart from sentimental retrospection, this *Zircon* and
her men make a puzzling mixture of past and present. Our ship
has to be thought out; an old voyager is compelled to start
afresh with her. The master and his chief officer, though only
in their middle years, learned seamanship under square rig, and
they speak familiarly of the famous clippers of long ago; yet
both of them wear most notable war decorations. Our chief
engineer went down in the *Lusitania*. At the mess table it is
plain enough that our juniors very often don't know what their
seniors are talking about, though our converse is over the deep,
which is said never to change. To them the famous sailing craft,
which did not quite reach as far as 1914, are no more beautiful
and attractive than wheelbarrows. They know nothing about
them and are not curious. They are untroubled because their
seniors have lived in a world which has no bearings for them.
The four black years of mines, convoys, and torpedoes are with
Nelson. They have another tradition. It is possible that never
before in history was there so deep a division between youth
and maturity. Our chief officer and our third have nothing in
common except language, food, and navigation.

I discovered something else. The first night of the voyage,
when passing a cabin, I thought I heard a contralto voice within,
rich and languorous, and paused to make sure of it. Yes; and
that, too, was the cabin of a young engineer and . . . but I
soon learned all was shipshape. Only men are in this ship; and
hardware, motor cars, and soap in the holds. That lady was as
far as Moscow or Paris or somewhere. The mystery was exposed in daylight next morning when on the forecastle deck
with the only other passenger, my son, he pointed to strange
wires leading out of the ventilators of the seamen's and the fire-
men's quarters. They were aerials. We have as many as seven
radio sets in this ship. There is a weekly football sweepstake,
and on Saturday nights the steward attends to a voice from
Regent Street, and we hear who has won.

I may get used to it presently. The fact of our contact with the noisy world is unescapable, for our ship is so small. You cannot promenade on the *Zircon*. You are brought up by a winch or a hatch or a rail or a life line in a few paces. A few mornings ago, while sitting on a bunker hatch within a recess of the engine-room casing, trying to get the sun without too much wind in it, and still cherishing some of the illusion that the sea is what it was, I got another jolt. Spain was growing higher over the port bow. Nothing was in sight but the shapes of the Asturian mountains, and they were noble. A man was near me chipping the deck. Then a messmate stopped to report a threatening word from Rome. What, I exclaimed, how do you know that? Oh, he had just picked it up. The horizon was clear, the sea was friendly, and the land was a configuration purple through distance; but here a good soul paused by a bunker hatch and handed to me a fresh and prickly lump of trouble out of Rome.

We used to talk of solitude, of going to sea to hear from our-selves. Once upon a time you could be separate from the disturb-ance and distraction of the cities. You could begin at sea, in lone-liness, to recognize your private thoughts; but you cannot do that now, unless you set out by yourself, sailing your own boat. We have abolished solitude. It is going to be hard in future to hear from ourselves. I should say there are as many charming sentimental rosebuds presented as thanks offerings for the mar-vellous benefits of science as were ever given to Cupid. Some research work might be done to discover whether our practical cleverness has not taken away benefits of greater value to us than the wonders it has given in exchange. This, I know, is the new blasphemy, but now and then one is liable to utter it when the ardent supporters of a better order of things are not standing about ready to denounce us to our august masters. Seclusion at sea? The topics of our mess table this voyage are often the same as the headlines of the city newspapers of the same day; and the energy and direction of the views I hear sailors express daily, on matters that used to be reserved for the morning trains to the metropolis, put our ship in another age. Our men might be me-chanics in a popular motor works. For that reason, when wakeful late at night, in the middle watch, when the cabin light is out, and there is but the familiar rocking of a ship and the pulse of her engines, even then, when alone with memory, I know I am on a voyage at the beginning of another phase of history. It is, in a sense, my first voyage.

Not that one should be surprised by human enterprise and ineptitude when viewing on a southerly course the Atlantic seaboard of Iberia. The names of nearly every landmark remind a voyager, especially if he is an Englishman, that that high coast has witnessed more than its share of the great events which have set men cheering, and then, presently, filled them with dread. He has the leisure to recall too, while the monody of the waves accompanies his thoughts, that in the long run very little of the resounding dramas came to anything. What has survived, chiefly, is that liability to caprice in statecraft which sets us cheering once more just before we are again filled with dread. There, now, is Finisterre. The sun has set, and the headland all travellers have seen has the black shape of a whale with a diamond flashing on its head. Between that mass and another promontory to the eastward, Cape Ortegal, is the town of Corunna. This lovely coast, apparently aloof from human folly, is a long reminder of man's pride and cruelty. The Douro enters the sea lower down the coast. The next evening we were off the Tagus, from which Philip's Armada set forth to disaster. And before sunrise the following morning we were roused to go to the bridge because we were nearing Cape St. Vincent. It is natural for English travellers to be curious and thoughtful in these waters.

Here and here did England help me: how can I help England?

Browning's question is not so easy to answer, in these years. And St. Vincent has the right terrible aspect, as your ship stands in towards it, of a significant landmark. As the Cape grew over our bows the clear gold light of a new day was laid along the rim of the high land abeam of us. A tramp steamer was just ahead of our ship. She cleared the over-shadowing promontory first and entered full morning, altering course southeast for Trafalgar. She saw the sun before us, and was so glorified on the instant that her underwriters could have believed she was immortal. Surmounting renowned St. Vincent is a lighthouse tower, with a convent beside it, exhibiting to the Western Ocean from a white wall a vast red cross. From St. Vincent we stood across for Casablanca, well down the western coast of Morocco. . . .

When the *Zircon* left Malta, and was on her way to Greece, Istanbul and the Black Sea, a sirocco met us, a foul wind blowing from the Sahara, both hot and strong. I read that night the twenty-seventh chapter of the Acts of the Apostles with a new interest and sympathy. The gale was on our beam, and the ship rolled till we had to hang dangling from the roof, as it were, and the next minute look up from the basement. Our chief officer called on me that night, and missed his catch as his glass jumped out of its stand. He desired then to meet the fool who said the Mediterranean is the blue sea. The posters for tourists always picture it as a permanent rapture, but my experience of the Mediterranean is that you cannot trust it for an hour. That sea is as fickle as some of the folk who make its shores so romantic.

Yet it can be very good. It might have been trying to live up to the expansive words of the poets when we had Cephalonia in sight, and could make out Ithaca. The morning was still and fair, the waters lustrous, the coasts lofty, spectral, and legendary. It was a conjuration; there was Hellas. While we were still grateful for this perfect approach—because it was our first sight of Greece—our steward, who is a cockney, reminded us that over there was the home of Odysseus; and from his further remarks, while leaning on the bulwarks, it became clear he knew things about Hellas that were unknown to Homer. He freely told us much that university professors would have been astonished to hear, though I fancy they might have asked for more of his short stories.

In the Gulf of Corinth we put into the shore of Achaia, and we moored at Patras, at an hour when the new sun was almost high enough to penetrate to the extremity of the Bay of Lepanto, which was opposite. Alongside us was another steamer, loading Christmas fruit for London out of local craft, traditional little ships with fine lines and lateen sails, though it must be reported that the smallest of them now has a motor to get her about when her pinions are folded. Beyond that London steamer busy with fruit was a French steamer, discharging bales of dried Newfoundland cod; and the morning smelt in awful variance with its light.

That evening we continued east along the Gulf of Corinth. The ship was trivial beneath a high coast close to either beam, and the chart for navigators was alive with such names as Delphi, Helicon, Eleusis, Salamis. What is there to say about that? It is better to say nothing. The superb shores lightly supported their tradition. It was morning again when we rounded the isle of Salamis into Piraeus. To the south was the bluish serration of the isle of Aegina. Our ship made fast, and we landed on the threshold of Athens, which was of concrete, amid gas pipes, cased motor-car bodies, galvanized iron, drums of oil, and what not. But just before we landed, a policeman came aboard to stamp our passports. He does that everywhere we go, and almost always he is armed. This routine with passports is as if Authority were as suspicious as an aged and timid spinster who sees a burglar every time a bowler hat passes her window. Heaven knows what would happen if we dared set foot in foreign mud and began dodging the stacks of imported gas pipes unless a policeman had examined our papers upside down for signs of Bolshevism, and had stamped them because he could not read them. Men with automatics on their hips guard our gangway wherever we anchor. It is possible that what our brave new world chiefly needs is not more food, nor even fewer guns, but merriment over itself. When shall we hear that happy awakening laughter?

Our ship, always uncertain in any port of the time it would take her to discharge and load, and therefore jealous of the movements of her two passengers, advised us reluctantly to go away; we could be absent almost as long as we liked. We did not wait but went then, while she was rattling hardware overside. Piraeus with its cabarets and boardinghouses for seamen and its money-changers' stalls, all looking over a tangle of tram lines and mooring ropes to its fishing fleet and its shipping, did not detain us. That musky and vivacious scene in a candid light is always welcome, but the Mediterranean displays it everywhere. We boarded an electric train for Athens, and from its window I watched an aridity of dust heaps, stucco houses, shabby palms, and tethered goats fly past. I saw fairly soon I was too late in life, or too late in history, for Athens. My son was also looking at the dusty plain with its villas and goats, though perhaps with greater expectation, and he startled me presently with an exclamation of wonder. I turned quickly, but our electric speed allowed only a bare glimpse; a gaunt factory instantly intervened. Yet I did see it, so exalted that it was only just below the blue roof of day; the Acropolis!

That pale phantom in the heavens above the factory stacks was incredible. How could I not suppose we had better take the next train back to Piraeus? To go on was unwise. Had we not seen it, even if it were not there? Experience tells us it is idle to follow a vision too far; that way madness lies. A glimpse is enough, and we are fortunate to get it. Perhaps what we had both seen was only the projection of a fond hope, a dream in a late and darkened year. Perhaps reverie had induced a symbol of lost values too vividly; that was all it was. That sign in the sky has been abolished. What it represented is nothing now, in an age when the politics of power must justify any divergence by unreason, and any excess by barbarians who are able to take what they want.

My companion, however, thought otherwise. His eyes are better than mine, for they believe, and he had me out at the next stopping place. There at once we saw that we really had been deceived. Here about us was the living Athens, without a Parthenon. Instead of that we found stacks of galvanized iron pails. The markets betrayed the fact that life in Athens must be cheap and at low ebb. The interminable streets had sidewalks from which a third of the paving stones were missing. The shops of the butchers were cheerless with festoons of tripes, and the furniture dealers selling ornaments for the home would have shocked the good taste of a seaside lodginghouse keeper at Coney Island or Blackpool. Pericles is dead.

We saw presently we were wandering without direction in a suburb where the walls of the villas were stencilled abundantly, not with the sign of Athena's owl, but with red hammers and sickles. On one wall this symbol of revolution was painted over the royal arms; so it may be the King of Greece cannot keep his mind on ancient standards all day long. It was time to take a taxi out of it. That cab landed us before the Propylaea just as rain began to spatter. The hills around had grown dark, though not so dark as the clouds which rested on them. But at least we could see that the Acropolis was abandoned; the rain gave the hill and its relics to us alone.

Perhaps there is no way to communicate the chance intimations which affect us most. An important experience transcends expression; it is a confirmation that must remain a secret. One may know little or nothing of the glory that was Greece, but to look up at the Parthenon, even through rain, is to see a manifestation of mind in a form beyond the interpretation of scholarship, as great music is. That temple is for everybody. It is magnanimous, and includes the lowly with the wise and important, as majesty would, while overlooking from its high throne the spread of palaces and factories of a modern and amorphous city. Against the overcast sky the massive colonnades strangely glowed, as if ancient fire were inextinguishable in the heart of their marble, and the columns were dilated with their original fervor. The temple pavements were bright, as though the one to whom the place was dedicate had left in them the virtue of morning.

The rain ceased towards sunset; and the sun, for a minute or two, peered through a break in the nimbus, over the summits of the hills. That western light and the temple looked across at each other from above the world. A pair of tortoiseshell butterflies sported through the colonnades, dancing in accord. Two ravens stood at the base of a column unnaturally black and lustrous. As we turned, for a last look up at the temple, a falcon floated out of the frieze.

It was time to return to the ship. We said nothing to each other of that day's experience. I suppose there is nothing to say of ravens posed against luminous marble, or of butterflies sporting in the glowing court of Athena, of a falcon whose aerial curve is consonant with the lift of imponderable masonry. We returned to Piraeus. That place is different. It is tumult, shipping, and crowds. It was also night there, when we were back in the dock. We made our way round barricades of merchandise and tangles of mooring ropes, down a long length of concrete from which the workmen had gone. Only the cold arc lights were left. One cold revealing arc light stood over the quay where our ship had been that morning. There was no doubt about that. We recognized some of the *Zircon's* Liverpool cargo. The fact was indisputable. The empty water was black and forlorn; our ship had gone.

When a seafarer ashore on a foreign coast goes back at his ease to the quay where he left his ship—which is his home and his salvation—to find only water at night, his jaw drops. For about a minute that is all that happens. His jaw takes all that time to return to a firm position. She has gone; and how can that be true? There is a mistake somewhere. He is too astonished at first to realize all that he is in for now; and when it is night, and he has only petty coins and no passport, he is in for much.

We continued to examine the place which our ship had occupied that morning, but we could find nothing except shards of electric light floating in the dock. This was serious. We visited the next ship with some anxious questions, but she was Dutch. We went to the steamer on the other side, but she was a Finn; I think she was Finnish. We found an ancient man crouched within a recess of our Liverpool wares, but he was Greek, and an imbecile, by the look of him. He didn't care. He surveyed us, spat, and turned away his eyes. We ourselves were but little short of doddering at that moment; so we did not curse him.

We were marooned. Now we should get to know the taste of it. We were on the beach, and at night, knew nobody there, could not speak Greek, and the ship had all our papers and property; and she was presumably on her way to Turkey. More than that, the rain had been wet that day. At the dock gates—we found it hard to sleep with barrels of paint on concrete—we met a Greek sailor who thought he understood the difficulty. He guided us to a place which had subdued colored lights, a saxophone, a violin, and softly spoken and multilingual girls; and he was definitely inclined to oppose our energetic protest that this could not be the office of our ship's agent. The names of Greek streets are very unlike English, especially after dark; so it was by chance that we found that office, though it was closed, of course, except for an antique watchman with a corrugated skin of brown leather, whose impassivity would have frustrated desperate Ulysses.

We had to give it up. We did not feel equal to arguments with
the police; so we found a room on the waterfront, discouraged
the intimacy of the cockroaches, and waited for morning. The
lights of the harbor were some compensation. We could watch
them, wonder what they meant, and calculate, from a timetable,
a map, the *Zircon's* rate of knots, and the ports at which she must
touch, what chance we had of finding her somewhere between
Salonika and Egypt. It became clear towards daylight that the
good luck of such a coincidence was about as likely as the prize in
a large sweepstake, and that may have been the reason why we
got no sleep; that, or lesser things, for the beds were dubious.

The Greek agent of our ship found us next morning, but
though his staff work with the problem was better informed than
our own, it appeared to leave our ship still below the horizon;
yet he did introduce us to a resident Englishman, who had been
trained in the Royal Navy, and that good man took us to Pha-
leron Bay. He set us under trellised grapes to moderate the sun,
and fed us on red mullet, dandelion leaves in olive oil, and resin
wine, while we looked towards Mount Hymettus across blue
water. We did not care, while with him, whether we found our
ship or not.

Yet presently the dark thought intruded again that we were
destitute. Worse than that we had no name and no country; we
could not prove we had ever been born. There was an odd
chance, our friend thought, that if we boarded a Polish ship,
which had unexpectedly arrived, and was sailing that night for
Istanbul, she might be there in time to catch our steamer. We
were unaware till that day that the Poles had steamers, anyhow,
one fast enough to catch the *Zircon* when she was active; but we
took the risk, without hope, for it needs a deal of faith to believe
that the Polish flag, so lately salted, could overtake the Red
Ensign.

Our surprise when we boarded the twin-screw *Kosciuszko* was
educational. She was a large and well-appointed liner. The signs
about her for the directions of passengers were in Hebrew and
five other languages. Her officers were sure she could catch anything afloat; indeed, we were soon learning aboard her that our
knowledge of the latest European economics and politics and of

modern geography was nothing but old rags and tatters. We met a young Pole aboard—naturally he was a Count—who spoke seven languages; he was there to teach English to the crew. Her captain, a courteous and elderly giant, approached us and was concerned for our comfort in his ship. He had much to say of Polish mariners, who went to sea soon after the war ended. As he talked of the lore and literature of the sea I began to be sure that I had a card to win over this Polish ship's master; so when he mentioned Joseph Conrad I told him casually—playing my ace on the instant—that I had known Conrad. It was no trump. The captain of the *Kosciuszko* brushed Conrad lightly aside. "I speak fourteen languages," was all he said.

This was in the Aegean Sea. We passed close to Homer's "lofty Skyros." In its way, our voyage was stranger than if we were early navigators, for the man is not born who would dare to attempt a modern Odyssey. It was curious to watch the shadow of Lesbos in the distance while Syrian girls in sailors' slacks promenaded the deck. They gave no attention to Lesbos, yet Sappho herself might have resembled one of those girls. It was still more strange to see Lemnos, and Imbros beyond, and Cape Helles, and remember the fateful landing of a British army, while leaning on the rail of a Polish ship beside a Rabbi. For the world is becoming inexplicably mixed, even though nationalism can be as rabid as an infected dog. Turks, Jews, Syrians, Greeks, and the rest of us, follow the same fashions. We are so very much alike. Only the Rabbi was a little distinguished in his black silk gaberdine and a black skullcap. A brisk and youthful Turkish officer, one of our passengers, with his Hitler mustache and fair complexion, would have passed unnoticed at Aldershot for the common British infantry subaltern. The Turkish women with us could have walked without attracting more attention than their sisters in London or the Rue St. Honoré.

For that reason we turned, instead, to the admonishing landmarks. To starboard was the Plain of Troy; near that point abeam the Scamander entered the sea. To port was Atchi Baba, and along the shore were the white tombs of the great failure of the Dardanelles campaign, testifying to the heroism of common men wasted in a later and greater war. The sunset was glorious but aloof. Its light made the graves along the Gallipoli peninsula as plain as numberless rebukes without meaning, for what they signify has become as legendary as the marks on the opposite coast of Troas, where men died for lovely Helen. The Rabbi beside us, who was very still, continued to contemplate the scene with us, but perhaps he was thinking of servitude in Babylon; or his evening thoughts might, indeed, have been where moth and rust and the sword cannot corrupt; he was a venerable man.

In the Narrows we were boarded by severe, suspicious, and energetic Turks armed with the usual automatics, and passengers were assembled in the smoke room, and subjected to so searching a scrutiny that one could have been sure not a goat was left among the sheep, only we know how easily in this world goats will pass through, while lambs are left to bleat in appeal at the implacable gate.

There was a waking moment when I suspected the liner was much too quiet, and went on deck. We were at anchor. The coming day was announced to a sleeping world from the minarets of the City of the Seven Hills. The dome of St. Sophia was glowing over the ship. Constantinople! But that was not what I was looking for, not so soon. I began to search, in a light that was dim over the water, for a familiar funnel among that plentiful shipping which had not yet come to life; but could not find it. I turned aft, in resignation; and there, at the buoys under our counter, was our little *Zircon*. I was free then to see at my ease what sunrise could do with modern Byzantium.

MONTAIGNE

By ANDRE GIDE

ONTAIGNE is the author of a single book—the Essays. But in this one book, written without preconceived plan, without method, as events or his reading chanced to suggest, he claims to give us his whole self. He published four surviving editions of it—four different settings, I might almost say—the first in 1580, when he was forty-seven years old. This text he revised, he corrected, he perfected, and at his death, in 1592, he left yet another copy of his work loaded with emendations and addenda which were incorporated in later editions. Meanwhile Montaigne travelled through South Germany and Italy, in 1580 and 1581, and then filled the important post of Mayor of Bordeaux; he gives his readers the benefit of the observations he gathered in foreign lands and of the experiences of his public life at a period when the wars of religion were profoundly troubling his country.

From this time onwards, leaving public affairs in order to occupy himself only with his own thoughts, he shut himself up in his library and for the rest of his life never left the little château in Périgord where he was born. Here he wrote the additional chapters that constitute the third book of the Essays; he revised the old ones, corrected, improved, and expanded them. Occasionally, he encumbered his first text, too, with a load of quotations gathered in the course of his continual reading, for Montaigne was persuaded that everything had already been thought and said, and he was anxious to show that man is always and everywhere one and the same. The abundance of these quotations, which turn some of his chapters into a compact pudding of Greek and Latin authors, might cast a doubt on Montaigne's originality. It must indeed have been exceptionally great to triumph over such a jumble of antiquities.

This show of erudition was not peculiar to Montaigne, for his was a time when men's heads had been turned by Greek and Latin culture. Gibbon has very justly remarked that the study of the classics, which dates from much further back than the beginning of the Renaissance, retarded rather than hastened the intellectual development of the peoples of the West. The reason for this is that writers were then hunting for models rather than for inspiration and stimulus. Learning, in the days of Boccaccio and Rabelais, weighed heavily on men's minds and, far from helping to liberate, stifled them. The authority of the ancients, and of Aristotle in particular, drove culture into a rut and during the sixteenth century the University of Paris turned out almost nothing but bookworms and pedants.

Montaigne did not go so far as to rebel against this bookish culture, but he succeeded so well in assimilating and making it his own that it was never a hindrance to his mind, and in this he differs from all other writers of his time. At most, he follows the fashion by interlarding his works with quotations. But he asks, "What avails it us to have our bellies full of meat, if it be not digested? If it be not transchanged in us? except it nourish, augment and strengthen us?" And again, and more prettily, he compares himself to the bees who "here and there suck this and cull that flower, but afterwards they produce the honey which is peculiarly their own; then is it no more thyme or marjoram."

The success of the Essays would be inexplicable but for the author's extraordinary personality. What did he bring the world, then, that was so new? Self-knowledge—and all other knowledge seemed to him uncertain; but the human being he discovers —and uncovers—is so genuine, so true, that in him every reader of the Essays recognizes himself.

In every historical period, an attempt is made to cover over this real self with a conventional figure of humanity. Montaigne pushes aside this mask in order to get at what is essential; if he succeeds, it is thanks to assiduous effort and singular perspicacity; it is by opposing convention, established beliefs, conformism, with a spirit of criticism that is constantly on the alert, easy and at the same time tense, playful, amused at everything, smiling, indulgent yet uncompromising, for its object is to know and not to moralize.

"Montaigne is the frankest and honestest of all writers," says Emerson, who places him in his constellation of six "Representative Men" with Plato, Swedenborg, Shakespeare, Goethe, and Napoleon. In his study on "Montaigne, or The Sceptic," he tells us that the Essays "is the only book which we certainly know to have been in the poet's library"—the poet here being Shakespeare. Leigh Hunt, he adds, "relates of Lord Byron, that Montaigne was the only great writer of past times whom he read with avowed satisfaction," and further on he says, "Gibbon reckons, in these bigoted times [the sixteenth century] but two men of liberality in France: Henry IV and Montaigne."

For Montaigne, the body is as important as the mind; he does not separate the one from the other and is constantly careful never to give us his thoughts in the abstract. It is particularly incumbent on us, therefore, to see him before we listen to him. It is he himself who furnishes us with all the elements of a full-length portrait. Let us look at it.

He is rather short; his face is full without being fat; he wears a short beard according to the fashion of the period. All his senses are "sound, almost to perfection." Although he has used his robust health licentiously, it is still very hearty and only slightly affected by gravel at the age of forty-seven. His gait is assured, his gestures are brusque, his voice is loud and sonorous. He is fond of talking and always talks vehemently and excitedly. He eats of everything and anything so gluttonously that he sometimes bites his own fingers—for in those days forks were not in use. He rides a great deal, and even in his old age he is not fatigued by long hours in the saddle. Sleep, he tells us, takes up a great portion of his life. And I would on no account omit a little detail which may make American readers smile: when he sits down, he likes to have his "legs as high or higher than his seat."

The importance of an author lies not only in his personal value but also and greatly in the opportuneness of his message. There are some whose message is only of historical importance and finds no echo among us to-day. In past times, it may have stirred men's conscience, fed their enthusiasms, aroused revolutions; we have no ears for it now. Great authors are not only those whose work answers to the needs of one country and one period, but those who provide us with a food which is able to satisfy the different hungers of various nationalities and successive generations. "A heedy reader," says Montaigne, "shall often discover in other men's compositions perfections far different from the author's meaning, and such as haply he never dreamed of, and illustrateth them with richer senses and more excellent constructions." Is he himself such an author and will he be able to answer such new questions as the "heedy reader" of young America may wish to put to him?

In our time and in all countries, constructive minds are in particular request; the authors who are most admired are those who offer us a carefully composed system, a method for solving the agonizing political, social, and moral problems which are tormenting almost all peoples and every one of us individually. Montaigne, it is true, brings us no method (how could a method that might have been valid at his time be practicable in ours?), no philosophical or social system. No mind could be less ordered than his. He leaves it free to play and run wild as it pleases. And even his perpetual doubt, which made Emerson consider him as the most perfect representative of skepticism (that is to say, of antidogmatism, of the spirit of inquiry and investigation), may be compared, it has been said, to those purgative medicines which the patient ejects together with the stuff of which they rid him. So that some people have seen in his maxim *"Que sçais-je?"* (What do I know?) at once the highest mark of his wisdom and of his teaching. Not that it satisfies me. It is not their skepticism that pleases me in the Essays, nor is that the lesson I draw from them. A "heedy reader" will find in Montaigne more and better things than doubts and questions.

To Pilate's cruel question, which re-echoes down the ages, Montaigne seems to have adopted as his own, though in a quite human and profane manner, and in a very different sense, Christ's divine answer: "I am the truth." That is to say, he thinks he can know nothing *truly* but himself. This is what makes him talk so much about himself; for the knowledge of self seems to him indeed as important as any other. "The mask," he says, "must as well be taken from things as from men." He paints himself in order to unmask himself. And as the mask belongs much more to the country and the period than to the man himself, it is, above all, by the mask that people differ, so that in the being that is really unmasked, it is easy to recognize our own likeness.

He even comes to think that the portrait he paints of himself may be more generally interesting in proportion as it is more peculiar to himself; and it is by reason of this profound truth that we do, in fact, take so great an interest in his portrait; for "every man beareth the whole stamp of human condition." And more than this: Montaigne is convinced that, "as Pindarus said, to be sincerely true is the beginning of a great virtue." These admirable words which Montaigne borrowed from Plutarch, who himself took them from Pindar, I adopt as my own; I should like to inscribe them in the forefront of the Essays, for there, above all, lies the important lesson I draw from them.

And yet Montaigne does not seem to have himself at first grasped the boldness and reach of this resolve of his to admit only the truth about himself and to paint himself as Nature made him. This accounts for a certain early hesitation in his drawing, for his attempt to find shelter in the thick undergrowths of history, for his piling up of quotations and examples—authorizations, I was tempted to say—for his endless gropings. His interest in himself is at first vague and confused; with no very clear idea as to what is important, and with a suspicion that perhaps the things that are most negligible in appearance and the most commonly disdained may in reality be just those that are most worthy of attention. Everything in himself is an object of curiosity, amusement, and astonishment: "I have seen no such monster or more express wonder in this world than myself. With time and custom a man doth acquaint and enure himself to all strangeness; but the more I frequent and know myself, the more my deformity astonisheth me, and the less I understand myself." How delightful it is to hear him talking like this of his "deformity," when what we like about him is precisely what enables us to recognize him as one of ourselves—just an ordinary man.

It is only when he gets to the third and last book of the Essays (which does not figure in the first edition) that Montaigne, in full possession not of himself (he will never be that—no one can be) but of his subject, ceases to grope his way; he knows what he wants to say, what he must say, and he says it admirably, with a grace, a playfulness, a felicity, and an ingenuity of expression that are incomparable. "Others," he says (speaking of moralists), "fashion man, I relate him." And a few lines further on and more subtly, "I describe not the essence but the passage." (Germans would say the *Werden,* the becoming.) For Montaigne is constantly preoccupied by the perpetual flux of all things, and in these words he points to the nonstability of human personality which never *is,* but is only conscious of itself in the evanescent moment of becoming. And as all other certainties break down around him, this one at least grows greater and stronger, that on this subject, at any rate—the subject of himself—he is "the cunningest man alive" and that "never man waded further into his subject, nor arrived more exactly and fully to the end he proposed unto himself," for which he has "need of naught but faithfulness"; and he immediately adds, "which is therein as sincere and pure as may be found."

I think the great pleasure we take in Montaigne's Essays comes from the great pleasure he took in writing them, a pleasure we feel, so to speak, in every sentence. Of all the chapters that compose the three books of the Essays, one alone is distinctly tedious; it is by far the longest and the only one he wrote with application, care, and a concern for composition. This is the "Apology for Raymond Sebond," a Spanish philosopher, born in the fourteenth century, who professed medicine in France at the University of Toulouse, and whose "Theologia Naturalis" Montaigne had laboriously translated at his father's request. "It was a strange task and new occupation for me: but, by fortune, being then at leisure and unable to gainsay the commandment of the best father that ever was, I came ere long (as well as I could) to an end of it." This chapter is the first that Montaigne wrote. It is one of the most celebrated and oftenest quoted, for Montaigne's mind, by nature so rambling and unordered, here strives to develop a sort of doctrine and give apparent consistency to his inconsistent skepticism. But just because he is keeping his mind on the lead, it loses almost all its grace, the exquisite charm of its indolent progress; he is directing it, we feel, towards an object, and we are never enchanted as we are later on when he allows it to venture tentatively down untraced paths and gather all the casually encountered flowers that grow by the wayside. No works, I should like here to remark, are more naturally perfect and beautiful than those which the author has most delighted in writing, those in which difficulty and effort are least apparent. In art, seriousness is of no avail; the surest guide is enjoyment. In all, or almost all, the other writings which go to make up the different chapters of the Essays, Montaigne's thought remains, as it were, in the fluid state, so uncertain, so changing, and even contradictory, that the most diverse interpretations of it were subsequently given. Some writers, as, for instance, Pascal and Kant, attempt to see in him a Christian; others, like Emerson, an exemplar of skepticism; others a precursor of Voltaire. Sainte-Beuve went so far as to look upon the Essays as a sort of preparation, of antechamber to Spinoza's "Ethics." But Sainte-Beuve seems to me nearest the truth when he says: "With an appearance of making himself out peculiar, of reducing himself to a bundle of odd manias, he has touched each one of us in his most secret heart, and while portraying himself with careless, patient, and incessantly repeated strokes, he has cunningly painted the majority of mankind, and all the more successfully as he has the more minutely dissected his single self—'wavering and diverse' as he says. Each one of us finds a morsel of his own property in Montaigne."

I consider it a mark of great strength in Montaigne that he succeeded in accepting his own inconsistencies and contradictions. At the beginning of the second book of the Essays, the following sentence sounds the alarm: "Those who exercise themselves in controlling human actions, find no such difficulty in any one part as to piece them together and bring them to one same lustre; for they commonly contradict one another so strangely, as it seemeth impossible they should be parcels of one warehouse." None of the great specialists of the human heart—whether Shakespeare or Cervantes or Racine—has failed to have at any rate fleeting glimpses of the inconsistency of human beings. But, no doubt, it was necessary to establish for the time being a somewhat rudimentary psychology, on general and sharply defined lines, as a preliminary to the construction of a classical art. Lovers had to be nothing but lovers, misers wholly misers, and jealous men a hundred per cent jealous, while good care had to be taken that no one should have a share of all these qualities at once. Montaigne speaks of those "good authors" (and what he says is even truer of those who followed him than of those he was acquainted with) "who choose an universal air and following that image, range and interpret all a man's actions; which, if they cannot wrest sufficiently, they remit them unto dissimulation." And he adds, "Augustus hath escaped their hands," in much the same tone as Saint-Evremond, who nearly a century later says, of Plutarch, "There are corners and twists in our soul which have escaped him. . . . He judged men too much in the rough and did not believe them to be so different from themselves as they are. . . . What he thinks contradictory he attributes to external causes, . . . which Montaigne understood far better." It seems to me that Montaigne, unlike Saint-Evremond, saw more than the mere "inconstancy" in man; I think that it is precisely under cover of this word that the real question lies hidden, and that it was not until much later that Dostoevsky, and then Proust, attacked it so that some people say, "What is at issue here is the very conception of man on which we are now living"—a conception which Freud and some others are now in process of breaking down. Perhaps the most surprising thing about Montaigne, the thing that touches us most directly, is the occasional sudden light he casts unexpectedly, and, as it were, involuntarily, upon the uncertain frontiers of human personality and upon the instability of the ego.

Montaigne's contemporaries no doubt slid over the few passages which shake us most to-day without having eyes to see them, or at any rate to judge of their importance. And, no doubt, Montaigne himself partly shared their indifference, just as he shared their curiosity as to things which no longer interest us; and if he were to come back to earth to-day, he might very well say, "If I had known that that was what you would care about, there is a great deal more I might have told you!"—Why in the world didn't you, then? It was not your contemporaries it was important to please, but *us*. The points which were criticised or overlooked by a writer's own epoch are often the very points by which he succeeds in reaching and communicating with us across the ages. To foresee in the midst of the day's preoccupations what will still deserve the interest of coming generations demands a peculiar penetration indeed.

Love does not seem to have played much of a part in Montaigne's life; sensuality played a larger one. He seems to have married without great enthusiasm. And if, in spite of this, he was a good husband, he, nevertheless, wrote towards the end of his life, "It is haply more easy to neglect and pass over all the sex than duly and wholly to maintain himself in his wife's company"—which does not point exactly to his having done so. He had the lowest opinion of women, and beyond the pleasure he takes with them, confines them to the cares of the household. I have noted all the passages in the Essays in which he speaks of them; there is not one that is not insulting. And yet towards the end of his life he made an exception to this severity in favor of Mlle. Marie de Gournay, his *"fille d'alliance,"* "and truly of me beloved with more than a fatherly love, and as one of the best parts of my being enfeoffed in my home and solitariness." And he even adds, "There is nothing in the world I esteem more than her." She was only twenty and Montaigne was fifty-four when she was taken with an affection "more than superabounding" for the author of the Essays. It would be ungrateful not to mention this mutual attachment, which was entirely spiritual in its nature, for it is to Mlle. de Gournay's care and devotion that we owe the extremely important new edition of the Essays which appeared in 1595—three years after Montaigne's death—as well as the preservation of the manuscripts which served later for the establishment of the most authoritative text.

As to his own children, "they all die out at nurse," he tells us perfunctorily. An only daughter "escaped this misfortune," and the successive bereavements do not seem to have affected him greatly.

Montaigne, however, was by no means incapable of sympathy, and particularly towards small and humble folk: "I willingly give myself . . . unto the meaner sort . . . through some natural compassion, which in me is infinitely powerful." But, for equilibrium's sake, his reason immediately demands a correction. "I have a very feeling and tender compassion of other men's afflictions, and should more easily weep for company's sake, if possible for any occasion whatsoever I could shed tears." La Rochefoucauld says at a later date, forestalling Nietzsche's famous, "Let us be hard": "I am little susceptible to pity, and wish I were not so at all." But such declarations as these touch me particularly when they come from those who, like Montaigne and Nietzsche, are naturally tenderhearted.

Of Montaigne's sentimental life, friendship alone has left any trace in his work. Etienne de La Boëtie, his elder by three years, and author of a single short work on "Voluntary Servitude," inspired him with a feeling which seems to have occupied an important place in his heart and mind. This little book is not enough to make us consider La Boëtie "the greatest man of the age," as Montaigne did, but no doubt it helps us to understand the nature of the attachment which the future author of the Essays felt for a singularly generous and noble character.

Notwithstanding the beauty of this friendship, we may wonder whether it did not put some constraint upon Montaigne, and ask ourselves what the voluptuous author of the Essays would have been like if he had not met La Boëtie, and, above all, what the Essays would have been like if La Boëtie had not died so young (at the age of thirty-three), and if he had continued to exercise his influence over his friend. Sainte-Beuve, our great critic, quotes a very fine saying of the younger Pliny's: "I have lost the witness of my life. I fear I may henceforth live more carelessly." But this "carelessness" is just what we like so much about Montaigne. Under La Boëtie's eyes, he draped himself a little in antique fashion. In this, too, he was as sincere as ever, for he was greatly enamored of heroism; but he did not like a man to be artificial, and liked it less and less; more and more, he came to fear that to grow in height must mean to increase in narrowness.

La Boëtie, in a piece of Latin verse addressed to Montaigne, says: "For you, there is more to combat, for you, our friend, whom we know to be equally inclined both to outstanding vices and to virtues." Montaigne, when once La Boëtie disappeared, withdrew more and more from the combat, as much from natural inclination as from philosophy. There is nothing Montaigne dislikes more than a personality—or rather an impersonality—obtained artificially, laboriously, contentiously, in accordance with morals, propriety, custom, and what he likens to prejudices. It is as though the true self which all this hampers, hides, or distorts, keeps in his eyes a sort of mystic value, and as if he were expecting from it some surprising kind of revelation. I understand, of course, how easy it is here to play upon words and to see in Montaigne's teaching nothing but a counsel to abandon oneself to Nature, to follow one's instincts blindly, and even to grant precedence to the vilest, which always seem the sincerest—that is, the most natural—those which, by their very density and thickness are invariably to be found at the bottom of the recipient, even when the noblest passions have shaken him. But I believe this would be a very wrong interpretation of Montaigne, who, though he concedes a large allowance, too large perhaps, to the instincts we have in common with animals, knows how to take off from them in order to rise, and never allows himself to be their slave or victim.

It is natural that with such ideas, Montaigne should feel very little inclined to repentance and contrition. "I am grown aged by eight years since my first publications," he writes in 1588, "but I doubt whether I be amended one inch." And again: "The disorders and excesses wherein I have found myself engaged, . . . I have condemned according to their worth. . . . But that is all." Such declarations abound in the last part of the Essays. He also says, again to some people's great indignation: "Were I to live again, it should be as I have already lived. I neither deplore what is past nor dread what is to come." These declarations are certainly as little Christian as possible. Every time Montaigne speaks of Christianity, it is with the strangest (sometimes, one might almost say, with the most malicious) impertinence. He often treats of religion, never of Christ. Not once does he refer to His words; one might almost doubt whether he had ever read the Gospels—or rather, one cannot doubt that he never read them seriously. As for the respect he shows Catholicism, there undoubtedly enters into it a large amount of prudence. (We must remember that the great massacre of Protestants throughout France on the eve of St. Bartholomew's Day took place in 1572.) The example of Erasmus was a warning to him, and it is easy to understand that he was far from anxious to be obliged to write his "Retractations." I know that, as a matter of fact, Erasmus never wrote his, but he had to promise the church that he would. And even a promise of this kind is a nuisance. Far better to be wily.

In the 1582 and 1595 editions of the Essays, a multitude of conciliatory additions have been introduced into the chapter entitled "Of Prayers and Orisons." During his travels in Italy in 1581, Montaigne had presented his book to Pope Gregory the Thirteenth, who was the founder of the Gregorian calendar now in use. The Pope complimented him but made a few reservations of which Montaigne took account in the passages he afterwards introduced into the Essays. In these and in others as well, Montaigne insists, to excess and with much repetition, on his perfect orthodoxy and submission to the church. The church, indeed, showed herself at that time extremely accommodating; she had come to terms with the cultural development of the Renaissance; Erasmus, in spite of the accusation of atheism which caused his books to be condemned in Paris, was put up as a candidate for the cardinalate; the works of Machiavelli, notwithstanding their profoundly irreligious character, had been printed in Rome by virtue of a "brief" of Clement the Seventh. This tolerance and relaxation on the part of the church incited the great leaders of the Reformation to a corresponding increase of intransigence. Montaigne could come to an understanding with Catholicism but not with Protestantism. He accepted religion provided it was satisfied with a semblance. What he wrote about princes applied in his mind to ecclesiastical authorities as well: "All inclination and submission is due to them, except the mind's.

My reason is not framed to bend or stoop; my knees are."

In order still further to protect his book, he felt impelled to insert other passages of a very reassuring nature, in which he is hardly recognizable, into those very parts of the Essays which are most likely to arouse alarm in the hearts of sincere Christians: "This only end, of another life, blessedly immortal, doth rightly merit we should abandon the pleasures and commodities of this our life." This passage (which for that matter was left in manuscript and only published after his death) and other similar ones seem to have been stuck into his book like so many lightning conductors—or better still, like labels of lemonade or ginger ale fixed upon bottles of whisky when a state has "gone dry." And, in fact, a few lines after the lightning conductor come the words: "We must tooth and nail retain the use of this life's pleasures, which our years snatch from us one after another."

This passage of the first edition, which the added lines attempt in vain to disguise, shows the true Montaigne, that "sworn enemy to all falsifications"; and I should be indignant at this cautious recantation if I did not think that it had perhaps been necessary in order to get his wares safely through to us. Sainte-Beuve says of him very justly: "He may have appeared a very good Catholic except for not having been a Christian." So that one might say of Montaigne what he himself said of the Emperor Julian: "In matters of religion he was vicious everywhere. He was surnamed the Apostate because he had forsaken ours; notwithstanding this opinion seems to me more likely, that he never took it to heart, but that for the obedience which he bare to the law he dissembled till he had gotten the empire into his hands"; and what he said later, quoting Marcellinus, again about Julian—he "hatched Paganism in his heart but forasmuch as he saw all those of his army to be Christians, he durst not discover himself." What he likes about Catholicism, what he admires and praises, is its order and ancientness. "In this controversy by which France is at this instant molested with civil wars, the best and safest side is no doubt that which maintaineth both the ancient religion and policy of the country," he says. For "all violent changes and great alterations, disorder, distemper, and shake a state very much." And "the oldest and best known evil is ever more tolerable than a fresh and unexperienced mischief." There is no need to look for any other explanation of his ignorance of the Gospels and his hatred of Protestant reformers. He wishes to keep the church's religion—France's religion—as it is, not because he thinks it the only good one but because he thinks it would be bad to change it.

In the same way, we feel throughout Montaigne's life and writings a constant love of order and moderation, care for the public good, refusal to let his own personal interest prevail over the interest of all. But he believes that the honesty of his own judgment and the preservation of that honesty are more valuable than any other considerations and should be set above them. "I would rather let all affairs go to wrack than force my faith and conscience for their avail." And I prefer to believe in the sincerity of this statement rather than ask myself whether he is not bragging a little; for it is as important nowadays that such words should be listened to as it was important in Montaigne's troubled times that there should be men to keep the integrity of their conscience and maintain their independence and autonomy above the herd instincts of submission and cowardly acceptance. "All universal judgments are weak, loose, and dangerous"; or again: "There is no course of life so weak and sottish as that which is managed by Order, Method, and Discipline." Passages of this kind abound in the Essays, and as they seem to me of the highest importance, particularly nowadays, I will quote one more: "The Commonwealth requireth some to betray, some to lie" (and, alas, he was obliged to add later) "and some to massacre: leave we that commission to people more obedient and more pliable." When he resigned his post of magistrate and later on too, when he retired from the mayoralty of Bordeaux to occupy himself henceforth exclusively with himself, he judged very rightly that the elaboration of his Essays would be the greatest service he could render to the state, and—let me add—to all mankind. For it must be observed that the idea of mankind for Montaigne predominates greatly over that of country. After a wonderful panegyric of France, or at any rate of Paris, "the glory of France and one of the noblest and chief ornaments of the world," which he loved "so tenderly that even her spots, her blemishes, and her warts are dear to me," he takes care to say that his love of the human race is greater still. I esteem, he says, "all men as my countrymen"; and as "kindly embrace a Polonian as a Frenchman, subordinating the national bond to universal and common." "Friendships," he adds, "merely acquired by ourselves do ordinarily exceed those to which we are joined either by communication of climate or affinity of blood. Nature hath placed us in the world free and unbound; we imprison ourselves into certain straits, as the Kings of Persia, who bound themselves never to drink other water than of the river Choaspez, foolishly renouncing all lawful right of use in all other waters."

> Each of us inevitable;
> Each of us limitless; each of us with his or
> her right upon the earth,

says Walt Whitman. How Montaigne would have delighted—Montaigne who was so unblushing on the subject of his person, so anxious not to oppose the soul to the flesh and to proclaim the latter's legitimate and healthy pleasures—how he would have delighted to hear Whitman sing, indecently and gloriously, the beauties and robust joys of his body!

One never comes to an end with Montaigne. As he speaks of everything without order or method, any man can glean what he likes from the Essays, which will often be what some other man would leave aside. There is no author it is easier to give a twist to without incurring the blame of betraying him, for he himself sets the example and constantly contradicts and betrays himself. "Verily (and I fear not to avouch it), I could easily for a need bring a candle to Saint Michael and another to his Dragon." This, it must be admitted, is more likely to please the Dragon than Saint Michael. Montaigne, indeed, is not beloved by partisans, whom he certainly did not love, which explains why after his death he was not held in much favor, at any rate, in France, which was torn in two by the bitterest factions. Between 1595 (he died in 1592) and 1635, there were only three or four re-issues of the Essays. It was abroad, in Italy, in Spain, and particularly in England that Montaigne soon became popular during this period of French disfavor or half-favor. In Bacon's essays and Shakespeare's plays, there are unmistakable traces of Montaigne's influence.

The British Museum has a copy of Florio's translation of Montaigne which bears, it is believed, one of the rare signatures of the author of "Hamlet." It is in this play in particular that English critics have found traces of Montaigne's philosophy. And in "The Tempest" he makes Gonzalo say:

Had I plantation of this isle . . .
And were the king on't, what would I do? . . .
I' the commonwealth I would by contraries
Execute all things; for no kind of traffic
Would I admit; no name of magistrate;
Letters should not be known; riches, poverty,
And use of service, none; contract, succession,
Bourn, bound of land, tilth, vineyard, none; . . .
No occupation; all men idle, all;
And women too, but innocent and pure;
No sovereignty . . .
All things in common nature should produce
Without sweat or endeavor; treason, felony,
Sword, pike, knife, gun, or need of any engine,
Would I not have; but nature should bring forth,
Of its own kind, all foison, all abundance,
To feed my innocent people.

These lines are almost a translation from a passage in the chapter of the Essays on "Cannibals," or, at any rate, are greatly inspired by it. Everything that Montaigne says in this chapter may be of particular interest to Americans, for his subject is the New World, which had been recently discovered, and towards which Europe was turning ecstatic glances. It hardly matters that countless illusions went to make up the prestige of these distant lands. Montaigne delights in describing their inhabitants and the purity of their manners and customs, just as Diderot, two centuries later, painted the manners of the Tahitians in order to shame those of the Old World. Both understand what instruction and guidance the whole of humanity might gather from the example of one happy man.

In his drift away from Christianity, it is to Goethe that Montaigne draws near by anticipation. "As for me, then, I love my [life] and cherish it, such as it hath pleased God to grant it us. . . . Nature is a gentle guide, yet not more gentle than prudent and just." Goethe would, no doubt, gladly have endorsed these lines which are almost the last of the Essays. This is the final flowering of Montaigne's wisdom. Not a word of it is useless. How very careful he is to add the idea of prudence, justice, and culture to his declaration of the love of life!

What Montaigne teaches us especially is what was called at a much later date "liberalism," and I think that it is the wisest lesson that can be drawn from him at the present time, when political or religious convictions are so miserably dividing all men and setting them against one another. "In the present intestine trouble of our State, my interest hath not made me forget neither the commendable qualities of our adversaries, nor the reproachful of those I have followed." He adds a little later: "A good orator loseth not his grace by pleading against me." And further on these admirable lines: "They will . . . that our persuasion and judgment serve not the truth but the project of our desires. I should rather err in the other extremity; so much I fear my desire might corrupt me. Considering, I somewhat tenderly distrust myself in things I most desire." These qualities of mind and soul are never more needed and would never be of greater service than at the times when they are most generally disregarded.

This rare and extraordinary propensity, of which he often speaks, to listen to, and even espouse, other people's opinions, to the point of letting them prevail over his own, prevented him from venturing very far along the road that was afterwards to be Nietzsche's. He is held back by a natural prudence, from which, as from a safeguard, he is very loth to depart. He shrinks from desert places and regions where the air is too rarefied. But a restless curiosity spurs him on, and in the realm of ideas he habitually behaves as he did when travelling. The secretary who accompanied him on his tour kept a journal. "I never saw him less tired," he writes, "nor heard him complain less of his pain" (Montaigne suffered at that time from gravel, which did not prevent him from remaining for hours in the saddle); "with a mind, both on the road and in our halting places, so eager for any encounters, so on the lookout for opportunities to speak to strangers, that I think it distracted him from his ills." He declared he had "no project but to perambulate through unknown places," and further: "He took such great pleasure in travelling that he hated the neighborhood of the place where he was obliged to rest." Moreover, he "was accustomed to say that after having passed a restless night, when in the morning it came to his mind he had a town or new country to visit, he would rise with eagerness and alacrity." Montaigne himself writes in his Essays: "Well I wot that being taken according to the bare letter, the pleasure of travelling brings a testimony of unquietness and irresolution, which, to say truth, are our mistress and predominant qualities. Yes, I confess it: I see nothing but in a dream or by wishing, wherein I may lay hold. Only variety and possession or diversity doth satisfy me, if at least anything satisfy me."

Montaigne was very nearly fifty years old when he undertook the first and only long journey of his life through South Germany and Italy. This journey lasted seventeen months and in all probability would have lasted still longer, considering the extreme pleasure he took in it, if his unexpected election as Mayor of Bordeaux had not suddenly recalled him to France. From that moment he directed towards ideas the high-spirited curiosity that had sent him hurrying along the roads.

It is very instructive to follow through the successive editions of the Essays the modifications of his attitude towards death. He entitles one of the first chapters of his book "That To Philosophize Is To Learn How To Die," in which we read: "There is nothing wherewith I have ever more entertained myself than with the imaginations of death, yea, in the most licentious times of my age." His idea was that, by familiarizing himself with these "imaginations," he would diminish their horror. But in the last edition of his Essays he reached the point of saying: "I am now by means of the mercy of God in such a taking that without regret or grieving at any worldly matter I am prepared to dislodge whensoever he shall please to call me. I am everywhere free; my farewell is soon taken of all my friends, except of myself. No man did ever prepare himself to quit the world more simply and fully, or more generally left all thoughts of it, than I am fully assured I shall do . . . nor can death put me in mind of any new thing." He almost comes to love this death as he loves all that is natural.

We are told that Montaigne made a very Christian end. All we can say is that he was by no means on the road to it. It is true that his wife and daughter were present at his last moments, and, no doubt, they induced him, out of sympathy as often happens, to die not that "death united in itself, quietly and solitary, wholly mine, convenient to my retired and private life," with which he would have been content, but more devoutly than he would have done of himself. Was it a presentiment of this that made him write of death, "If I were to choose, I think it should rather be on horseback than in a bed, away from my home, and far from my friends"?

If I am accused of having sharpened Montaigne's ideas to excess, my answer is that numbers of his commentators have busied themselves with blunting them. I have merely removed their wrappings and disengaged them from the wadding that sometimes chokes the Essays and prevents their shafts from reaching us. The great preoccupation of pedagogues, when they are faced with authors of some boldness, who yet are classics, is to render them inoffensive; and I often wonder that the work of years should so naturally contribute to this. After a little, it seems as if the edge of new thoughts gets worn away, and, on the other hand, we are able to handle them without fear of injury.

During his travels in Italy, Montaigne is often surprised to see the loftiest monuments of ancient Rome half buried in a mass of fallen litter. Their summits have been the first to crumble, and it is their own fragments that strew the earth around them and gradually raise its level. If, in our day, they do not seem to tower so high above us, it is also because we do not stand so far below them.

THE GREATEST LOVE STORY
IN THE WORLD

By CLARENCE DAY, JR.

I F a crown were awarded to the greatest love story, there
might be many candidates, but surely only one would seem
pre-eminent to a competent jury. Most of the famous love
stories are entirely too smoky, too turgid. Abélard and
Héloïse, Paolo and Francesca, Tristan and Iseult—none has the
clear note of beauty. No, the noblest and best of such tales was
written by a Victorian, a troubadour disguised as a jester—the
good Edward Lear.

The characters in his drama are, first, Handel Jones, Esquire,
who is the head of Handel Jones & Company, a great English
firm. Second, his wife, Lady Jingly Jones, who does not like her
husband. Third, a small, lonely hermit, with the heart of a Ro-
meo or Leander, whose musical and mysterious name is the
Yonghy-Bonghy-Bò.

An uninspired writer would either begin with the woes of the
Joneses, or else he would have the third person appear in their
home and plant complications. But why describe the old familiar
details of an unhappy marriage? As well describe the spots in
each case of measles—they are always the same. And why dwell
on the complications of a triangle? That is quite as banal to free
spirits, in spite of the ever-fresh interest taken in them by pris-
oners.

Edward Lear, being a man of genius, omits the whole business. He begins by introducing us, not to the husband and wife,
but to the true hero, the Other Man. And where does he ingeniously place him? Why, far off in the wilds. We are made to
feel at first as though he were utterly alone in the world. He sets
him before us so simply that we are attracted at once:

> On the Coast of Coromandel
> Where the early pumpkins blow,
> In the middle of the woods
> Lived the Yonghy-Bonghy-Bò.
> Two old chairs, and half a candle—
> One old jug without a handle—
> These were all his worldly goods:
> In the middle of the woods
> These were all the worldly goods
> Of the Yonghy-Bonghy-Bò.

We hardly need to know any more of his nature than that. Compared to him, Thoreau on his river was a collector of bric-a-brac. The Bò had even fewer requirements than a saint in the desert.

But unlike the usual recluse he had no hard austerity; he was not a misanthrope but a warm-hearted lover of life.

Hence there comes that great day—once to every man—when he finds the right woman; and never has that poignant moment been more sweetly sung:

> Once, among the Bong-trees walking
> Where the early pumpkins blow,
> To a little heap of stones
> Came the Yonghy-Bonghy-Bò.
> There he heard a Lady talking
> To some milk-white Hens of Dorking—
> " 'Tis the Lady Jingly Jones!
> On that little heap of stones
> Sits the Lady Jingly Jones!"
> Said the Yonghy-Bonghy-Bò.

He is so intensely moved that he immediately springs into action. When an instantaneous recognition of the right woman is vouchsafed to a man, the right thing to do is not to shilly-shally but to wed her at once. "Will you come and be my wife?" he begs:

> I am tired of living singly
> On this coast so wild and shingly.

He tells her in the first place how happy she would make him; and then, in the second, to reassure any womanly doubts of hers about what they would live on, he describes how plentiful the food is in Coromandel—at least the shrimps, prawns, and watercresses. In addition he offers her all his possessions. He holds nothing back:

> You shall have my chairs and candle,
> And my jug without a handle.

And for occupation she and he can gaze on the rolling deep, he suggests. "As the sea, my love is deep," he adds quietly, and awaits her reply.

She is entranced. Who would not be? She has already perceived that he is the ideal lover for whom all women long. But imagine her anguish. To marry this dear hermit is a happiness that she cannot have—she has forfeited the right to it by already having a husband.

> Lady Jingly answered sadly,
>   And her tears began to flow—
>   "Your proposal comes too late
>   Mr. Yonghy-Bonghy-Bò!
> I would be your wife most gladly"
> (Here she twirled her fingers madly)
>   "But in England I've a mate!
>   Yes! you've asked me far too late,
>   For in England I've a mate,
>   Mr. Yonghy-Bonghy-Bò!"

England seems a far-away place to the Bò, but Lady Jingly is tied to it. She describes her incumbrance and how he still sends Dorking fowls to her. He must have been an affectionate man, for he delights to do this, it seems. She says if he sends her any more she will give the Bò three of them. A woman of finer sensibilities would hardly have made such an offer, but wives get callous in married life and don't realize that lovers are sensitive. Yet she means to be considerate of the Bò and his feelings—she will not let herself play with them. She sends him away. She wishes she didn't have to say it, she tells him, but

> Will you please to go away?
> That is all I have to say,
> Mr. Yonghy-Bonghy-Bò.

He goes. It is over. His one crowded hour of love-life is dead. Down the slippery slopes of myrtle he flees to the bay, and there he finds "a large and lively Turtle" on which he departs.

> Through the silent-roaring ocean
> Did the Turtle swiftly go;
> Holding fast upon his shell
> Rode the Yonghy-Bonghy-Bò.
> With a sad primeval motion
> Towards the sunset isles of Boshen
> Still the Turtle bore him well.
> Holding fast upon his shell,
> "Lady Jingly Jones, farewell!"
> Sang the Yonghy-Bonghy-Bò.

There's our clear note of beauty. Lohengrin on his swan and the Bò on his turtle—those are the two finest lyrics.

When Ibsen wrote the "Doll's House" his fame spread round the world. But long before the "Doll's House" was written, Lear gave us this sequel. Ibsen's play ended with Nora's going out of the door to achieve independence. Lear shows us what she did with it, nothing: except to wreck one more life. But the Bò had so beautiful a spirit that he hardly seems wrecked, as he sails away into the sunset, singing that longing farewell.

And then in the last scene of all, we are given a glimpse of the woman. As the Bò disappears on the ocean, Lear turns back our eyes and shows us that small huddled figure alone on her stones, weeping into a jug without a handle, among the incurious hens.

THE AMERICAN WRITERS AND THE NEW WORLD

By ARCHIBALD MACLEISH

I T was apparent even before the war began that there was a new world in being and that the existence of that world created obligations—obligations and difficulties—for those who followed the profession of writer. One cause of our disastrous difficulties was our failure to occupy—imaginatively and understandingly to occupy as only the writer can give us to occupy it—the world in which we lived. Certain scientific discoveries, certain inventions now commonplace, had altered not only the possibilities of the world but its actualities also: not only its dreams but its geography. And our failure to occupy, not only intellectually but imaginatively, not only practically but emotionally, the world thus created, was in large part responsible for the maladjustment and insecurity from which we suffered. It is not physical nature alone which abhors a vacuum nor is it only air and water which flood in to fill the empty space. If men do not occupy for themselves the new continents, the enemies of men will occupy them.

But if it was apparent even before this war that there was a new world in process of creation it is even more obvious now. There are some, I realize, who still find it possible to believe that the vast struggle of our time is nothing but another "European war" which we may notice or decline to notice as we please. They are not, however, people whose good judgment—whatever may be said for their good intentions—has impressed their fellow citizens. Aside from this minority and a handful of equally earnest but decidedly less honest people engaged in propagandizing the sword-and-pistol Marxian theory of the imperialist war, the great majority of our contemporaries believe that they have seen what they have seen and heard what they have heard.

They believe, that is to say, that fascism is world revolution aimed at the overthrow not only of political systems and economic systems but of social systems as well, and of the entire fabric of moral and cultural values upon which the world as men have known it for many centuries has rested. They differ among themselves only in this—that some of them believe the new order of discipline, authority, and war which fascism proposes to substitute, and has already in many places substituted, for these systems and fabrics is the true shape of the future and must, therefore, be accepted, while others believe the true shape of the future is the very different order of freedom, responsibility, and life which those who hate and fear fascism will be obliged to raise against it as a weapon of their own defense.

But neither those of the first opinion nor those of the second, nor any others who have watched this time with honesty and courage, doubt for a moment that the world we are in process of creating will be a world unlike the world which went before. Those who believe that fascism is the shape of the future can see their future mirrored in a dozen countries and in the faces of the men and women of a hundred once great towns. The rest of us, who believe that democracy, menaced by forces darker, bloodier, and more brutal than those which forced its birth, will of necessity become democracy again and labor and create, can guess our future also. Both worlds are very different from the world we know.

Those who follow the profession of writer seriously and honestly now and in the years which will follow these years will face, therefore, a great obligation and a great difficulty.

The central problem of any art, but, above all, of the art of letters, is the problem of the reduction of experience to form; and a revolutionary change in the structure of experience presents of necessity a revolutionary problem to the artist. The scientist who deciphers experience by abstracting from it absolute quantities can let his absolute quantities stand however violently the reactions of men to each other and the earth may alter; and the philosopher who explains experience by fixing it in abstract terms may pin his abstract terms to the world's skin however the world's skin wrinkles. The artist has no such freedom from change and time. His labor is the labor of translating one form of experience—his life—to another form of experience—his art —and the second must change as the first changes. His labor is to communicate experience in such a way that, by the very act of communication, by the forms of art in which the communication is accomplished, experience itself is recreated—but recreated with coherence and made whole.

As experience alters, therefore, the forms in which experience is recreated and made coherent must alter also. But—and this is the heart of the difficulty—the alteration of forms is never free alteration, pure invention, but always an adaptation of the forms which went before. It is not a new art the artist is contriving but a new use of an art which before had many uses. The artist's problem is to use the formal disciplines which have accomplished the miracle of sensuous translation in other times and with other materials, to accomplish a new miracle of sensuous translation. He brings forward as his tools and implements the inherited devices of his art. And his labor, in a time of profound and unexampled change, is the difficult and arduous labor of compelling the inherited forms of his art to adapt themselves to the necessities of an experience for which they were not devised.

All writers in all countries in which the art of writing continues to be practised will be committed, in the years which follow the war, to this labor in one form or another, and all will find it difficult. But if it is at all possible in a matter such as this to judge the future by the past—and there is, so far as I know, no other means by which to judge the future—then it is possible, I think, to say that the writers of the Americas will find the difficulties somewhat less than will the writers of other countries. And for this reason: that the history of American letters is precisely the history of a long and difficult apprenticeship in the adaptation of an inherited art of letters to an experience for which that inherited art of letters was in no way devised—an apprenticeship in the adaptation of an art of letters developed in Europe to the experience of life in a country geographically, meteorologically, socially, psychologically, and otherwise unlike the country and the life of Europe.

This, I am well aware, is not the usual description of the literatures of the Americas. The general view, taught in the schools and treated in the scholarly texts, is the view that the literatures of the Americas, certain exceptions duly noted, are principally interesting for two reasons: first, that they are inferior to the European literatures from which they derived and, second, that their inferiority is to be attributed to the fact that they are colonial. The problem, as the historians have generally seen it, has been the colonial problem, not the problem of the New World. It has been, that is to say, the problem seen from the point of view of Europe and the European tradition, not the problem seen from the point of view of the Americas and the American experience. The weakness of American writers, if you are to believe the books written about them, has been their tendency to the imitation of European writers; and their final enfranchisement will be—or has been—their creation of an American tradition of their own equal in merit to the European tradition from which they derive.

To think at all realistically about the future of American writing or about the work of American writers in the foreseeable future of our world, it is necessary, I think, to re-examine the colonial theory of American art and letters and to inquire how far this theory does really explain what it purports to explain, and how far it leaves out of consideration what no theory dealing with these matters can leave out of consideration. How far, that is to say, are the inadequacies of literature in the Americas explained by explaining merely that literature in the Americas has been colonial? And to what extent is it necessary to have recourse to other theories and explanations to account for the many generations of failure and for the moments of miraculous success?

The colonial theory as I understand it goes something like this: the people of an old world—say, of Europe—have developed certain arts, as for example the arts of cooking and house-building and hide-tanning, and the representation of persons and scenes in colored oils upon canvas, and the composition of accounts and descriptions in words, and the performance of music upon various instruments. These arts and skills are passed along in the usual manner from one generation to another with a minimum of fuss and a variety of consequences but with little or no loss by the way. The new generation learns what it can from the old, does what it must do and what it can do with the means at its disposal, and passes the inheritance on down to those who come after.

This process goes on, interrupted by wars, varied by individual talents, but more or less simply and naturally over long periods of time until, sooner or later, a new land—a new continent or new islands or whatever—is discovered overseas and a migration to those newly discovered countries follows. At which point and without warning, everything is changed. The emigrants—part of the living generation of the old country and co-inheritors, therefore, of its various skills and arts—carry their part of the inheritance out to the new land. They practise there the arts of cooking and house-building, of hide-tanning and oil painting, of stone masonry and music, of the manufacture of textiles and the manufacture of books, which their brothers and their cousins and their contemporaries continue to practise at home.

But the results of their practice are now not at all what they would have been had they remained in the country from which they came. Certain of their arts and skills become more artful, more skilful than they were at home. The emigrants come in time to build better drains. They slaughter better beef. They produce better crops. They manufacture more and better bath-tubs. They produce better dentists, better doctors, better engineers, better athletes. But other arts, other skills, deteriorate. And the arts and skills which deteriorate most are always the fine arts, the pure skills—painting, music, and, above all, poetry and letters.

Why poetry and letters should deteriorate among a colonial people, while other inherited arts and skills do not deteriorate, the historians of these matters fail to explain. At least, they fail to explain to those most interested in the problem—the writers and artists of the countries called colonial and so disposed of. American writers wish to learn not that their work is difficult—for they know very well that it is difficult—and not that many American writers in the past have failed—for that, too, is obvious enough—but rather why their difficulties have been so great and why the history of their art in these countries is strewn with so rich and tragical a wreckage. To that sincere and long-asked question the word "colonial" gives back ambiguous answers.

There is, for one example, the common answer, known to every schoolboy, that the new countries—the colonies—because they are geographically new are also culturally new: because they lack a geographic past, lack also a literary past, and must wait for a past to be accumulated before they can produce a literature of their own. Another is the answer that new countries provide no audiences for the arts and, therefore, can produce no arts. Still another answer is the explanation that the emigrants who go to new countries are not men of the kind who produce poems or music or paintings; and, therefore, poems and music and paintings must wait for a different kind of man to develop. All of these statements are accepted as gospel truth by most of those who talk about the literature of the Americas. And none of them, I suspect, is even superficially true. I suspect, indeed, that it would be difficult to think of many generally accepted notions which are more completely false.

Take first the thesis that the new American countries failed to produce a great literature throughout their early history because they were settled by men of adventurous, hardy, and active types who were incapable of art themselves and incapable of breeding art in their descendants. The thought apparently is that artists and particularly writers are bred by other writers—or at the very least by sedentary persons such as professors, parsons, dilettantes, and stock-brokers. Nothing could be farther from the fact. The fact is that writers descended from other writers, as Mrs. Woolf was from Thackeray, are the exceptions. Writers rarely breed good writers and professors almost never. Writers, painters, and musicians are capable of turning up in the most unlikely families—and usually do.

Furthermore, it is pure romance to assert that the Americas were peopled principally by soldiers and bold adventurous people without nerves, minds, or the capacity of observation. New countries attract all sorts and kinds, including many of the principal producers of literary materials, and the Americas were not exceptions. Soldiers there were, but there were also convicts, parsons, disappointed revolutionists, politicians out of favor, younger sons, illegitimate children, persons luckless in love, merchants with a nose for bargains, speculators, fanatics, people who valued liberty, people who respected their own convictions, and a thousand more beside—all the sorts, kinds, and species which produce between them artists, poets, and musicians in any country and at any time.

And as for the soldiers and adventurers themselves—some of the best writing ever done has come precisely from such people. I cite, for one, Bernal Diaz del Castillo; for another, Thucydides.

The same thing is true of the second explanation, which explains that newly settled countries are countries without background, without culture, without tradition, and, therefore, without the possibility of art and letters: the explanation which says: "But America is a new country: it must wait for time to ripen it." The explanation which says: "There is no American culture—yet." As geographical units, the American countries are "new" perhaps—though by no means as new as the European critics imagine. But as societies considered in terms of background, of inherited culture, they are no more new than are the countries of Europe from which their people came. For their people brought with them to America the same tradition and the same culture they left behind them.

The settlers were quite as much the inheritors of the culture and the tradition of the mother countries as were the brothers and the first cousins and the first cousins once removed and the schoolfellows and the contemporaries they left behind them. If anything, they were inheritors and heirs more conscious and more zealous than the rest who stayed at home, for the inheritance had to them the added value of all things carried overseas and displayed like a chest of drawers or a box of family silver or a portrait of an ancestor or a leather-bound book in a Boston parlor or a drawing room in Salta or a hacienda in the Vale of Chile or a sod-house on the Dakota plains.

It is a matter of common knowledge to all who have travelled in this world that there are no inheritors of tradition or heirs of culture more devoted or more passionate or more opinionated than those who have taken their household goods and their possessions and their memories to the provinces of a new land. Indeed, it is precisely this that the word "provincial" in its pejorative sense implies. The taste of Boston or of Buenos Aires or of Rio de Janeiro was provincial in the last century because it admired too slavishly and protected too sedulously and possessed too entirely the arts and culture of Britain or of Portugal or of Spain.

The truth is that the people of the newly settled countries possessed the great stream of the inherited tradition down not only to the time of separation but well beyond—and possessed it with a fervor unknown to those who stayed behind. They were snobs of the tradition in a degree far beyond the snobbishness of the mother countries. One has only to consider the unquestioning and pious enthusiasm with which the women of the United States accepted British novelists and British poets, regardless of merit, throughout the nineteenth century and into this.

But if it was not tradition which was lacking in the new countries, or human stock capable of producing writers and artists, neither was it a potential audience. The theory which explains American literary history in terms of the colonial audience is the familiar theory that the people of a newly discovered country are so busy building houses and hewing forests and running surveyor's lines and shooting Indians that they have no time to serve as ears for music or as eyes for poems. It is a plausible theory but it has no basis in fact. It is true, undoubtedly, that the first years of the first settlements in the American countries were laborious and uneasy years. No one in the early years of San Francisco or Plymouth or Deerfield or Jamestown or Vera Cruz or Lima or Rio de Janeiro had much leisure for book-reading— to say nothing of tables, chairs, and candle fat to read by. But in the settlements which endured, this period was always brief— a generation at the most or barely two.

Far from having little time or little need for books, the people of these settlements required books and had time to read them as their descendants never would again. It was in the new settlement, and along the frontier as settlement moved westward, that men had time to read the great books through from end to end, and not once alone but many times—Shakespeare, Camoëns,

Cervantes, and the Bible. And it was not only on the frontier that men in the United States had time and appetite for reading. Jefferson's library, the purchase of which was the true founding of the Library of Congress, was not the only great library in Virginia, nor was Virginia the only State of the United States to possess magnificent collections of great works. Neither in the United States nor elsewhere in the Americas was there any lack of men with appetites for books and means to possess them.

The truth, in other words, is that the theory of American letters which explains the inadequacies of American literature over many generations, and even centuries, on the ground that the American countries were colonial countries is considerably less than adequate. For one thing it does not explain what it purports to explain. For another it is mischievous. The young American writer who thinks of American letters as the critics have taught him to think of American letters, begins very shortly to think of his own work in the same terms: begins, that is, to tell himself that his task is to produce not a poem or a novel or a play but "literature"—"literature" equal if possible to the literature of Europe but in any case "literature."

A very considerable part of the self-consciousness which afflicted American writing a generation ago, and even less, was the direct and natural consequence of this attitude. The preoccupation with "literature," the preoccupation with The Tradition which was so familiar a decade or so ago, was an American contribution to the art of letters and could have been nothing else. Only Americans bred in the colonial theory of American letters could have thought of the art of writing as the art of adding to the tradition of English literature. To less self-conscious men the purpose of the art of writing is writing; and the tradition is a means which one employs if one can—a means which becomes an end only when the work is finished and the tradition accepts it or rejects it as history determines.

But the chief indictment of the colonial theory of American letters is graver than this. The chief indictment of the colonial theory is that it leaves out of account the true reason, the honorable reason, for the many and repeated failures of the art of letters in these countries, and neglects, therefore, the considerations upon which a true understanding of the American literatures or of their future may be based. The colonial theory is the theory of a new literature as it appears to those who continue to occupy, either physically or psychologically, the countries from which the colonists went out. But the problem with which the serious writers of the Americas have wrestled for centuries is not the problem of the emulation of Old-World writers, nor the self-conscious attempt to escape from emulation into a new American tradition.

The problem with which the writers of the Americas have struggled has been the problem of the New World: the problem of a new literature as it looks to those who have brought the older culture with them to conditions and surroundings in which the forms of the older culture are foreign, inappropriate, and strange. The colonial problem is a problem imposed by emigration from a known country; the problem of the New World is a problem imposed by the occupation of a new. To European critics it is only important that the ancestors of American writers went *from* Spain or Portugal or England or the continent of Europe. To American writers, it is infinitely more important that their ancestors—or they themselves—came *to* America.

The difference is real. But it is not merely geographical. It involves also a difference—an ancient and frequently embittered difference—between the poet's concept of the art of letters and the critic's: between the concept which sees the art of letters as the art of creating *this* poem, *this* novel, *this* play, and the concept which sees it as a great number of poems, plays, and novels already written and now to be arranged together in a certain order, or a certain organism, called the literature or the tradition of the tongue. To the critic, feeling backward down his coral reef from the surface-present to the deep and crumbling rubble far below, the labor of the creation of a single coral cell or branch of cells has small importance. To the poet it has the supreme importance of an act unique and single in the world. To the critic the art of letters is literature, and literature is in the past—an old existing country which needs but roads and road maps to be known. To the poet the art of letters is an art, and art is in the present—a process frequently repeated and never finally performed: the process of reducing to a form at once sensuous and intelligible the fragmentary, reluctant, and inarticulate experience of men upon this earth—the process, that is to say, the one known process, by which men present to themselves an image of their lives and so possess them. The art of letters to the poet is the mirror of time—the only mirror men have ever found of time.

The problem of the New World, then, is a poet's problem not a critic's. It is the problem faced by those to whom the practice of the art of letters is the practice of the art by which experience is reduced to form—and who practise that art in a world in which the experience of men is new and unaccustomed—and the forms are old. It is, in other words, *the* poet's problem carried to the farthest point of difficulty. The labor of the poet is difficult in any country and at any time. But in a new country—in a continent in which the experience of men alters but the forms of art are old—it is a labor of which the difficulty is almost immeasurable. The raw material, the stubborn facts, of an experience never before resolved into art must be resolved: the raw material of geography, climate, the nervous reactions of men, their tricks and gestures, what they do here that they have not done elsewhere and what they do not do, how they get on with the new sun and the new rain and the animals, how they are with each other and how not, how they sleep and what images come to their sleep. But this is not the whole difficulty. It is not even the principal difficulty. The principal difficulty is that this experience must be communicated in forms of art never intended for its communication—forms of art unrelated to the experience on which they move.

In an old country, an ancient civilization like that of China in its great period, or a less ancient but, none the less, habitual civilization like that of England in the seventeenth century— a society which continues from generation to generation in surroundings more or less unchanged—in such a country, the relation between the forms of art and the pattern of experience is easy and familiar: so easy and so familiar that the two are tangled into one and cannot be untangled. The references are immediate and immediately understood, the allusions are a second speech and equally intelligible, the responses of emotion are as natural and certain as echoes from an old-built wall.

But in a new country, and, above all, in a new country in which everything is different—seasons, geography, and men—there is no such familiar and habitual relation between art and lives. There is, on the contrary, a lack of relation which is more than a mere absence of that quality: which becomes instead a positive obstacle, an intrusive discord. The inherited forms of art carried to the new country by settlers and there employed are not only not forms developed in the new country for the communication of its experience but, instead, forms developed in a different country for the communication of a different experience. They are, therefore and necessarily, forms which carry with them the tone, the color, the remembrance of the old experience. The principal reason why the labor of the poet in a new country is difficult is that this tone, this color, bred into the forms of his art, twisted into the sounds and meanings of his words, impossible therefore to avoid or evade, falsifies and discolors and distorts the image of the world he lives in, out of which he writes.

It is this fact, a fact well known to every sensitive writer of this hemisphere whether he writes in English or in Spanish or in Portuguese, which defines the true American problem in the art of letters. To represent by the use of a medium which carries in the fibre of its structure reflections and refractions of an altogether different experience—to represent by such a medium the experience of a new and altered world—is the labor to which the writers of the Americas have been committed from the beginning of their history. It, and not the colonial problem, not the problem defined by European critics, not the problem described by American writers in violent revolt against their work, their fellow workers, and themselves, is the problem common to us all.

The entire history of letters in this continent demonstrates that fact. Early writers in all our countries have been blamed by later critics because they wrote of America as though it lay in the valley of the Tagus or the yellow hills of Navarre or the sheep pastures of Devon. Nature, the critics complained, came to Anne

Bradstreet, the seventeenth-century New England poetess, not directly but "as something which had to be translated into the regular rhythm and rhetorical exaggerations of the English school of the time." But it was not Anne Bradstreet or her contemporaries of the other Americas who were at fault. Nor are later writers chargeable with moral turpitude and artistic dishonesty because they continued for two hundred years and still sometimes continue to write of American life in books and poems which could have been written equally well by Europeans who had never crossed the Atlantic.

The literary suicides of the Americas—the many Americans who destroyed themselves as American writers by one means or another—testify not to the indifference of the writers of these countries but to the difficulty of their task. These suicides—for suicides they are—are commonplaces in our literary history both north and south. Some men of talent, unable to compel the art to serve their purposes, resigned the effort altogether. Some, although they continued to write, gave up the attempt to write as men living in their own time and in the Americas, and wrote instead and deliberately as though they had lived a hundred years before and in a different country. Others again emigrated physically, as these last emigrated psychologically, returning from the New World to the Old and settling again in the surroundings and the society to which the forms they had inherited belonged. Still others escaped in an opposite direction, emigrating not from the new experience but from the tradition of the art, destroying themselves in anarchy and ignorance. Even the best, the most courageous and most skilful, were incapable over many generations of mastering the American experience *and* communicating it in forms derived from the traditions of the art.

It was not until Mark Twain that writers of the United States forced their art to serve them as Americans, and it was not until the present generation—the generation of Hemingway and Dos Passos and Faulkner—that an American novel was written which could at once move easily in the great tradition of English letters and at the same time occupy and master the American experience of living men. The same thing is true of the poetry of the United

States. Although Whittier wrote out of New England, and although Whitman broke hugely and violently through the English tradition of the art of poetry, it was not until the present generation of men now writing that a poetry native both to the tradition and to the country appeared in the United States. It was not until Eliot and Pound that the current of poetic influence was turned back eastward across the Atlantic.

It would be untrue and unwise beside to say, in conclusion of this matter, that American writers have solved for themselves the problem with which they have struggled for so long. Latin American poetry is as fine as any poetry now written, and the novel in the United States has surpassed the British novel with which it was so long and so unfavorably compared; but it would be presumptuous notwithstanding to pretend that the American experience and the old inherited forms of the art of letters have now at last been matched. Nevertheless, if it is true as I believe it to be true that the labor of letters in our own time and in the time beyond us is the labor imposed upon us by a new and undiscovered world, then the work done and the failures suffered in these continents will have their use. For in that labor the writers of the four Americas have served a long apprenticeship and gained some knowledge.

There are those I know who doubt that writers have played or can play an effective part in the histories of their peoples. There are, among others, the contemporary determinists who inform us that the proper role of the writer is merely to give words to a popular will which would have existed in any case without him— a will driven by economic and historic forces beyond the power of any man to direct or control. But though the opinion is very broadly held, I doubt that it has reason. I doubt that fatalism is a truer formula since Marx than it was before, or that it is any more admirable to surrender the will of men to the will of fate under a scientific name than under a mythological. But whether it is true or not that writers should be the followers of human destiny rather than the instigators of human purpose, one thing is clear and certain: that no purposed human action is conceivable without an image of the world which is coherent and distinguishable, and that the creation of such an image of the world, recognizable to the emotions as well as to the mind, is the work of which the artist moving in the forms and words of art is capable.

Without such an image of the world and of their lives, men inevitably fall into such a surrender of the will, such a mute reliance upon mechanistic forces, as our time, and the generation particularly to which I belong, has made. It is because the world of our time seems to most of those who live in it to have lost its coherence and its meaning that the economic fatalities of the communists, and the wave-like and inevitable futures of the fascists, have had such power in men's minds. In a shadowy and chaotic world where nothing has reality and all the enemies are shadows, surrender to the mechanistic fates, the predetermined futures, becomes the only sure escape for frightened men. Those of us, therefore, who do not love the mechanistic fates or the predetermined futures will continue to believe that the writers of our own time and of the time beyond us must undertake to reduce to sunlight and recognition the shadowy chaos of our world, providing us, in place of the unopposable and terrifying shadows, with an understandable experience of life with which the will of men can deal. For it is only by seeing their experience of the world for what it is—however terrible—that men can act upon it.

I have no wish to prophesy and no authority to read the future. But it seems to me possible, notwithstanding, that the writers of the four Americas—writers to whom the problem of the New World is a known and a familiar problem—may perhaps undertake this labor more willingly, and accomplish it with greater courage, than other writers will in other countries. It seems to me conceivable, in other words, that the long apprenticeship of the Americans, the centuries of labor and the fierce defeats, may perhaps end now in such a literature—so strong, so boldly knowing, so perfect to its time—that others who come after us will say the labor was the prologue to a noble art, and all the pain worth bearing.

HOUSMAN'S POETRY

By CHAUNCEY BREWSTER TINKER

I T IS unusual for a poet to cultivate his reputation by a policy of silence. It seems strange that one should create an appetite for a particular kind of verse, and then deliberately refuse to gratify it. Nevertheless, in such a policy there may be a kind of weary wisdom, as of one who has apprehended the awful dangers of satiety. In the creation of a public demand for one's work—even for poetry—there is nothing very unusual. Many in this century, whose names still recur, have had their bright day, have formed their little circle, created a demand, satisfied it, and then passed into oblivion. Men in later middle age can well remember when the appetite for Mr. Kipling's poetry seemed insatiable. That demand was fully met, and the poet, whose collected verse now fills a stout volume of nearly a thousand pages, has passed into (perhaps temporary) eclipse. For the moment, nobody, not even his King, will do him any reverence. And those who remember the rise and decline of poor dear dead Stephen Phillips have a poignant theme on which to meditate: for what seemed fresher and more fragrant in its day than "Marpessa"? But Mr. Phillips, alas, wrote himself out, and died, I make no doubt, of a broken heart. A dozen cases, nearer our own day, may be passed over in merciful silence. Poets give the public too much. Mr. Housman has followed the proud policy of giving too little.

When, in 1922, he put forth his second volume of verse, entitled "Last Poems," there were some among his readers who refused to take his implied threat seriously. This could not be the end. Can a poet, even a successful one, hold his peace? But those who knew the poet better realized at once that he would rather die than publish another line of verse. His career as poet was ended:

To air the ditty,
And to earth I.

Mr. Housman was sixty-three years old when that second volume, with its haughty preface, was published.

His poetry, as one begins to see it in perspective, reveals an incredibly high level of worth. He is, *par excellence*, the poet who has produced nothing poor. His poems all measure up to a mark, and a mark which is set very high. He has no juvenilia; if he has preserved his first sketches, the work of his 'prentice hand, the world has been permitted to know nothing about them. They have, no doubt, perished in flames, so that the secret of his early training and practice may die with him. Hardly more than a hundred poems in all have escaped his ruthlessness: there are sixty-three poems in the first volume and forty-one in the second. Only one extends to more than a hundred lines; and the first of them betrays the same skilled hand that fashioned the last. All this gives the impression, as the preface of 1922 explicitly asserts, that he has written only when he felt the goad of the Muse. If so, his case is almost unique in the annals of poetry, for the very greatest poets have cluttered up their volumes with the second-rate and the trivial, in all honesty of conviction that they were still giving us of their best. What scoffing Mephistopheles has pointed his critical finger to Housman's worthless lines, and caused them to be blotted out forever?

Perhaps the poet guessed that the public, even such readers as are concerned for the good of poetry, could not bear too much of him. Fastidious as he is, Mr. Housman is often repetitious. One may assert too often that youth and beauty must presently lie down in the lonely grave. For, as we might easily have too long a "Rubáiyát," so we might speedily have too much of Mr. Housman and his lads. (The word "lad," by the way, occurs sixty-seven times in the first volume.) Terence, one remembers, is a performer on the flute, an instrument which, in a master's hand, utters a deliciously pure and limpid note, but one of which we presently grow weary. It is valued in proportion to its infrequency; so that we are not displeased when it is absorbed into larger harmonies.

He himself knows the folly of trying to prolong one's success unduly. With the bitter knowledge that comes only in middle age he realizes that the flowers from his garden may not always be "the wear." He is not the man to linger on the scene till his audience begins to melt away, but rather prefers to make an end before his admirers have realized their delight.

Characteristic of middle age, again, is the atmosphere of disillusion that prevails in his poetry. His are not the swift vicissitudes of joy and sorrow that mark a passionate youth; his moods are deep-seated, never to be changed. He ceases not to sing of the land of lost content and happy highways where he cannot come again. In all the endless road we tread there's nothing but the night. These are the expressions of a man who has long since settled his philosophy and taken his stand. There are moments when he recalls the work of an earlier bard who also knew that the world can give us nothing equal in value to what it takes from us:

> For the sword wears out the sheath,
> And the soul wears out the breast,
> And the heart must pause to breathe,
> And Love itself have rest . . .
> So we'll go no more a roving
> By the light of the moon.

These lines were written when the author, Lord Byron, was nearing his twenty-ninth birthday, the age at which Housman, if we may trust his dates, wrote the first poem in "A Shropshire Lad." The bulk of it, he says, was produced as late as 1895, when he was thirty-six; so that despite the perpetual assumption of the rôle of youth, the sentiments are actually those of middle age. It is all reminiscential. About that there is nothing incredible: a poet may sing of "liquor, love, and fights" long after he has ceased to be a practitioner of the arts with which they are related.

It is not given to youth to speak with the professional skill of a Housman, whose manner, for all its apparent and engaging simplicity, results from a mature knowledge of the art of rhetoric (as it was once universally called, before modern colleges had brought it into disrepute), the French *éloquence*. Every phrase tells. His climax catches us unaware like a blow upon the mouth, a blow carefully placed, delivered, with full knowledge of its deadly force, by a professional. Not even in Browning can you find opening strains more blinding in their suddenness than

> Shot? so quick, so clean an ending?
> Oh that was right, lad, that was brave.

It is only when we turn to his scholarly prose, and particularly to his reviews of the publications of rivals, that we see how awful a power this may be when mercilessly applied. Professor Housman, who is professionally concerned with late Latin poetry, belongs to that extinct and evil school of reviewers, headed by Jeffrey and Brougham, who regarded the authors under their scrutiny as headhunters do their captives. The wretched victims are neatly slaughtered, their heads cut off, and shrunken to the size and smiling contours of a wax doll's, and henceforward serve as trophies, proofs of the artist's skill—*sein Hand zu weisen*. There are those who admire this art, and if they wish to study it in detail may examine Professor Ferguson's essay, "The Belligerent Don." He cites an example (which, I fear, he admires) of a poor devil who had ventured to publish a translation of the elegies of Propertius, or "Cynthia," as the first book of those somewhat artificial love poems used to be called. The translator modestly asked the reader's pardon for his "bald" rendering. Rash man! Professor Housman (a student of that lyric poet who courteously referred to a rival as "stinking Maevius," and hoped that the ship on which he was putting forth to sea might go to the bottom) remarked in a review:

" 'Scholars will pardon an attempt, however bald, to render into English these exquisite love poems.' Why? Those who have no Latin may pardon such an attempt, if they like bad verses better than silence; but I do not know why bald renderings of exquisite love poems should be pardoned by those who want no renderings at all."

Such blows are not unrelated to the art of the bully, nor are they unrelated to the art of the poet, as Horace and the Latin satirists have taught the Cambridge don. Those who enjoy

British arrogance at its best may pursue this subject exhaustively in the classical and philological reviews to which Professor Housman has contributed.

I am not further concerned with all this than as it relates to the poet's very beautiful art, for, as I have said, the relation is there. The skill behind the savage prose and the force behind the poetry are the same shattering power. There is death in the words. In the simplest poems there is *passion* wound up to the intensest pitch. Take a poem like "The New Mistress." There is nothing really satirical about it, and a stanza chosen at random reads like one of the "Barrack Room Ballads":

> I will go where I am wanted, to a lady born and bred
> Who will dress me free for nothing in a uniform of red;
> She will not be sick to see me if I only keep it clean:
> I will go where I am wanted for a soldier of the Queen.

This obviously is Tommy Atkins speaking, but there is a subtlety in the poem to which Mr. Kipling never attains, a recurrent *motif* of sickness, which extends from the scornful sweetheart's "Oh, sick I am to see you," all the way through to the final line with its insistence upon the theme,

> And the enemies of England they shall see me and be sick.

These verses are the product of a man who esteems workmanship as one of the best things to be found in poetry.

Mr. Housman is fond of writing about soldiers; but he is not forgetful of the bitterness in their lot:

> What evil luck soever
>   For me remains in store,
> 'Tis sure much finer fellows
>   Have fared much worse before.
>
> So here are things to think on
>   That ought to make me brave,
> As I strap on for fighting
>   My sword that will not save.

It is perhaps natural that, among the elegies upon the dead who fell in the Great War none is so powerful as that of Housman, who realizes and stresses the unmitigated and abiding horror of it. No poem produced by that conflict sums up quite so well the terror and the grim realism, not of the battlefield, but of the cowering nations huddled watchfully behind their armies:

> These, in the day when heaven was falling,
>   The hour when earth's foundations fled,
> Followed their mercenary calling,
>   And took their wages and are dead.
>
> Their shoulders held the sky suspended;
>   They stood, and earth's foundations stay;
> What God abandoned, these defended,
>   And saved the sum of things for pay.

An "epitaph on an army of mercenaries"! For sheer irony where shall be found anything superior to "took their wages and are dead"? Pathos, pity, and all the fine sentimentalities about death on the field of glory drop out of mind and leave only the stark finality of dying. Were a soldier's wages a shilling a day? Yes, and death into the bargain. But compare it with the great Greek epitaph on the soldiers who fell at Thermopylae, and you shall see a difference: "Traveller, go tell the Lacedemonians that here, obedient to their word, we lie." It is no less forceful, but it is without bitterness.

Mr. Housman may idealize youth, but he never forgets its temptation to violence and even to crime; and this may account, in some degree, for his strange preoccupation with death by hanging. Nobody is likely to forget the pieces on this subject in "Last Poems," or that horrible burlesque of the Crucifixion in the earlier volume, entitled "The Carpenter's Son," a poem that I prefer to pass without comment. It is not the poet's only satire on the Christian way of life.

> And if your hand or foot offend you,
>   Cut it off, lad, and be whole;
> But play the man, stand up and end you,
>   When your sickness is your soul.

This simple counsel and the oft-repeated theme that, though death is cruel, life is more cruel still, accounts, I suppose, for the adjective "pagan" that is so often applied to Housman's poetry; but this is hardly the correct term, for the pagan, properly so-called, is intensely religious in his way, "other-worldly" in truth; and to religion and its consolations Mr. Housman never makes a concession. Yet I cannot convince myself that such poems as "The Immortal Part," "The Carpenter's Son," and the ones on suicide are a considered message that it is better to enter into death than to endure the ignominy of life. I cannot even believe that they are intended to overthrow a consolatory religion and set up a grim and tight-lipped stoicism in its place. Mr. Housman does not use his poetry for "messages," and I doubt whether it is intended to influence our conduct in any special way.

Poems of this sort have no ethical relations. If they were seriously intended as lessons of conduct, their author himself might reasonably be expected to apply them and make his stormy way to the grave. And we, the readers of this verse, can we be said really to have taken it to heart unless we too play the man and set the pistol to our head? However much we may admire this verse, our use of it is confined to the realm of the imagination, and never touches the more practical problems of conduct. If the function of a poem is merely to persuade the reader to mend his ways or to adopt some high principle or noble standard of living, such verse is of secondary import, nothing more, indeed, than means to an end, means which may very properly be forgotten when the end is attained.

Take such a type of verse, for example, as the hymn. It releases within us certain emotions and instincts, memories and pieties, which transcend poetry altogether and touch higher and more lasting concerns. A hymn which remains merely a poem, without influencing our walk and conversation, has not properly discharged its function. This is why it is impossible to evaluate hymns as literature; and it is also the reason why poetry that is employed for propaganda can never be of a high order. This is what is wrong with the lyrics that William Morris wrote for the socialist party of his day, and this is what is wrong with such a thing as Mr. W. H. Auden's "Dance of Death," because, effective as that satire on the modern world may be, it concludes with the triumph of Karl Marx and his young adherents. Like Mrs.

Browning's "Bitter Cry of the Children," it is dedicated to a cause and not to the Muse.

The cause served by poetry is a peculiarly elevated one, because it enriches our spirit by giving us vicarious experience, and so enabling us to understand ways of life that are never to be ours. Hence it is that among the hosts who have loved the "Rubáiyát of Omar Khayyám," few have tried to live by it, few have become winebibbers as a result of reading it, and fewer still have filled a drunkard's grave. We read Swinburne's most macabre ballads, without sinking into degeneracy. We may read and admire "The City of Dreadful Night" without ourselves falling into melancholia, and may delight in the most sinister lyrics in "A Shropshire Lad" without the temptation to make way with ourselves or even to embrace the austerities of the Stoic school. But we are wiser and more experienced for having read these things, and have a larger conception of the incredible variety and intensity of human life.

No critic has been more insistent upon the non-ethical view of poetry than Mr. Housman himself, who has gone so far as to say that poetry is not the thing said but a way of saying it. His lecture on "The Name and Nature of Poetry," delivered at the University of Cambridge in the spring of 1933, is a highly characteristic utterance, designed to annoy as well as to invigorate— a perfect irritant. "Meaning," he asserted, "is of the intellect, poetry is not." He affects to be wholly serious about this, and blandly announces that poetry is frequently the product of persons who have gone mad. He seems, throughout, to be thinking (like Poe) of poetry as consisting exclusively of brief lyric poems, what used to be called "ejaculations" or "effusions." Having told us that it is frequently "inadvisable" to draw the meaning out of such poems, he leaves us to decide for ourselves what to think of such vast works as the "Agamemnon" of Aeschylus, the "Oedipus" of Sophocles, the sixth book of the "Aeneid," "King Lear" and the "Divine Comedy." If these things be not poetry, and, moreover, poetry at its most majestic, what are they henceforth to be deemed? If they are what the world has thought them hitherto, we must find a place for them in some poetic category, and we shall find it both possible and highly advisable to draw a meaning out of them. Such things, as Mr. Housman's own career reveals, are worth the attention of a lifetime.

But all this is from the point. The significant thing about the lecture is its complete revelation of the personality of the author. It may be read with emotions similar in kind, if not in degree, to those awakened by his verse, and may, furthermore, serve as a commentary upon it. Like his poetry, the lecture is meant to startle and waylay. It succeeds in doing so. It proclaims that the effect of poetry is more physical than intellectual, that the seat of poetic sensation is the pit of the stomach, that poetry at its most intense makes the flesh creep and the hair of the head stand up. It is unwise to recite poetry to oneself while shaving. As for the act of creation, a certain deadening of the intellect is apparently desirable, and in Mr. Housman's case, at least in the days of the Shropshire Lad, the poet before composing drank a pint of beer at luncheon as a "sedative to the brain."

Those may take this seriously who can. For my part I cannot forget Housman's besetting temptation to jostle the Ark of the Covenant. I cannot forget that he must be aware of the activity in Cambridge of Mr. I. A. Richards and his young school. I can imagine his delight in telling the dons and the bluestockings in his audience how he had answered a foolish American who had asked him for a definition of poetry. (An English lecturer can always get a laugh by girding at Americans.) Housman replied that one "could no more define poetry than a terrier can define a rat, but that I thought we both recognized the object by the symptoms which it provokes in us." In which there is, of course, something deliciously unregenerate, something pungent and slightly sulphurous, highly amusing and quite unacceptable.

There is nothing in the lecture to indicate any waning of the poet's powers, so that the reader cannot but wish that instead of this vigorous and provocative lecture, we might have had another slender volume of perfect and provocative verse. But this is to cry for the moon. Housman has spoken eloquent words about the exhaustion that ensues for the poet upon the completion of his work: "I can no longer expect to be revisited by the continuous excitement under which . . . I wrote the greater part of my other book ["A Shropshire Lad"], nor indeed could I well sustain it if it came."

That is his *apologia*. He has bidden us farewell in one of the most beautiful translations that has ever been wrought in English:

> We'll to the woods no more,
> The laurels all are cut,
> The bowers are bare of bay
> That once the Muses wore;
> The year draws in the day
> And soon will evening shut:
> The laurels all are cut,
> We'll to the woods no more.
> Oh we'll no more, no more
> To the leafy woods away,
> To the high wild woods of laurel
> And the bowers of bay no more.

Here is that power to pierce the breast with unutterable emotion of which Mr. Housman lectured so eloquently, and which he would, rather rashly, hold to be the sole and complete mark of poetry.

Whether it be so or not is a question that does not concern us here: if not the highest power possessed by poets, it is certainly among the highest. It is one which we shall, I think, seek in vain among other living poets in England. Who, now that Mr. Housman has fallen silent, stabs the heart with the sudden and unforgettable word? Who speaks the word that conquers and controls the breast, and gives utterance to the deepest emotions of the spirit, and so becomes a partner in the will of the Creator? Mr. Kipling has remarkable gifts—gifts which at the moment are perhaps too lightly esteemed—but this has never been reckoned among them. The Laureate has depended upon other means to touch the emotions and to hold the interest. The younger poets are preoccupied with their own emotions and their exciting programme, and are probably unaware that the public has a heart to stab.

Although Mr. Housman has condemned himself to silence, he has not been without his active influence upon the literary world. He has remained a symbol of sanity and intelligibility, and has reminded us that a poet may have a larger audience than his own narrow circle of personal friends. The enduring steadiness of his poetic reputation has served as a commentary on the rise and fall of the paltry poetic fashions of the day. As a poet he has displayed a becoming modesty in strange contrast to his native arrogance. He has never pandered to the public taste or solicited the discipleship of poets; but he has kept alive the notion that a poet has a profession to learn and a duty to fulfil. His pride in his craft has been contagious. Meanwhile he has been content to be Professor of Latin and an authority on Manilius. His activity in this chosen field he has been pleased to describe as his "proper job"; posterity will remember him for a "job" of a very different kind, but one discharged with no less professional skill.

BACK TO NATURE

By HENRY SEIDEL CANBY

N O ONE tendency in life as we live it in America to-day is more characteristic than the impulse, as recurrent as summer, to take to the woods. Sometimes it disguises itself under the name of science; sometimes it is mingled with hunting and the desire to kill; often it is sentimentalized and leads strings of gaping "students" bird-hunting through the wood lot; and again it perilously resembles a desire to get back from civilization and go "on the loose." Say your worst of it, still the fact remains that more Americans go back to nature for one reason or another annually than any civilized men before them. And more Americans, I fancy, are studying nature in clubs or public schools—or, in summer camps and the Boy Scouts, imitating nature's creatures, the Indian and the pioneer—than even statistics could make believable.

What is the cause? In life, it is perhaps some survival of the pioneering instinct, spending itself upon fishing, or bird-hunting, or trail hiking, much as the fight instinct leads us to football, or the hunt instinct sends every dog sniffing at dawn through the streets of his town. Not everyone is thus atavistic, if this be atavism; not every American is sensitive to spruce spires, or the hermit thrush's chant, or white water in a forest gorge, or the meadow lark across the frosted fields. Naturally. The surprising fact is that in a bourgeois civilization like ours, so many are affected.

And yet what a criterion nature love or nature indifference is. It seems that if I can try a man by a silent minute in the pines, the view of a jay pirating through the bushes, spring odors, or December flush on evening snow, I can classify him by his reactions. Just where I do not know; for certainly I do not put him beyond the pale if his response is not as mine. And yet he will differ, I feel sure, in more significant matters. He is not altogether of my world. Nor does he enter into this essay. There are enough without him, and of every class. In the West, the very day laborer pitches his camp in the mountains for his two weeks' holiday. In the East and Middle West, every pond with a fringe of hemlocks, or hill view by a trolley line, or strip of ocean beach, has its cluster of bungalows where the proletariat perform their *villeggiatura* as the Italian democracy did in the days of the Renaissance. Patently the impulse exists, and counts for something here in America.

It counts for something, too, in American literature. Since our writing ceased being colonial English and began to reflect a race in the making, the note of woods-longing has been so insistent that one wonders whether here is not to be found at last the characteristic "trait" that we have all been patriotically seeking.

I do not limit myself in this statement to the professed "nature writers" of whom we have bred far more than any other race with which I am familiar. In the list—which I shall not attempt—of the greatest American writers, one cannot fail to include Emerson, Hawthorne, Thoreau, Cooper, Lowell, and Whitman. And every one of these men was vitally concerned with nature, and some were obsessed by it. Lowell was a scholar and man of the world, urban therefore; but his poetry is more enriched by its homely New England background than by its European polish. Cooper's ladies and gentlemen are puppets merely, his plots melodrama; it is the woods he knew, and the creatures of the woods, Deerslayer and Chingachgook, that preserve his books. Whitman made little distinction between nature and human nature, perhaps too little. But read "Out of the Cradle Endlessly Rocking" or "The Song of the Redwood-Tree," and see how keen and how vital was his instinct for native soil. As for Hawthorne, you could make a text-book on nature study from his "Note-Books." He was an imaginative moralist first of all; but he worked out his visions in terms of New England woods and hills. So did Emerson. The day was "not wholly profane" for him when he had "given heed to some natural object." Thoreau needs no proving. He is at the head and forefront of all field and forest lovers in all languages and times.

These are the greater names. The lesser are as leaves in the forest: Audubon, Burroughs, Muir, Clarence King, Lanier—the stream broadening and shallowing through earnest forest lovers, romantic "nature fakers," literary sportsmen, amiable students, and tens of thousands of teachers inculcating this American tendency in another generation. The phenomenon asks for an explanation. It is more than a category of American literature that I am presenting; it *is* an American trait.

The explanation I wish to proffer in this essay may sound fantastical; most explanations that explain anything usually do—at first. I believe that this vast rush of nature into American literature is more than a mere reflection of a liking for the woods. It represents a search for a tradition, and its capture.

Good books, like well-built houses, must have tradition behind them. The Homers and Shakespeares and Goethes spring from rich soil left by dead centuries; they are like native trees that grow so well nowhere else. The little writers—hacks who sentimentalize to the latest order, and display their plot novelties like bargains on an advertising page—are just as traditional. The only difference is that their tradition goes back to books instead of life. Middle-sized authors—the very good and the probably enduring—are successful largely because they have gripped a tradition and followed it through to contemporary life. That is what Thackeray did in "Vanity Fair," Howells in "The Rise of Silas Lapham," and Mrs. Wharton in "The House of Mirth." But the back-to-nature books—both the sound ones and those shameless exposures of the private emotions of ground hogs and turtles that call themselves nature books—are the most traditional of all. For they plunge directly into what might be called the adventures of the American sub-consciousness.

It is the sub-consciousness that carries tradition into literature. That curious reservoir where forgotten experiences lie waiting in every man's mind, as vivid as on the day of first impression, is the chief concern of psychologists nowadays. But it has never yet had due recognition from literary criticism. If the sub-consciousness is well stocked, a man writes truly, his imagination is vibrant with human experience, he sets his own humble ob-

servation against a background of all he has learned and known
and forgotten of civilization. If it is under-populated, if he has
done little, felt little, known little of the traditional experiences
of the intellect, he writes thinly. He can report what he sees, but
it is hard for him to create. It was Chaucer's rich sub-consciousness that turned his simple little story of Chauntecleer into a
comment upon humanity. Other men had told that story—and
made it scarcely more than trivial. It is the promptings of forgotten memories in the sub-consciousness that give to a simple
statement the force of old, unhappy things, that keep thoughts
true to experience, and test fancy by life. The sub-consciousness
is the governor of the waking brain. Tradition—which is just
man's memory of man—flows through it like an underground
river from which rise the springs of every-day thinking. If there
is anything remarkable about a book, look to the sub-consciousness
of the writer and study the racial tradition that it bears.

Now, I am far from proposing to analyze the American sub-
consciousness. No man can define it. But of this much I am certain. The American habit of going "back to nature" means that
in our sub-consciousness nature is peculiarly active. We react to
nature as does no other race. We are the descendants of pioneers
—all of us. And if we have not inherited a memory of pioneering experiences, at least we possess inherited tendencies and desires. The impulse that drove Boone westward may nowadays
do no more than send some young Boone canoeing on Temagami,
or push him up Marcy or Shasta to inexplicable happiness on the
top. But the drive is there. And furthermore, nature is still
strange in America. Even now the wilderness is far from no
American city. Birds, plants, trees, even animals have not, as in
Europe, been absorbed into the common knowledge of the race.
There are discoveries everywhere for those who can make them.
Nature, indeed, is vivid in a surprising number of American
brain cells, marking them with a deep and endurable impress.
And our flood of nature books has served to increase her power.

It was never so with the European traditions that we brought
to America with us. That is why no one reads early American
books. They are pallid, ill-nourished, because their traditions are
pallid. They drew upon the least active portion of the American

sub-consciousness, and reflect memories not of experience, contact, live thought, but of books. Even Washington Irving, our first great author, is not free from this indictment. If, responding to some obscure drift of his race towards humor and the short story, he had not ripened his Augustan inheritance upon an American hillside, he, too, would by now seem juiceless, withered, like a thousand cuttings from English stock planted in forgotten pages of his period. It was not until the end of our colonial age and the rise of democracy towards Jackson's day, that the rupture with our English background became sufficiently complete to make us fortify pale memories of home by a search for fresher, more vigorous tradition.

We have been searching ever since, and many eminent critics think that we have still failed to establish American literature upon American soil. The old traditions, of course, were essential. Not even the most self-sufficient American hopes to establish a brand-new culture. The problem has been to domesticate Europe, not to get rid of her. But the old stock needed a graft, just as an old fruit tree needs a graft. It requires a new tradition. We found a tradition in New England; and then New England was given over to the alien and her traditions became local or historical merely. We found another in border life; and then the Wild West reached the Pacific and vanished. Time and again we have been flung back upon our English sources, and forced to imitate a literature sprung from a riper soil. Of course, this criticism, as it stands, is too sweeping. It neglects Mark Twain and the tradition of the American boy; it neglects Walt Whitman and the literature of free and turbulent democracy; it neglects Longfellow and Poe, and that romantic tradition of love and beauty common to all Western races. But, at least, it makes one understand why the American writer has passionately sought anything that would put an American quality into his transplanted style.

He has been very successful in local color. But then local color is *local*. It is a minor art. In the field of human nature he has fought a doubtful battle. An occasional novel has broken through into regions where it is possible to be utterly American even while writing English. Poems too have followed. But here lie our great failures. I do not speak of the "great American novel," yet to come. I refer to the absence of a school of American fiction, or poetry, or drama, that has linked itself to any tradition broader than the romance of the colonies, New England of the 'forties, or the East Side of New York. The men who write for all America are mediocre. They strike no deeper than a week-old interest in current activity. They aim to hit the minute because they are shrewd enough to see that for "all America" there is very little continuity just now between one minute and the next. The America they write for is contemptuous of tradition, although worshipping convention, which is the tradition of the ignorant. The men who write for a fit audience though few are too often local or archaic, narrow or European, by necessity if not by choice.

And ever since we began to incur the condescension of foreigners by trying to be American, we have been conscious of this weak-rootedness in our literature and trying to remedy it. This is why our flood of nature books for a century is so significant. They may seem peculiar instruments for probing tradition —particularly the sentimental ones. The critic has not yet admitted some of the heartiest among them—Audubon's sketches of pioneer life, for example—into literature at all. And yet, unless I am mightily mistaken, they are signs of convalescence as clearly as they are symptoms of our disease. These United States, of course, are infinitely more important than the plot of mother earth upon which they have been erected. The intellectual background that we have inherited from Europe is more significant than the moving spirit of woods and soil and waters here. The graft, in truth, is less valuable than the tree upon which it is grafted. Yet it determines the fruit. So with the books of our nature lovers. They represent a passionate attempt to acclimatize the breed. Thoreau has been our most original writer, barring only Whitman. He and his multitudinous followers, wise and foolish, have helped establish us in our new soil.

I may seem to exaggerate the services of a group of writers who, after all, can show but one great name, Thoreau's. I do not think so, for if the heart of the nature lover is sometimes more active than his head, the earth intimacies he gives us are vital to literature in a very practical sense. Thanks to the modern science of geography, we are beginning to understand the profound and powerful influence of physical environment upon men. The geographer can tell you why Charleston was aristocratic, why New York is hurried and nervous, why Chicago is self-confident. He can guess at least why in old communities, like Hardy's Wessex or the North of France, the inhabitants of villages not ten miles apart will differ in temperament and often in temper, hill town varying from lowland village beneath it sometimes more than Kansas City from Minneapolis. He knows that the old elemental forces—wind, water, fire, and earth—still mould men's thoughts and lives a hundred times more than they guess, even when pavements, electric lights, tight roofs, and artificial heat seem to make nature only a name. He knows that the sights and sounds and smells about us, clouds, songs, and wind murmurings, rain-washed earth, and fruit trees blossoming, enter into our sub-consciousness with a power but seldom appraised. Prison life, factory service long continued, a clerk's stool, a housewife's day-long duties,—those things stunt and transform the human animal as nothing else, because of all experiences they most restrict, most impoverish the natural environment. And it is the especial function of nature books to make vivid and warm and sympathetic our background of nature. They make conscious our sub-conscious dependence upon earth that bore us. They do not merely inform (there the scientist may transcend them), they enrich the subtle relationship between us and our environment. Move a civilization and its literature from one hemisphere to another, and their adapting, adjusting services become most valuable. Men like Thoreau are worth more than we have ever guessed.

No one has ever written more honest books than Thoreau's "Walden," his "Autumn," "Summer," and the rest. There is not one literary flourish in the whole of them, although they are done with consummate literary care; nothing but sound honest observation of the world of hill-slopes, waves, flowers, birds, and beasts, and honest, shrewd philosophizing as to what it all meant for him, an American. Here is a man content to take a walk, fill his mind with observation, and then come home to think. Repeat the walk, repeat or vary the observation, change or expand the thought, and you have Thoreau. No wonder he brought his first edition home, not seriously depleted, and made his library of it! Thoreau needs excerpting to be popular. Most nature books do. But not to be valuable!

For see what this queer genius was doing. Lovingly, laboriously, and sometimes a little tediously, he was studying his environment. For some generations his ancestors had lived on a new soil, too busy in squeezing life from it to be practically aware of its differences. They and the rest had altered Massachusetts. Massachusetts had altered them. Why? To what? The answer is not yet ready. But here is one descendant who will know at least what Massachusetts *is*—wave, wind, soil, and the life therein and thereon. He begins humbly with the little things; but humanly, not as the out-and-out scientist goes to work, to classify or to study the narrower laws of organic development; or romantically as the sentimentalist, who intones his "Ah!" at the sight of dying leaves or the cocoon becoming moth. It is all human, and yet all intensely practical with Thoreau. He envies the Indian not because he is "wild," or "free," or any such nonsense, but for his instinctive adaptations to his background,—because nature has become traditional, stimulative with him. And simply, almost naïvely, he sets down what he has discovered. The land I live in is like this or that; such and such life lives in it; and this is what it all means for me, the transplanted European, for us, Americans, who have souls to shape and characters to mould in a new environment, under influences subtler than we guess. "I make it my business to extract from Nature whatever nutriment she can furnish me, though at the risk of endless iteration. I milk the sky and the earth." And again: "Surely it is a defect in our Bible that it is not truly ours, but a Hebrew Bible. The most pertinent illustrations for us are to be drawn not from Egypt or Babylonia, but from New England. Natural objects and phenomena are the original symbols or types which express our thoughts and feelings. Yet American scholars, having little or no root in the soil, commonly strive with all their might to confine themselves to the imported symbols alone. All the true growth and experience, the living speech, they would fain reject as 'Americanisms.' It is the old error which the church, the state, the school, ever commit, choosing darkness rather than light, holding fast to the old and to tradition. When I really know that our river pursues a serpentine course to the Merrimack, shall I continue to describe it by referring to some other river, no older than itself, which is like it, and call it a meander? It is no more meandering than the Meander is musketaquiding."

This for Thoreau was going back to nature. Our historians of literature who cite him as an example of how to be American without being strenuous, as an instance of leisure nobly earned, are quite wrong. If any man has striven to make us at home in America, it is Thoreau. He gave his life to it; and in some measure it is thanks to him that with most Americans you reach intimacy most quickly by talking about "the woods."

Thoreau gave to this American tendency the touch of genius and the depth of real thought. After his day the "back-to-nature" idea became more popular and perhaps more picturesque. Our literature becomes more and more aware of an American background. Bobolinks and thrushes take the place of skylarks; sumach and cedar begin to be as familiar as heather and gorse; forests, prairies, a clear, high sky, a snowy winter, a summer of thunderstorms, drive out the misty England which, since the days of Cynewulf, our ancestors had seen in the mind's eye while they were writing. Nature literature becomes a category. Men make their reputations by means of it.

No one has yet catalogued—so far as I am aware—the vast collection of back-to-nature books that followed Thoreau. No one has ever seriously criticised it, except Mr. Roosevelt, who with characteristic vigor of phrase, stamped "nature-faking" on its worser half. But everyone reads in it. Indeed, the popularity of such writing has been so great as to make us distrust its serious literary value. And yet, viewed internationally, there are few achievements in American literature so original. I will not say that John Muir and John Burroughs, upon whom Thoreau's mantle fell, have written great books. Probably not. Certainly it is too soon to say. But when you have gathered the names of Gilbert White, Fabre, Maeterlinck, and in slightly different *genres,* Izaak Walton, Hudson, and Kipling, from various literatures you will find few others abroad to list with ours. Nor do our men owe one jot or tittle of their inspiration to individuals on the other side of the water.

Locally, too, these books are more noteworthy than may at first appear. They are curiously passionate, and passion in American literature since the Civil War is rare. I do not mean sentiment, or romance, or eroticism. I mean such passion as Wordsworth felt for his lakes, Byron (even when most Byronic) for the ocean, the author of "The Song of Roland" for his Franks. Muir loved the Yosemite as a man might love a woman. Every word he wrote of the Sierras is touched with intensity. Hear him after a day on Alaskan peaks: "Dancing down the mountain to camp, my mind glowing like the sunbeaten glaciers, I found the Indians seated around a good fire, entirely happy now that the farthest point of the journey was safely reached and the long, dark storm was cleared away. How hopefully, peacefully bright that night were the stars in the frosty sky, and how impressive was the thunder of icebergs, rolling, swelling, reverberating through the solemn stillness! I was too happy to sleep."

Such passion, and often such style, is to be found in all these books when they are good books. Compare a paragraph or two of the early Burroughs on his birch-clad lake country, or Thoreau upon Concord pines, with the "natural history paragraph" that English magazines used to publish, and you will feel it. Compare any of the lesser nature books of the mid-nineteenth century— Clarence King's "Mountaineering in the Sierra Nevada" for example—with the current novel writing of the period and you will feel the greater sincerity. A passion for nature! Except the New England passion for ideals, Whitman's passion for democracy, and Poe's lonely devotion to beauty, I sometimes think that this is the only great passion that has found its way into American literature.

Hence the "nature fakers." The passion of one generation becomes the sentiment of the next. And sentiment is easily capitalized. The individual can be stirred by nature as she is. A hermit thrush singing in moonlight above a Catskill clove will move him. But the populace will require something more sensational. To the sparkling water of truth must be added the syrup of sentiment and the cream of romance. Mr. Kipling, following ancient traditions of the Orient, gave personalities to his animals so that stories might be made from them. Mr. Long, Mr. Roberts, Mr. London, Mr. Thompson-Seton, and the rest, have told stories about animals so that the American interest in nature might be exploited. The difference is essential. If the "Jungle Books" teach anything it is the moral ideals of the British Empire. But our nature romancers—a fairer term than "fakers," since they do not willingly "fake"—teach the background and tradition of our soil. In the process they inject sentiment, giving us the noble desperation of the stag, the startling wolf-longings of the dog, and the picturesque outlawry of the ground hog,—and get a hundred readers where Thoreau got one.

This is the same indictment as that so often brought against the stock American novel, that it prefers the gloss of easy sentiment to the rough, true fact, that it does not grapple direct with things as they are in America, but looks at them through optimist's glasses that obscure and soften the scene. Nevertheless, I very much prefer the sentimentalized animal story to the sentimentalized man story. The first, as narrative, may be romantic bosh, but it does give one a loving, faithful study of background that is worth the price that it costs in illusion. It reaches my emotions as a novelist who splashed his sentiment with equal profusion never could. My share of the race mind is willing even to be tricked into sympathy with its environment. I would rather believe that the sparrow on my telephone wire is swearing at the robin on my lawn than never to notice either of them!

How curiously complete and effective is the service of these nature books, when all is considered. There is no better instance, I imagine, of how literature and life act and react upon one another. The plain American takes to the woods because he wants to, he does not know why. The writing American puts the woods into his books, also because he wants to, although I suspect that sometimes he knows very well why. Nevertheless, the same general tendency, the same impulse, lie behind both. But reading nature books makes us crave more nature, and every gratification of curiosity marks itself upon the sub-consciousness. Thus the clear, vigorous tradition of the soil passes through us to our books, and from our books to us. It is the soundest, the sweetest, if not the greatest and deepest inspiration of American literature. In the confusion that attends the meeting here of all the races it is something to cling to; it is our own.

THE POWER OF THE WRITTEN WORD

By STEPHEN VINCENT BENET

THE title of this discussion—the power of the written word—may seem a little pretentious. I do not mean it in that way. Words happen to be our way of getting to know one another; that is all. Words—and the use and recording of words—are one of the few things that justifiably distinguish us from the animals. I have known cats with an interesting and extensive vocabulary—very possibly a learned one, for all that I could discern—but what they had to say perished with the saying of it. It is only the human race, as far as one can know, that is able to record its own past. In our brief life, we seem to have a passionate desire to put down what we saw and felt and knew—as it was, as it appeared to us—so that later people can know what sort of world we lived in and how we felt about it. It is that impulse which has made all writers write, from the first poet to the latest novelist. And it seems to be built into the human race.

Why do we do it? There are many reasons. The written word—the word set down—is not only a sword and a trumpet for the present but a link which binds us to all humanity. When we lose touch with the great words of the past—when they seem meaningless to us and we can make no new good words for our own day—then history changes. "No man is an island, entire of itself; every man is a piece of the continent, a part of the main. If a clod be washed away by the sea, Europe is the less; . . . any man's death diminishes me because I am involved in Mankind. And therefore never send to know for whom the bell tolls. It tolls for thee."

The words I have just quoted were written by the great poet and great preacher John Donne in the seventeenth century. They appear, more than three hundred years later, on a flyleaf of the finest novel of 1940—and so apposite are they both to the theme of that novel and to our own times that they might have been written yesterday. Yes, words do have power, and live on.

Not only do they live on, but, with time and change, they sometimes gather an importance not dreamed of by their first makers. Let me take a rather simple sentence—a fairly banal one—such a sentence as "I am a citizen of the United States." Now the actual fact stated there is a fact that most of us take for granted. We are used to it—so used that we don't talk of it. You would as soon think of beginning a conversation with the blunt remark, "I am a mammal." And yet, what I say in that particular sentence—"I am a citizen of the United States"—has rather more meanings than appear on the surface. For if I am a citizen, I am not a slave—and if I am a citizen, I need not be a lord. I have a state to which I owe certain responsibilities—and which, at the very least, owes certain responsibilities to me. That may not seem very much, but it has taken a good many centuries to establish that much. Neither baron nor serf of the Middle Ages knew it. What I say in that one word "citizen" represents a dream in men's minds—a dream as old as the city-states of Greece, as new as last week's election. That dream has been trampled upon, wiped out for dark ages of history—and recurred and recurred again, like the grass growing back after drought. To me, it is an essential dream. And yet part of it is there in one word.

Let us take some of the rest of the sentence—the mere words "United States." Well, of course, we know what the United States means—we know it so well that we do not even have to think about it. And yet do we? For it took five years of active revolution to make the one word, "States"—twelve years of confederation and argument and, later on, four years of Civil War to make the word "United" an effective word. When you say those particular words—United States—you are not just talking of geography or even of a flag. You are talking of an idea in action—an idea as strong, as deeply rooted as any that has moved the minds of men—an idea that has been served, at one time or another, with singular devotion. I agree that we do not often think of it in that particular way. And yet it is there, in the words. And without the words, and the thought behind the words, it would not be there.

It is well to be thoughtful, then, when we use words. For sometimes the words that we write down are going to go on in ways that we did not expect and of which we could have no fore-knowledge. A few men, gathered together on a crowded ship, set down and signed the Mayflower Compact—"to combine our-selves together in a civil body politick . . . for our better order-ing . . . and by virtue hereof to enact, constitute and frame such just and equal laws . . . as shall be thought most meet and convenient for the general good of the colony."

The historians will tell us, and quite correctly, that this par-ticular document was an emergency measure for a particular case. It did not mean that the men who signed it wanted either a republic or a democracy, as we conceive of them, on these shores. It did not mean free speech—it did not mean religious tolerance. It merely meant that those few men wanted some sort of worka-ble government once they got ashore. And yet once the thing is written down, it is written down and the men who come after remember it and put their own meanings to it. Once you have said "just and equal laws . . . for the general good," you have planted the seed for an unexpected harvest. As Sandburg says— be careful how you use proud words.

Be careful and yet be bold—for it is the bold words and the direct ones that live—and neither a nation nor an art can endure for long in a state of continuous apology. We have had bold words in the past—we shall have them again. There were very bold words in our Declaration of Independence—bold and novel words in the Constitution. We do not recognize their boldness because we have for so long enjoyed their benefits. And yet cer-tain of these phrases have become part of the unconscious stream of our minds—the stream that lies at the back of all thought. The boldness is still in them, whenever we wish to rediscover it.

I am not saying, of course, that words will do it all. Any writer knows better than that. If at times he is proud of his craft, at other times he is humble about it. For he knows as well as anyone how words can be distorted, defaced, and misconstrued. And then, he is very fallible. He spends a good deal of time creating, as he thinks, a thing of beauty—and discovers, to his annoyance, when he has created it that it has six legs and four ears. He may spend a good deal of time trying to describe a certain section of life honestly and discover that, in the opinion of eminent persons, he has tried to corrupt the public morals. Now, it is really very difficult for a writer to corrupt the public morals all by himself—even with the best will in the world, he has to have considerable help from his constituency. And, what is worse, such a charge is apt to flatter the writer's vanity, and that isn't very good for him either.

No—words will not do it all—and the writer knows that. But sometimes they may take the step ahead, the step that means much to to-day and even more to to-morrow. The stone is thrown into the water and the ripples spread to far shores. In a troubled time—and ours is a troubled one indeed—it is easy to lose heart, to give in, to think there is no solution for the difficulties that perplex us. And yet, out of troubled times, the great artists have always looked forward. The greatest writers have shown what human life is—they have also shown what human life may be. Through their work runs continual wonder and continual questioning. Yet through the long roll of time, few of them have praised tyranny; most have denounced injustice; few have hated man.

I think it will continue to be so. And it must be so indeed. We have seen, in the last few years, a dark wave rise from the past to engulf free nations—we have seen a tyranny set out to bind the minds of men such as has not bound the minds of men for many ages. Where that tyranny has passed, art has ceased. And yet so fearful is that tyranny of the mere power of words that it does not—and dares not—allow its subjects to listen to or read the words and the books of freedom. Perhaps that one single fact may show as well as anything the power of words.

It remains for those of us who are free, and who mean to stay free, to consider what words we shall say and how we shall say them. For those of us who are interested in the arts know very well, by now, for whom the bell tolls. We have heard it toll for men of genius who had no crime but their genius. We have talked to distinguished colleagues who have been hunted from nation to nation because they refused to abandon that freedom of thought and expression which is the creative birthright of every artist. We have seen this happen in our time. I do not see how it can leave us untouched, unaffected and at ease.

I do not mean that we should all immediately begin to propagandize, or all suddenly join in the singing of a medley of patriotic airs. It is not quite so simple a problem as that. I wish it were. It is more a question of thinking certain things through. My own generation of writers has recently been the target of criticism from a number of angles. That criticism has its justifications. We were not wiser than the statesmen or more foreseeing than the prophets. We moved with the mood of our time. Yet we did try to tell the truth about our time as we saw it—and that I do not regret.

To the charge of disillusion, we may perhaps plead guilty. We wanted to clear the ground, and clear it of bunk and cant. We wanted to enlarge the scope of fiction so that it could deal with all sides of life, not just carefully selected sectors. We wanted to experiment in new ways of saying things—new ways of breaking ground. Any generation that tries to do these things is apt to destroy certain illusions. And yet, in so doing, we were neither singular nor alone.

For two moods have been in the mind of America from the very first. From the first discoverers, what are "these loathly and savage woods" to one man become "these delicious prospects" to another. "The face of nature was a weather-beaten face" to the Pilgrims—but "We sat down and drank our first New England water with as much delight as ever we drank drink." It is this double mood of enthusiasm and self-criticism that has made the American mind. It shows in the folk songs of the people. For, in the march west, you might be singing, "O'er the hills in legions, boys . . . Freedom's bright star"; but you might equally well be singing, "Hurrah for Greer County, the land of the free, / The land of the grasshopper, bedbug and flea, / I'll sing of its praise, I'll tell of its fame, / While starving to death on my goverment claim." And the double edge shows in the work of Whitman himself. The very spokesman of the democratic idea, the man who sang of democracy as few have sung of it, could yet write in "Democratic Vistas," "Never was there perhaps more

hollowness at heart than at present here in the United States."
Did that mean he was lying when he said one thing or lying when
he said the other? I do not think so. It meant that he had a concern with the Republic as most of our great writers have had a
concern—a concern so passionate that it saw both faults and virtues. For both laughter and criticism are also part of democracy.

Am I wrong in saying that? Somehow, I do not think so. For
democracy is often talked about but seldom defined. I will give
a very old definition of it and it is this: "Democracy, which is a
charming form of government, full of variety and disorder, and
dispensing a sort of equality to equals and unequals alike." The
definition happens to be Plato's—it might just as well be Mr.
Dooley's. It is hundreds of years old and extremely contemporary. It would be entirely incomprehensible to Dr. Goebbels.
He would not see how such a system could possibly work. And
yet we have been able to work it here in this country for more
than a century and a half.

I recommend it to your attention, because there is this to be
said, and said in all seriousness. There are those who say or im-
ply—and not only the official spokesmen for the totalitarian
states—that democracy is dead and finished—that the future belongs to another and different concept of man and man's fate. I
do not think they know the deep-rooted, inarticulate thing that
democracy is in the lives and hearts of our people. I do not think
they realize how swiftly, once that deep, inarticulate thing is
really threatened, Americans can unite and put aside petty concerns and petty quarrels. I do not think they realize—quite—
how well we know what we don't like. And yet that is something
written across all our history—sometimes with a jest, sometimes
with a deeper stain.

There are others—and this is to me a curious point of view—
who suggest that because we have a good many automobiles as a
nation and go to the movies now and then, we have therefore lost
the manly virtues. Women, it appears, have feminized us and
done us a great deal of damage—though the entire abolition of
women has not yet been suggested by these critics. Yet that
would be the logical step. We could all then be extremely manly,
until, necessarily, we perished from the continent in one genera-

tion. I confess I cannot follow this particular line of reasoning. No nation has ever yet fallen because it treated its women like human beings. Nor is it necessary to be merely a hard-fisted brute in order to lead a nation to success. George Washington was a good many things, but, if he was merely a hard-fisted brute, the fact has escaped history. He and all the men of our own Revolution—all the great leaders—were civilized men. They had faults —they were human—but none of them, as far as we know, was in favor of abandoning all civilization because they were making a new country. On the contrary, it was upon the civilization they knew that they built their great new dream. I think it is to such men we should turn for example—not to those who have left the world nothing but a wasted land and the memory of a sword.

But we were considering writers, and the written word. And, after all, in this discussion that is our chief concern. I have tried to point out one or two things by the way. I have tried to point out that free words and free thinking are an essential part of our democratic process, and that disillusion, for a time, does not mean everlasting despair. For I think there is a new tide—and a deep one—setting in American letters, a tide that has nothing to do with brag or false optimism, but a tide of deep conviction in certain essential things.

It must be so, for the issue has been joined. There is that abroad in the world which would destroy the freedom of the' artist as it would destroy the free thinking of every man. And that issue must be met. For the war in the world to-day is a war of ideas and minds, as well as a war of armed forces.

We can call upon the great men, the great words of our own past—and that we should do—for in looking back at our past we can see at what a price, by what endurance and fortitude, the freedom we have inherited was bought. But that is only part of the task. We need new words also—and great ones—to match the present, to build for the future that must be. That is a great task indeed, and a very hard one. I do not know by whom these words will be made. They will not be made by the summer soldier or the sunshine patriot. And yet, if we believe in freedom, if we believe in life itself, they must be made.

Some have been made—in the last book of a man now dead,

who attacked and cried out upon certain follies and shams as bitterly as any satirist and yet never lost belief in a greatness here. The voice speaks from the dead.

"I believe that we are lost here in America, but I believe we shall be found. . . . I think these forms are dying and must die just as I know that America and the people in it are deathless, undiscovered, immortal, and must live.

"I think the true discovery of America is before us. I think the true fulfilment of our spirit, of our people, of our mighty and immortal land is yet to come. I think the true discovery of our own democracy is still before us. And I think that all these things are as certain as the morning, as inevitable as noon. I think I speak for most men living when I say that our America is Here, is Now and beckons on before, and this assurance is not only our living hope but our dream to be accomplished."

There is little I can add to these words of Thomas Wolfe. But that is our task—the living hope—the dream to be accomplished. It will not be accomplished easily—there are times when we may well think that it cannot be accomplished. There are always such times. But men have still gone forward. The day is troubled and the night full of voices. But if we are men we shall go forward. We shall still go forward to the hills.

PUBLIC AFFAIRS

MAKING DEMOCRACY SAFE
IN THE WORLD

By CARL BECKER

WHEN the Roosevelt-Churchill Eight Points of Peace were published, August 14, 1941, it was reported that the English people were not much interested in them. They took the very British position that since their political existence was at stake it would be eminently sensible, before talking about the terms of peace, to make sure that they would have something to do with making it. But that was last August. Since then the resistance of Russia, the entry of the United States into the war, and the adherence of twenty-six countries to the Atlantic Charter have materially changed the situation—so much so that we may assume, with some confidence I think, that Hitler will be defeated, and that the British Commonwealth of Nations and the United States will accordingly play an important role in making the peace. It is perhaps not too early, therefore, to consider what kind of "new order" it would be possible and desirable for them and their allies to work for, if and when they are in a position to work for it by other means than war.

During the last five centuries, three methods have been proposed or employed for maintaining the peace and unity of Europe—imperial unification, balance of power, and a federation of states. Imperial unification was tried in vain by Charles the Fifth, Louis the Fourteenth, and Napoleon; and is now being tried, we hope in vain, by Hitler. A federation of states, often proposed, was never seriously tried until the creation of the League of Nations in 1919. The balance of power was less an adopted method than a rationalization of existing practice, and the most that could be claimed for it was that it reduced the number of wars, or at least prevented any one country from destroying permanently the political or cultural independence of the others. In this sense it worked not too badly in the eighteenth century, but collapsed under the impact of Napoleon's conquests. It was restored in the nineteenth century, only to be destroyed again by the conquests of Hitler. We know what kind of "new order," if it can be called either new or an order, Hitler would establish if he could win the war. When he loses it, the democratic countries might rehabilitate the old balance of power; but to do that would seem, in the light of past and present experience, to be asking for a repetition of the present situation. To do anything more than that, anything in the way of creating a democratic new order, would call for some kind of federation, confederation, league, or union of states. The question is, what kind?

The idea that a "new order" in Europe could and should be created by a federation of states is not itself new. It could hardly have failed to occur to anyone capable of being distressed by the fact that the European community of nations, although sharing a common tradition and culture, seemed always threatened with dissolution by persistent political and military conflicts. It occurred to Dante in the thirteenth century, and since his time innumerable projects have been drafted for creating a new international order in Europe. All these projects, unless we except Kant's work on "Perpetual Peace," have proposed a federation or league of states designed solely, or at least primarily, to prevent war. Two efforts have been made to translate the idea into practice; and although both efforts failed, I infer, from the reference in the Eight Points to "the establishment of a wider and permanent system of general security," that President Roosevelt and Prime Minister Churchill are prepared to make one more effort of the same sort. A brief account of the nature and history of these projects should enable us to determine whether it is worth while to make the effort—whether, that is to say, a league or federation primarily designed to prevent war is a proper method of attaining the end desired.

The essential nature of all the projects to prevent war by means of a league or federation was briefly but clearly indicated by Grotius in his famous book, "The Rights of War and Peace," published in 1625. "It would be useful," he says, "and indeed it

seems almost necessary, that certain congresses of Christian powers should be held, in which disputes between some of them may
be decided by others that are disinterested; and in which means
may be taken to compel the parties to accept peace on equitable
terms."

This idea Grotius did not, so far as I know, ever mention again.
He perhaps never saw a little book by an obscure French humanist, Emeric Cruce, published in 1623, entitled "The New Cyneas." The title refers to that Cyneas who, as Plutarch relates,
asked his master, King Pyrrhus, what good it would do him to
conquer all the world. "Why," said Pyrrhus, "we will live at our
ease, my dear friend, and drink all day, and divert ourselves with
pleasant conversation." To which Cyneas replied: "And what
hinders us now, sir, if we have a mind to be merry, . . . since
we have at hand without trouble all those necessary things, to
which through much blood and labor, and infinite hazards and
mischief to ourselves and others, we design at last to arrive?"
Emeric Cruce's little book is a humane and an engaging commentary on this theme. He endeavors to convince princes that
all desirable things can be better obtained without war, and lays
before them a simple plan for getting rid of it. Let all the princes
of the world send ambassadors to some central city, such as Venice, "in order that the differences that might arise shall be settled
by the judgment of the whole assembly. . . . If anyone re-
belled against a decree of so notable a company, he would receive
the disgrace of the princes, who would find means to bring him
to reason."

"The New Cyneas" was scarcely noticed until our own time,
but during the seventeenth and eighteenth centuries there appeared many other works of a similar nature. Of these, the most
widely read were the so-called "Grand Design of Henry the
Fourth," and the Abbé Saint-Pierre's "Project for Making
Peace Perpetual in Europe." Among those who were familiar
with Saint-Pierre's work was Alexander the First of Russia, the
first statesman to bring the idea of a federation of states into the
realm of practical politics. He proposed a general alliance of all
the European states which would bind all and several to prevent
war by a mutual guarantee of existing boundaries and forms of

government. Such an alliance was not formed, but for ten years after the defeat of Napoleon the great powers, following the suggestion of Metternich, endeavored to act in concert for suppressing any revolutionary activities that might, by disturbing the settlement of 1815, threaten the peace of Europe. This half-hearted attempt to replace the balance of power by a confederation of states had never more than a partial success, and failed altogether in dealing with the Greek revolution of 1821. It failed because, in every particular crisis, each state was apt to regard its own national interest as more important than the suppression of revolution or the preservation of peace; and in 1823 Canning described the situation by saying: "Things are getting back to a wholesome state again. Every nation for itself and God for us all. The time for Areopagus and the like of that is gone by."

Nevertheless, the idea of a federation survived. Throughout the nineteenth century, schemes for disarmament, an international tribunal, and a federation of states were persistently propagated by the peace societies, and repeatedly recommended to governments by the international peace congresses. In 1899 the first steps towards establishing an international tribunal were taken at the Hague Conference. On the eve of the first World War, William H. Taft and other men prominent in public affairs organized the League to Enforce Peace; and finally, after the most destructive war in the history of Europe, a League of Nations, for three centuries advocated by humanitarians and philosophers, was incorporated into the battered and broken structure of international law.

The various projects for a federation of states, from Emeric Cruce to Woodrow Wilson, although differing in detail, are all essentially alike in their presuppositions, their aims, and the means proposed to attain the end desired. Stripped of nonessentials, the argument implicit in all of them runs somewhat as follows. War is admittedly an evil of the first magnitude, and it is accordingly a prime interest of all governments to abolish it. But no one government can afford to renounce war unless the others also renounce it. Therefore, let all governments bind themselves, in a solemn treaty, to do certain things: (1) to recognize the form of government and the territorial limits (with such adjustments as may be agreed upon) of each of the contracting parties; (2) to establish an international tribunal for settling disputes between any two or more governments that cannot be settled by the governments concerned; (3) to unite in applying such sanctions (diplomatic, economic, military) as may be provided in the treaty against any government that refuses to accept the decision of the tribunal.

Such, in essence, is the argument implicit in all the projects for preventing war by means of a federation. Obviously, the argument is sound; and any such federation would prevent war —*provided* the contracting governments would always do what they promised to do. The fundamental assumption of the argument implicit in all such federations may, therefore, be stated as follows: the great majority of governments will always do what they have promised to do because war is an evil of such magnitude that the prevention of any particular war will always be, for the governments not directly involved in it, more important than any other interest that might dispose them to condone it.

On this major assumption, the League of Nations was established in 1919. Its primary purpose was to prevent war, and the Covenant provided a carefully considered and precisely defined procedure for attaining that end. Yet the League failed—so completely that it now seems strange that anyone could ever have supposed it might succeed. The cause of its failure has usually been attributed to some defect in the procedure: "teeth," it is said, should have been put into the sanctions—which means, I suppose, that the League should have been equipped with an army of its own to enforce its decisions. But this, in the circumstances, would surely have been useless. The failure did not arise from lack of sanctions to enforce the decisions, but either from lack of decisions to be enforced at critical junctures, or failure of the contracting governments to apply the sanction provided. Any military force that might conceivably have been placed at the disposal of the League would have been inadequate against the chief member states if those states were not disposed to follow the procedure provided in the Covenant; and if they were disposed to follow the procedure provided, no military force would have been needed. The League failed because, being nothing but an agent of the member states, it could do only what the member states used it for doing; and the chief member states were unwilling to use it for the purpose for which they had created it. The defects of the League were not incidental, but inherent; it was created on false assumptions for inadequate purposes.

It was created on the false assumption that the prevention of war is a major interest of states. Generally speaking, neither war nor peace is one of the concrete positive interests of men or nations. Nations, like individuals, seek to obtain certain real or imagined concrete goods or to avoid certain concrete evils. Neither nations nor individuals are ever, except in an academic discussion, offered a choice between peace and war; they are offered a choice between doing this or doing that in order to obtain the concrete good or to avoid the concrete evil. War is no doubt recognized as an evil to be avoided if possible; but in any actual situation war will always be accepted if it is thought to be the only means of avoiding some evil that is greater, or of obtaining some good if the good desired can only be obtained by war and is thought to overbalance the evil of the means employed to obtain it. The prevention of war can never be a major interest of nations so long as war, in certain situations, is regarded as the only means of preserving or promoting what are thought to be the vital interests of the particular nations concerned.

Not only was the League founded on false assumptions, but for too limited, too negative, and therefore inadequate purposes. Existing only or chiefly to prevent war, it could act only after it was too late, only when the conflict of interests, being fully matured, could no longer be settled by peaceful means. The history of the League provides sufficient evidence of all this. In all the crucial situations—the Ethiopian affair, the Japanese invasion of China, the Spanish revolution in its international implications, the German aggressions that led to the war of 1939—the League failed to prevent war, for the same reason that Metternich's Concert of Europe failed to prevent revolution; that is to say, because in each situation it could not act until too late, and because then the nations concerned subordinated the desire to prevent war to other interests which, at the time, were thought to be more important. I venture to think that any league founded on similar assumptions and for similar purposes would likewise fail—if for no other reason than because it could, as a last resort, prevent war only by waging war.

Any league or federation of states designed to prevent war should be primarily concerned not with the negative task of preventing war but with the positive task of eliminating the causes of it. The essential conditions for undertaking that enterprise with some chance of success are: first, that the league or federation should function all the time and be concerned with reconciling the conflicting and promoting the common interests of the member states; and, second, that the particular interests that are likely from time to time to divide the member states should be less fundamental and of less consequence than the common and permanent interests that unite them.

Such federations now exist, and have been notably successful. We are all familiar with them—the Swiss and Dutch confederations, the British Commonwealth of Nations, the federal republic of the United States. The one we are most familiar with is the federal republic of the United States. We do not think of it (or of any of the other federations) in connection with the League of Nations, because it was not created for the sole purpose of preventing war. It was created "in order to form a more perfect union, establish justice, insure domestic tranquillity, provide for the common defense, promote the general welfare, and secure the blessings of liberty to ourselves and our posterity." It was created, that is, for positive political ends—one of these being the promotion of the common interests of the member states, another, the maintenance of peace among them. This was its strength, that by being chiefly concerned with the emergencies of peace it did all that any federation could do to prevent war.

I do not mean to say that this was the only, or even the principal reason for the success of the American federal republic. No federation will succeed merely because its constitution is a good one, and because its purposes are properly understood and defined. The indispensable condition for the success of any federation is that the people included in it should have common interests to be promoted and that they should be willing to work together for promoting them. This implies that they should have essentially similar ideas about the fundamentals of life—morality and religion, political and economic institutions, and the foundations of public authority, to say nothing of such apparently trivial but really important matters as stars and garters, dress coats, and how to behave mannerly at table. The success of the American federal republic, of the Swiss and Dutch confederations, and of the British Commonwealth of Nations must be attributed, in the last analysis, to the fact that their constitutions were but the formal expression of a union potentially existing and easily cemented because the people included had all much the same needs and interests, and much the same ideas about how they could be best safeguarded and promoted.

Knowledge of the past does not, as I am often told it should, enable one to predict the future. Whether the democratic countries will establish an international federation at the close of the war or not, no one can say; but, supposing them disposed to do so, what is known about the league that failed and the federations that have succeeded should enable us to discriminate, with some confidence, between the kind of federation it would be useless for them to establish and the kind that might conceivably accomplish something worth while.

It would surely be useless to establish a world federation, with or without a super-world government. All nations are animated and united by love of peace and a common humanity, no doubt; but these are sentiments too intangible to be the basis of a political structure. It would be equally useless, I think, to attempt to establish, at the close of the war, a federation of all the European countries. Such unity of ideas and institutions as once existed in Europe has been, temporarily at least, destroyed. Between the democratic countries and the fascist totalitarian countries there is no common basis for intelligent discussion even, to say nothing of co-operative action. If Hitler is defeated the totalitarian philosophy might indeed lose its hold on the minds of men in Germany and elsewhere, but this is not likely to happen all at once; and, in any case, the present conflict has generated hatreds so intense that, for the immediate future, no union between Germany and the countries she has conquered and despoiled would, I think, have any chance of success. If a world federation is out of the question, and a federation of all European countries impracticable at the present time, there remain, for our federation, if one is to be formed, the democratic countries. What then are the democratic countries, and what interests and aims have they in common that might be the basis of a workable union?

The term "democratic countries" lacks precision and covers a multitude of virtues and defects. In listing the democratic countries, we think at once, and with confidence, of the United States and the British self-governing Dominions, of Great Britain and France, Switzerland, Belgium and Holland, the Scandinavian countries, and Czechoslovakia. We think of some other countries also, with less confidence, perhaps, because their institutions are so different from ours.

Assuming that these countries are all democratic, what else have they in common that might be the basis of a federation? Not a great deal, certainly. To say nothing of the fact that they are widely separated geographically, the differences between many of them are numerous and deep-seated—differences in racial origin and language, in political tradition and procedure, in real or imagined national interest. Taking all of the democratic countries together, there is obviously no sufficient community of interest or habit for a federation on the model of the United States or the British Commonwealth of Nations. Even limited to the nations that speak the same language and have essentially similar ideas about law and political procedure, a federation, if it implies a federal government limiting the sovereignty of the member states, is clearly not an end that as yet lies within the realm of practical politics.

Any union of the democratic countries, if there is to be one, must then be a pretty loose and flexible one, since it must be based on the aims and interests that do in fact unite them, and these, if real, are somewhat intangible, and may not prove to be enduring. At the present moment, the democratic countries are in fact united by certain aims and interests that are real enough to keep them united for the duration of the war, and will probably keep them sufficiently united to agree upon the terms of peace. In the Eight Points, President Roosevelt and Prime Minister Churchill have stated what they suppose these common aims and interests to be; and an examination of the Eight Points, by disclosing which of the enumerated aims and interests are genuine and may prove to be reasonably permanent, should give some indication of the kind of union it might be worth while to establish after the peace is made.

Briefly stated, the Eight Points are: (1) no territorial aggrandizement; (2 and 3) self-determination of nations; (4) access by all nations, on equal terms, to the trade and raw materials of the world needed for their economic prosperity; (5) collaboration of all nations in the economic field to secure improved labor conditions and social security; (6) a peace that will "afford to all nations the means of dwelling in safety within their own boundaries"; (7) freedom of the seas; (8) the ultimate abandonment of force by all nations, and, "pending the establishment of a wider and permanent system of general security," the disarmament of nations "which threaten, or may threaten, aggression outside their frontiers."

Even a casual reading enables us to classify these eight points under two heads: a statement of explicit intentions; a statement of generous hopes. The explicit intention is to restore the conquered countries to their former political independence, to disarm the present aggressor nations, and to re-establish the old system of international trade and maritime police of the seas. The generous hope is that all nations will collaborate to improve social conditions within the nations, to effect a more equitable distribution of economic resources among them, and to create some sort of international organization ultimately designed to enable all nations to dispense with the use of force.

We may, for the moment, dismiss the generous hopes. The explicit intentions reveal well enough the two dominant interests of the allied countries—that is, the group, led by the British and American democracies, that signed the Twenty-six Nation agreement subscribing to the Atlantic Charter—at the present moment—defense of their respective countries against aggression and conquest, and the preservation of their political institutions against the impact of the Nazi philosophy. When Hitler is defeated, these will no doubt still be the dominant interests of these countries in making peace. In making peace, so far as Europe is concerned, the allied countries will be confronted with the crucial fact that, however completely Hitler is defeated, there will still be in central Europe seventy or eighty million Germans; and the chief aim of these countries in making peace in Europe will be to safeguard their political independence against a repetition of German aggression and conquest. How can this be done?

It might conceivably be done in one of three ways: by exterminating the Germans; by keeping them down as the Nazis now keep the people of the conquered countries down; or by consolidating the power of the democratic countries in some form of union. Since the extermination of seventy million Germans seems somewhat impracticable, the allied countries will probably try a modification of the second method. Russia will no doubt insist upon terms of peace designed to strengthen her western frontier against future German aggression. The Eight Points of Peace call for the disarmament of Germany, temporarily at least; Britain, Russia, and the conquered countries will undoubtedly think this necessary; and some of them may very well desire to weaken Germany still more by indemnities, territorial cessions, or political partition. Such half-hearted attempts to apply the Nazi methods to the Germans would, I think, be unwise. They would only irritate without in the long run essentially weakening the Germans, and thereby prove no less futile than the indemnities and disarmament imposed by the Treaty of Versailles. The allied countries would do better to leave Germany to the Germans, accord to them the same freedom they claim for themselves, and rely upon their own power rather than upon German weakness as the means of providing for their common defense and promoting their common welfare.

Providing for the common defense certainly calls for a cooperative effort or union of some sort; but a union of all the democratic countries after the war, based upon a fixed constitution or covenant imposing uniform obligations on all alike, would amount to a revival of the League of Nations, and prove no less impractical. It is not enough that all the democratic countries should be united by the desire to defend themselves against aggression and conquest; for the danger from aggression and conquest is not equally pressing for all, nor does it arise for all from the same source. Any union of the democratic countries for defense, to be workable, must take account of these variations in the concrete situation of the countries concerned.

Taking account of such variations, the European democracies might very well work out a military *entente* for mutual defense after the war, in fact if not in name against the only countries that, as it then appears, are likely in any near future to be able, whether disposed or not, to disturb their peace or security in Europe. The futility, for the small countries, of relying upon the law of neutrality, and, for the large countries, of waiting to see what turns up, should be sufficiently evident by now to convince them that some form of defensive alliance is desirable. That the United States or the South American republics would be willing to underwrite such an alliance is extremely unlikely. But the United States, the South American republics, Canada, and Great Britain, having a common interest in the "defense of the Western Hemisphere," might reach a workable agreement to maintain the Monroe Doctrine and the "freedom of the seas" in the Atlantic; while the democracies having common interests in the Far East might reach a workable agreement for mutual defense against any likely and potential disturber of the peace in that area. Such agreements would not amount to a federation; but they could be so drawn that each would supplement the others, and thereby constitute a loose and flexible union of the democratic countries designed to provide for the common defense.

If it be said that all this would be no more than a manipulation and readjustment of the old balance of power, I agree. By itself it would, obviously, be no more than that—like all military defensive alliances, no more than a negative, dead thing, in the nature of a concrete wall erected to stop something after it has gained momentum, a momentum too great, as like as not, to be effectively resisted. Such a military alliance for the common defense might, indeed, have the temporary value of permitting the several countries to reduce their respective military and naval establishments; but it would have permanent value only if supplemented by another sort of alliance—an alliance designed to promote the general welfare, an alliance, that is to say, which would function positively, in time of peace, in the effort to remedy the conditions that generate the totalitarian philosophy and reinforce the impulse to aggression and conquest.

President Roosevelt and Prime Minister Churchill are at least aware that such conditions exist. They realize, therefore, that crushing Hitler and disarming Germany are not enough. In the Eight Points they declare for a peace that will accord to all nations, on equal terms, access to the trade and raw materials of the world needed for their economic prosperity, and call upon all nations to collaborate in the economic field to secure improved labor conditions and social security. This may be, on their part, no more than a political gesture—the expression of a generous hope; but it touches the heart of the two-fold problem that confronts all democratic societies in our time—the problem of effecting a more satisfactory distribution of economic possessions and opportunities within and among the nations.

During the last half century, competition between the have and the have-not classes, in all industrial societies, has provided a fertile field for generating the totalitarian philosophy; and it is widely recognized that a more rational method of distributing economic possessions is essential to the preservation, or better working, of democratic institutions. During the same time, unrestrained competition between nations for the trade and raw materials needed by every industrial society has been one of the causes of war. Not by any means the only cause, or perhaps ever a justifiable cause. That Hitler and Mussolini and the Japanese imperialists are inspired by other motives; that they might have obtained the trade and raw materials needed for their countries by other and better means than war; that their countries may, therefore, be rightly described, in the present war, as aggressor nations—all this I would be the last to deny.

I am also aware that the distinction between the have and the have-not nations is not so clear cut as it is often taken to be. All countries are in some respects have-not countries—countries that lack at least some of the economic resources needed by every industrial society. This would not matter if no barriers obstructed free commercial intercourse among nations, and if no nation ever needed to fear that such intercourse as exists in time of peace might be interrupted by war. But the fact is that political power can be and is used to obtain exclusive or preferential access to the trade, the raw materials, and the economic exploitation of the industrially undeveloped regions of the earth; and in this competitive political struggle for economic possessions and opportunities, the strong countries have an advantage over the weak, and those that are best supplied, within their own boundaries and colonial possessions, with needed economic resources have an advantage over those that are less well supplied. In the world as it is politically organized, the politically weak countries have to accept this disadvantage, and rely for their economic security upon the good will of the strong countries and the law of neutrality. But the politically strong countries that are most lacking in needed economic resources (and it is significant that Germany, Italy, and Japan are notable examples) regard this as a precarious situation, and for that reason are apt to resort to political means, including war, for obtaining what they think essential for their economic security.

The two essential problems thus presented to democratic countries in the modern world—the mitigation of the social conflict, and the prevention of war—are related, since war intensifies the social conflict, and the social conflict, if sufficiently intensified and prolonged, is a contributory cause of war. The fundamental conditions that create this vicious circle can neither be abolished nor essentially improved by military alliances, however strong. They can be abolished or improved only in so far as the competitive struggle, within and among the nations, is replaced, or at least supplemented and restrained, by more co-operative and rational methods of distribution. If, then, the democratic countries wish to create anything in the way of a "new order," in Europe or elsewhere, if they wish to safeguard effectively their democratic institutions against the totalitarian philosophy and their national independence against the aggression of dictators, they should undertake in all seriousness and good faith the difficult task of giving some reality to the generous hopes expressed in the Eight Points of Peace—they should endeavor, that is to say, within their own countries to secure better labor conditions and social security, and, in international relations, to devise a more rational and co-operative method of dealing with the conflict of economic interests that arise among them.

To insinuate anything co-operative and rational into the methods traditionally employed by states for settling their disputes would be, I am fully aware, sufficiently difficult; but that something could be done in that way if much were attempted in good faith, I think not unlikely. It is obvious, however, that nothing can be accomplished in the way of co-operation unless the principal democratic countries are willing to co-operate, are willing, that is, to form some sort of union, however loose and flexible. Let us not irritate their pride of sovereignty by inaugurating the union with flourish of trumpets and impressive ceremonies and solemn pledges. The union will have a better chance of success if it begins, so to speak, "unbeknownst to itself," without a name, or drafted covenant defining its functions and procedure—if it begins, in short, merely as a tentative and experimental effort, on the part of the countries that at the close of the war are able to make the effort, to deal by familiar methods with the insistent problems that the war will surely bequeath to the victors as its accustomed but unwanted heritage.

The most urgent problems at the close of the war will obviously be the political restoration and economic and financial rehabilitation of the conquered and devastated countries. Of these two problems, political restoration may well be left to the countries concerned; but for their economic and financial rehabilitation they will need assistance, and the two countries, almost the only countries, likely to be able to give that assistance are the United States and Great Britain. Great Britain and the United States are now united to win the war, and they have announced certain common aims to be realized at the close of it. Their commitments therefore, and their interests no less so, should dispose them to remain united after the war for effecting, as rapidly as possible, by whatever means are available, political order and economic stability in Europe. Their first concern should no doubt be for the countries conquered and despoiled by the Nazis; but if, as may well be, the defeat of Hitler leaves

Germany and Italy economically disordered and financially helpless, those two countries should, so far as possible, be given assistance too, since political order and economic stability cannot be effectively established in some European countries if the others, especially if Germany is one of them, remain in a state of economic as well as political confusion.

Such co-operative effort on the part of Great Britain and the United States, undertaken in their own interest, for dealing with immediate problems, might conceivably be the beginning of a wider, and perhaps a permanent union. The countries most likely to be at first included in this wider union (we may at this point perhaps venture to call it an economic *entente*) would be those that are now virtual allies of Great Britain, and likely to be, after the war, disposed to co-operate with Great Britain and the United States for mutual defense and economic advantage— without any intention of being exclusive or snobbish about it, let us say, for example, France, Switzerland, Belgium and Holland, the Scandinavian countries, Czechoslovakia, and China. It would certainly be to the advantage of these countries to recognize the fact that, in a world so highly integrated economically, their several interests can no longer be best served by the traditional method of free competitive political enterprise. Recognizing this fact, the governments of these countries might conceivably regard certain matters (for example, trade and tariffs, the gold standard or a managed currency, labor conditions and the standard of living, the need for raw materials, and the value of colonial possessions) as constituting a single interrelated international problem, and attempt to deal with it co-operatively, on the basis of scientific knowledge, instead of competitively, in response to unreal notions of national power and prestige. In such an enterprise, they would have less need for professional diplomats, trained in the fine art of getting something for nothing, than for experts in economics and finance, trained to approach problems objectively and to offer solutions suggested by an analysis of the relevant facts. They would probably need an international commission of experts. Well, there is the late League of Nations, lying in state in its palatial dwelling at

Geneva. Dismantled of its war-prevention paraphernalia, it might well be salvaged by the democratic countries to serve them as an international fact-finding agency, its name being retained as a useful symbol of their union.

Such a union, beginning as a tentative and experimental effort to deal with immediate problems, by familiar methods, without assuming the godlike prerogative of foreseeing the future, of drawing indictments against nations or pronouncing judgment upon them, might conceivably accomplish something worth while; whether much or little, temporarily or permanently, would depend upon the shape of things to come. Nothing would exclude the South American republics or the Eastern European countries except their own reluctance or inability to share in the co-operative effort. Whether the union could later be extended to include other countries—even Germany and Japan—would depend upon the people of those countries, upon the kind of governments they might establish, and the disposition of those governments to adhere to agreements entered into and to co-operate in good faith for the achievement of common aims. Less in the nature of a predetermined, created mechanism than a developing organism, such a union would at any time be what it could be used for doing; and would ultimately become, in respect to functions and procedure, what it could from time to time do to preserve the peace by composing the conflicts of political and economic interests that so often, when prolonged and aggravated, lead to war.

The country that could do most either to make or to break such a union is the United States. It was said at the close of the last war, and will be said at the close of this one, that we have nothing to do with the European mess, and should keep out of it. But if that is so, why are we in the European mess now, why were we in it from 1917 to 1919? It seems that the European mess, when it is a war mess, has something to do with us—so much to do with us that we inevitably have, after all, something to do with it. The mistake is to suppose that the mess is merely European, and a mess only when it assumes the form of war. In truth, the war mess is only an exacerbation of the peace mess, and the peace mess is worldwide. Let us not then continue in the error of supposing that even if we always have to do something about the war mess, we can, so far as the peace mess is concerned, either take it or leave it alone.

The disposition to stand aside is not peculiar to the United States. England has also traditionally followed a policy of splendid isolation, except when war compelled her to abandon it. The small European countries have, once too often, followed the same policy: have assumed that they had nothing to do with the conflicts of the great powers only to find that the present conflict had something disastrous to do with them. It should be sufficiently evident by now that, in a world so highly integrated economically, no country can, in the emergency of war, safely follow a policy of political isolation. If, then, we would avoid the entangling alliances that war is sure to impose upon us, we should cultivate the less entangling peace-time alliances that would do nothing to impair our freedom, and might do much to safeguard it.

What I am suggesting is a military and an economic union, however loose and flexible, led by the chief democratic countries, designed to provide for their common defense and to promote their common welfare. If it be said that such a union has all the appearance of a democratic power combination, directed by the British Commonwealth of Nations and the United States and capable of world domination, I do not deny it. But the present situation seems to me to indicate that if the chief democratic countries cannot, by united action, acquire the power to say what shall and shall not happen in a considerable part of the world, they may again run the risk of not being able to say what shall and shall not happen in *any part* of it.

If it be asked whether the democratic countries can be trusted to use so much power wisely, one answer is, no: there can be no guarantee that power will ever be used wisely. But another answer is that power exists and will be used by the countries that have it; and if some countries are to hold a commanding position in the world, I at least prefer that it should be the democratic rather than the totalitarian countries that hold it: for one reason, because the United States is one of the democratic countries; for another, because it is evident that the democratic countries can be more safely trusted than the totalitarian to use great power with some regard for justice and humanity.

Taking the world as it is, it seems to me no more than political prudence and common sense for the democratic countries to consolidate their power for the promotion of their own interests. Beyond political prudence and common sense, there is, nevertheless, something else. There is political wisdom; and the democratic countries, however impressive the power at their command may be, will lack political wisdom if they fail to remember that the quality of their own freedom, and the ultimate value of the force that sustains it, can be displayed with best advantage to themselves only by maintaining a scrupulous regard for the rights and possessions of all nations.

THE UNIQUENESS OF MAN

By JULIAN HUXLEY

MAN'S opinion of his own position in relation to the rest of the animals has swung pendulum-wise between too great or too little a conceit of himself, fixing now too large a gap between himself and the animals, now too small. The gap, of course, can be diminished or increased at either the animal or the human end. One can, like Descartes, make animals too mechanical, or, like most unsophisticated people, humanize them too much. Or one can work at the human end of the gap, and then either dehumanize one's own species into an animal species like any other, or superhumanize it into beings a little lower than the angels.

Primitive and savage man, the world over, not only accepts his obvious kinship with the animals but also projects into them many of his own attributes. So far as we can judge, he has very little pride in his own humanity. With the advent of settled civilization, economic stratification, and the development of an elaborate religion as the ideological mortar of a now class-ridden society, the pendulum began slowly to swing in the other direction. Animal divinities and various physiological functions such as fertility gradually lost their sacred importance. Gods became anthropomorphic and human psychological qualities pre-eminent. Man saw himself as a being set apart, and the rest of the animal kingdom created to serve his needs and pleasure, with no share in salvation, no position in eternity. In Western civilization this swing of the pendulum reached its limit in developed Christian theology and in the philosophy of Descartes: both alike inserted a qualitative and unbridgeable barrier between all men and any animals.

With Darwin, the reverse swing was started. Man was once again regarded as an animal, but now in the light of science rather than of unsophisticated sensibility. At the outset, the consequences of the changed outlook were not fully explored. The unconscious prejudices and attitudes of an earlier age survived, disguising many of the moral and philosophical implications of the new outlook. But gradually the pendulum reached the furthest point of its swing. What seemed the logical consequences of the Darwinian postulates were faced: man is an animal like any other; accordingly, his views as to the special meaning of human life and human ideals need merit no more consideration in the light of eternity (or of evolution) than those of a bacillus or a tapeworm. Survival is the only criterion of evolutionary success: therefore, all existing organisms are of equal value. The idea of progress is a mere anthropomorphism. Man happens to be the dominant type at the moment, but he might be replaced by the ant or the rat. And so on.

The gap between man and animal was here reduced not by exaggerating the human qualities of animals, but by minimizing the human qualities of men. Of late years, however, a new tendency has become apparent. It may be that this is due mainly to the mere increase of knowledge and the extension of scientific analysis. It may be that it has been determined by social and psychological causes. Disillusionment with *laisser faire* in the human economic sphere may well have spread to the planetary system of *laisser faire* that we call natural selection. With the crash of old religious, ethical, and political systems, man's desperate need for some scheme of values and ideals may have prompted a more critical re-examination of his biological position. Whether this be so is a point that I must leave to the social historians. The fact remains that the pendulum is again on the swing, the man-animal gap again broadening. After Darwin, man could no longer avoid considering himself as an animal; but he is beginning to see himself as a very peculiar and in many ways a unique animal. The analysis of man's biological uniqueness is as yet incomplete. This essay is an attempt to review its present position.

The first and most obviously unique characteristic of man is his capacity for conceptual thought; if you prefer objective terms, you will say, his employment of true speech, but that is only another way of saying the same thing. True speech involves the use of verbal signs for objects, not merely for feelings. Plenty of animals can express the fact that they are hungry; but none except man can ask for an egg or a banana. And to have words for objects at once implies conceptual thought, since an object is always one of a class. No doubt, children and savages are as unaware of using conceptual thought as Monsieur Jourdain was unaware of speaking in prose; but they cannot avoid it. Words are tools which automatically carve concepts out of experience. The faculty of recognizing objects as members of a class provides the potential basis for the concept: the use of words at once actualizes the potentiality.

This basic human property has had many consequences. The most important was the development of a cumulative tradition. The beginnings of tradition, by which experience is transmitted from one generation to the next, are to be seen in many higher animals. But in no case is the tradition cumulative. Offspring learn from parents, but they learn the same kind and quantity of lessons as they, in turn, impart: the transmission of experience never bridges more than one generation. In man, however, tradition is an independent and potentially permanent activity, capable of indefinite improvement in quality and increase in quantity. It constitutes a new accessory process of heredity in evolution, running side by side with the biological process, a heredity of experience to supplement the universal heredity of living substance.

The existence of a cumulative tradition has as its chief consequence—or if you prefer, its chief objective manifestation—the progressive improvement of human tools and machinery. Many animals employ tools; but they are always crude tools employed in a crude way. Elaborate tools and skilled technique can develop only with the aid of speech and tradition.

In the perspective of evolution, tradition and tools are the characters which have given man his dominant position among organisms. This biological dominance is, at present, another of man's unique properties. In each geological epoch of which we have knowledge, there have been types which must be styled biologically dominant: they multiply, they extinguish or reduce competing types, they extend their range, they radiate into new modes of life. Usually at any one time there is one such type— the plac ntal mammals, for instance, in the Cenozoic period; but sometimes there is more than one. The Mesozoic is usually called the Age of Reptiles, but in reality the reptiles were then competing for dominance with the insects: in earlier periods we should be hard put to it to decide whether trilobites, nautiloids, or early fish were *the* dominant type. To-day, however, there is general agreement that man is the sole type meriting the title. Since the early Pleistocene, widespread extinction has diminished the previously dominant group of placental mammals, and man has not merely multiplied, but has evolved, extended his range, and increased the variety of his modes of life.

Biology thus reinstates man in a position analogous to that conferred on him as Lord of Creation by theology. There are, however, differences, and differences of some importance for our general outlook. In the biological view, the other animals have not been created to serve man's needs, but man has evolved in such a way that he has been able to eliminate some competing types, to enslave others by domestication, and to modify physical and biological conditions over the larger part of the earth's land area. The theological view was not true in detail or in many of its implications; but it had a solid biological basis.

Speech, tradition, and tools have led to many other unique properties of man. These are, for the most part, obvious and well known, and I propose to leave them aside until I have dealt with some less familiar human characteristics. For the human species, considered as a species, is unique in certain purely biological attributes; and these have not received the attention they deserve, either from the zoological or the sociological standpoint.

In the first place, man is by far the most variable wild species known. Domesticated species like dog, horse, or fowl may rival or exceed him in this particular, but their variability has obvious reasons, and is irrelevant to our inquiry.

In correlation with his wide variability, man has a far wider range than any other animal species, with the possible exception of some of his parasites. Man is also unique as a dominant type.

All other dominant types have evolved into many hundreds or thousands of separate species, grouped in numerous genera, families, and larger classificatory groups. The human type has maintained its dominance without splitting: man's variety has been achieved within the limits of a single species.

Finally, man is unique among higher animals in the method of his evolution. Whereas, in general, animal evolution is divergent, human evolution is reticulate. By this is meant that in animals, evolution occurs by the isolation of groups which then become progressively more different in their genetic characteristics, so that the course of evolution can be represented as a divergent radiation of separate lines, some of which become extinct, others continue unbranched, and still others divergently branch again. Whereas in man, after incipient divergence, the branches have come together again, and have generated new diversity from their Mendelian recombinations, this process being repeated until the course of human descent is like a network.

All these biological peculiarities are interconnected. They depend on man's migratory propensities, which themselves arise from his fundamental peculiarities, of speech, social life, and relative independence of environment. They depend again on his capacity, when choosing mates, for neglecting large differences of color and appearance which would almost certainly be more than enough to deter more instinctive and less plastic animals. Thus divergence, though it appears to have gone quite a long way in early human evolution, generating the very distinct white, black, and yellow subspecies and perhaps others, was never permitted to attain its normal culmination. Mutually infertile groups were never produced: man remained a single species. Furthermore, crossing between distinct types, which is a rare and extraordinary phenomenon in other animals, in him became normal and of major importance. According to Mendelian laws, such crosses generate much excess variability by producing new recombinations. Man is thus more variable than other species for two reasons. First, because migration has recaptured for the single interbreeding group divergences of a magnitude that in animals would escape into the isolation of separate species; and secondly, because the resultant crossing has generated recombinations which both quantitatively and qualitatively are on a far bigger scale than is supplied by the internal variability of even the numerically most abundant animal species.

We may contrast this with the state of affairs among ants, the dominant insect group. The ant type is more varied than the human type; but it has achieved this variability by intense divergent evolution. Several thousand species of ants are known, and the number is being added to each year with the increase of biological exploration. Ways of life among ants are divided among different subtypes, each rigidly confined to its own methods. Thus even if ants were capable of accumulating experience, there could exist no single world-wide ant tradition. The fact that the human type comprises but one biological species is a consequence of his capacity for tradition, and also permits his exploitation of that unique capacity to the utmost.

Let us remind ourselves that superposed upon this purely biological or genetic variability is the even greater amount of variability due to differences of upbringing, profession, and personal tastes. The final result is a degree of variation that would be staggering if it were not so familiar. It would be fair to say that, in respect to mind and outlook, individual human beings are separated by differences as profound as those which distinguish the major groups of the animal kingdom. The difference between a somewhat subnormal member of a savage tribe and a Beethoven or a Newton is assuredly comparable in extent with that between a sponge and a higher mammal. Leaving aside such vertical differences, the lateral difference between the mind of, say, a distinguished general or engineer of extrovert type and of an introvert genius in mathematics or religious mysticism is no less than that between an insect and a vertebrate. This enormous range of individual variation in human minds often leads to misunderstanding and even mutual incomprehensibility; but it also provides the necessary basis for fruitful division of labor in human society.

Another biological peculiarity of man is the uniqueness of his evolutionary history. Writers have indulged their speculative fancy by imagining other organisms endowed with speech and conceptual thought—talking rats, rational ants, philosophic dogs and the like. But closer analysis shows that these fantasies are impossible. A brain capable of conceptual thought could not have been developed elsewhere than in a human body.

The course followed by evolution appears to have been broadly as follows. From a generalized early type, various lines radiate out, exploiting the environment in various ways. Some of these comparatively soon reach a limit to their evolution, at least as regards major alteration. Thereafter they are limited to minor changes such as the formation of new genera and species. Others, on the other hand, are so constructed that they can continue their career, generating new types which are successful in the struggle for existence because of their greater control over the environment and their greater independence of it. Such changes are legitimately called "progressive." The new type repeats the process. It radiates out into a number of lines, each specializing in a particular direction. The great majority of these come up against dead ends and can advance no further: specialization is one-sided progress, and after a longer or shorter time, reaches a biomechanical limit. The horse stock cannot reduce its digits below one; the elephants are near the limits of size for terrestrial animals; feathered flight cannot become more efficient than in existing birds, and so on.

Sometimes all the branches of a given stock have come up against their limit, and then either have become extinct or have persisted without major change. This happened, for instance, to the echinoderms, which with their sea urchins, starfish, brittle stars, sea lilies, sea cucumbers, and other types now extinct had pushed the life that was in them into a series of blind alleys: they have not advanced for perhaps a hundred million years, nor have they given rise to other major types.

In other cases, all but one or two of the lines suffer this fate, while the rest repeat the process. All reptilian lines were blind alleys save two—one which was transformed into the birds, and another which became the mammals. Of the bird stock, all lines came to a dead end; of the mammals, all but one—the one which became man.

Evolution is thus seen as an enormous number of blind alleys, with a very occasional path of progress. It is like a maze in which almost all turnings are wrong turnings. The goal of the evolutionary maze, however, is not a central chamber, but a road which will lead indefinitely onwards.

If now we look back upon the past history of life, we shall see that the avenues of progress have been steadily reduced in number, until by the Pleistocene period, or even earlier, only one was left. Let us remember that we can and must judge early progress in the light of its latest steps. The most recent step has been the acquisition of conceptual thought, which has enabled man to dethrone the non-human mammals from their previous position of dominance. It is biologically obvious that conceptual thought could never have arisen save in an animal, so that all plants, both green and otherwise, are at once eliminated. As regards animals, I need not go through the early steps in their progressive evolution. Since some degree of bulk helps to confer independence of the forces of nature, it is obvious that the combination of many cells to form a large individual was one necessary step, thus eliminating all single-celled forms from such progress. Similarly, progress is barred to specialized animals with no blood-system, like planarian worms; to internal parasites like tapeworms; to animals with radial symmetry and consequently no head, like echinoderms.

Of the three highest animal groups—the molluscs, the arthropods, and the vertebrates—the molluscs advanced least far. One condition for the later steps in biological progress was land life. The demands made upon the organism by exposure to air and gravity called forth biological mechanisms, such as limbs, sense organs, protective skin, and sheltered development, which were necessary foundations for later advance. And the molluscs have never been able to produce efficient terrestrial forms: their culmination is in marine types like squid and octopus.

The arthropods, on the other hand, have scored their greatest successes on land, with the spiders and especially the insects. Yet the fossil record reveals a lack of all advance, even in the most successful types such as ants, for a long time back—certainly during the last thirty million years, probably during the whole of the Tertiary epoch. Even during the shorter of these periods, the mammals were still evolving rapidly, and man's rise is contained in a fraction of this time.

What was it that cut the insects off from progress? The answer appears to lie in their breathing mechanism. The land arthropods have adopted the method of air tubes or tracheae, branching to microscopic size and conveying gases directly to and from the tissues, instead of using the dual mechanism of lungs and bloodstream. The laws of gaseous diffusion are such that respiration by tracheae is extremely efficient for very small animals, but becomes rapidly less efficient with increase of size, until it ceases to be of use at a bulk below that of a house mouse. It is for this reason that no insect has ever become, by vertebrate standards, even moderately large.

It is for the same reason that no insect has ever become even moderately intelligent. The fixed pathways of instinct, however elaborate, require far fewer nerve cells than the multiple switchboards that underlie intelligence. It appears to be impossible to build a brain mechanism for flexible behavior with less than a quite large minimum of neurones; and no insect has reached a size to provide this minimum.

Thus only the land vertebrates are left. The reptiles shared biological dominance with the insects in the Mesozoic. But while the insects had reached the end of their blind alley, the reptiles showed themselves capable of further advance. Temperature regulation is a necessary basis for final progress, since without it the rate of bodily function could never be stabilized, and without such stabilization, higher mental processes could never become accurate and dependable.

Two reptilian lines achieved this next step, in the guise of the birds and the mammals. The birds soon, however, came to a dead end, chiefly because their forelimbs were entirely taken up in the specialization for flight. The subhuman mammals made another fundamental advance, in the shape of internal development, permitting the young animal to arrive at a much more advanced stage before it was called upon to face the world. They also (like the birds) developed true family life.

Most mammalian lines, however, cut themselves off from indefinite progress by one-sided evolution, turning their limbs and jaws into specialized and therefore limited instruments. And, for the most part, they relied mainly on the crude sense of smell, which cannot present as differentiated a pattern of detailed knowledge as can sight. Finally, the majority continued to produce their young several at a time, in litters. As J. B. S. Haldane has pointed out, this gives rise to an acute struggle for existence in the prenatal period, a considerable percentage of embryos being aborted or resorbed. Such intrauterine selection will put a premium upon rapidity of growth and differentiation, since the devil takes the hindmost; and this rapidity of development will tend automatically to be carried on into postnatal growth.

As everyone knows, man is characterized by a rate of development which is abnormally slow as compared with that of any other mammal. The period from birth to the first onset of sexual maturity comprises nearly a quarter of the normal span of his life, instead of an eighth, a tenth or twelfth, as in some other animals. This again is in one sense a unique characteristic of man, although from the evolutionary point of view it represents merely the exaggeration of a tendency which is operative in other Primates. In any case, it is a necessary condition for the evolution and proper utilization of rational thought. If men and women were, like mice, confronted with the problems of adult life and parenthood after a few weeks, or even, like whales, after a couple of years, they could never acquire the skills of body and mind that they now absorb from and contribute to the social heritage of the species.

This slowing (or "foetalization," as Bolk has called it, since it prolongs the foetal characteristics of earlier ancestral forms into postnatal development and even into adult life) has had other important by-products for man. Here I will mention but one—his nakedness. The distribution of hair on man is extremely similar to that on a late foetus of a chimpanzee, and there can be little doubt that it represents an extension of this temporary anthropoid phase into permanence. Hairlessness of body is not a unique biological characteristic of man; but it is unique among terrestrial mammals, save for a few desert creatures, and some others which have compensated for loss of hair by developing a pachydermatous skin. In any case, it has important biological consequences, since it must have encouraged the comparatively defenseless human creatures in their efforts to protect themselves against animal enemies and the elements, and so has been a spur to the improvement of intelligence.

Now, foetalization could never have occurred in a mammal producing many young at a time, since intrauterine competition would have encouraged the opposing tendency. Thus we may conclude that conceptual thought could develop only in a mammalian stock which normally brings forth but one young at a birth. Such a stock is provided in the Primates—lemurs, monkeys, and apes.

The Primates also have another characteristic which was necessary for the ancestor of a rational animal—they are arboreal. It may seem curious that living in trees is a prerequisite of conceptual thought. But Elliot Smith's analysis has abundantly shown that only in an arboreal mammal could the forelimb become a true hand, and sight become dominant over smell. Hands obtain an elaborate tactile pattern of what they handle, eyes an elaborate visual pattern of what they see. The combination of the two kinds of pattern, with the aid of binocular vision, in the higher centres of the brain allowed the Primate to acquire a wholly new richness of knowledge about objects, a wholly new possibility of manipulating them. Tree life laid the foundation both for the fuller definition of objects by conceptual thought and for the fuller control of them by tools and machines.

Higher Primates have yet another prerequisite of human intelligence—they are all gregarious. Speech, it is obvious, could never have been evolved in a solitary type. And speech is as much the physical basis of conceptual thought as is protoplasm the physical basis of life.

For the passage, however, of the critical point between subhuman and human, between the biological subordination and the biological primacy of intelligence, between a limited and a potentially unlimited tradition—for this it was necessary for the arboreal animal to descend to the ground again. Only in a terrestrial creature could fully erect posture be acquired; and this was essential for the final conversion of the arms from locomotor limbs into manipulative hands. Furthermore, just as land life, ages previously, had demanded and developed a greater variety of response than had been required in the water, so now it did the same in relation to what had been required in the trees. An arboreal animal could never have evolved the skill of the hunting savage, nor ever have proceeded to the domestication of other animals or to agriculture.

We are now in a position to define the uniqueness of human evolution. The essential character of man as a dominant organism is conceptual thought. And conceptual thought could have arisen only in a multicellular animal, an animal with bilateral symmetry, head and blood system, a vertebrate as against a mollusc or an arthropod, a land vertebrate among vertebrates, a mammal among land vertebrates. Finally, it could have arisen only in a mammalian line which was gregarious, which produced one young at a birth instead of several, and which had recently become terrestrial after a long period of arboreal life.

There is only one group of animals which fulfils these conditions—a terrestrial offshoot of the higher Primates. Thus not merely has conceptual thought been evolved only in man: it could not have been evolved except in man. There is but one path of unlimited progress through the evolutionary maze. The course of human evolution is as unique as its result. It is unique not in the trivial sense of being a different course from that of any other organism, but in the profounder sense of being the only path that could have achieved the essential characters of man. Conceptual thought on this planet is inevitably associated with a particular type of Primate body and Primate brain.

A further property of man in which he is unique among higher animals concerns his sexual life. Man is prepared to mate at any time: animals are not. To start with, most animals have a definite breeding season; only during this period are their reproductive organs fully developed and functional. In addition to this, higher animals have one or more sexual cycles within their breeding seasons, and only at one phase of the cycle are they prepared to mate. In general, either a sexual season or a sexual cycle, or both, operates to restrict mating.

In man, however, neither of these factors is at work. There

appear to be indications of a breeding season in some primitive peoples like the Eskimo, but even there they are but relics. Similarly, while there still exist physiological differences in sexual desire at different phases of the female sexual cycle, these are purely quantitative, and may readily be overridden by psychological factors. Man, to put it briefly, is continuously sexed: animals are discontinuously sexed. If we try to imagine what a human society would be like in which the sexes were interested in each other only during the summer, as in songbirds, or, as in female dogs, experienced sexual desire only once every few months, or even as in ants, only once in a lifetime, we can realize what this peculiarity has meant. In this, as in his slow growth and prolonged period of dependence, man is not abruptly marked off from all other animals, but represents the culmination of a process that can be clearly traced among other Primates. What the biological meaning of this evolutionary trend may be is difficult to understand. One suggestion is that it may be associated with the rise of mind to dominance. The bodily functions, in lower mammals rigidly determined by physiological mechanisms, come gradually under the more plastic control of the brain. But this, for what it is worth, is a mere speculation.

Another of the purely biological characters in which man is unique is his reproductive variability. In a given species of animals, the maximum litter size may, on occasions, reach perhaps double the minimum, according to circumstances of food and temperature, or even perhaps threefold. But during a period of years, these variations will be largely equalized within a range of perhaps fifty per cent either way from the average, and the percentage of wholly infertile adults is very low. In man, on the other hand, the range of positive fertility is enormous—from one to over a dozen, and in exceptional cases to over twenty; and the number of wholly infertile adults is considerable. This fact, in addition to providing a great diversity of patterns of family life, has important bearings on evolution. It means that in the human species differential fertility is more important as a basis for selection than is differential mortality; and it provides the possibility of much more rapid selective change than that found in wild animal species. Such rapidity of evolution would, of course, be

effectively realized only if the stocks with large families possessed a markedly different hereditary constitution from those
with few children; but the high differential fertility of unskilled
workers as against the professional classes in England, or of the
French Canadians against the rest of the inhabitants of Canada,
demonstrates how rapidly populations may change by this means.

Still another point in which man is biologically unique is the
length and relative importance of his period of what we may
call "post-maturity." If we consider the female sex, in which
the transition from reproductive maturity to non-reproductive
post-maturity is more sharply defined than in the male, we find,
in the first place, that in animals a comparatively small percentage of the population survives beyond the period of reproduction; in the second place, that such individuals rarely survive
long, and so far as known never for a period equal to or greater
than the period during which reproduction was possible; and
thirdly, that such individuals are rarely of importance in the
life of the species. The same is true of the male sex, provided we
do not take the incapacity to produce fertile gametes as the criterion of post-maturity, but rather the appearance of signs of
age, such as the beginnings of loss of vigor and weight, decreased
sexual activity, or graying hair.

It is true that in some social mammals, notably among rumi-
nants and Primates, an old male or old female is frequently
found as leader of the herd. Such cases, however, provide the
only examples of the special biological utility of post-mature
individuals among animals; they are confined to a very small
proportion of the population, and it is uncertain to what extent
such individuals are post-mature in the sense we have defined.
In any event, it is improbable that the period of post-maturity is
anywhere near so long as that of maturity. In civilized man, on
the other hand, the average expectation of life now includes over
ten years of post-maturity, and about a quarter of the population
enjoys a period of post-maturity almost as long as that of maturity. What is more, in all human societies above the lowest, a large
proportion of the leaders of the community has always been post-
mature.

This is truly a remarkable phenomenon. Through the new

social mechanisms made possible by speech and tradition, man has been able to utilize for the benefit of the species a period of life which in almost all other creatures is a mere superfluity. We know that the dominance of the old can be overemphasized; but it is equally obvious that society cannot do without the post-mature. To act on the slogan "Too old at forty"—or even at forty-five—would be to rob man of one of his unique character-istics, whereby he utilizes tradition to the best advantage.

We have now dealt in a broad way with the unique properties of man both from the comparative and the evolutionary point of view. Now we can return to the present and the particular and discuss these properties and their consequences a little more in detail. First, let us remind ourselves that the gap between human and animal thought is much greater than is usually supposed. The tendency to project familiar human qualities into animals is very strong, and colors the ideas of nearly all people who have not special familiarity both with animal behavior and scientific method.

Let us recall a few cases illustrating the unhuman character-istics of animal behavior. Everyone is familiar with the rigidity of instinct in insects. Worker ants emerge from their pupal case equipped not with the instincts to care for ant grubs in general, but solely with those suitable to ant grubs of their own species. They will attempt to care for the grubs of other species, but ap-pear incapable of learning new methods if their instincts kill their foster children. Or again, a worker wasp, without food for a hungry grub, has been known to bite off its charge's tail and present it to its head. But even in the fine flowers of vertebrate evolution, the birds and mammals, behavior, though it may be more plastic than in the insects, is as essentially irrational. Birds, for instance, seem incapable of analyzing unfamiliar situations. For them some element in the situation may act as its dominant symbol, the only stimulus to which they can react. At other times, it is the organization of the situation as a whole which is the stimulus: if the whole is interfered with, analysis fails to dissect out the essential element. A hen meadow-pipit feeds her young when it gapes and squeaks in the nest. But if it has been ejected by a young cuckoo, gaping and squeaking has no effect, and the rightful offspring is neglected and allowed to die, while the usurper in the nest is fed. The pipit normally cares for its own young, but not because it recognizes them as such.

Mammals are no better. A cow deprived of its calf will be quieted by the provision of a crudely stuffed calfskin. Even the Primates are no exception. Female baboons whose offspring have died will continue carrying the corpses until they have not merely putrefied but mummified. This appears to be due not to any profundity of grief, but to a contact stimulus: the mother will react similarly to any moderately small and furry object.

Birds and especially mammals are, of course, capable of a certain degree of analysis, but this is effected, in the main, by means of trial and error through concrete experience. A brain capable of conceptual thought appears to be the necessary basis for speedy and habitual analysis. Without it, the practice of splitting up situations into their components and assigning real degrees of significance to the various elements remains rudimentary and rare, whereas with man, even when habit and trial and error are prevalent, conceptual thought is of major biological importance. The behavior of animals is essentially arbitrary, in that it is fixed within narrow limits. In man it has become relatively free— free at the incoming and the outgoing ends alike. His capacity for acquiring knowledge has been largely released from arbitrary symbolism, his capacity for action, from arbitrary canalizations of instinct. He can thus rearrange the patterns of experience and action in a far greater variety, and can escape from the particular into the general.

Thus man is more intelligent than the animals because his brain mechanism is more plastic. This fact also gives him, of course, the opportunity of being more nonsensical and perverse: but its primary effects have been more analytical knowledge and more varied control. The essential fact, from my present standpoint, is that the change has been profound and in an evolutionary sense rapid. Although it has been brought about by the gradual quantitative enlargement of the association areas of the brain, the result has been almost as abrupt as the change (also brought about quantitatively) from solid ice to liquid water. We should remember that the machinery of the change has been an increase in plasticity and potential variety: it is by a natural selection of ideas and actions that the result has been greater rationality instead of greater irrationality.

This increase of flexibility has also had other psychological consequences which rational philosophers are apt to forget: and in some of these, too, man is unique. It has led, for instance, to the fact that man is the only organism normally and inevitably subject to psychological conflict. You can give a dog a neurosis as Pavlov did, by a complicated laboratory experiment: you can find cases of brief emotional conflict in the lives of wild birds and animals. But, for the most part, psychological conflict is shirked by the simple expedient of arranging that now one and now another instinct should dominate the animal's behavior. I remember in Spitsbergen finding the nest of a Red-throated Diver on the shore of an inland pool. The sitting bird was remarkably bold. After leaving the nest for the water, she stayed very close. She did not, however, remain in a state of conflict between fear of intruders and desire to return to her brooding. She would gradually approach as if to land, but eventually fear became dominant, and when a few feet from the shore she suddenly dived, and emerged a good way farther out—only to repeat the process. Here the external circumstances were such as to encourage conflict, but even so what are the most serious features of human conflict were minimized by the outlet of alternate action.

Those who take up bird-watching as a hobby tend at first to be surprised at the way in which a bird will turn, apparently without transition or hesitation, from one activity to another—from fighting to peaceable feeding, from courtship to uninterested preening, from panic flight to unconcern. However, all experienced naturalists or those habitually concerned with animals recognize such behavior as characteristic of the subhuman level. It represents another aspect of the type of behavior I have just been describing for the Red-throated Diver. In this case, the internal state of the bird changes, presumably owing to some form of physiological fatigue or to a diminution of intensity of a stimulus with time or distance; the type of behavior which had been dominant ceases to have command over the machinery of action, and is replaced by another which just before had been subordinate and latent.

As a matter of fact, the prevention of conflict between opposed modes of action is a very general phenomenon, of obvious biological utility, and it is only the peculiarities of the human mind which have forced its partial abandonment on man. It begins on the purely mechanical level with the nervous machinery controlling our muscles. The main muscles of a limb, for instance, are arranged in two antagonistic sets, the flexors bending and the extensors straightening it. It would obviously be futile to throw both sets into action at the same time, and economical when one set is in action to reduce to the minimum any resistance offered by the other. This has actually been provided for. The nervous connections in the spinal cord are so arranged that when a given muscle receives an impulse to contract, its antagonist receives an impulse causing it to lose some of its tone and thus, by relaxing below its normal level, to offer the least possible resistance to the action of the active muscle.

Sherrington discovered that the same type of mechanism was operative in regard to the groups of muscles involved in whole reflexes. A dog, for instance, cannot very well walk and scratch itself at the same time. To avoid the waste involved in conflict between the walking and the scratching reflex, the spinal cord is constructed in such a way that throwing one reflex into action automatically inhibits the other. In both these cases, the machinery for preventing conflicts of activity resides in the spinal cord. Although the matter has not yet been analyzed physiologically, it would appear that the normal lack of conflict between instincts which we have just been discussing is due to some similar type of nervous mechanism in the brain.

When we reach the human level, there are new complications; for, as we have seen, one of the peculiarities of man is the abandonment of any rigidity of instinct, and the provision of association-mechanisms by which any activity of the mind, whether in the spheres of knowing, feeling, or willing, can be brought into relation with any other. It is through this that man has acquired the possibility of a unified mental life. But, by the same token, the door is opened to the forces of disruption, which may destroy any such unity and even prevent him from enjoying the efficiency of behavior attained by animals. For, as Sherrington has emphasized, the nervous system is like a funnel, with a much larger space for intake than for outflow. The intake cone of the funnel is represented by the receptor nerves, conveying impulses inward to the central nervous system from the sense organs: the outflow tube is, then, through the effector nerves, conveying impulses outwards to the muscles, and there are many more of the former than of the latter. If we like to look at the matter from a rather different standpoint, we may say that, since action can be effected only by muscles (strictly speaking, also by the glands, which are disregarded here for simplicity's sake), and since there are a limited number of muscles in the body, the only way for useful activity to be carried out is for the nervous system to impose a particular pattern of action on them, and for all other competing or opposing patterns to be cut out. Each pattern when it has seized control of the machinery of action, *should* be in supreme command, like the captain of a ship. Animals are, in many ways, like ships which are commanded by a number of captains in turn, each specializing in one kind of action, and popping up and down between the authority of the bridge and the obscurity of their private cabins according to the business on hand. Man is on the way to achieving permanent unity of command, but the captain has a disconcerting way of dissolving into a wrangling committee.

Even on the new basis, however, mechanisms exist for minimizing conflict. They are what are known by psychologists as suppression and repression. From our point of view, repression is the more interesting. It implies the forcible imprisonment of one of two conflicting impulses in the dungeons of the unconscious mind. The metaphor is, however, imperfect. For the prisoner in the mental dungeon can continue to influence the tyrant above in the daylight of consciousness. In addition to a general neurosis, compulsive thoughts and acts may be thrust upon the personality. Repression may thus be harmful; but it can also be regarded as a biological necessity for dealing with inevitable conflict in the early years of life, before rational judgment and control are possible. Better to have the capacity for more or less unimpeded action, even at the expense of possible neurosis, than an organism constantly inactivated like the ass between the two bundles of hay, balanced in irresolution.

In repression, not only is the defeated impulse banished to the unconscious, but the very process of banishment is itself unconscious. The inhibitory mechanisms concerned in it must have been evolved to counteract the more obvious possibilities of conflict, especially in early life, which arose as by-products of the human type of mind.

In suppression, the banishment is conscious, so that neurosis is not likely to appear. Finally in rational judgment, neither of the conflicting impulses is relegated to the unconscious, but they are balanced in the light of reason and experience, and control of action is consciously exercised.

I need not pursue the subject further. Here I am only concerned to show that the great biological advantages conferred on man by the unification of mind have inevitably brought with them certain counterbalancing defects. The freedom of association between all aspects and processes of the mind has provided the basis for conceptual thought and tradition; but it has also provided potential antagonists, which in lower organisms were carefully kept apart, with the opportunity of meeting face to face, and has thus made some degree of conflict unavoidable.

In rather similar fashion, man's upright posture has brought with it certain consequential disadvantages in regard to the functioning of his internal organs and his proneness to rupture. Thus man's unique characteristics are by no means all beneficial.

In close correlation with our subjection to conflict is our proneness to laughter. So characteristic of our species is laughter that man has been defined as the laughing animal. It is true that, like so much else of man's uniqueness, it has its roots among the animals, where it reveals itself as an expression of a certain kind of general pleasure—and thus in truth perhaps more of a smile than a laugh. And in a few animals—ravens, for example,—there are traces of a malicious sense of humor. Laughter in man, however, is much more than this. There are many theories of laughter, most of them containing a partial truth. But biologically the important feature of human laughter seems to lie in its providing a release for conflict, a resolution of troublesome situations.

This and other functions of laughter can be exaggerated so that it becomes as the crackling of thorns under the pot, and prevents men from taking anything seriously; but in due proportion its value is very great as a lubricant against troublesome friction and a lightener of the inevitable gravity and horror of life, which would otherwise become portentous and overshadowing. True laughter, like true speech, is a unique possession of man.

Those of man's unique characteristics which may better be called psychological and social than narrowly biological spring from one or other of three characteristics. The first is his capacity for abstract and general thought: the second is the relative unification of his mental processes, as against the much more rigid compartmentalization of animal mind and behavior: the third is the existence of social units, such as tribe, nation, party, and church, with a continuity of their own, based on organized tradition and culture.

There are various by-products of the change from pre-human to the human type of mind which are, of course, also unique biologically. Let us enumerate a few: pure mathematics; musical gifts; artistic appreciation and creation; religion; romantic love.

Mathematical ability appears, almost inevitably, as something mysterious. Yet the attainment of speech, abstraction, and logical thought, bring it into potential being. It may remain in a very rudimentary state of development; but even the simplest arithmetical calculations are a manifestation of its existence. Like any other human activity, it requires proper tools and machinery. Arabic numerals, algebraic conventions, logarithms, the differential calculus, are such tools: each one unlocks new possibilities of mathematical achievement. But just as there is no essential difference between man's conscious use of a chipped flint as an implement and his design of the most elaborate machine, so there is none between such simple operations as numeration or addition and the comprehensive flights of higher mathematics. Again, some people are by nature more gifted than others in this field; yet no normal human being is unable to perform some mathematical operations. Thus the capacity for mathematics is, as I have said, a by-product of the human type of mind.

We have seen, however, that the human type of mind is distinguished by two somewhat opposed attributes. One is the capacity for abstraction, the other for synthesis. Mathematics is one of the extreme by-products of our capacity for abstraction. Arithmetic abstracts objects of all qualities save their enumerability; the symbol π abstracts in a single Greek letter a complicated relation between the parts of all circles. Art, on the other hand, is an extreme by-product of our capacity for synthesis. In one unique production, the painter can bring together form, color, arrangement, associations of memory, emotion, and idea. Dim adumbrations of art are to be found in a few creatures such as bowerbirds; but nothing is found to which the word can rightly be applied until man's mind gave the possibility of freely mingling observations, emotions, memories, and ideas, and subjecting the mixture to deliberate control.

But it is not enough here to enumerate a few special activities. In point of fact, the great majority of man's activities and characteristics are by-products of his primary distinctive characteristics, and therefore, like them, biologically unique.

On the one hand, conversation, organized games, education, sport, paid work, gardening, the theatre; on the other, conscience, duty, sin, humiliation, vice, penitence—these are all such unique by-products. The trouble, indeed, is to find any human activities which are not unique. Even the fundamental biological attributes such as eating, sleeping, and mating have been tricked out by man with all kinds of unique frills and peculiarities.

There may be other by-products of man's basic uniqueness which have not yet been exploited. For let us remember that such by-products may remain almost wholly latent until demand stimulates invention and invention facilitates development. It is asserted that there exist human tribes who cannot count above two; certainly some savages stop at ten. Here the mathematical faculty is restricted to numeration, and stops short at a very rudimentary stage of this rudimentary process. Similarly, there are human societies in which art has never been developed beyond the stage of personal decoration. It is probable that during the first half of the Pleistocene period, none of the human race had developed either their mathematical or their artistic potentialities beyond such a rudimentary stage.

It is perfectly possible that to-day man's so-called supernormal or extra-sensory faculties are in the same case as were his mathematical faculties during the first or second glaciations of the Ice Age—barely more than a potentiality, with no technique for eliciting and developing them, no tradition behind them to give them continuity and intellectual respectability. Even such simple performances as multiplying two three-figure numbers would have appeared entirely magical to early Stone Age men.

Experiments such as those of Rhine and Salter on extra-sensory guessing, experiences like those of Gilbert Murray on thought transference, and the numerous sporadic records of telepathy and clairvoyance suggest that some people at least possess possibilities of knowing which are not confined within the ordinary channels of sense perception. Salter's work is particularly interesting in this connection. As a result of an enormous number of trials with apparatus ingeniously designed to exclude all alternative explanation, he finds that those best endowed with this extra-sensory gift can guess right about once in four times when once in five would be expected on chance alone. The results are definite, and significant in the statistical sense, yet the faculty is rudimentary: it does not permit its possessor to guess right all the time or even most of the time—merely to achieve a small rise in the percentage of right guessing. If, however, we could discover in what this faculty really consists, on what mechanism it depends, and by what conditions and agencies it can be influenced, it should be capable of development like any other human faculty. Man may thus be unique in more ways than he now suspects.

So far we have been considering the fact of human uniqueness. It remains to consider man's attitude to these unique qualities of his. Professor Everett, of the University of California, in an interesting paper bearing the same title as this essay, but dealing with the topic from the standpoint of the philosopher and the humanist rather than that of the biologist, has stressed man's fear of his own uniqueness. Man has often not been able to tolerate the feeling that he inhabits an alien world, whose laws do not make sense in the light of his intelligence, and in which the writ of his human values does not run. Faced with the prospect of such intellectual and moral loneliness, he has projected personality into the cosmic scheme. Here he has found a will, there a purpose; here a creative intelligence, and there a divine compassion. At one time, he has deified animals, or personified natural forces. At others, he has created a superhuman pantheon, a single tyrannical world ruler, a subtle and satisfying Trinity in Unity. Philosophers have postulated an Absolute of the same nature as mind.

It is only exceptionally that men have dared to uphold their uniqueness and to be proud of their human superiority to the impersonality and irrationality of the rest of the universe. It is time now, in the light of our knowledge, to be brave and face the fact and the consequences of our uniqueness. That is Dr. Everett's view as it was also that of T. H. Huxley in his famous Romanes lecture. I agree with them; but I would suggest that the antinomy between man and the universe is not quite so sharp as they have made out. Man represents the culmination of that process of organic evolution which has been proceeding on this planet for over a thousand million years. That process, however wasteful and cruel it may be, and into however many blind alleys it may have been diverted, is also in one aspect progressive. Man has now become the sole representative of life in that progressive aspect and its sole trustee for any progress in the future.

Meanwhile it is true that the appearance of the human type of mind, the latest step in evolutionary progress, has introduced both new methods and new standards. By means of his conscious reason and its chief offspring, science, man has the power of substituting less dilatory, less wasteful, and less cruel methods of effective progressive change than those of natural selection, which alone are available to lower organisms. And by means of his conscious purpose and his set of values, he has the power of substituting new and higher standards for change than those of mere survival and adaptation to immediate circumstances, which alone are inherent in pre-human evolution. To put the matter in another way, progress has hitherto been a rare and fitful by-product of evolution. Man has the possibility of making it the main feature of his own future evolution, and of guiding its course in relation to a deliberate aim.

But he must not be afraid of his uniqueness. There may be other beings in this vast universe endowed with reason, purpose, and aspiration: but we know nothing of them. So far as our knowledge goes, human mind and personality are unique and constitute the highest product yet achieved by the cosmos. Let us not put off our responsibilities onto the shoulders of mythical gods or philosophical absolutes, but shoulder them in the hopefulness of tempered pride. In the perspective of biology, our business in the world is seen to be the imposition of the best and most enduring of our human standards upon ourselves and our planet. The enjoyment of beauty and interest, the achievement of goodness and efficiency, the enhancement of life and its variety —these are the harvest which our human uniqueness should be called upon to yield.

LAW AND LITERATURE

By BENJAMIN N. CARDOZO

I AM told at times by friends that a judicial opinion has no business to be literature. The idol must be ugly, or he may be taken for a common man. The deliverance that is to be accepted without demur or hesitation must have a certain high austerity which frowns at winning graces. I fancy that not a little of this criticism is founded in misconception of the true significance of literature, or, more accurately perhaps, of literary style. To some a clearer insight has been given. There are those who have perceived that the highest measure of condensation, of short and sharp and imperative directness, a directness that speaks the voice of some external and supreme authority, is consistent, none the less, with supreme literary excellence. A dictum of Henri Beyle's, recalled not long ago by Mr. Strachey, will point my meaning. The French novelist used to say that "there was only one example of the perfect style, and that was the Code Napoléon; for there alone everything was subordinated to the exact and complete expression of what was to be said." The poor man succumbed to its charm to such an extent that he was in the habit of reading a few paragraphs every morning before breakfast. I do not seek to substitute this regimen for the daily exercise in calisthenics. Some of us prefer our literature like our food in less concentrated tablets. I do no more than suggest that the morsel hastily gulped down may have a savor all its own for the discriminating palate. But I overemphasize and exaggerate if I seem to paint the picture of any active opposition that is more than sporadic and exceptional to so amiable a weakness as a love of art and letters.

A commoner attitude with lawyers is one, not of active opposition, but of amused or cynical indifference. We are merely wasting our time, so many will inform us, if we bother about form when only substance is important. I suppose this might be true if anyone could tell us where substance ends and form begins. Philosophers have been trying for some thousands of years to draw the distinction between substance and mere appearance in the world of matter. I doubt whether they succeed better when they attempt a like distinction in the world of thought. Form is not something added to substance as a mere protuberant adornment. The two are fused into a unity. Not long ago I ran across a paragraph in the letters of Henry James in which he blurts out his impatience of these attempts to divide the indivisible. He is writing to Hugh Walpole, now a novelist of assured position, but then comparatively unknown. "Don't let any one persuade you—there are plenty of ignorant and fatuous duffers to try to do it—that strenuous selection and comparison are not the very essence of art, and that Form *is* not substance to that degree that there is absolutely no substance without it. Form alone *takes*, and holds and preserves substance, saves it from the welter of helpless verbiage that we swim in as in a sea of tasteless tepid pudding." This is my own faith. The argument strongly put is not the same as the argument put feebly any more than the "tasteless tepid pudding" is the same as the pudding served to us in triumph with all the glory of the lambent flame. The strength that is born of form and the feebleness that is born of the lack of form are in truth qualities of the substance. They are the tokens of the thing's identity. They make it what it is.

Up to this point at least, I have little fear of opposition. We shall, most of us, be agreed, I think, not merely that style is not an evil in the Sahara of a judicial opinion, but even that it is a positive good, if only it is the right style. *There* is the disquieting condition which checks the forward movement of triumphal demonstration. What is to be deemed the right style, or the right styles if there are more than one of them? Do the examples of the great masters reveal some uniformity of method for the instruction of the tyro? If uniformity is not discoverable, may there not at least be types or standards? If types or standards do not exist, shall we not find stimulus and interest in the coruscations of genius, however vagrant or irregular? If at times there is neither stimulus nor interest, may there not in lieu of these be the awful warning of example?

I suppose there can be little doubt that in matters of literary style the sovereign virtue for the judge is clearness. Judge Veeder in his interesting and scholarly essay, "A Century of Judicature," quotes the comment of Brougham upon the opinions of Lord Stowell: "If ever the praise of being luminous could be bestowed upon human compositions, it was upon his judgments." How shall his successors in the same or other courts attain that standard or approach it? There is an accuracy that defeats itself by the over-emphasis of details. I often say that one must permit oneself, and that quite advisedly and deliberately, a certain margin of misstatement. Of course, one must take heed that the margin is not exceeded, just as the physician must be cautious in administering the poisonous ingredient which magnified will kill, but in tiny quantities will cure. On the other hand, the sentence may be so overloaded with all its possible qualifications that it will tumble down of its own weight. "To philosophize," says Holmes in one of his opinions—I am quoting him from uncertain and perhaps inaccurate recollection—"to philosophize is to generalize, but to generalize is to omit." The picture cannot be painted if the significant and the insignificant are given equal prominence. One must know how to select. All these generalities are as easy as they are obvious, but, alas! the application is an ordeal to try the souls of men. Write an opinion, and read it a few years later when it is dissected in the briefs of counsel. You will learn for the first time the limitations of the power of speech, or, if not those of speech in general, at all events your own. All sorts of gaps and obstacles and impediments will obtrude themselves before your gaze, as pitilessly manifest as the hazards on a golf course. Sometimes you will know that the fault is truly yours, in which event you can only smite your breast, and pray for deliverance thereafter. Sometimes you will feel that the fault is with counsel who have stupidly misread the obvious, in which event, though you rail against the bar and the imperfect medium of speech, you will be solaced, even in your chagrin, by a sense of injured innocence.

Sometimes, though rarely, you will believe that the misreading is less stupid than malicious, in which event you will be wise to keep your feelings to yourself. One marvels sometimes at the ingenuity with which texts the most remote are made to serve the ends of argument or parable. But clearness, though the sovereign quality, is not the only one to be pursued, and even if it were, may be gained through many avenues of approach. The opinion will need persuasive force, or the impressive virtue of sincerity and fire, or the mnemonic power of alliteration and antithesis, or the terseness and tang of the proverb and the maxim. Neglect the help of these allies, and it may never win its way. With traps and obstacles and hazards confronting us on every hand, only blindness or indifference will fail to turn in all humility, for guidance or for warning, to the study of examples.

Classification must be provisional, for forms run into one another. As I search the archives of my memory, I seem to discern six types or methods which divide themselves from one another with measurable distinctness. There is the type magisterial or imperative; the type laconic or sententious; the type conversational or homely; the type refined or artificial, smelling of the lamp, verging at times upon preciosity or euphuism; the type demonstrative or persuasive; and finally the type tonsorial or agglutinative, so called from the shears and the pastepot which are its implements and emblem.

I place first in order, for it is first in dignity and power, the type magisterial or imperative. It eschews ornament. It is meagre in illustration and analogy. If it argues, it does so with the downward rush and overwhelming conviction of the syllogism, seldom with tentative gropings towards the inductive apprehension of a truth imperfectly discerned. We hear the voice of the law speaking by its consecrated ministers with the calmness and assurance that are born of a sense of mastery and power. Thus Marshall seemed to judge, and a hush falls upon us even now as we listen to his words. Those organ tones of his were meant to fill cathedrals or the most exalted of tribunals. The judicial department, he tells us, "has no will in any case. . . . Judicial power is never exercised for the purpose of giving effect to the will of the judge; always for the purpose of giving effect to the will of the legisla-

ture; or in other words, to the will of the law." The thrill is irresistible. We feel the mystery and the awe of inspired revelation. His greatest judgments are framed upon this plane of
exaltation and aloofness. The movement from premise to conclusion is put before the observer as something more impersonal
than the working of the individual mind. It is the inevitable
progress of an inexorable force. Professor Corwin in an interesting volume (in "The Chronicles of America") "John Marshall
and the Constitution," shows how even his contemporaries, the
bitterest critics of his aggrandizement of federal power, were
touched by this illusion. "All wrong, all wrong," lamented John
Randolph of Roanoke, "but no man in the United States can tell
why or wherein." I have re-read a few of the most famous of his
judgments: Marbury vs. Madison; Gibbons vs. Ogden; Mc-
Culloch vs. Maryland; they are all in the grand style.

Listen to the voice of the magistrate in Marbury vs. Madison:
"The distinction between a government with limited and unlimited powers is abolished if those limits do not confine the
persons on which they are imposed, and if acts prohibited and
acts allowed are of equal obligation. It is a proposition too plain
to be contested: that the Constitution controls any legislative act
repugnant to it; or that the legislature may alter the Constitution
by an ordinary act. Between these alternatives there is no middle
ground. . . . If two laws conflict with each other, the courts
must decide on the operation of each. So if a law be in opposition
to the Constitution; if both the law and the Constitution apply to
a particular case, so that the court must either decide that case
conformably to the law, disregarding the Constitution, or conformably to the Constitution, disregarding the law, the court
must determine which of these conflicting rules governs the case.
This is of the very essence of judicial duty." Nothing is here of
doubt; nothing of apology; no blurred edges or uncertain lines.
"There is no middle ground." The choice that is made is "of the
very essence of judicial duty." The voice has pealed forth. Let
the wicked heed it and obey.

One will find this same suggestion of sure and calm conviction in some of the judgments of Lord Mansfield. The slave
Somerset captured on the coast of Africa, is sold in bondage in

Virginia, and brought to England by his master. The case comes before Mansfield on the return to the writ of habeas corpus: "The state of slavery is of such a nature that it is incapable of being introduced on any reasons, moral or political, but only positive law, which preserved its force long after the reasons, occasions, and time itself from whence it was created, are erased from memory. It is so odious that nothing can be suffered to support it, but positive law. . . . I care not for the supposed *dicta* of judges, however eminent, if they be contrary to all principle. The *dicta* cited were probably misunderstood, and at all events they are to be disregarded. Villainage, when it did exist in this country, differed in many particulars from West India slavery. The lord never could have thrown his villain, whether *regardant* or *in gross,* into chains, sent him to the West Indies, and sold him there to work in a mine or in a cane field. At any rate villainage has ceased in England, and it cannot be revived. The air of England has long been too pure for a slave, and every man is free who breathes it. Every man who comes into England is entitled to the protection of English law, whatever oppression he may heretofore have suffered, and whatever may be the color of his skin. '*Quamvis ille niger, quamvis tu candidus esses.*' Let the negro be discharged."

It is thus men speak when they are conscious of their power. One does not need to justify oneself if one is the mouthpiece of divinity. The style will fit the mood.

I have said that in dignity and power there is no method that can be matched with the method which I have characterized as magisterial or imperative. A changing philosophy of law has tended, none the less, to the use of other methods more conciliatory and modest. The development of law is conceived of, more and more, as a process of adaptation and adjustment. The pronouncements of its ministers are timid and tentative approximations, to be judged through their workings, by some pragmatic test of truth. I find a striking statement of this attitude of mind in a dissenting opinion by Mr. Justice Brandeis, filed not many months ago. Arguing for the restriction of a rule which had proved itself unworkable, he says: "Such limitations of principles previously announced and such express disapproval of *dicta* are often necessary. It is an unavoidable incident of the search by courts of last resort for the true rule. The process of inclusion and exclusion, so often applied in developing a rule, cannot end with its first enunciation. The rule as announced must be deemed tentative. For the many and varying facts to which it will be applied cannot be foreseen. Modification implies growth. It is the life of the law."

One cannot face the law in this spirit of cautious seeking without showing the changing point of view in a changing style and form. Universals will be handled more charily under the dominance of such a philosophy than in days when the law of nature supplied us with data that were supposed to be eternal and unyielding. Yet there are times even now when the magisterial method is utilized by men who know that they are masters of their calling. It is still utilized in fields where some established principle is to be applied to new facts or where the area of its extension or restriction is fairly obvious or narrow. But alas! even then it is the masters, and no others, who feel sure enough of themselves to omit the intermediate steps and stages, and leap to the conclusion. Most of us are so uncertain of our strength, so beset with doubts and difficulties, that we feel oppressed with the need of justifying every holding by analogies and precedents and an exposure of the reasons. The masters are content to say, "The elect will understand, there is no need to write for others." Perhaps there are opinions by Mr. Justice Holmes in which this mood can be discerned. The sluggard unable to keep pace with the swiftness of his thought will say that he is hard to follow. If that is so, it is only for the reason that he is walking with a giant's stride. But giants, after all, are not met at every turn, and for most of us, even if we are not pygmies, the gait of ordinary men is the safer manner of advance. We grope and feel our way. What we hand down in our judgments is an hypothesis. It is no longer a divine command.

I pass to other types which run into each other by imperceptible gradations, the laconic or sententious and the conversational or homely. There has been no stage of our legal history in which these methods have been neglected. The Year Books are full of wise saws and homely illustrations, the epigram, the quip, the jest. Perhaps this is but a phase of that use of the maxim or the proverb which is characteristic of legal systems in early stages of development. Dean Pound in a recent paper has traced the growth and function of the maxim with all the resources of his learning. If the maxim has declined in prevalence and importance, now that the truths of the law have become too complex to be forced within a sentence, there has been no abatement of recourse to the laconic or sententious phrase, to drive home and imbed what might otherwise be lost or scattered. Who will resist Lord Nottingham's adjuration: "Pray let us so resolve cases here, that they may stand with the reason of mankind when they are debated abroad"? Is there any armor proof against a thrust like the dictum of Lord Bowen's: "The state of a man's mind is as much a fact as the state of his digestion"? Next door to the epigram is the homely illustration which makes its way and sinks deep by its appeal to every-day experience. In the wielding of these weapons, the English judges have been masters. The precept may be doubtful in the beginning. How impossible to fight against it when the judge brings it down to earth and makes it walk the ground, the brother of some dictate of decency or of prudence which we have followed all our lives. Perhaps the kinship is not so close or apparent as it is figured. Who of us will have the hardihood to doubt the reality of the tie when it is so blandly assumed to be obvious to all? The common denominator, silences and satisfies. The rule that is rooted in identities or analogies of customary belief and practice is felt and rightly felt to be rooted in reality. We glide into acquiescence when negation seems to question our kinship with the crowd. Something must be set down also to the sense of fellowship awakened when judges talk in ways that seem to make us partners in the deliberative process. "I entirely agree with my right honorable and learned friend upon the woolsack." We seem to be let into the mysteries of the conference, the sacrosanct "arcana," to quote Professor Powell's phrase, to which "the uninitiated are not admitted." Given such an atmosphere, with point and pungency thrown into it, the product makes its way into every crack and crevice of our being.

I limit my illustrations, though many are available. Take this by Lord Bramwell: "It does not follow that if a man dies in a fit in a railway carriage, there is a *prima facie* case for his widow and children, nor that if he has a glass in his pocket and sits on it and hurts himself, there is something which calls for an answer or explanation from the company." Take this by Lord Blackburn in Smith *vs.* Chadwick: "If with intent to lead the plaintiff to act upon it, they put forth a statement which they know may bear two meanings, one of which is false to their knowledge, and thereby the plaintiff, putting that meaning upon it, is misled, I do not think they can escape by saying he ought to have put the other. If they palter with him, in a double sense, it may be that they lie like truth, but I think they lie, and it is a fraud." One could cite other examples without number. What a cobweb of fine-spun casuistry is dissipated in a breath by the simple statement of Lord Esher in *Ex parte* Simonds, that the court will not suffer its own officer "to do a shabby thing." If the word shabby had been left out, and unworthy or dishonorable substituted, I suppose the sense would have been much the same. But what a drop in emotional value would have followed. As it is, we feel the tingle of the hot blood of resentment mounting to our cheeks. For quotable good things, for pregnant aphorisms, for touchstones of ready application, the opinions of the English judges are a mine of instruction and a treasury of joy.

Such qualities on the whole are rarer close at home, yet we have one judge even now who can vie with the best of his English brethren, past as well as present, in the art of packing within a sentence the phosphorescence of a page. If I begin to quote from the opinions of Mr. Justice Holmes, I hardly know where I shall end, yet fealty to a master makes me reluctant to hold back. The sheaf will be a tiny one, made up haphazard, the barest sample of the riches which the gleaner may gather where he will. Some hint of the epigrammatic quality of his style may be found in this: "The Fourteenth Amendment, itself a historical product, did not destroy history for the States and substitute mechanical compartments of law all exactly alike." In this: "We are in danger of forgetting that a strong public desire to improve the public condition is not enough to warrant achieving the desire by a shorter cut than the constitutional way of paying for the change." In this: "Legal obligations that exist but cannot be enforced are ghosts that are seen in the law but that are elusive to the grasp." And finally in this, words of solemn dissent, their impressiveness heightened by the knowledge that the cause has been already lost: "Persecution for the expression of opinions seems to me perfectly logical. If you have no doubt of your premises or your power and want a certain result with all your heart you naturally express your wishes in law and sweep away all opposition. To allow opposition by speech seems to indicate that you think the speech impotent, as when a man says that he has squared the circle, or that you do not care whole-heartedly for the result, or that you doubt either your power or your premises. But when men have realized that time has upset many fighting faiths, they may come to believe even more than they believe the very foundations of their own conduct that the ultimate good desired is better reached by free trade in ideas—that the best test of truth is the power of the thought to get itself accepted in the competition of the market, and that truth is the only ground upon which their wishes safely can be carried out. That at any rate is the theory of our Constitution. It is an experiment, as all life is an experiment. Every year if not every day we have to wager our salvation upon some prophecy based upon imperfect knowledge. While that experiment is part of our system I think that we should be eternally vigilant against attempts to check the expression of opinions that we loathe and believe to be fraught with death, unless they so imminently threaten immediate interference with the lawful and pressing purposes of the law that an immediate check is required to save the country."

There is another type or method which I have spoken of as the refined or artificial, smelling a little of the lamp. With its merits it has its dangers, for unless well kept in hand, it verges at times upon preciosity and euphuism. Held in due restraint, it lends itself admirably to cases where there is need of delicate precision. I find no better organon where the subject matter of discussion is the construction of a will with all the filigree of tentacles, the shades and nuances of differences, the slender and fragile tracery that must be preserved unmutilated and distinct. Judge Finch of the Court of Appeals of New York was an adept in the writing of opinions which carried with them this suggestion of precision and refinement. Occasionally, it shades into a faint and gentle sarcasm which is sometimes the refuge of the spokesman of a minority expressing his dissent. As an illustration, let me quote from the dissenting opinion in an election controversy which provoked in its day no little warmth of difference. The majority had held that despite the provision of the Constitution making each house of the legislature the judge of the elections, returns, and qualifications of its own members, the courts would refuse affirmative aid to a claimant for such an office if it found him ineligible in its own view of the law. Judge Finch protested against this holding. "And so," he said, "I deny the asserted doctrine of 'Invocation'; of a right to do evil that good may come; of excusable judicial usurpation; and if the doctrine has anywhere got its dangerous and destructive hold upon our law, which I do not believe, it should be resolutely shaken off. But let us not deceive ourselves. The excess of jurisdiction is not even excusable, for it has neither occasion nor necessity." A moment later, he has his fears that he has been betrayed into excessive warmth. His closing words are those of apology and deference: "If what I have said does not convince the majority of the court, nothing that I can say will do so. I have tried faithfully, and, I hope, with proper respect, for certainly I have not meant to be wanting in that, to point out the mistake which, it seems to me, they are about to make. Theirs, however, must be both the responsibility and its consequences."

Such a method has its charm and its attraction, though one feels at times the yearning for another more robust and virile. It is here that I pass into the type which I have characterized as demonstrative or persuasive. It is not unlike the magisterial or imperative, yet it differs in a certain amplitude of development, a freer use of the resources of illustration and analogy and history and precedent, in brief, a tone more suggestive of the scientific seeker for the truth and less reminiscent of the priestess on the tripod. One might cite many judges who have used this method with distinction. I think the work of Charles Andrews, for many years a judge and then the Chief Judge of the New York Court of Appeals, is a shining illustration. I can best describe the quality of his opinions in the words of a memorial written upon his death: "The majesty of his personal appearance," it was said, "is reflected in the majesty of his judicial style, the steady and stately march of his opinions from established premises to inevitable conclusions." Such a method, well pursued, has a sanity and a clarity that make it an admirable medium for the declaration of considered judgments. The form is no mere epidermis. It is the very bone and tissue.

My summary of styles may leave a cheerless impression of the solemn and the ponderous. Flashes of humor are not unknown, yet the form of opinion which aims at humor from beginning to end is a perilous adventure, which can be justified only by success, and even then is likely to find its critics almost as many as its eulogists. The story is told by Bernard Shaw of a man who wished to consult the writings of the great naturalist Buffon, and who startled the clerks in the bookstore by the pompous and solemn query, "Have you the books of the celebrated Buffoon?" One of the difficulties about the humorous opinion is exposure to the risk of passing from the class of Buffons where we all like to dwell and entering the class of the celebrated Buffoons. The transition at times is distressingly swift, and when once one has entered the new class, it is difficult, if not indeed impossible, to climb over the fences and back into the old. None the less, there are subjects which only the most resolute have been able to discuss without yielding to the temptation of making profert of their sense of humor. A dog or a cat, or a horse if it is the occasion of a horse trade, has been the signal for unexpected outbursts of mirth and occasionally of pathos from judges slowly stirred to emotion by the cinema of life.

Judge Allen's opinion on the "code duello" among dogs was on the whole a fine success, but it has been responsible for the writing of some others that were not. There is an opinion by Baron Bramwell which deals with the propensities of pigs. A fence was defective, and the pigs straying did mischief to a trolley car. The decision was that the barrier should have been sufficient to protect the adjoining owner against the incursions, not of all pigs, but of pigs of "average vigour and obstinacy." "Nor do we lay down," said the learned Baron, "that there must be a fence so close and strong that no pig could push through it, or so high that no horse or bullock could leap it. One could scarcely tell the limits of such a requirement, for the strength of swine is such that they would break through almost any fence, if there were a sufficient inducement on the other side. But the company are bound to put up such a fence that a pig not of a peculiarly wandering disposition, nor under any excessive temptation, will not get through it." Perhaps the humor of this ruling was more unwitting than designed. Some may agree with Sir Frederick Pollock that the decision is "almost a caricature of the general idea of the 'reasonable man.'" In all this I would not convey the thought that an opinion is the worse for being lightened by a smile. I am merely preaching caution. Other flights and digressions I find yet more doubtful than the humorous. In days not far remote, judges were not unwilling to embellish their deliverances with quotations from the poets. I shall observe towards such a practice the tone of decent civility that is due to those departed.

I have had in mind in this excursus a humor that was conscious and intended. Perhaps I should have classed the opinion that is humorous or playful as an independent type, but I have preferred to treat it incidentally since I am not aware that any judge has employed it consistently or except on rare occasions. Humor also that is unconscious and unintended may be dug out of the reports if we take the trouble to extract it. I once gathered together for my own edification and amusement some gems that I had unearthed from the opinions of one of our local courts in days when it had an appellate branch of its own and handed down opinions which were faithfully reported. Unluckily, I have lost my memorandum, but a few of the items are still vivid in my mind. The question to be determined was the extent of the amendment of a pleading to be permitted upon the trial. The decisive principle was thus expounded: "The bed that litigants make and lie in up to the trial, should not be then vacated by them. They should continue to lie therein until the jury render their verdict." I understand that the modern Practice Acts have swept this principle away, and that the suitor, who seems to his adversary to be innocently somnolent, may now jump out of bed at the last moment and prove to be very much awake. This is the new doctrine, but where will you find a more vivid statement of the doctrine of an elder day which decried surprise and haste, and was satisfied that justice herself should have the privilege of a nap? I recall, too, a charge to a jury, never reported, but surely fit to be preserved. "In this case," said the trial judge, "I believe that Mr. A. (the counsel for the plaintiff), knows as much law as Mr. B. (the counsel for the defendant), and I believe that Mr. B. knows as much law as Mr. A., but I believe that I in my judicial capacity know as much law as both of them together." Whereupon he forgot to tell the jury anything else, but said they were to consider of their verdict and decide the case in accordance with the rules he had laid down. Well, his charge was sparse, but it enunciated an important truth. Our whole judicial system is built upon some such assumption as the learned judge put forward a trifle crassly and obscurely. This is the great convention, the great fiction, which makes trial in court a fair substitute for trial by battle or by casting lots. The philosopher will find philosophy if he has an eye for it even in a "crowner's" court.

I must not forget my final type of judicial style, the tonsorial or agglutinative. I will not expatiate upon its horrors. They are known but too well. The dreary succession of quotations closes with a brief paragraph expressing a firm conviction that judgment for plaintiff or for defendant, as the case may be, follows as an inevitable conclusion. The writer having delivered himself of this expression of a perfect faith, commits the product of his hand to the files of the court and the judgment of the ages with all the pride of authorship. I am happy to be able to report that this type is slowly but steadily disappearing. As contrasted with its arid wastes, I prefer the sunny, though rather cramped and narrow pinnacle of a type once much in vogue: "We have carefully examined the record and find no error therein; *therefore* the judgment must be affirmed with costs." How nice a sense of proportion, of the relation between cause and effect, is involved in the use of the illative conjunction "therefore," with its suggestion that other minds less sensitively attuned might have

drawn a different conclusion from the same indisputable premises.

I have touched lightly, almost not at all, upon something more
important than mere felicities of turn or phrase. Above and beyond all these are what we may term the architectonics of opinions. The groupings of fact and argument and illustration so as to
produce a cumulative and mass effect; these, after all, are the
things that count above all others. I should despair, however, of
any successful analysis of problems at once so large and so difficult within the limits of this paper. One needs a larger easel if
one is to follow such a map. Often clarity is gained by a brief and
almost sententious statement at the outset of the problem to be
attacked. Then may come a fuller statement of the facts, rigidly
pared down, however, in almost every case, to those that are
truly essential as opposed to those that are decorative and ad-
ventitious. If these are presented with due proportion and selection, our conclusion ought to follow so naturally and inevitably
as almost to prove itself. Whether it succeeds in doing this or
not, is something about which the readers of the opinion are not
always in accord. To gain a proper breadth of view, one should
consult counsel for the vanquished as well as counsel for the
victor.

The thought of the vanquished brings me to the opinion that
voices a dissent. The protests and the warnings of minorities
overborne in the fight have their interest and significance for
the student, not only of law itself, but of the literary forms
through which law reaches its expression. Comparatively speaking at least, the dissenter is irresponsible. The spokesman of the
court is cautious, timid, fearful of the vivid word, the heightened
phrase. He dreams of an unworthy brood of scions, the spawn of
careless *dicta*, disowned by the *ratio decidendi*, to which all legitimate offspring must be able to trace their lineage. The result is
to cramp and paralyze. One fears to say anything when the peril
of misunderstanding puts a warning finger to the lips. Not so,
however, the dissenter. He has laid aside the rôle of the hiero-
phant, which he will be only too glad to resume when the chances
of war make him again the spokesman of the majority. For the
moment, he is the gladiator making a last stand against the lions.

The poor man must be forgiven a freedom of expression, tinged at rare moments with a touch of bitterness, which magnanimity as well as caution would reject for one triumphant.

A French judge, M. Ransson, a member of the Tribunal of the Seine, wrote some fifteen years ago an essay on the art of judging, in which he depicts the feelings of a judge of the first instance when a judgment is reversed. I suppose the state of mind of one reversed is akin in quality to the state of mind of one dissenting, though perhaps differing in degree. "A true magistrate," says M. Ransson, "guided solely by his duty and his conscience, his learning and his reason, hears philosophically and without bitterness that his judgment has not been sustained; he knows that the higher court is there to this end, and that better informed beyond doubt, it has believed itself bound to modify his decision. Ought we even to condemn him, if having done his best, he maintains in his inmost soul the impression that perhaps and in spite of everything he was right? *Causa diis victrix placuit, sed victa Catoni.*" Cato had a fine soul, but history does not record that he feared to speak his mind, and judges when in the minority are tempted to imitate his candor. We need not be surprised, therefore, to find in dissent a certain looseness of texture and depth of color rarely found in the *per curiam*. Sometimes, as I have said, there is just a suspicion of acerbity, but this, after all, is rare. More truly characteristic of dissent is a dignity, an elevation, of mood and thought and phrase. Deep conviction and warm feeling are saying their last say with knowledge that the cause is lost. The voice of the majority may be that of force triumphant, content with the plaudits of the hour, and recking little of the morrow. The dissenter speaks to the future, and his voice is pitched to a key that will carry through the years. Read some of the great dissents, the opinion, for example, of Judge Curtis in Dred Scott *vs.* Sandford, and feel after the cooling time of the better part of a century the glow and fire of a faith that was content to bide its hour. The prophet and the martyr do not see the hooting throng. Their eyes are fixed on the eternities.

I shall be travelling away from my subject if I leave the writing of opinions and turn to arguments of the bar. A word of digression may be pardoned, however, for the two subjects are allied. One is called upon often to make answer to the question, what sort of argument is most effective in an appellate court? Shall it be long or short, terse or discursive? Shall it assume that the judges know the rudiments of law, or shall it attempt in a brief hour to supply the defects in their early training? Shall it state the law or the facts? Shall it take up the authorities and analyze them, or shall it content itself with conclusions and leave analysis for the study? There is, of course, no formula that will fit all situations in appellate courts or elsewhere. If, however, I had to prepare a list of "Don'ts" for the guidance of the novice, I think I would say that only in the rarest instances is it wise to take up one decision after another for the purpose of dissection. Such autopsies have their value at times, but they are wearisome and gruesome scenes. In my list of Don'ts, I would add, don't state the minutiae of the evidence. The judges won't follow you, and if they followed, would forget. Don't attempt to supplement the defects of early training. Your auditors are hardened sinners, not easily redeemed. Above all, don't be long-winded. I have in mind a lawyer who argues the appeals for one of the civil sub-divisions of the State. His arguments last about a quarter of an hour. He tells us his point and sits down. The audience in the rear of the court room may not applaud, but the audience in front does—at least in spirit—and as the latter audience has the votes, it is best to make your play for them. If you faithfully observe these cautions, let not your spirits droop too low when the decision is adverse, even though there be the added gall and wormwood of a failure of the court to crown your brilliant effort with the dignity of an opinion. Many a gallant argument has met the same unworthy fate.

Young men as they approach admission to the bar must some-times say to themselves that the great problems have been solved, that the great battles of the forum have been fought, that the great opportunities are ended. There are moods in which for a moment I say the same thing to myself. If I do, the calendar of the following day is as likely as not to bring the exposure of the error. It is a false and cramping notion that cases are made great solely or chiefly by reason of something intrinsic in themselves. They are great by what we make of them. McCulloch *vs.* Maryland—to choose almost at random—is one of the famous cases of our history. I wonder, would it not be forgotten, and even perhaps its doctrine overruled, if Marshall had not put upon it the imprint of his genius. "Not one of his great opinions," says Professor Corwin, speaking of Marshall's work, "but might easily have been decided on comparatively narrow grounds in precisely the same way in which he decided it on broad, general principles, but with the probable result that it would never again have been heard of outside the law courts." So, too, the smaller issues await the transfiguring touch. "To a genuine accountant," says Charles Lamb, "the difference of proceeds is as nothing. The fractional farthing is as dear to his heart as the thousands which stand before it. He is the true actor, who, whether his part be a prince or a peasant, must act it with like authority." That is the spirit in which judge or advocate is to look upon his task. He is expounding a science, or a body of truth which he seeks to assimilate to a science, but in the process of exposition he is practising an art. The Muses look at him a bit impatiently and wearily at times. He has done a good deal to alienate them, and sometimes they refuse to listen, and are seen to stop their ears. They have a strange capacity, however, for the discernment of strains of harmony and beauty, no matter how diffused and scattered through the ether. So at times when work is finely done, one sees their faces change, and they take the worker by the hand. They know that by the lever of art the subject the most lowly can be lifted to the heights. Small, indeed, is the company dwelling in those upper spaces, but the few are also the elect.

SECOND-BEST STATESMEN

By WALTER LIPPMANN

M R. BERNARD SHAW has convinced himself that the art of civilization is too long for short-lived men. What can be expected, he asks, from a breed of novices and "flappers" who die off when they are still politically adolescent, and temporize with every great issue because they will not live long enough to care whether it is settled or not?

Viewed on the scale of thirty-one thousand years through eyes made confident by an insider's knowledge of creative evolution, Mr. Shaw's question and Mr. Shaw's answer may be indisputable. For, if you calculate in aeons, many urgent questions come out in the wash and much that seems troublesome is ironed away. But what of our statesmen now and in the next generation? Is it true, as Mr. Shaw says, that we are ruled by freshmen who will never mature?

My own opinion is that we do not know whether it is true or not. We have not any conception, I believe, of the present powers of man, short-lived as he is. We have a hint of his enormous mechanical ingenuity, of his astounding physical courage, of his unbelievable patience. But of his latent capacity for bringing order out of the tohubohu of human relations we know very little because he is not seriously trying. We have learned almost to think that satisfaction with the second best is a mark of good humor and wisdom, that it is gauche not to discount the pretensions of all public characters, not to conclude almost any discussion of public affairs with an "Ah well! they're pretty good fellows, I suppose, and doing the best they know."

Now, we may all be pretty good fellows, but in the art of civilization we are emphatically not doing the best we know how. Our public men are in fact quite dismayed, when they have the leisure and candor to stop and think. Again and again, in critical matters they find themselves doing what they know to be foolish. As they reflect they are amazed when they watch themselves upholding policies they know will not work, making promises they know they cannot keep, purveying cheap and second-rate goods which privately they despise, and evading today or postponing for posterity what should be dealt with at once. For real criticism of the statesman you do not need to go to Mr. Shaw's Burge and Lubin; you have only to go to the statesmen themselves, when they are off duty and are not talking for publication.

You may come away from such a talk still convinced that man is congenitally incapable of civilization. But you are just as likely to come away feeling elated at the candor of which men are capable in private, and depressed by their apparent inability to let their best insight govern their public life. That, at least, is the feeling I have brought away with me from many journalistic interviews. And only, I think, by recalling that public men lead this double life, can you account for some of the inexplicable devotion they so often arouse. The thick-and-thin followers see the private character rather than the public personage. Did they see only the carefully constructed façades they, too, would be discouraged. For public men, in spite of their press agents, usually put their worst foot forward in public life. But those who are behind the façade can like the man for the possibilities he really possesses. Those out front have to judge by his display. After a while, perhaps after prolonged contemplation of a performance like that of Congress with the bonus, they are bound to think with Mr. Shaw that all public characters are a total loss and no insurance.

And yet, what if it were possible, taking men as they are, to liberate the possibilities that in moments of candor are revealed to the devoted? We do not know what would happen. We know a little of what has happened in the conquest of nature when this liberation took place—when men shook themselves free of their own taboos. In the physical sciences little remains of the disproportion between what a discoverer really thinks and what in the interests of his reputation he sees fit to tell the world. There it is not considered wiser and better form and more mellow to be rather inaccurate and decently secretive. Why, then, should there be a cult of the second-rate in our public relations?

Mr. Shaw thinks that man practises this cult because he has not a sufficient stake in the world. According to what he calls, in "Back to Methuselah," the Gospel of the Brothers Barnabas, man's attitude towards civilization is that of a transient and untidy tenant without interest in the upkeep or improvement of the property. Others think that the root of the trouble lies in "capitalism"; some think it lies in commercialism; some in Puritanism; some in the great tide of immigration; some in the primitive state of our knowledge; some in the inherent difficulty of the subject matter of the social sciences.

I think the argument can be pursued for a while on different lines. For grant that it is desirable to breed and educate and select better men, grant everything the eugenicist and educator and creative evolutionist demand; still it is possible to argue from the fact that there is such a gap between public and private character, that this world would soon be a better place to live in if everyone who exercises authority or helps to shape public opinion acted according to such lights as he now has. It is possible to argue that the improvement following the closing of the gap would be cumulative.

Very easily one can talk nonsense in these matters, but personally I am convinced that almost no one to-day who deals with large electorates, with great circulations, with anonymous publics, is wholly without a kind of inner stultification. Something it seems has obtruded between the individual and the public which acts as a depressant and self-censor upon a candid first-rate relationship. In their public dealings, most men are much less than themselves. They assume that a certain insincerity is necessary to success, that a little less than common sense is appropriate, that the best is the enemy of the better. They have the attitude of a nurse to a patient. They involve themselves deeply in considerations of manner and tact. They become so preoccupied with the eternal question of how to "put something across," and how much to ladle out at one dose, and how good is the digestion of the public, that their own interest in the subject matter is diverted and distracted. In their anxiety about the sugar-coating, they forget the pill. Their own powers of invention and judgment are starved through disuse, while their powers of promotion and salesmanship grow constantly more elaborate.

The fashionable thing to do in this connection is to pronounce the phrase "herd instinct" with a sense of finality. At the moment, these are magic words yielding glamour and ironical relief. The leaders huddle with the herd. They are afraid to be alone as the crowd is afraid of people who are different. There is nothing to do about it but repeat "herd instinct" whenever your feelings need expression.

Or if you do not share this biological fatalism, you can insist with good three-dimensional invective that man is naturally timid and lazy, and that he will always take the easiest way. If the quickest way to fame and fortune is to catch votes, collect audiences, and increase the circulation by saying faintly insincere and second-rate things, Adam will indulge. Man will take that way. You can preach against it. You can exhort him to "the search and expectation of greatest and exactest things," but your success will in the main be negative. You may put a brake on the deterioration of standards. You may stir up that conscience in the community which does somehow manage to set a lowest limit for the panderer. You can do little more because the conscience of the community deals with the minimum. When it comes to setting standards of excellence, preaching is likely to be feeble, rhetorical, and ineffective.

For there is something that conflicts with an unexamined premise of our culture in a sermon aimed to incite men to pursue their highest good. We ought to look for that premise. I believe that the trouble can be located: that what some call the herd instinct, and others natural laziness and timidity, has surreptitiously acquired the sanction of conscience in democracy; and that the older conceptions of duty, honor, and excellence are undercut by a myth that passes for the latest science and the most modern conception of democracy. I believe this myth is partly a survival from the days when democracy was fighting for existence and improvising a creed, and partly confusion due to the absence of a really friendly and drastic criticism of democratic

ideas; that it has no more to do with the intrinsic virtues of democracy than Alexandrine speculation had to do with the teach-
ings of Jesus; and that it has no more to do with the substance of
popular government than the mediaeval picture of the heavens
had with the Gospels.

A distracting error has worked itself into the democratic tradition which is corrupting to the will because it sanctifies the cult
of the second best.

The man who in a roomful of up-to-the-minute people ventured to use the word reason in connection with public affairs
would soon discover that he was naïvely endangering his reputation. There would be an embarrassed silence, almost as awkward
as if he had smuggled himself into a congress of scientists and
was asserting that the earth is flat. Savvy Barnabas, who is Mr.
Shaw's incarnation of an advanced intellect, would probably
bounce out of the room choking with laughter. Or if she stayed
long enough to argue, she would tell the apostle of reason that
apparently his brain is upholstered with red plush, and, therefore, he does not know that the function of reason in politics is to
find pretexts for realizing the wishes of men. She would insist
that a wish clothed in a reason constitutes an interest, and that
interests are the only guide in public affairs.

Savvy is proud of this discovery. She regards it as a touchstone
for telling fossils from freemen. It seems to work well. She can
employ it with devastating effect upon academicians whose habits
of thought hardened before the discovery was generally known.
And since there are still many of these academicians left, and
since there is even a renewal of the supply from certain centres of
learning, and since these unemancipated people write a greater
percentage of the books and make a greater percentage of the
speeches than they are entitled to make according to the population statistics, Savvy is under the impression that they speak the
accepted doctrine of the great mass of the people. Because her
battle-ground is among the books and the reviews, she does not
know that the real intellectual battle-ground has shifted, that
fact has run far ahead of theory, and that she is a good half-turn
behind in the cycle of thought. Observing that the conservative
academicians arrive at much the same conclusions about the Re-

publican party as her uncles, Savvy thinks these academicians do the thinking for the community, and goes for them head on.

But Savvy is mistaken. Her own doctrine is far more popular as a working philosophy than that of this older generation. She is, without knowing it, rushing eagerly to the support of the victors. For, except among a few authors and professors, the doctrine of interests is triumphant in everyday life.

Modern teaching about the rôle of the interests has been transfigured much as was the theory of evolution two generations ago. What was intended as a mere statement of probable fact has been twisted into an absolute moral precept. In the case of evolution, the idea that change is unending was hastily moralized into the belief that change for the better was inevitable. Then it followed that to-morrow was inevitably better than yesterday. And merely to come after was an improvement on what had gone before. All the generations since Aristotle stood on each others' shoulders, and he who would stand on ours could almost touch the sky.

The theory of interests was at first as neutral, as much beyond good and evil, as evolution. The discoverers claimed nothing for it but that they had observed in somewhat greater detail than people had ever observed it before that a wish was father to most thoughts. They taught that most of the time when men imagined they were acting on reason they were in truth finding reasons for acting as they desired. Few of them claimed that men could never act on reason, for such an admission would have tainted their own inquiries. Certainly they did not say that men could not, or ought not to try, to follow reason, but only that, more often than was currently believed, reason was an apologist and an advocate rather than a counsellor and a judge.

The new technique for going under the other fellow's skin and exposing him in the act of rationalizing his impulses satisfied Savvy's lust of battle. The technique came to her at first or second hand from the writings of James, Bergson, and Freud; and their heresy became her orthodoxy. Because the anti-intellectualists had been fighting men, as well as scientists, all of them wrote with an eye on their academic colleagues, and they stated their position in a series of polemics against opponents who were dogmatic rationalists. Savvy has inherited the polemics along with the doctrine. And, if the truth be told, it is the polemics that she likes best. She imagines, anyhow, that she is championing the newest truth by brandishing the sticks which men old enough to be her grandfather used in order to beat their grandfathers. She has not realized that she is thrashing a straw man. She has not waked up to the fact that, however hard-shelled the opposition of scholars may have been, the new knowledge spread like a prairie fire. Often it assumed strange shapes that would have horrified the pioneers; but it passed quickly into usage, and was acclaimed with shouts of joy by everyone who was glad he could now believe that to be timid and time-serving was to be at once ultra-modern and scientific and an advanced democrat.

For by a twist in the association of ideas, the theory of interests coalesced with that of government by consent of the governed. The statement in scientific jargon that the wish is father to the thought amalgamated with the faith that the will of the people should be supreme. Out of this confusion emerged the conviction that the wish which is father to the thought should be supreme in politics, the newspapers, the movies, and the theatre. In consequence, the people who take the doctrine very literally go about by day, and make sure they have pencil and pad within reach when they are in bed at night, so that they may listen in for their impulses, and obey them. They move on tiptoe so that they may overhear the voice of the unconscious. Politicians speak their real thoughts in whispers for fear of creating commotion in the ether that might interfere with their deciphering the wishes of the public. The final answer to any proposal is that the people do not want it; the final excuse for anything is that the people want what they want when they want it.

In our world this has become the chief substitute for the old architecture of heaven and hell, the ancient springs of revelation, the oracles and the sacred books, and the authoritative code of morals which they sanctioned. To a limited extent the older views survive, but they seem clearly archaic and are threatened with extinction. For behind this new attitude there is a great pride, a great sense of emancipation from ancient error. So great a pride is it, so great a sense of freedom, that the faults of the old are sufficient to float the new. The doctrine of watchful waiting, of mysterious popular guidance, of purely receptive and purely passive leadership, has an air about it of democratic humility, of unpretentiousness, of nobly serving great things. What is man on the scale of time? A mere spokesman, a transmitter, a dictograph.

It is quite easy to become mystical on the subject. You can say that out of the vasty deeps of our modern minds, out of the eternal caverns of the unconscious, out of the collective super-soul and over-soul, profounder than reason, impregnated with the everlasting memories of the race, instinctive with primal knowledge and heavy laden with immemorial wisdom, comes the will of the people. Not your half-hearted views and mine, not our compound of prejudices and headlines and inattention, but something other and utter. And all the politician or the editor has to do is to wait and listen and strain his ear, and he will know just what to do about the sales tax and the bonus, ship subsidies and the tariff, reparations and the integrity of China.

Thus, by sleight-of-hand, popular government embraced a mythology. Beginning with a theory based on the vision of a very simple village community where everyone knew everybody else's character and affairs, and inspired by a high sense of human equality, the democrat found himself in an unmanageable civilization. No man's wisdom seemed to be great enough for the task. A somewhat more mystical wisdom was necessary. But about the steadiness of the supply of that wisdom he still had inner doubt. Then came the doctrine of interests to relieve the tension. It was said, apparently on the highest scientific authority, that all men instinctively pursued their interests; that their reason need not be dealt with because it was a mere pretext for their wishes; and that all you had to do was to probe for the interests of the people, and you were in touch with reality.

But as a practical matter, it was not at all easy to tell offhand what were the interests which the will of the people expressed. The popular will had a way of formulating itself in abstract nouns like Justice, Right, Honor, Americanism. It proved to be rather a puzzle, therefore, just how the leaders were to detect the interests which the unconscious collective soul was uttering. At that critical moment the sophists stepped in, and by manipulating the double meaning of "interest" they laid to rest the scruples of conscience.

It happens that "interest" may mean either the feeling of concern or the fact of being concerned. The difference is often very great. A child has, for example, a very great interest in his father's business affairs. They will determine many of his opportunities in life. But the child in not in the least interested in any discussion of his father's business. Similarly, the people of the United States have an enormous interest in the settlement of German reparations, but they were far more interested in reading about the wedding gown of the Princess Mary. When the Reparations Commission makes a decision, no courier takes an airplane for the nearest ocean greyhound, carrying the full text in a water-tight packet specially designed to float, and casts it overboard where a fast destroyer can pick it up, and rush it to Boston Harbor twenty-four hours and eighteen minutes before the ocean greyhound docks in New York. We are not sufficiently interested in some of our biggest interests to take that much trouble.

But by confusing the two meanings of the word interest, the sophists could satisfy themselves that the degree of interest felt was a true index in a democracy of the amount of interest at stake. They could pose as servants of the public by identifying interest subjectively felt with interest as an objective reality. They could confuse what the public seems to demand now with what the public in the long run needs. It is a deep and corrupting ambiguity. It is to say that a taste for marshmallows is the clue to a diet.

No such grossly obvious play upon words would, of course, have found wide acceptance, were there not in the background a powerful will to believe. The desire to think that our wishes are instinctively directed to the satisfaction of our own best interests, and of society's, has grown as the older systems of authority in government, religion, and morals have disintegrated. In a world complicated beyond their powers, men who were deprived of external guidance have had to fall back upon themselves. But on what selves were they to fall back? The traditional Higher Self, consisting of a code of Duty and Rights and Purposes, had disintegrated with the institutions of which it was a part.

For a brief time, the individual reason acting deductively on its own premises was elected to carry the burden. But it did not take long to discover that individual reason working on accidental premises in people's minds was more often than not a mere intellectualization of their hopes and fears. Its authority collapsed at the approach of the analytical psychologists. But there remained the sheer human necessity of believing in something that could be trusted as a guide to conduct. What was that something to be? It could not be a revealed religion nor a revealed political system; it could not be the individual reason acting alone, for that was now understood to take its direction not from the facts of the environment but from the stresses and urgencies of each person. Apparently, the instinctive needs and appetites were the governing forces of human life.

And then, because we all have a tendency to worship whatever is powerful and certain, the cult of instinct was taken up by nineteenth-century liberalism. Since it had been demonstrated more or less convincingly that most of our reasoning and most of our beliefs were dominated by desire, men proclaimed that desire was the ultimate reality. Being ultimate, it must be ultimately right. Being ultimately right, it must be intelligent. Being intelligent, it must be capable of expressing itself. And therefore in reverse order, the intensity and quantity of whatever was expressed was the sign of an intelligent pursuit of what was ultimately right.

This is, I think, a true statement of the prevailing belief about human nature. Few hold it in a pure form or act upon it all the time. The older ideas survive to modify it somewhat in practice, and there is also a check upon it in certain of the newer schools of thought. But the realm over which the doctrine presides is, nevertheless, immense. It determines the characteristically "modern" attitude in innumerable fields of activity.

There is none more obvious than that in the recent agitation about self-determination and nationalism. These agitations receive their impetus from the conflict with imperial authority. They are phases of the general revolt against external and arbitrary limitation of men's lives. They run true to form in that they set up the expressed wish of any group of people as the one proper and unanswerable guide to political organization. But such guidance is just exactly what no plebiscite can give. The expressed will of any group at any particular moment is the product of a whole series of essentially accidental factors, such as the effects of certain laws, the temperament of certain officials, the strength of certain propagandist organizations, the dramatizing of certain incidents. The expressed will of the group is determined by one form of external relationship which it dislikes, rarely if ever by a considered judgment of all the external relationships which arise, not out of imperialism alone, but out of geography, economic organization, and the distribution of the human race.

That the state of mind engendered by opposition to a particular form of authority, say the old Austro-Hungarian Empire, is an element of great importance, no one could deny. That as a matter of historic fact, the break-up of so evil an authority can be brought about only by a temporary cultivation of self-determining nationalism, I should not dispute. But that self-determination by and in itself alone can reconstruct anything is clearly not so. How can one believe that it will, unless one accepts the prevailing dogma about human nature and says that every man is by instinct an economist, a constitutional lawyer, and a diplomat? For every man would have to be just that, if the doctrine of self-determination in all its universal pretensions were true.

The popular modern theory of the instincts is a vestibule to several different conflicting schools of thought. It leads, for example, to many naïve theories about the economic interpretations of politics. Usually, these theories assume that men group themselves more or less infallibly by economic classes, and that the programmes they adopt express their economic interests. But is there any evidence for thinking that this rule holds? Do people never vote foolishly, do they never vote for laws that injure them? Is the fact that a group asks for a measure any evidence that a measure is really to their advantage? It seems to me clear that it is no evidence at all. And if it is no evidence, it follows that the word "self-interest," which has such an air of reality about it, has no reality. It is used with assurance only by people who are confused by the two meanings of the word interest, and who imagine that the measures in which a group of working-men, or a farmers' bloc, or a manufacturers' association happen to be interested, are equivalent to a policy which will in fact further their economic interests.

The cult of instinct has turned out to be an illusion. And if we read more carefully what modern psychology actually teaches, we can see readily enough why it is an illusion. The instincts are not stimulated to activity, as perhaps they were in primitive ages, by a true picture of the relevant environment in which they must find their satisfaction, but oftener than not in our civilization by quite false fictions, accidentally encountered or deliberately de-vised. They are not set in motion by obvious truth, and the action to which they are habituated has no necessary connection with the end desired. For this reason it is impossible in the modern world to trust instinct alone, once it is seen that our instincts are not in gear with the facts, and that they are not equipped by habit with a knowledge of ways and means.

Perhaps it will be denied that anyone proposes to trust instinct in the way I have described the cult here. It is true that no one does wholly trust it in practice, not even the most pagan of the anti-Puritans. Practice is often better than the theory. But I in-sist that this theory is central in our modern liberal culture, and that it has very serious consequences.

The most serious is that the theory undermines the intellectual resistance of those who see the evil of trying to run modern civi-lization on the notion that what happens to be interesting is, therefore, the measure of the public interest, and a guide to the conduct of the politician, the editor, the popular artist, and the teacher. In every one of the popularizing professions you will find among the ablest a feeling of frustration and a vein of cyni-cism. Their pride of craft and their love of excellence encounter not only the inevitable resistances which are part of the game, but a certain moralized and highfalutin doubt about whether it is not undemocratic, unpleasantly superior, and almost sinful to do what they feel to be the first-rate thing.

They lack, in other words, the support of the authoritative dogma of their time, the dogma of instinct, when they seek the highest good. It is as if the intellect of mankind had conspired against itself and had lamed its right arm in the eternal war of light against darkness. It is the business of criticism to destroy this cult of the second best. Destroying it will not, of course, insure the victory, or suddenly transform the timid and time-serving—the Burges and the Lubins—into courageous and candid men. But at least it will deprive the tempter of his scripture when he whispers seductively in men's ears that by drifting idly with the eddies of popular interest they are serving the interests of a free people.

GREEK IDEALS IN MODERN CIVILIZATION

By SIR RICHARD LIVINGSTONE

W HEN Plato is about to consider the nature of the state, he starts with the smallest possible unit that can supply the necessaries of life, the embryo that contains the essentials of the complete and full-grown organism. What the "minimum state" is to the developed adult community, Greek civilization is to our own. It is the skeleton outline of our own world. It contains, reduced to their simplest form, but fully conceived and clearly grasped, the main principles which underlie modern society. Our world rests on three fundamental conceptions: science; technology, by which I mean those applications of science which have given us the material fabric of our society; and a certain ideal of human nature and conduct. Now, all these are to be found in ancient Greece. The Greeks created the idea of science and technology. Like us, they regarded these as the basis of civilization. And, as for the third conception, they had, I think, a clearer ideal of what life should be than we have.

Let me try to explain in what sense it is true to say that the Greeks had our attitude to science and (in the germ) our idea of the place of technology in life. First, science—the idea of finding a rational explanation of the universe, of continually extending knowledge of it, and of building on knowledge a progressive civilization. This idea comes from Greece. The Greek started at the very bottom of the ladder, with rain magic and crop magic. Unhelped except by his own instinct and intelligence he created a civilization based on the scientific attitude to life.

It is easy to overlook the magnitude and difficulty of this feat. Probably it is the greatest intellectual achievement of man. I am not, of course, thinking of the actual scientific work of the Greeks —of such achievements as Aristarchus' discovery of the heliocentric theory, Archimedes' statement of the fundamental principles of hydrostatics, Eratosthenes' calculation of the earth's circumference at 7,850 miles; or of such brilliant premonitions of modern science as Democritus' idea that the universe consists of atoms in infinite space, or the anticipation of Darwinism in Anaximander's notion that "man originated from animals of a different species," or Antiphon's statement of a view to which medicine has paid some attention in the last thirty years—"In all men the mind controls the body, for good health and for bad." These discoveries, considering that the first Greek scientist was born into a world which believed that the sun and moon were gods and that thunder was produced by Zeus, are remarkable achievements. But time antiquates all scientific discovery, and Greek science for us has only a historic interest. Infinitely more remarkable, in the thick darkness of savagery and primitive superstition, is the emergence of a temper not too common even in our own times—the scientific temper.

If a man were preaching sermons on the cardinal virtues of science, it would be easy to find a text in Greek for each of them. What are the cardinal virtues of science? Among them are the passion to know, which is the source and spring of all discovery; the belief in the supreme arbitrament of reason; modesty; caution and patience; industry. It would be difficult to better the following Greek texts for these, taken from such writers as Heraclitus, Democritus, Anaxagoras, and Plato.

For the passion to know: "I would rather discover one scientific fact than become king of Persia"; "The happiness of man lies not in the body or in wealth but in rightness and fulness of understanding"; "Life is worth living because it enables us to contemplate the heavens and the order of the universe." For the belief in the supreme arbitrament of reason: "No law or ordinance whatever has the right to sovereignty over knowledge; it is a sin that reason should be the subject or servant of anyone; its place is to be ruler of all." For the modesty of science: "In reality we know nothing; truth lies in the depths"; "The opinions of men are like children's play." For its caution and patience: "Sobriety and skepticism are the sinews of the mind." For its industry: "The price at which God sells us all good things is labor." And there is the contemptuous comment of Thucydides on certain historians—"So unlaborious for most people is the quest for truth; they prefer to have recourse to what lies to their hand." We can find in Democritus the justification of the specialist: "Do not seek to know everything or you will be ignorant of everything"; and in Heraclitus a warning to the learned: "Abundance of knowledge does not teach men to be wise."

It is no paradox to say that the authors of these sayings understood the scientific temper as well as it has ever been understood, and that to live with them should be a training in it which would satisfy Huxley's definition of education as "the instruction of the intellect in the laws of Nature . . . and the fashioning of the affections and of the will into an earnest and loving desire to move in harmony with these laws."

There is a sense in which perhaps their attitude to science was saner and juster than ours. It is revealed in their term for science. If we wish to translate into Greek what we mean by science, there are two ways of doing it. If we have natural science in mind, we should use a Greek term meaning "inquiry into nature." The phrase has two merits: it is more precise and free from ambiguity than "science"; and it suggests not a secure body of ascertained truth but quest and investigation. In both these points it has advantages over our word. But an equally good translation of "science" is *philosophia*, "the love of wisdom." This Greek word has a richness and vitality absent from our cold and nondescript term. It suggests at once to the mind what "science" does not suggest—wisdom, the highest goal and achievement of man, and the love which wisdom inspires. Further, the Greek word suggests the real empire and ideal of knowledge. To-day science, like "philosophy," has been narrowed in scope: each has resigned its claim to survey all existence and has accepted a province which if great is yet smaller than the whole. But the Greek started at least with the idea that in conceiving its ultimate goal science must draw no distinctions between the knowledge of nature and of man; that it was the mark of the philosopher "to desire wisdom, not this part of it or that, but all"; that you knew him by his wishing "to taste every kind of knowledge and attacking his studies joyfully and with an insatiable appetite."

It may seem that I am overemphasizing a linguistic detail, and that it makes little difference whether a man who spends half a lifetime in classifying streptococci is called a scientist or a lover of wisdom. But if specialism is the duty of the scientist, the ideal of science is a wider view and a more splendid ambition. The word *philosophia* reminds us that knowledge is a whole, concerned with "all time and all existence," whose aims and ideals hold in politics, morals, and every other field of human activity no less than in the kingdom of nature. There was never any cleavage between science and humanism in Greece, and no Greek would have understood how there could be a cleavage. Both were provinces of *philosophia*. We sometimes need to be reminded of that.

Our civilization stands on two closely connected bases, the scientific spirit and applied science. The Greeks had the scientific spirit. But in what sense had they applied science? Certainly no motor car tore along the primitive Greek roads, no airplane broke the silence where the eagles of the "Agamemnon" wheeled; and the "books of Anaxagoras," which the Athenian bought for a drachma in "the orchestra," were not written in printer's ink. Yet Plato's summary description of civilization includes technology and might have been written about our own civilization: "States and constitutions and arts and laws and much evil and much good." The arts, by which the Greeks meant not the fine arts but the useful ones, are to Plato an integral part of human life. The Greeks had grasped the conception of a progressive civilization built on advancing science and the development of the "arts." It appears, complete in its outline, as early as 460 B.C. in the writings not of a professed philosopher but of the dramatist Aeschylus. Prometheus, in the play called by his name, describes the early state of men, living in caves, without fire, the meaningless chaotic life of figures in a dream. Then Prometheus traces the stages of progress: the gift of fire; the use of animals for transport; the invention of the sailing ship; the discovery of writing, of medicine, of mathematics, of the metals. The picture is crude, but Aeschylus has grasped that idea of civilization which is at the root of our society, the conception of man climbing upward from the life of a beast to heights beyond the reach of imagination. He has grasped, too, the material base of this progress, the development of the arts. There may have been no technology in Greece, but it was not from a failure to conceive the notion of it. The words of Aeschylus are a hymn to applied science. The tiny seed of flame which Prometheus hid in a fennel stalk and gave to men is the obscure and distant ancestor of the boiler house and factory chimney of modern industry.

A few years later, we find the picture repainted in the same colors by a far less speculative writer than Aeschylus. Here the conservative Sophocles shares the views of his predecessor, and expounds them in the famous ode of the "Antigone," which, starting from the trick of a Greek girl, passes into the praise and prophecy of civilization. The features of progress are the same as in "Prometheus"—the discovery of the arts, of sea transport and agriculture, hunting and fishing. Sophocles has varied the list slightly and has emphasized the advances of the future, to which he sets only one limit—the conquest of death. Here is no question of Prometheus as an intermediary. Man has done the work for himself. "He taught himself" each new knowledge. Not that man is strong; his is no work of superhuman power or effortless wisdom. This poet of human progress also wrote, "Ah! generations of mortals, how like to nothingness do I count your life!" Yet with the knowledge of human feebleness goes pride in man and in his achievement and a sense of infinite vistas opening before the race—"There are many wonderful things, and nothing is more wonderful than man." The words are the epitome and explanation of the Greek achievement. If anyone wants a motto for a history of civilization, they might serve his purpose, and with them two other passages. The first was written in the sixth century B. C.:

> Knowledge came not to men from the first by divine revelation,
> But man's search, with time, all things more clearly reveals.

The second passage dates from the fourth century:

> . . . All that is sought, is found,
> Unless you leave the quest or shun its toil.

For see how man's discovery has mastered
Provinces of the heavenly world remote,
The rising, setting, wheeling of the stars,
The sun's eclipse! What, then, shall 'scape man's search
In the related, kindred world below?

The Greeks were the first to conceive the idea of civilization and of progress based on human effort and advancing knowledge. It is the essential spirit of the modern world. Greece is the source not only of powerful influences in our literature, architecture, and many other fields but of what is most characteristic of our civilization; and from that source flows the current which is carrying us along, in its purest form and uncontaminated strength. One function of Greek studies, therefore, is to interpret our world to itself.

But another and more important function is to heal it. Science and unfettered thought—these twin children of Greece—have created a civilization which puzzles us by its complexity and appalls us by its tendency to escape our control. Like the imprisoned djinn in the casket of the "Arabian Nights," science, once released, has become too powerful for its liberator. The value of many of our discoveries is wasted because we have not learnt to use them wisely. Mankind cannot have too much of material resources, material power—but only if it remains their master, if at each moment it can say of them, "I possess them, not they me." If we told the truth, we should often say the opposite.

That is where we can learn from Greece, where its example can correct us. We have realized its dream; we have our applied science, the "arts," as the Greeks called them, carried to a perfection which they never conceived. But, I had almost said, we have stopped there. The Greeks did not stop. Had they done so, we should have owed them the least part of our debt. They would have used their intelligence to great purpose on nature, as we have done, and remained indifferent to the human problem. At one time in their history this seemed likely. The early speculation of Greece dealt with the physical world, and its acutest brains were occupied with questions of cosmology. Socrates himself was once absorbed by it, as he, or Plato, tells us in words that still keep the freshness of the curiosity out of which science was born: "When I was young, I was passionately attracted by what is called physical science; I thought it splendid to know the causes of each thing, why it comes into being, why it exists, why it perishes. I was always worrying over problems like these."

Socrates abandoned science because he thought that its explanations, not indeed of the cosmos but of human nature and human conduct, were superficial and unsatisfactory. It is as if some modern scientist of genius suddenly felt that chemistry and physics and biology could not solve our difficulties and that the real problem lay elsewhere; as if he abandoned the study of natural science but attacked the problem of conduct by the methods of intelligence, knowledge, and hard thinking which he had employed in his scientific inquiries, gathering round him a band of students who after his death carried on his work, though the quest led all of them further than their master, and some of them to ideals remote from his. As that happens more and more frequently to-day, while physical science continues to advance, religion, ethics, political science, and psychology will come to seem no less fascinating and even more important. Socrates taught his countrymen a lesson which they never forgot, that life is essentially a human problem.

What life did the Greeks conceive that men should lead against the background of material civilization? Here again, as in their view of nature, they started on the lowest rung of the ladder, in a world where a hero sacrificed captives at the grave of his friend, and gods feasted and quarrelled on a high mountain top. Four hundred years later, they had reached a very different conception of life. "Evil, Theodorus, can never pass away," Plato makes Socrates say. "There must always remain something which is antagonistic to good. It has no place in heaven; so of necessity it haunts our mortal nature and this earthly sphere. Therefore we ought to escape to heaven from earth: and to escape is to become like God, so far as this is possible; and to become like him is to become holy, just, and wise." How did the Greeks achieve this transition from the ideals of Homer to those of Plato?

It is almost true to say that one clue guided them through and

out of the jungle of childish belief to this serene air. They noticed
that everything is capable of "perfection," a "best": or, as they
put it, that everything has a "virtue." This is true of an eye, a
knife, a foot, whose respective "virtues" are to see well, to cut
well, to walk or run well. But it is also true of human beings.
They, too, have their "virtues," which they aim at achieving and
which we expect them to achieve. The "virtue" of a cobbler is to
make good boots, of a sculptor to carve fine statues, of a salesman
to sell goods effectively.

But beyond the "virtue" of which each of us is capable in his
peculiar occupation, age, or condition of life, there is a "virtue"
of man as human being. It is difficult to be sure what it is. But it
exists. We cannot admit that a knife and a horse may have a perfection but that man has none; and man's business is to discover
it, and success or failure in life is measured by the degree in which
he achieves or falls short of this, the supreme goal of human
effort. The Greek word *areté* sometimes means virtue in our
sense, but it always keeps a hint of an older and wider meaning
for which English has no equivalent. This Greek conception appears in the passage where Meno, when asked to define it, re-
plies: "Let us take first the virtue of a man—he should know
how to administer the state. . . . A woman's virtue . . . is to
order her house and keep what is indoors and obey her husband.
Every age, every condition of life, young or old, male or female,
bond or free, has a different virtue: there are virtues numberless
and no lack of definitions of them; for virtue is relative to the
actions and ages of each of us in all that we do." In this sense
there are innumerable virtues in the world. But the most important and the most puzzling is the virtue of man, not in his capacity of cobbler, or sculptor, or salesman, or statesman, not as male
or female, but as human being. The history of Hellenism is the
discovery of human virtue.

This idea of virtue seems very elementary. Yet it is extraordi-
narily potent and fruitful. Out of it came, and could not fail to
come in the hands of a people with genius, a noble human ideal.
The story of Greece is much more than one of war and economic
growth and political experiment and artistic achievement. It is
the story of the making of an ideal of human life: an ideal which

has all the cardinal features of a great moral system; which is disinterested, progressive, free from narrowness, and which compels men to accept, desire, and pursue it.

Let me show, very briefly, how this is so. Take in your hands this clue of virtue, this idea that each of us, as a human being, is capable of a "best," and see, if you follow it, to what scheme of morals, what path of life you will be implicitly committed and naturally drawn; what type of character it will tend to create. First, its power to draw men away from lesser aims to follow it— a power such as Aristotle ascribes to his Final Cause which, itself unmoved, "moves by the love which it inspires." We start with the conception that human nature has an excellence. But the best, once its existence is known, must be desired and sought. Once we realize that man has a "perfection" of his own, we are afloat on a stream that will take us far. If human nature has a perfection, it is self-evident that this perfection must be desired and sought. There is a categorical imperative as peremptory as Kant's. That is one fruit of this conception of virtue. Implicit in it is the desire to achieve it. The mere idea of human perfection justifies itself and constitutes a self-evident claim on the human spirit.

Implicit in it, too, is an impulse to progress. There is nothing fixed or static in this virtue. The definition of it grows with the growth of the intellect and rises as high as the imagination can take it. The virtue of a knife remains the same in all ages; the virtue of a horse will change with the uses to which a horse is put; but the virtue of a human being admits of almost infinite interpretation, at least among a race with the intellectual and imaginative power of the Greeks. So for every successive age of their history, virtue is incarnated afresh and her lineaments change with each incarnation. For Homer it is courage and steadfastness in war. It may decline to a lower idea. "For most men," says Theognis, "the one is money; there is no profit, they think, in anything else, either in knowledge, or in right-mindedness." (This is a view which, if less frankly expressed in our theory of life, is not absent from its practice.) Pindar, living with the well-to-do and writing poems on the athletic successes of his friends, sees virtue in perfect physical fitness, and in the color, brilliance, and hospitality of an aristocratic society, and transfigures, as none has done before or

since, the race-course and the running-track and the life of the
rich into poetry and almost into a moral ideal. These views mark
a decline from Homer. But meanwhile there come from Asiatic
Greece, from Ephesus and Miletus, two other interpretations:
"The supreme virtue is thought, and wisdom consists in saying
what is true and acting according to nature, listening to her";
"All virtue is summed up in justice." Perhaps these statements
do not impress us. They are so simple that it is easy to ignore
the immense spiritual progress which they reveal. Hellenism
never got beyond, though its later writers amplified and illus-
trated, the statement that the perfection, the greatness, of man
lies in thought and in justice.

Another trait of a life ruled by the idea of virtue is disinter-
estedness. Admit perfection as an ideal, and it cannot but be
desired for itself. The athlete is rewarded by the perfection of
his bodily powers, not by prizes or applause; the poet or scientist,
by his own supreme achievements, apart from fame or money.
Enough for the thinker to see the world as it is, for the artist to
enjoy it for itself. So with every faculty: its perfect exercise is its
own reward.

Again, a life based on this conception of virtue must be rich
and many-sided. There is nothing restricted in the Greek view
of human perfection. From the first it was free of the narrowness
which has been a besetting danger to Christianity, and which has
left its mark in different ways in different ages—in the contempt
of Tertullian for literature and learning, in the extravagances
of the ascetics, in the broken statues of English cathedrals, in the
life of Victorian Nonconformity. There is nothing of this in
Greece. Everything has its virtue, and each virtue in its sphere
is admirable and desirable. There is room for the athlete and the
intellectual, for the statesman and the artist—even for flying
round the world and breaking motor records. But none of these
is enough in itself. There is a virtue of an athlete, a painter, a
statesman; and it might seem sufficient for a man to achieve any
of these, to be a world champion, a great artist, a President or
Prime Minister. But besides these virtues there must be a virtue
of man as man—an ideal of human nature quite apart from any
special gifts or occupations, and, obviously, higher than any of

these. Specialism, however exalted and successful, is not enough. So it is realized that a man is something more than any part of himself, more than his profession or occupation; and there is no danger of people's supposing that his excellence lies in his feet or in his muscles, or of their regarding athletic success or professional capacity or any technical gift as a supreme or complete ideal. Success in politics, scholarship, business, or sport does not make the perfect life or the complete human being.

Whom, then, did the Greeks regard as the perfect man? Different ages would have given different answers, according to the changing views of human virtue. The ideal of the fifth century B.C., as Pericles states it in Thucydides' report of his Funeral Speech, was a man versatile and intensely active, both in public duty and in his private occupation, combining practical pursuits with intellectual interests and artistic enjoyment. Pericles describes the ideal man as public-spirited, respecting the law of the land and, above all, the unwritten moral code, living in a state which is prosperous, rich in noble buildings and in festivals and recreations, which oppresses neither poor nor rich, but gives all full opportunity to make the best of themselves. Already we have a rich conception of human nature and the state. In the next century the philosophers developed the subject with method and logic.

Aristotle has enumerated the qualities which, in his opinion, compose the perfect character, and his list reveals the generous and ample ideal of life to which the conception leads us. There are the intellectual virtues: wisdom, intelligence, and that practical wisdom which is the virtue of a ruler, of Prime Ministers and Presidents, of Congressmen and Members of Parliament. There are the moral virtues: not only the four cardinal virtues of courage, wisdom, temperance, and justice, which Plato recognized, but truthfulness, liberality, good temper, amiability, and two qualities which may be roughly translated as "magnificence" and "greatness of soul." These are the things which make the complete man. If we knew nothing else of Greek civilization, this list would be sufficient to reveal the breadth and richness of its existence.

But, it may be said, the list is becoming overcrowded. There is almost an excess of virtues. Life may be too rich as well as too poor. Here the Greeks were guided by the same instinct which drove them to make a cosmos, an ordered system of the universe. It saved them in morals from the confusion to which the very richness of their life might have led. Here, too, they are an example to an age which has indeed its ordered view of the universe but is content to live in spiritual chaos. Their philosophers devised a calculus and ranked the virtues in a hierarchy of values which assigned its place to each but excluded none.

This is Plato's scale: "There are two kinds of good things, the human and the heavenly; and the former are dependent on the latter; if a state achieves the greater, it acquires the lesser also, and if not, it loses both. First among lesser goods is health; second, beauty; third, strength in racing and in all other bodily movements; and, fourth, wealth—not blind but keen-sighted and guided by wisdom. Among the heavenly goods the first and foremost is wisdom; second, a reasonable habit of mind allied with insight; third, and resulting from the combination of these qualities with courage, is justice; and fourth, courage. All these rank naturally before the lesser goods, and in this order the lawgiver must rank them."

Aristotle says even more plainly that the noblest power of man is the reason, and that the supreme human virtue is the exercise of reason. The Anglo-Saxon will be shocked by this idea that the highest existence is that of the theologian, the philosopher, the poet and artist, the man of science. Yet we cannot deny that it is noble, that it is tenable, that its definiteness contrasts favorably with the intellectual chaos of our own day, and that it is easier to reject than refute. Christianity indeed developed and enriched Hellenism. It gave to those who accepted its revelation a definiteness and sense of certainty about the nature and will of God which is absent from the Greek view of life. By insisting that the supreme virtue is love, it put the highest spiritual good within the reach of the humblest of mankind. By its doctrine of a suffering God, it suggested an attitude to sorrow and pain other than mere endurance or defiance. But thereby it corrected and completed Hellenism rather than superseded it.

The Greek view of life based on the conception of virtue grew slowly and under various influences. The foundations were laid in ages of war and disorder, when those survived who had courage never to submit or yield. In the social misery and lawlessness of the succeeding centuries the ideal of justice was born. Aristocracy contributed its splendid and picturesque virtues. In Ionia wealth, leisure, and contact with foreign peoples (from whom the Greeks were not too proud to learn) stimulated intellectual curiosity; and the enterprise which had brought the Greek colonists across the Aegean carried them into the stranger seas of thought. The composite and slowly fashioned ideal that resulted is throughout the work of the unaided human mind, pondering on itself. It is a product of the human intellect and imagination, studying the capacities and character of man, analyzing his nature and so determining his virtue. The work, once done, has never needed to be done again and remains the greatest spiritual achievement of European man.

In these fundamental conceptions of Hellenism we recognize a kinship with our inner spirit and ideal which owe so much to them. That kinship is easily explained. It springs from the fact that the Greeks took reason as their guide, and by the use of critical intelligence and methodical inquiry explored both the material universe and the capacities of man. In Greece we perceive the natural trend of human development, unassisted by divine revelation, undeflected by religious or political terrorism, unimpeded by grinding poverty, unseduced by excessive wealth. That is the real reason why we still read Greek. The classics are not in education—it is a paradox that they should be there at all in this modern mechanical, scientific, economic age—by accident or even by tradition or even because they open to us one great and one supreme literature. It is because some people find in them a training for life and help in living it. It was not of literary enjoyment that Goethe was thinking when he said that of all men the Greeks had dreamt the dream of life best; or Cicero when he wrote to his son, starting for Athens, "You are going to visit men who are supremely men." Cicero and Goethe found in Greece something more than a great literature. They saw in it a supreme ideal for life. If they were right, there is some truth in the belief that the study of that ideal can help both to interpret our age and to correct it.

THE VOTER: HIS RIGHTS AND DUTIES

By JAMES TRUSLOW ADAMS

IN somewhat more than a century and a half the two great
English-speaking nations, the British Empire and the
United States, have passed from a firm belief in representative government to the practice, at least, of an almost pure
democracy. The change has been coincident with a vast extension
of the suffrage which has given to nearly all but children, a few
selected criminals, and such idiots only as have been unlucky
enough to have got themselves certified as such, an equal voice
in the selection of the overseers of their destinies. It is conceivable that such a vast increase in the numbers of the electors might
have occurred without a change in the theory of *representation*.
A group of ten thousand might just as reasonably have elected
a man who was to be a representative, and not an errand boy or
a rubber stamp, as the earlier group of a few hundred in the same
borough or district. Indeed, theoretically, as the size of the electorate increased it might have been considered that the importance of representation as contrasted with direct participation in
legislation of the individual elector might also have increased.

For the most part, the Americans who framed our Constitution certainly believed so, and nothing was further from their
desires or hopes than that every Tom, Dick, and Harry who
could vote would have a direct voice in Congress and other lawmaking bodies. Times, nevertheless, were already changing, and
the freshets which were to swell the stream of democracy had
begun to rise. In addressing the men who had just elected him to
parliament from Bristol in 1774, Edmund Burke made what has
become the classic speech on the difference between representation and direct democracy.

"Your representative owes you," he told the men of Bristol,
"not his industry only, but his judgment; and he betrays, in-

stead of serving you, if he sacrifices it to your opinion. . . . If government were a matter of will upon any side, yours without question ought to be superior. But government and legislation are matters of reason and judgment, not of inclination; and what sort of reason is that, in which the determination precedes the discussion; in which one set of men deliberate, and another decide? . . . To deliver an opinion is the right of all men; that of constituents is a weighty and respectable opinion, which a representative ought always to rejoice to hear; and which he ought always most seriously to consider. But *authoritative* instructions, mandates issued, which the member is bound blindly and implicitly to obey, . . . these are things utterly unknown to the laws of this land, and which arise from a fundamental mistake of the whole order and tenor of our constitution. Parliament is not a *congress* of ambassadors from different and hostile interests, which interests each must maintain, as an agent and advocate, against other agents and advocates; but parliament is a *deliberative* assembly of *one* nation, with one interest, that of the whole; where not local purposes, not local prejudices ought to guide, but the general good, resulting from the general reason of the whole."

On those terms Burke was allowed to retain his seat for six years, but at last he was defeated, as was also to be the doctrine he so manfully and lucidly set forth. What a "congress of ambassadors from different and hostile interests" may do in the way of legislation our own has shown all too often. Last spring the good of the whole, which was obviously the passing of a tax measure to balance the budget, had to wait on the miserable tactics of the "ambassadors" from the hostile interests.

For months Congress reeled in its course like a drunken man while the clear good of the nation was made subservient to the interests of this or that group. This inability of Congress to act was due in largest measure to its abandonment of the doctrine of representation and its complete yielding, even in a crisis of the first magnitude, to the pressures from direct democracy. The Babel in Congress itself but echoed the Babel in the electorate, organized, to a great extent, into pressure groups—copper, ex-service men, timber, agriculture, cheap money advocates, wets, drys, and what not. The congressmen, unlike Burke, seemed unable to use their own minds and to act for the best as the representatives of the whole people; they considered themselves incapable of doing anything opposed to the direct mandates of their constituents; and, their constituents being a mob, Congress has become a mob.

All this is hackneyed commonplace, although the situation has long been of appalling and increasing seriousness. Much, but not too much, has been written of the effect on governing bodies of the substitution for the old representative idea of the more modern one of the legislator as receiving his mandate direct from the electors on every topic which he may have to consider, yielding, often against his own better judgment, to the balance of ayes and noes in a barrage of telegrams and postcards or other more gross or subtle means of influence.

A point which has troubled me, however, and I believe many others, with regard to the effects now showing themselves of the abandonment of representative government is quite a different one. It has to do with the effect of the mandate-rubber-stamp-messenger-boy theory not on the governing bodies but on the members of the electorate itself. It is not what we may be doing to the character of legislation enacted by representatives whom we no longer regard as such, but what we are doing, by forsaking the old doctrine, to our own private lives. For a moment, let us turn from the horrors of legislation as performed by demos and pressure groups, to the individual life of that citizen whom American doctrine proclaims a king, and whom democratic doctrine insists upon giving a direct voice in all public affairs.

"Public affairs"—the old *res publica*, republic, of the Romans. Until comparatively recently we were quite free, ethically, to give our time and thought to them or not as we chose, except on the small stage of village, parish, vestry, or town, where our daily occupations and contacts afforded us all the information needed to act wisely. Public-spirited citizens of such so-called democracies and city states as Athens, Florence, and others were in this happy condition. They could get tremendously excited and take their part in politics which were purely local and in which they knew all the chief actors as fellow members of a small community.

In greater states, such as the Oriental despotisms or the European nations which gradually emerged after the Middle Ages, the individual had practically no share in the central government. That government might impinge on his private life most unpleasantly at times, just as the weather might ruin his crops, a fire destroy his house, or the soldiery of an invading army assault his family. These were all, more or less alike, acts of God. But outside his small sphere of local interests he had no responsibility for running the state any more than he had for running the universe. His leisure time was his own to do with as he would. He could sing, dance, idle, dream of the Virgin, walk under the stars, carve utensils, recite poetry—in fact, do anything which his own errant instincts and tastes might lead him to wish to do.

Even with the growth of the modern concept of "liberty" and the rise of representative government, he was as yet free to do as he would and remain a good citizen, so long as he obeyed the laws and chose his representatives, if he were allowed to do so, as wisely as he could. The representatives did the rest, and the ordinary citizen did not need to trouble himself overmuch as to what they were doing save when he was faced with the final result of their deliberations.

With the passing of the representative idea and the advent of modern democracy, however, a new situation has come about. When citizens decided that representatives could no longer be trusted and that they themselves must dictate legislation, they assumed tremendous responsibilities. As Burke said to the electors of Bristol, "To be a good member of parliament, is, let me tell you, no easy task." As the pressure of the elector on the member of parliament or Congress became more and more marked, it meant that the conscientious citizen had to assume more and more of the duties which had belonged to his representative. In other words, in addition to being a farmer, a doctor, a mechanic, poet, or shopkeeper, he had also to undertake to perform the duties of a congressman.

As it was impossible that he could perform this double duty successfully, the ship of state began to wallow. We were told that the cure for the ills of democracy was more democracy. The past generation saw the rise of the initiative, the referendum, the recall, the direct primary, and other experimental methods of making the individual citizen more of a legislator and the representative less. In some States, the inroads on the time of the citizen merely to cast ballots at all sorts of elections and referendums became serious. Far more serious, however, for the conscientious citizen, have become the inroads on his time and thought if there is to be well-considered and worth-while opinion back of ballot, telegram, postcard or other effort at lawmaking by the democracy at large.

Let us take, for example, a few of the problems on which the citizen in a democracy which has abandoned the representative idea must have an opinion arrived at with as great knowledge as possible. These include farm relief, private or public ownership of power plants, international trade, regulation of banking, inflation or deflation of the currency, taxation, the bonus, disarmament, the Far Eastern situation, prohibition, tariffs, the League of Nations, education, reorganization of the government departments, and a host of others.

It may be pointed out that there is a large and highly technical literature on all of these topics; that specialists in them disagree as readily as the proverbial doctors; that there is nowhere an "authoritative" opinion to be had for the seeking; and that the public press, as well as private propaganda, frequently does its best to mislead the enquirer after truth.

The so-called "opinions" of the ordinary man are usually a mixture of the veriest smattering of information and misinformation, with a large injection of his favorite newspaper's attitude and the influence of his personal environment. But obviously if legislation is to be based on no better foundation than that, we might as well install a sandwich boy from a drug-store counter as president of General Electric or United States Steel. We pride ourselves on saying that this is the age of the specialist, and that there is no longer place, either in science or business or education, for the untrained. Clearly then, if we are to have democracy and not representative government; if John Doe and Richard Roe in Richmond and Seattle are to settle the legislation in Washington, Doe and Roe will have to sit up nights studying the problems on which they are to legislate. If they do not do so, or if having done so, they and all the rest of us have not been able to form sound opinions on all the topics, what possible hope is there for even reasonably sound legislation?

Again, I return, however, to the point that I am not thinking at present so much of the *legislation* as of the *legislator*, that is, of all of us who are being forced to take on in addition to the more than arduous task at present of making a living the complete duties formerly assigned to our political representatives; in other words, of our having to be doctor, salesman, janitor, or portrait painter, *plus* congressman. Burke was right. It is no easy job to be a legislator. It is also no easy one to be a private citizen and to bring up a family in decency and comfort. To combine the jobs is impossible.

Most of us, when we have work, have little leisure time except evenings, Saturday afternoons, Sundays, and occasional holidays —even when we have all of those. Such time is none too much, after we have taken out of it adding up the grocer's bills, writing checks, doing odd jobs, attending committees, and so on, for us to devote to our families, general reading, exercise, the enjoyment of the hobby every sane individual should have, and certain other things. Such disposition of it as we chose to make we could make before the days when we were kings and democracy did away with the representative function of the legislator. There might be things going on in Congress of which we highly disapproved, but we were not called upon to do much about them, at least not until election time. The issues in the older days, moreover, were comparatively simple. The sphere in which a national government functioned was rather limited, and the rest was local politics which we could understand without sitting up nights to read volumes on finance and currency, on what the League really is like, on whether the theory of the Farm Board's operations has been right or wrong, and all the rest of it. In 1824 Andrew Jackson stated that "the duties of all public offices are, or at least admit of being made, so plain and simple that men of

intelligence may readily qualify themselves for their performance." This was true, at any rate in so far as the tasks may be compared with those of to-day.

At present the conscientious citizen finds himself in an un-
pleasant predicament. Under the old representative system,
there was no more perfect justice meted out to all classes than
there ever has been, or probably ever will be, under any other
system. Because of the perennial dissatisfaction of certain classes
whose noses were not quite close enough to the trough, an effort
was made to bring the millennium nearer by controlling the
votes of the representatives. Under the old system, there had
been "pressure groups" of the landed interest and what not.
Under the new system, we have added numerous other pressure
groups to these—the tariff-favor hunters, American Legion,
Anti-Saloon League, and the rest of the two thousand who, it
has been stated, maintain lobbyists at Washington.

Under the old system, however, the conscientious citizen
could curse the government and go for a walk, shoot rabbits or
read his favorite author. Under the new system, if he *is* conscientious, he should spend laborious nights studying the problems of legislation, and does not know whom to curse.

What is he to do? Theoretically he ought to use his influence
to bring about wise legislation. To do that, he must know his subject. Practically, he knows not only that, according to the theory
of democracy instead of representation, it is his duty to make the
congressional rubber stamps register his opinions but that his
fellow citizens by the hundreds of thousands are trying to do
the same thing, either singly or in powerful groups.

If he is conscientious and wishes to have really considered
opinions, the study of one topic after another—if undertaken
seriously and if his opinions are not to be cribbed from newspapers and a weekly or two—will occupy his entire leisure time.
Even if he spent all of it on the complexities of the modern world
and the topics before Congress, he would not be a tithe as well
posted as a congressman can be who has his entire working as
well as leisure hours for the task. If anyone wants to try it out,
let him take one or two of what are considered minor problems,
such as the administration of our dependencies or the administra-

tion of the Indian Department, and see how long it will take him to decide on actual conditions and wise measures.

The ordinary citizen simply has not got the time for all this. But there is another point. Even if he spent all his time trying to be a wise legislator, would he even then achieve good citizenship? The problems of the moment at any time are largely problems of organization, of how to form a structure within which to lead a sane and balanced life. How sane is it to devote all one's working hours to making a living, and then devote all one's leisure ones to studying the problems of organizing life, and never begin really to live, that is, to savor life itself and to enjoy the best possible which it may afford, whether in literature, art, or other pleasures according to personal inclination?

What, after all, is the end of government? Aristotle claimed that it was to permit of a happy and virtuous life on the part of the citizens. Our Declaration of Independence stated it to be the securing of the rights of "life, liberty, and the pursuit of happiness." Is not the result of the modern theory of democracy much the same as that of the modern theory of mass production: that man is a consumer who must buy goods chiefly for the sake of keeping the machinery of trade turning, not for his own enjoyment? The citizen, under modern conditions of complex problems in an unrepresentative democracy, would appear to exist for the sake of keeping the government functioning rather than to enjoy his private life.

I have perhaps exaggerated the situation, and yet I do not think I have. If my member of Congress is not to have any mind of his own but is to vote only in response to the mandate of his constituents; if it is considered the duty of the constituents to issue the mandates by sending telegrams; and if all the constituents except myself are considering the problems and sending the telegrams, am I a good citizen if I get fed up with it all and read the classics in the evenings instead of articles on farm relief and cancellation of war debts? Or can I be eighteenth-century, decide that I have elected a man to go to Washington, whom I pay for the express purpose of wrestling with these national problems as I wrestle with those of my own job, and chuck the whole thing? I cannot be omniscient. I cannot have a real opinion on all the congressman's problems without giving all my small amount of spare time to it, and may not have a real opinion then. Am I to allow my short remaining span of private leisure to be absorbed entirely by the problems of the day so that I may bring my small pressure to bear on the member from my district, like the other pressure-bringers; or become a bad citizen, selfish, and un-public-spirited? Does modern democracy expect us to issue mandates to our ex-representatives hypocritically without real knowledge of the subject, or does it expect that we shall merge our private lives wholly in our service to the state, and lose our humanism in our citizenship?

Nor can we lose sight of the fact that in this complex modern era, with government impinging on every side of our private lives, it has become almost impossible to disentangle the public from the private interest. It is not only a question of the age-old power of government to drive us to war or to take our property in taxation. War debts, farm relief, bonus legislation, a thousand things which the people now undertake to decide, affect us powerfully as individuals, while in minor ways the government, whether merely recording the sum total of pressures brought by various groups or not, enters our homes at a hundred doors and tells us how we must keep our personal accounts, what we can drink at our tables, what books we can have on our library shelves, what knowledge we may obtain and impart. It has become almost impossible to separate ourselves as citizens from ourselves as individuals.

I am beginning to suspect that the decline of the representative theory, like the fall of earlier forms of governing, came because some groups wanted the extra pickings from the government trough that other groups had been getting. From that quite simple and human desire sprang the theory that I must not consider my congressman as a representative but that I must send mandates in the interest, theoretically, of liberty and, practically, of spoils. Eternal vigilance, we have been told, is the price of liberty, but eternal vigilance is a frontier or a war condition. It cannot be expected of peaceful and civilized generation after generation. Neither the frontier nor war develops the finest qualities in the private life. A man who sleeps with a gun to protect his family from savage or civilized enemies is not in the best situation to become a contented, happy, and cultured human being.

Life, that moment of self-consciousness which we enjoy between the mysteries of two unknowns, is extremely brief. As we grow older, it appears briefer with every fleeting year and month. For hundreds of thousands of years, man has slowly advanced while paying but scant attention to the *res publica*, the public things, as contrasted with the affairs of his own private interests. The world is immensely interesting, but many of its most absorbing interests lie remote from the problems before Congress, whether our own are golf, motoring, the excavation of Sumerian ruins, the study of Chaucer, or any one of a million things as far from politics as is Hindu philosophy from the splitting of the atom. Each human being must find his own interest, find that which fascinates him most in a transient world of marvels. Some will find theirs in the handling of public affairs, but why should all the rest suddenly be turned into unwilling and unaccomplished amateurs of legislation?

The progress we have made has come largely from the division of labor. Why reverse the process now and make us all members of Congress? It is to be hoped that as many able and honest men as possible should find their private ambition coincide with a career as a politician or statesman, but why should those who do not find this to be so have to sacrifice their whole leisure to a study of problems which do not interest them when they themselves would be far more valuable members of the great society by devoting themselves to other pursuits? Forms of government continually shift and are innumerable. Under all of them, some groups or classes or individuals will probably always get somewhat more than their rightful share of the favors going round. This is certainly still happening under democracy in the year 1932.

It is needless to say that nothing in this article need be taken as detracting from the supreme importance of the right sort of men entering on political careers as representatives of the people; or from the duty of the citizen to encourage their doing so, and to try to choose his representative with care as a man of honesty, courage, independence, and knowledge. Such men would be far more likely to enter politics to serve the state under the old formula of Burke than under the threat of instant dismissal from office if their acts displeased demos at any moment. Such a system would relieve the individual citizen of much of the pretense of being capable of expressing an opinion on subjects in which the accumulated mass of learning and the complexity of problems have become infinitely great as compared with days of a Bacon or an Erasmus. We are supposed to know a great deal as contrasted with our grandparents; but in fact, as any dinner table conversation will most lamentably prove, ninety-nine per cent of our chatter about the problems of the world is nothing but high-class gossip. To base a sound Oriental policy for the nation on what the average intelligent citizen really knows about the rights of the Sino-Japanese question, would be as sensible as to base it on the peeping of bullfrogs. Yet theoretically and to a great extent practically, that is what has to be done to-day. The effect on the individual is to make him hypocritical, or if not that, to lead him to believe that public affairs can be run without a tithe of the thought and knowledge which he knows are essential in his private business. The moral and intellectual effects are disastrous.

The democratic theory which has rejected the theory of the legislator as a representative has brought us only to the point of the present Congress, and to parties and platforms which dodge every real issue so as to return rubber stamps to seats in the next Congress, and so on year after year. The complexity of governmental problems will increase and not decrease in the future. If we are all to assume the functions which ought to belong to our representatives, either our hypocrisy must increase or our private life will disappear. We must either try to force Congress to vote as we wish without having given adequate consideration to the legislation, basing our wishes perhaps on our selfish interest as we see it without thought of the good of the whole; or else, if we try to play the rôle of the conscientious legislator, we must devote our leisure life to the study of problems about most or all of which we shall never, in any case, gain more than a very amateurish knowledge. Is he who declines to accept either of these alternatives, and tries instead to be a rounded and sane human being, a bad citizen? It is worth pondering, and the answer may be found in what we consider the values of a humane life and the functions of a government.

There is, perhaps, one possible and practical way of escape from the present demoralizing and increasingly difficult situation. Human nature being what it is, we cannot look for any immediate diminution of the mass pressure brought to bear on those who are in high office. If we cannot at present diminish that pressure we may, however, consider the alternative possibility of increasing the resistance to it on the part of those against whom it is brought. As our central government has waxed in power and prestige, both nationally and internationally, there has been a marked falling off in interest in the local governments—town, county, and state. It may as well be confessed that power and prestige are the two goals of the ambition of most Americans. It has been these and not money which have kept men toiling at amassing ever more tens of millions as they have grown old, and have already possessed every other gratification which money can buy.

As the nation grows older, however, and the prizes offered by economic exploitation, and the chance of securing them, become somewhat less, we may come to regard the work which is good in itself as of satisfying value to us. Few of us have the ability to play a national rôle in politics or statesmanship; just as few of us can become billionaires. If there is less glitter about working for the good of the nation in a state legislature, for example, than in the halls, not to say lobbies, of Congress, the work to be done in the former, as also in town and county, is of national importance. Our national political system, whether controlling men in office or a nominating convention, goes straight down through the hierarchy of bosses to the local unit. At the bottom of all is the ability of the small bosses to deliver given quantities of votes, from groups of individual voters, boards of aldermen, or state legislatures.

Down in this now neglected part of our political life, the average man can find himself, if he will, more in the position of the old voter in Greece. He can know the local leaders and the local issues. The voter may not see or be able to learn all the intricacies of national problems, but he knows, or can know, whether the men of his own community, whom he is placing in office in town board or state capitol are honest and able. This is not so easy, of course, in a great municipality, like New York or Chicago, as it is in a rural section or a smaller town or city, but even in the greatest of all there are still the lesser units of wards or other divisions.

I do not wish to be understood as advocating that we should not take as active and intelligent an interest in national affairs and policies as our time and knowledge will permit. All I wish to warn against, for the effect on ourselves quite as much as on government, is the vain and absurd effort on the part of all voters to legislate themselves on such matters before Congress simultaneously with, if not even prior to, discussion by that body. It may well prove that in largely abandoning the good old Democratic doctrine of States' Rights, the greatest danger which we have incurred is that of forcing the individual citizen out of a sphere in which he can be useful into one so large that his usefulness is destroyed by ignorance—and ignorance that can be overcome only at a price in time and energy which he is both unable and unwilling to afford. By shifting the whole of our interest to the national government, we have done nothing to improve that, and much to ruin the entire structure by neglecting to think of the foundations. If one wants to make a plant thrive, one waters the roots and not the topmost branch.

The point I would make is that if, instead of keeping our minds mainly on national problems, with the results which I have already suggested, we would undertake to make ourselves familiar with the local ones of our own States, we should be attempting something within the limits of our leisure and ability; and not only that but we should be rendering a service of incalculable value to the national life. A body of informed opinion on local matters, a large addition to the number of voters insistent on honesty in administration and on high quality in local officials, and a group of men in every state legislature large enough to affect legislation, backed by a similarly extended section of an interested and informed electorate, would all have enormous influence on the ability and character of the candidates for office all the way up the line to Congress itself. Much narrower limits would be set to the power of the bosses, and even if we could not, as I have said, diminish the pressure brought to bear on national officials, we could in that way increase their power of resistance. If we became more sure that they would not supinely yield to the pressure of one group or another, we would not remain under the same necessity as we are now of trying to make our own pressure felt, either with or against some other body of citizens. In other words, we could get back more to the old idea of the representative. We could lessen the difficulties which this article has pointed out, and could once more combine a private life with the life of a conscientious citizen in a community.

The day may come—there are signs it has already come—when more men may be willing to enter public life for the sake of rendering service on the stages of our smaller political units. The desire for the spectacular may give place among us to a saner valuation of what is worth while. We may also as individual citizens come to the conclusion that it is just as important to seek to have an honest and able administration in each of our forty-eight commonwealths as it is to try to direct the solution of all the problems before the national government from the country store or the club smoking room. When that day comes, we shall have gone far towards settling one of the greatest of our national problems,—how to get able, fearless, and independent men to administer the government of the nation, with or without postcards and telegrams. Meanwhile, whether this is an impossible ideal or not, there would seem little hope of improving national conditions politically, or of reconciling the citizen's rights with his duties, by merely bringing more and more pressures to bear at the top of the political system while leaving all the local fields to take care of themselves, allowing every evil force to entrench itself. Good citizenship, like charity, should begin at home. If enough of us acted on that belief, the result might well be that we could once more in peace balance the demands of the public and the private life.

PATTERNS OF SUCCESS

By JOHN HODGDON BRADLEY

BY implying motivation through purpose, success is a typical concept of the human mind. Men, who believe with some reason that their own behavior may be consciously purposive, have frequently inferred some comparable actuation for the behavior of other creatures. Inasmuch as no amount of undirected manipulation might conceivably create so intricate and useful a mechanism as a watch, it is difficult for men to believe that any amount of random activity might conceivably create so intricate and useful a device as a beehive.

It is easy for them, on the other hand, to assume that effort towards desired and envisioned ends is the power that drives the entire living world. Many, indeed, have so assumed, and a few like Henri Bergson have beautifully and persuasively urged the truth of their assumption. But the men who have seen most in the lives of plants and animals have rather generally failed to see there a convincing equivalent of human purpose. If they have seen any suggestion of divine purpose in a world of boundless cruelty and waste, they have rather generally yielded to others the embarrassing task of discovering its justification.

Biologic success is measured by the fitness of creatures for the lives they lead. With the sole known exception in man, the attainment of this fitness—so far as the science of biology may surely say—is as automatic as breathing during sleep; neither the site nor the equipment of success may be consciously chosen or altered by species or individuals. Conditions just happen to combine in some cases to the advantage and in other cases to the disadvantage of the organism.

Since Darwin first anchored the doctrine of chance to a base of observable fact, innumerable observations and experiments have been made which in small part discredit but in large part confirm his views. Post-Darwinian investigations have added very little to Darwin's meagre knowledge of the fundamental causes for the variations which underlie the fate of organisms. They have detracted little from Darwin's general argument for the shaping of that fate by environment and competition. Given the inventive fertility of flesh on an earth too lean to satisfy its needs and the stage would seem to be adequately set for the drama of life.

Most men do not enjoy finding economy where they have sought morality, especially when the economy is uneconomical and cruel. That some chance advantage should have been at the bottom of every achievement in the living world for more than a billion years is a concept which they can scarcely stomach with pleasure. That the lucky should have ruthlessly and invariably pressed their advantages at the expense of the luckless is even less palatable to the moral taste. It is not surprising in view of the traditional inconsistency of that taste that many have preferred to exchange these bitter likelihoods for sweeter fictions.

Unfortunately, biologic success may not be reliably described with reference to the moral sense of man. Neither may it be reliably measured with reference to the human sense of time, space, and relativity. Practically speaking, there is no human sense of time, space, and relativity because only a few men think less briefly and parochially than they live. Were it possible to view the living world as Einstein has viewed the physical world, expanding the imagination to the size and complexity of the subject it attempts to grasp, the ramifications of biologic success and failure might appear both endlessly and indistinguishably interwoven.

For even the less cosmic eye may see that biologic success and failure are neither pure nor stable values. The clam who sits in the mud may be a failure with reference to the bird who flies in the sky, but he is also a success with reference to those who must die because he sits there. The tapeworm, who has lost many organs through degeneration, is in one sense a failure with reference to his ancestors, who retained them. In another sense, he has succeeded, and his ancestors have failed because he is alive and they are not. Gauged by the relative duration of their existence, the sharks, who ruled the seas for part of the Devonian period in geologic history, were less successful than the dinosaurs, who ruled the lands for the whole of the Mesozoic era. But even the dinosaurs eventually perished. Gauged by the ultimate inevitability of death, all success is a phase of failure because all living is a phase of dying.

What, then, remains of success? Nothing essential, it would seem, but the ability to eat and to avoid being eaten until reproduction is attained. Any individual that reproduces before it dies, any species that propagates itself however briefly, completes the basic cycle of life and achieves thereby the one fundamental success. The stagnant and the degenerate, the spectacular and the dull, are all equally successful in the economy of Nature if they succeed in this. Paltry though such success may seem to those who are able to dream of higher goals, many individuals have failed to achieve it. The adaptations which have enabled a minority to succeed are the most marvellous phenomena in the world. They are also the most mysterious.

Before natural history grew up into biology, the student of plants and animals went to the field to observe. Now, for the most part, he goes to the laboratory to experiment. The shift was more than a change of method and location. It was also a change of approach to the problems of Nature. One need not exaggerate the achievements of the naturalist or belittle those of the biologist to see that something valuable was lost in this evolution.

Gilbert White could not have known and probably would not have cared about the rôle of chromosomes in the genesis of earthworms. But he knew and cared about the rôle of earthworms in his little world of Selborne. He knew that life is more than the isolated facts and principles of anatomy, function, and descent. It is not always obvious that the specialist of to-day knows as much. He too often obscures the forest of life by magnifying the trees that compose it.

Stimulated by the evolutionary philosophy of Nature, modern biology stresses, above all other relationships, the genetic relationships of living creatures. From a professional point of view, it is important to know that both spiders and flies have jointed appendages, but that the former have eight, the latter only six. Facts of this sort put spiders and flies in their proper anatomical and genealogical places with reference to one another, and also with reference to the rest of the living world.

Such facts, however, do not orient spiders and flies with reference to the dynamic business of living. They do not reveal the very different methods whereby the two make their bargains with a flinty world. The possession of jointed appendages does not constitute a bond of sympathy when the two meet, nor does the difference in the number of appendages determine the outcome of the meeting. However valuable such facts may be in disciplining the minds of freshmen and in labelling specimens in museums, they do not elucidate life as it is lived in the flesh. To know life only by such facts is like knowing football by the weight, position, and parentage of the players while remaining ignorant of the plays.

One is not likely to find the significant plays and rules of living in any of the conventional sciences of life. Life is far broader and less arbitrary than these sciences. Whole categories of data that have no meaning and no standing there are significant in a more realistic study of living.

Especially significant in such a study are certain basic patterns of existence, which do not lie within the limits of any orthodox department of biologic thought, and which cannot be explained by any orthodox theory of evolution. Theories of evolution, indeed, have practically neglected the similarities of creatures in the attempt to explain their differences. The most striking aspect of these patterns is the universality with which they apply to the motley multitudes that people the earth. Again and again have creatures of dissimilar origin been similarly shaped to fit them. They embrace, in fact, all living things, the active and the progressive no less than the stagnant and degenerate. They are deadly to the myth that Nature never repeats.

The trilobites that once ruled the earth, to be sure, are dead. They will almost certainly remain so to the end of time. The mole is not apt to regain its lost sight, the snake its legs, or the tapeworm its ambition. Nature has never been known to return a life, an organ, or an attitude, once she has taken it away. But in a general fashion she does repeat certain favorite designs for the bodies and behavior of her children.

She repeats because the world is not so variable nor are its inhabitants so various as they might seem from a specialized point of view. It is true that the compromises which creatures make with a shifting world and with one another are multiple and diverse beyond hope of complete enumeration and description. As long as men remain curious, the catalogue of examples will doubtless grow. But it has already grown large enough to show that it does not grow at random. It expands by departments, which are as rigid in form and limited in number as the items they contain are varied and abundant. It does so because these departments represent the only fundamentally different methods of living.

Whatever power may decide what kinds of individuals shall be born, environment decides, to a considerable extent, what kinds shall survive to maturity. Adjustment to the physical environment is life's first command. Unless this adjustment is successfully made, no felicity in the adjustment of a creature to his fellows can save him from destruction. Inasmuch as there are but few decidedly different types of physical environment, there are but few decidedly different designs for living.

Though in detail the earth has been changing these many aeons, and with it the creatures who have clung to its back, the sea, the land, and the air have always existed somewhere since geologic history began. There have always been the sunlit surface waters of the sea, where creatures might bask and drift at ease, the sombre abyss, where they might sink to a stagnant security, the turbulent shores, where they might find their weakness and their strength.

On land there have always been the dynamic rivers to develop the dynamic powers of flesh, and the placid lakes to foster its placidity. There have been the swamps for amphibious pursuits, the plains and deserts for running, the hills for walking and burrowing. In the air there have always been buoyancy for those who could use it to fly, and more recently trees for climbing and leaping. Conspicuously in some cases and inconspicuously in others, these places and ways of living have placed their peculiar brands on all who have ever come under their jurisdiction.

The sea, in the belief of many, was the earliest home of life.

Certainly by the testimony of the geologic record it has long been the home of a numerous and varied society. The reason is not far to seek. The sea is the most dependable medium of life, the safest place to live. Its temperature and gases are relatively constant. Its water is much like the blood of its inhabitants, and it never fails.

Even the simplest performances of life are difficult on land. The mere act of going from here to there is made hard by the lightness of the atmosphere. Suitable food for most land animals is too heavy to float in the air. It stolidly clings to the ground. Animals must move to their meals through their own exertions, or filch a ride.

Living is more idyllic in the sea. Because water is 814 times as heavy as air and almost as heavy as protoplasm, sea creatures are all but exempt from the drag of gravitation. A bit of gas or a drop of oil and they become as airy as angels. One-celled plants and animals in untold billions float near the surface of the sea, like motes in a shaft of light. They live with ease themselves, and they enable their larger neighbors to do likewise.

Jellyfishes, molluscs, crustaceans, and certain diminutive back-boned creatures have long abided in the sunlit paradise of the open ocean. Varied though they are in heritage, they have come through living alike to looking alike. They are uniformly unencumbered by heavy skeletons because buoyancy is the first requisite of their lives. They are characteristically shaped like parachutes rather than projectiles because they are moved by wind and current rather than by their own exertions. Their ineptitude as swimmers is offset by their ability to sink below the waves in time of storm and to rise when the storm subsides. Colorless as the water they inhabit, they represent a comparably colorless compromise between progress and stagnation.

Far from both the surface and the shore is the abyssal underworld of the sea. Live creatures have been caught in the dredges of the oceanographers at depths as great as twenty-six thousand feet. Representatives of every major group of organisms, excepting the green plants and the air-breathing animals, have been collected below the lowest limit of wave action and light. Of these the fishes are the most interesting because they show best the standardization imposed by the most unvarying environment in the world.

Like the other dwellers of the deep, they appear not to have originated there but to have migrated from shallower zones at comparatively recent epochs of geologic time. Though a few are quaintly fierce of face, most are frail and faded, flabby, slim, and small. A few are blind, but many have saucerlike eyes for gathering such light as may come their way, and phosphorescence for enhancing it. Most of them possess elaborate feelers for additional guidance through the endless night of their lives. Descended variously from sharks, eels, herring, cod, and pike, they have been uniformly shaped by the uniformity of their strange environment.

The morphologists of the laboratory are inclined to consider such resemblances skin-deep and unimportant. They deplore the easy inaccuracies of slack observation, which once made vegetables of sponges and corals merely because they are rooted to the ground, and which yet beget error in the establishment of genetic affiliations. But when the obviously dissimilar in blood are yet strikingly similar in body and behavior, the similarities may just possibly be as significant as the differences. It does not further the attempt to understand the mechanics of life to dismiss the similarities merely because it is fashionable to do so.

Some convergent resemblances, indeed, go very much deeper than the shallow externals of form and function. Only the amateur or the careless observer would mistake a swallow for a swift, but only a prejudiced or a blind one would deny a real resemblance in the "telescope eyes" of certain fishes and molluscs that live in the abyssal sea. Fishes and molluscs belong to totally different divisions of the animal kingdom, yet, in the deep-sea forms of both, the eyes project from the head like opera glasses. In both, the optical lens is large and far from the retina that receives the image, a marvellous adaptation for conserving the light of the depths.

The most remarkable aspect of this convergence is not that the same complex organs develop in widely different organisms, but that they also develop in different ways from different types of tissue. The eyes of the fishes originate in the brain and those of the molluscs in the skin. Those who seek evidence of a guiding intelligence in Nature should be glad to consider these facts. A series of happy Darwinian accidents might conceivably have led once to an organ as intricate as a telescope eye. That a quite different series of accidents should do it again is all but too much for the power of belief, rugged though it is.

While stagnation marks the creatures at the surface of the sea and degeneracy those at the bottom, no one condition would appear at first sight to characterize the hordes that live along the shore. They would seem to be as various as the moods of the region they haunt. Darting fishes and wriggling worms, barnacles clinging to the rocks and starfishes clambering over them, sea anemones that are rooted in the sand, crabs that run upon it, clams that burrow beneath it—these are but a few of the diversities of the shore. At first sight it would seem that the only uniformity to be found in this cradle of evolution is the uniformity of divergence.

On second sight, however, it may be seen that the variable strand is invariable in one regard. Each day it is alternately bared to the air and buried beneath the water. The creatures that cling or crawl or dig in the tide-swept zone must alternately avoid being dried up by the air and driven away by the water. Animals dissimilar in blood have repeatedly achieved this ability. By doing so in similar ways with the help of similar organs, they have come in not a few cases to resemble one another.

Seashores may be roughly classified as hard or soft. The inhabitants of rocky strands—seaweeds, limpets, barnacles, crabs, and a host of others—are universally hardened to withstand the pounding of the waves, and strengthened with organs of adhesion to resist the drag of the tides. Most creatures of sandy and muddy shores, on the other hand, either burrow or root themselves in the bottom. The clogging of their breathing mechanism is a daily threat. A great variety of molluscs, crustaceans, and other marine invertebrates have developed essentially the same sort of straining apparatus for protection against this menace.

The strongest animals that dwelt in the oceans during most of the periods of geologic history were those that were built for speed. Most of them came from the land, where speed is a common commandment. The fishes were the first to go down to the sea from the rivers of the land, but they were followed in succession by a great variety of reptiles, birds, and mammals. The same type if not the same degree of change took place in all. Their bodies were streamlined towards the shape of a cigar. Their necks grew shorter, their tails longer, and their limbs became paddles or fins. Such surface adornments as ears, hair, feathers, and armor, tended to be smoothed away. Three different times in the history of life, three different types of animals achieved perfection in marine locomotion: the shark, the ichthyosaur, and the porpoise. Though the first is a fish, the second a reptile, and the third a mammal, the three are so similar in form that a lay observer may fail to tell them apart.

The physical conditions of the lands above the shore are far more diversified and variable than those of the waters below it. Yet each of a number of conditions has repeatedly remained stable sufficiently long for the Procrustes of standardization to do its work. Even such comparatively evanescent environments as rivers, lakes, and swamps, have been known to stamp their inhabitants with their own peculiar marks.

All who would know the bounty of such places must meet one unvarying requirement. Salt is an indispensable ingredient of blood, and it is likely to seep out of vessels which are in intimate contact with fresh water. The first need of all fresh-water animals is the ability to maintain the composition of their blood despite fluctuations in the composition of their environment. Unable to meet this requirement, such animals as sharks and their relatives are rare in rivers and lakes. Many other animals of diverse origin, however, can turn the trick. Their ability to do so creates a true blood relationship which is wholly independent of ancestry.

Lean in salt, fresh waters are likewise lean in buoyancy. Their people as a result are uniformly smaller than the people of the denser sea. Because the bodies of water are also, for the most part, small the winds play upon them less boisterously than upon the sea. Lakes and rivers are relatively smooth, and abundantly coated with the membranous film which is a peculiar property of the surface of unruffled water. A diversity of lives is adjusted to this film in but a few fundamentally different ways. Various insects have practically the same equipment for skating through life on its upper side. Various snails and insect larvae have essentially uniform mechanisms for clinging and crawling on its under side. Many plants like the duckweed and the water lily live beneath the surface of the water and float their leaves in similar fashion on the film.

Freezing and evaporation are general hazards of living in fresh water against which Nature has provided a general type of protection. The life cycles of most fresh-water creatures include resting stages, which are much the same whether they take the form of seed, egg, or chrysalis. Wells, Huxley, and Wells, in "The Science of Life," cite a remarkable convergent adaptation of this sort. Certain unrelated fresh-water rotifers and crustaceans produce only females during summer. These multiply by virgin birth until autumn, when normal males and females make a belated appearance. Before winter brings its gift of death, these normal individuals produce a great many hard-skinned, cold-resisting eggs. Though fertilized in autumn, the eggs lie under the ice until the following spring, when they give rise to another troop of unsexed females.

This strange and complicated cycle is remarkable not only because it has arisen in species of different blood but because it has arisen in species whose ancestors resided in the sea. It demonstrates again how living needs are a stronger compulsion than dead traditions, and how a common problem may beget a truer kinship than a common inheritance.

The striking physical differences between standing and running fresh water are reflected in the physique of their inhabitants. The denizens of the former are characterized by indolence, which in certain cases is translated into convergent anatomical terms. The frog, the crocodile, and the hippopotamus, for example, are unrelated excepting in their love of the amenities of sluggish water and in their need for air. With time this need has ceased to be a bother. Lazy floaters for countless generations, all three have grown knobs for lifting their nostrils to the air while the rest of their bodies remains coolly and safely in the water.

Streams, on the other hand, impart their energy to their inhabitants. The shiftless floaters of sea and lake are absent there. Fast water moulds the flesh along sterner lines. Like all other environments, it promotes certain favorite body styles among its devotees. It flattens and smooths many backboneless animals to a uniform pattern of resistance, and it provides them with the same sort of hooks and suckers for clinging to the rocks. It uniformly streamlines and muscles its backboned inhabitants for fighting the current more aggressively.

Creatures of the higher land, like creatures elsewhere, have always been most uniformly and conspicuously marked by the most widespread and persistent conditions. Viewed against the background of all the lands during all of their known history, the most significant condition in this connection is dearth of moisture. The annual plants of the desert, unlike ancestors and relatives of moister realms, spend most of their lives underground in seeds. They aestivate through heat in much the same way that certain animals hibernate through cold. Only during the few wet weeks of spring do they show their faces in bloom. The perennials, too, have their crowded hour of glorious life in spring. Though they do not wither away in summer with the annuals, their real life retires into underground bulbs and fleshy roots when the vernal holiday is over.

More plants than one might suspect, however, stand sturdily enough in the dry desert air throughout the year. Cactus, agave, yucca, mesquite, smoke tree, tamarisk, and many other shrubs and trees have learned to live and even to thrive in the earth's least friendly places. Though varied in origin they are alike in one regard. All have mechanisms for conserving the precious moisture which their roots have been able to suck from the stony ground.

These mechanisms vary in detail, but they are similar in fundamentals. The central principle in all is the reduction of surfaces from which water might be lost by evaporation. The result is that all desert shrubs and trees have small leaves or no leaves at all, the normal work of leaves being transferred to the less extensive surfaces of trunks and stems. Nearly all have spines or thorns, an added safeguard for hoarded moisture in a world of thirsty animals.

Desert climates are no more friendly to animals than to plants. Throughout geologic history they have repeatedly come to wither the food and waste the water on which the lives of animals depend. Only those animals that could swiftly make the round of the oases could possibly survive. Creatures as biologically diverse as lizards and dogs, and as geologically distant from one another as dinosaurs and horses, have met the challenge of the desert in the only way it might possibly be met with success.

Their bodies were moulded to reduce friction with the medium through which they moved. Legs grew longer, toes grew shorter and tended with time to disappear. Many lizards, dinosaurs, rodents, and the kangaroo, took to running on their hind limbs. In all of them the neck and the fore limbs shortened, the tail lengthened to provide counterpoise. Like automobiles, they were similarly styled for similar performance regardless of make. Like automobiles, those that failed to conform failed also to survive.

Animals that bury themselves in the earth are as surely shaped by the exigencies of their rôles as are those that run on its surface. Whether snake, lizard, swallow, owl, gopher, badger, rat, or mole, they grow to a single pattern. That pattern requires the degeneration of eyes, ears, and tails, which are superfluous underground. It requires the development of strongly clawed fore limbs, sharp incisor teeth, and tapered snouts, which are needed there. Similarly in caverns, which are the terrestrial counterpart of the abyssal sea, animals of varied ancestry grow blind, thin, and pale in the manner of their fellow degenerates of the deep.

Yet another pattern applies to those who climb. Their chests, hips, and shoulders are strengthened for the endless struggle with gravitation, their hands and feet develop prehensile hooks for clinging to the rocks and trees, their ribs are shaped to support the viscera in any outlandish position. Many different creatures have at various times been modelled in this fashion for a life of acrobatics; certain lizards, sloths, and monkeys with considerable success. More than thirty times in the history of the backboned animals alone have climbers attempted to fly. The same old story of convergence may be told of the three that succeeded. Though wholly unrelated in blood, the pterosaur, the bird, and the bat all developed the wings, rudder, keel, and hollow air-filled bones which are the indispensable mechanisms of flight.

So, endlessly, may examples of the basic patterns of successful living be recorded. The difficulty is not to illustrate them but to explain them.

Most theories of evolution deal with these patterns by the simple expedient of neglecting them. They are concerned primarily with the origin of species, with the diversities rather than the similarities in the living world. As late as the sixth edition of "The Origin of Species," Darwin believed that blood relationship is the major cause of close similarities among plants and animals. To-day, however, we know that resemblances which have no basis in blood are common; that in many cases they involve the most essential organs of the creatures that exhibit them.

In so far as Darwin was aware of such resemblances he attempted to cram them into the frame of his natural selection hypothesis. "I am inclined to think," he wrote in the sixth edition, "that as two men have sometimes independently of one another hit on the same invention, so . . . it appears that natural selection, working for the good of each being, and taking advantage of all favorable variations has produced similar organs, as far as function is concerned." Most of Darwin's successors in the science of biology have been followers with regard to this particular tenet of his belief.

A few, however, have demurred. Inasmuch as every useful variation, according to the doctrine of natural selection, arises by chance from an infinity of possible variations, it is incredible to these skeptics that the same variation should arise in two species of totally different ancestry. To assume that coincidences of this sort should occur repeatedly seems to them absurd.

Though they may be willing to admit that variation and selection played a part in such an evolutionary sequence as that which led from Eohippus to the horse, they doubt that these factors alone created the horse. It may be true that an immortal monkey pounding a typewriter might ultimately produce all the books in the British Museum. Some of these books, indeed, would seem to have been written in that fashion, yet it is a known fact that not one of them actually was. An average horse is a more subtle, intricate, and intelligent fabrication than an average book. It may have been made by the monkey of random variation on the typewriter of mechanical selection, but the skeptic is inclined to suspect that both the monkey and the typewriter had some help.

One need not be a mathematician to sense the improbability that such a long and logical process should have been only a succession of fortuitous events. One need not be a mathematician to sense the far greater improbability that many grazing contemporaries of the horse should have evolved through almost precisely the same succession of fortuitous events. The automobile was not the result of a series of lucky accidents, nor are the similarities between the different makes of automobile the accidental result of a number of such series of accidents. It is hard to believe that the horse and the other grazing mammals were any more accidental.

The skeptics, in short, may suspect the presence of forces in Nature which cannot be proved in the laboratory to exist. They may even open their minds to the teleological heresies of the vitalists. Unfortunately, these heresies are no more convincing than the orthodox assumptions of the mechanists. Aristotle's "internal perfecting tendency," Schopenhauer's "will," Driesch's "entelechy," Bergson's "*élan vital*," and a host of other conceptions of a vital force which transcends the known limits of physical and chemical laws, are all unacceptable to the skeptical mind. The assumption of such a force is not explanation but belief, and the belief has been impotent in the scientific attack upon the mysteries of creation.

Where, then, may the scientific skeptic go for light? How may the curious layman who desires to accept the universe know what manner of universe to accept? The answer is all too simple. There is no certain light, no unequivocal universe. There is only the hope that somewhere in the wilderness between the doctrines of chance and design a solution to the enigma of life may someday be discovered.

Pending that discovery there remains the marvellous fitness of creatures for the lives they lead. It is the most striking aspect of vital phenomena. To be sure, there are strange deviations from the general rule, where death rather than life would seem to be the goal of existence. There are moths that destroy themselves in fire and females that devour their young. But these impulses towards death are exceptional. The adaptations of most creatures are for the improvement and prolongation of their lives.

Because adaptation is predominantly beneficial even when it leads to stagnation and degeneracy, because it cleaves to certain definite and stable patterns of success, life may be truly called purposive. Purposive adaptation of structure and behavior is neither sophistry nor myth, but an easily apparent property of living creatures. It is as much a property of flesh as irritability and contractility, as significant in the adjustments of plants and animals as the capacity to eat and to reproduce. It is as much a force as magnetism, electricity, and gravitation—and probably as much a law.

No one can formulate that law in terms of human purpose. No one, indeed, can state it precisely in any terms. But this is no proof that the law does not exist. The nearly universal spectacle of fitness argues that it must exist. It argues that the doctrine of chance, despite its gain in intellectual respectability since Empedocles first gave it to the world, is yet not the complete and final answer to the riddle of creation.

The tendency to fitness, whatever its motivation, is the rock on which the edifice of life has been built. However strong the winds of chance may blow, the rock remains. Men in the swirl of their lives may feel that the winds blow strong indeed, but the rock is there for men no less than for mice. The successful ones will find it and hold fast.

THE HAPPY VALLEY

By ALVIN JOHNSON

WHERE the happy valley lies we cannot yet know. Somewhere on one of our hundreds of rivers, lovelier than their beautiful names— Merrimac, Connecticut, Delaware, Susquehanna, Tennessee, Colorado, Sacramento, Willamette, Niobrara, Floyd, Wind River. Or on one of the innumerable lesser streams; glittering brooks, hurrying down from the heights to join in a powerful river branch winding through alluvial plains rich with field or meadow. Or in the very middle of the wide coastal plain, where great islands of rich land loom out of the sandy barrens; or on the red soil of the foothills, looking towards a range of mountains crowned with shining rocks, or with ice playing eternally with the colors hidden in the sunlight. It does not matter much where, in our infinity of beautiful lands, the happy valley shall first become a reality. The acids of a disorderly industrialism have dissolved our hopes into a solution saturated with yearning. We need nothing more than a catalyst, and one brilliant crystal will shape itself and then another. Give us one happy valley, and soon no one will need to range far to find another.

If I were but a geographer—not one of these mechanized moderns who entangle you in a maze of contours, like a fly in a dusty cobweb, deserted by summer and even by the spider himself—but a geographer of the fine old school of chart makers, with their arrows indicating the compass, their spyglass hills and deep grassed savannas, their black crosses subscribed *Treasure buried here*—were I but such a geographer, I would draw you a map that would of itself awaken you out of the inertia that blocks the road to the happy valley. But let us poor amateurs join our imaginations and make a map of a sort, with apologies to the artists that have gone before.

Shall it actually be a valley? Agreed. We shall thrust from us, with regret, the picturesque upper reaches among the wooded mountains, for what we must have above all else is land, good land, free from stone and hardpan, with soil that is rich, or not hard to enrich, soil that is easy to work and pleasant to the hand of man. On either side, as you look down the valley, a range of hills, crowned with low trees crouching against the winds. The steeper slopes and jutting spurs are wooded; below the woods are upland pastures, dotted with sheep of the community flock. Still lower the fields descend softly to the river and rise again beyond, to the upland pastures on the other side. From pasture line to pasture line the distance is about two miles; from the upper end of our map to the lower, along the river, the distance is three miles. Six square miles of fields, with perhaps an equal space of grassy and wooded upland.

At once I am charged with playing unfairly with our imaginations. We were to create our valley; but what is this but a bald description of a valley everyone of us has seen from the Pullman window, or has driven through by motor car? Wait. The worth of the old maps we loved lay in the cross, with the words *Treasure buried here.* The treasure in our valley is happiness. And it is to be found in the cottages set thickly among the green fields— three hundred of them, in this narrow realm. It is to be found in the central village, with a community building which serves as a schoolhouse for the children by day, for the adults in the evening, which provides a hall for town meetings, for plays, for music and the dance. There will be, too, a community store, storage warehouse, creamery, mill, machine shop, small factories equipped for spinning and weaving wool, for making furniture, pottery.

If I were a poet I could make you see and feel this hidden treasure of life in the happy valley: the sunrise and sunset drawn back into the circle of daily experience; the clear black shadows of the morning lying immensely long over the sparkling green; the thrill of early spring and the bursting buds and the returning birds calling to each other from tree to tree; the fertile exultation of May when all nature is conceiving; the soil pouring forth its excellent bounties; the hush of autumn and the distant music of the woodsman's axe; the setting in of winter and the friendly clustering of man and beast in the warm shelter of house and barn. Or I could evoke for you the white light of the summer moon: two anxious households, for Genevieve and Robert have not come home, though the play was over an hour ago; and down by the rivulet where the moonlight trembles in the ripples, two graceful figures are trembling with new emotions, hitherto unknown in the world. No more of that. I am an economist held to answer the question, Will it pay? Yet one word more. Myself when young did live in the open country, in a happy valley in miniature. The ineffable glamour of the fields and sky was my own possession, and I treasured it. Nevertheless, I fled from the country, because at that time commercialism was turning the happy valleys of the West into corn-and-hog wallows. Only the landscape remained: the beautiful slave of slaves.

To the economics of the problem. There are now available an immense number of inventions that can be applied to free our happy valley from the grinding toil that once afflicted life on the farm. For close settlement electric power may be had at not too high a cost, and this means the solution of the crucial problem of farm life—an abundant supply of flowing water. Just as the pioneers built first of all the hearth and chimney, and then built one room, two rooms or more, around it, so in our happy valley we shall provide first equipment for cold and hot water, and then as many rooms as we need and can afford. Electric power also will grind our grain, and we shall eat meal fresh from the clean ear, full of vital force, instead of the commercial powders guaranteed not to sustain even insect life. With the marvellous versatile tractor, we shall turn our soil as often as we like, stir it as deeply as appears wise, pulverize the surface against drought, suppress the weeds as we never were able to do with traction made of horseflesh and pain. With the truck, markets are open to us, far and wide. Agricultural science shows us how best to fertilize the soil; it produces an endless succession of improved varieties of the familiar plants, and assembles new plants from the ends of the earth.

Thus we have the technical basis for a rural community in which intensive agriculture may be practised without the infinite

hand labor of the older intensive cultures. Machinery will do
away with the heavy drudgery. For the rest, what is most needed
is mind: close and accurate observation, eagerness for experiment, promptness to necessary action, ability to transform the
gifts of nature into the values of human life. But by these speci-
fications I appear to have defeated the hope of a happy valley.
For where shall we find settlers with mental qualifications like
these? Not among the dejected tenantry of our commercialized
countryside; not among the exhausted owners of stony hillside
farms; not among the successful possessors of broad fields and
fat feeding troughs. Where then?

We shall not look for any large proportion of our settlers
among the present farming population. They have their bread,
and a roof over their heads. Heavily victimized as they have
been by our economic system, they know, nevertheless, that life
holds a place for them, and that it is possible for prosperity to
return to them, through politics or chance. We shall look for our
settlers among the dwellers in our cities, and not in the slums,
either, but in the better quarters. It is there where you find care
at its grimmest.

One of our greatest universities reports 480 of its Ph.D.'s now
in the ranks of the unemployed, or at best holding temporary
jobs that merely afford a precarious minimum of subsistence.
From all the universities there must be 5,000 Ph.D.'s in a similar
condition, not to mention the thousands who are indeed attached
to the universities, but are without hope of advancement. There
are even greater numbers of doctors, lawyers, engineers, architects, writers who have no hope whatever of arriving. Add the
college graduates who have been unable to resolve themselves
upon any vocation, but are hunting vainly for jobs, and we have
an enormous army of despair. Nor are these the unfit or inferior.
In their number there is a large proportion of the finest men
and women America produces, men and women who would
make their mark if they but had a chance. But in our society, as it
is organized to-day, a chance comes not by merit alone, but by
chance. To many of these people it will never come where they
now are; and they know it.

For the army of unemployed intellectuals is no mere problem

of depression that may be expected to solve itself with the return of prosperity. Our educational machine is gauged to turn out more Ph.D.'s, doctors, lawyers, engineers, teachers, than society can use. It must be so gauged, for the impetus towards higher academic and professional education is still gathering speed among the masses of the population. Like every other social force, this impetus does not check itself when it has attained to the theoretical optimum, but plunges on, even gaining in strength when the optimum has been overpassed. Besides, it is doubtful whether we should check it, if we could. We need good doctors, lawyers, teachers, and how shall we get them except through selection from among superfluous numbers? But alas, selection implies rejection, and the rejected are human beings, bred upon hopes, trained with much love and sacrifice, often more deserving, from any human point of view, than the accepted. Indeed, our process of selection is so arbitrary, so shot through with irrelevancies, that there will often be found among the rejected the very cream of the human life.

Granting, however, that the selection proceeds with automatic correctness and that the man best fitted is set in the way of becoming a successful lawyer, doctor, professor, it remains true that society cannot afford to waste the valuable qualities in the rest. When I was a boy I knew a farmer who had come to the country beaten in his professional ambitions. All his family's fortune had gone to his training for surgery; but when he encountered the blood and agony of the operating room his nerve broke and he fled, crippled in spirit, to a pioneer homestead. When he came to the land, he could not distinguish a field of ripe wheat from a field of barley. He did not know what corn looks like when it comes up, nor did he know a spavined horse from one with heaves. Many an amusing tale of his early blunders lingered in the community; many a good story of the shocking abuse of his good faith by his rustic neighbors. But by the time when I was old enough to judge his merit, he had the most magnificent farm in the whole country. He had learned how to defeat drought by tillage and had taught the art to his neighbors. By selection of seed and proper cultivation, he had made each of his acres grow the crops of two. He built up a herd of thoroughbred cattle which has improved the art of cattle-breeding throughout the prairie States. Though an incurable stutterer, he entered county politics as kingmaker, threw out a corrupt political ring, and set up an efficient administration of honest men. While he lived, there was no room in county office for a scoundrel. He was a great man, though he never suspected it. God rest his soul. To-day a man like that would be thrown on the rubbish heap.

Can we stand by and see such a hideous waste of human values? We certainly would not, except for the fear of encountering financial impracticabilities. To acquire the six square miles of good land, with the appurtenant uplands, and to set up three hundred cottages would cost a million dollars. Another half million would be required to supply all the holdings with the necessary stock and equipment, to erect schoolhouse and community centre, and the minimum of factory and mill structures. Immediately one asks, why not try the enterprise on a smaller scale? Why not begin with the simplest possible shacks to live in and secondhand farm equipment? Why not leave out the community centre, until enough money is accumulated by the settlers to finance it?

It is a sound principle of practical action that nothing should ever be undertaken unless with sufficient force to put it through. Do not shoot a bear with birdshot. Do not strike a king unless you kill him. Our settlers could begin in shacks, but half of them would leave within six weeks. They must have good water and plumbing, else they would break their hearts over the minor inconveniences of living. They must have good machinery, good livestock, good seed, fertilizer, or they are beaten at the start. There must be about three hundred of them. That is the number that can be settled within walking distance of the community centre: hence we do not want more. We do not want less, because with less we should not have adequate power to draw in the free services of the Department of Agriculture, the agricultural colleges, the architects and engineers. We should not have power enough to interest manufacturers in designing an economical set-up for the all-important water supply, to interest business men in finding us the best markets. Above all, we need a community large enough to have a fair representation of all sorts of abilities, technical, business, educational, literary, artistic, that it may be not a surrender but a victory to join it.

We must have a million and a half, more or less—about the cost of an apartment building housing three hundred families, deep in grim care. It is about the capital required to endow ten professorships. Wait! Can't we have our happy valley and the professorships, too? Our million and a half would be invested as safely and productively as the majority of university investments. Why should not five or ten of our great universities transfer some small part of their endowments to this use, and for the first time in their existence, launch real university extension? Were I but an orator, equipped with so obvious, so cogent a plan, no college president could resist my plea. But I am a plain economist and can only hope that some one of my readers, possessed of a silver tongue, will come to my aid and supply the necessary eloquence, for lack of which, and for no other reason, our happy valley may remain, after all, only a dream.

Finance presents no insuperable problem. The real difficulty, our university administrator would say, lies elsewhere. Ours is a lily pure tower of the liberal arts; our Ph.D.'s are fit to teach Sanskrit, or Greek epigraphy, or higher mathematics, but fit for nothing else. These men want jobs, but the world has no jobs for them, and there you are. The country? Why, they do not know a cabbage plant from a mustard weed. But the whole art of intensive cultivation can be learned with less effort than a single variant Sanskrit dialect. One needs initial instruction, but our happy valley would make provision for that. After an initial period three hundred intelligent experimenters would soon have a volume of technical skill that any agricultural college would envy.

Whether the plan would work or not would indeed depend on the selection of settlers. Ex-farm boys and girls, you say. Not necessarily. It is better that the prospective settler should know a food plant from a weed, but this is something he could soon learn. It is better that he should be physically robust, but man acquires good muscles with incredible speed, if he sets about it. The real qualifications are of another nature.

First of all, our settler must have, or be capable of acquiring, the right attitude towards a cow. He must regard her, not as a milk machine or a bore, but as a friend whose timid advances are to be welcomed and whose simple wants it is pleasant to gratify. For without a cow—and each holding should have two—there is no security against temporary lapses in income. Any family can live on milk for months, and be in better condition for it. The cows will force the farmer to watch every bit of ground, and when it is yielding nothing else he will make it yield pasture or hay. This is the first secret of good tillage—never let any land lie idle. Most important of all, the cows will make a man stay at home. They must be milked morning and night, and hence they rule out the long aimless expeditions that weaken a man's purpose and weed out his purse.

Second, our settler must have, or be capable of acquiring, philosophy. He must realize that in the eyes of God beet roots are quite as important as Sanskrit roots; and that it is a thrilling thing to carry forward the work of the god-like paleolithic men and women, who did not despair when they found that celery and parsnips and carrots were poisonous, but set about breeding the poison out, who were not discouraged when the kernels dropped from the wheatear when one touched it and were lost in the dust. They bred an ear that patiently awaited the flail. We have fairly well-bred plants now, yet there is plenty of work for the devotees of Demeter and Bacchus and Pan. There is something that any man can grow more beautifully than it was ever grown before, if he but has the true religion of the rural gods in his blood.

Third, he must have a wife, or acquire one. The unwed man may thrive tolerably in Wall Street or in a den of outlaws, but in the country he will almost inevitably go to seed. There is no real thrift in the flowers or fruits of the seasons unless they are viewed by at least two pairs of eyes. There is no future in a bachelor's establishment. Who can think of him as planting trees or laying out a vineyard? With what spirit can he be expected to put away in the cellar, year after year, the woodsy flavored new wine, that when ripe will bring the faculty of his alma mater for a joyous visit?

Fourth, she must be the right kind of wife. She, too, must have philosophy, but this is a less difficult qualification for women, since they are not so likely to have cobwebs in their eyes. Both wife and husband must be free from the ghastly disease that has wasted a good part of American life—the sense of gentility. No wife can be anything but a disaster to our community unless she is willing and eager to put on overalls and learn every outdoor operation that her husband engages in, nor can she be worth much unless she compels her husband to put on an apron and learn to perform well every indoor operation. True, the sex division of labor does prevail in most of our rural territory, but that is a major cause of our farm problem. The indoor wife, preparing and eating outdoor food, becomes a semi-invalid and throws a pall over life from which there is no escape but by drink or money-making. Down to the close of the pioneer period the ruling escape was drink, and the country society survived somehow. Since then the graver vice has become firmly rooted, and country society is gone.

Fifth, there must be children, or hope of children, or adopted children. For what man can look out upon the burst of spring, the young shoots starting from the soil, buds breaking, birds nesting, all the world yearning towards the future, if the coming time is for him merely a time of declining years, dimming eyesight, stiffening limbs, and the final gray wind that obliterates the universe? To what end the community swimming pool, the dance floor on the hillcrest, where the folk dance will celebrate the full moon? To what end the most marvellous opportunity for a progressive school, where all the talents of the whole community will be pooled to teach, for the joy of teaching, children fresh from field and garden, sharers in the enterprise and knowledge of their households, not dear little nurse-bred cares that know so little of their parents' work that they cannot even do it over into childish play and day-dreams?

As we think it over, we shall be forced to the conclusion that this is the most important qualification of all. Something can be done even with a pedantic husband who feels that it is a degradation to pass from the condition of a learned proletarian into a blooming garden where God himself walks in the cool of the evening. Something can be done with the gentility-crippled wife who imagines that it is somewhat humiliating to occupy herself with the flow of life under the open sky, or even with the exchanging of smiles with her own baby at her breast. In a child's world such as this happy valley will be, even these unlucky defectives may be brought back into a fair semblance of health. In my time I have seen persons who at first sight appeared to be wholly irredeemable artificial fools transformed into live and beautiful women by the benignant influence of children and gardens.

But this you will say is a play world. To be sure: for that is what the real world was meant to be, a place where play and work merge unconsciously and the creative spirit of the one penetrates deeply into the other. Yes; but how can such a world compete with the stark reality of the great commercialized farm, with its huge acreage, its vast machinery for the sowing and harvest? You can't compete with an elephant in eating salad, but you still eat salad. Our community will at least supply itself, securely and abundantly, with its own requirements, and thus go a long way towards the solution of the problem. Beyond that it simply can't help devising innumerable quality products in which it can outclass any mechanized farm enterprise. Three hundred experimenters, or better, counting the wives, six hundred, or better still, counting the children who early evolve new ideas and techniques—is it not preposterous to suppose that they will approach the market only with wheat and corn and hogs?

What our community will do, first of all, is to assure itself of a year's food supply and a reserve for a less promising year. The most important part of the supply will be provided individually by the abundant flow of milk. Corn and wheat will be stored for grinding in the community mill; fruits and vegetables will be kept in community cold storage or canned; wine and cider will be stored individually—to allow for differences of moral opinion. The community as a whole will grow its own meat supply, and wool from the upland pastures. It will know how to spin and weave, and if worse comes to worst, outside economic society can go to the Devil, if it must.

But not one of these small farms would occupy the whole

time of the holder alone, still less the whole time of the holder and his wife, working side by side. In sowing time they would work from dawn to dusk, also at harvest time, but on the average, the utopian four hours would suffice. What in the world would these people do with the rest of their time? Many of them, remember, have scholarly or artistic ambitions. Our Sanskrit friend, for example—why could he not write to one of the numerous scholars in the Indian universities and have copies made for him of parts of that amazing dramatic literature that has never yet been accessible to a Western eye? Our essayist who has been eaten up by overhead in the city and has had to slave out an existence by hasty book reviewing—why should he not read and think, write and polish and recast and rethink, under the flowering lilacs? Our artist can still paint, with a hand not much damaged by the strength it wins from the field. At least he will not be reduced into an abhorrent mode that for the present moment commands the markets. Our scientist may have to change his objective, but all the world is material for a scientist if he is capable of invention, without which no scientist is more than a jailyard inmate, breaking the big rocks of fact into rubble of small facts for which there is scarcely any use in the modern world.

The conditions of our happy valley are quite compatible with an immense amount of artistic and intellectual activity. Our artists and poets and scientists will not lack a sympathetic and stimulating society. It will be the better society because no one will be under the pressure for immediate results. No one will rhyme away desperately in the hope that the rhymes may turn into bread and butter and cheese.

I do not deny that this scheme of life is a compromise. Were I now setting out in life I would, like Vergil, offer my whole services to the sweet Muses. But I would say with Vergil, if the Muses found that the blood flowed too coldly around my heart for this service, I would transfer my allegiance to the rustic gods and live inglorious but happy where each season brought me of its own free will the good fruits of life. Yet being a modern instead of a downright Roman I would cheat a bit! I would trust that the gods of the countryside would warm up my blood and fit me, after all, for the service of the Muses, as supernumerary at least, if not as a great and mighty pillar of the legion.

IMAGINATIVE LITERATURE

DISILLUSION

By THOMAS MANN

I CONFESS that the remarks of the singular gentleman I met in Venice that evening thoroughly mystified me, and I fear I shall not be able, even now, to repeat them so that they will affect others as they did me at the time. Perhaps the effect of his words was due merely to this amazing frankness, coming from a total stranger.

It is now about two months since that autumn morning when the stranger first attracted my attention in the Piazza San Marco. Only a few people were moving about in the wide square. But the banners were fluttering in the light sea breeze before the gorgeous, wonderful building, whose splendid and fantastic contours with their ornament of gold stood out with enchanting clearness against the delicate, light blue sky. In front of the main portal, a great flock of doves had gathered around a young girl who was scattering corn for them, while more and more kept flying down from all sides—a vision of incomparably bright and radiant beauty.

It was then that I came upon the stranger, and now, as I write, I still see him before me with extraordinary distinctness. He was rather below middle height and bent forward as he walked quickly along, clasping his stick behind him with both hands. He had on a stiff black hat, a light summer overcoat, and dark striped trousers. For some reason I took him to be an Englishman. He might have been anywhere from thirty to fifty years old. His face, with its rather thick nose and weary gray eyes, was clean shaven, and a baffling and somewhat foolish smile played continually around his mouth. From time to time he would raise his eyebrows and glance searchingly around, then look down at the ground again, mumble a few words to himself, shake his head, and smile. He kept on walking back and forth across the square.

After that I saw him daily, for he seemed to have nothing to do but pace up and down the piazza, from thirty to fifty times every morning and afternoon, in good weather and bad—always alone and always behaving in the same odd manner.

On the evening I have especially in mind there had been a military band concert. I was sitting at one of the Café Florian's little tables set far out in the square. At the end of the concert, when the crowd, which had been surging about in dense currents, began to scatter, the stranger, smiling as absent-mindedly as ever, sat down at one of the unoccupied tables beside me.

Time passed, it grew more and more quiet around me, and soon all the other tables far and near were empty. Now and then someone would go sauntering by. A majestic peace settled down upon the square; stars spread over the sky, and poised above the gloriously theatrical façade of St. Mark's a half-moon hung.

I was reading my newspaper with my back to my neighbor and was on the point of leaving him there alone when I was forced to turn towards him; for though up to that moment I hadn't heard from him the slightest sound, or even movement, now he suddenly began to speak to me.

"Is this your first visit to Venice?" he asked in bad French; and after I had struggled to reply in English, he took up the conversation again in German, without any foreign accent. His voice was low and hoarse, and he tried to clear his throat frequently by a little cough.

"You're seeing all this for the first time? Does it come up to your expectations?—Does it, perhaps, even exceed them?—You didn't imagine it would be more beautiful?—That's the truth?—You're not saying this merely to appear happy and enviable? Ah, really?"

He leaned back and regarded me with a strange expression, while he blinked his eyes rapidly.

The pause that followed lasted a long time. Not knowing how to continue this strange conversation, I was on the point of rising again when he leaned forward abruptly.

"Do you know, sir, what disillusion is?" he asked in a low, intense tone, as he clasped his stick firmly with both hands. "I don't mean failure and disappointment in little things or in single instances, but that great, general disillusion, the disillusion that all things, that all life brings to us? Clearly, you don't know it. But I have gone about under it from my youth, and it has made me lonely, unhappy, and a bit queer. I don't deny it.

"How could you understand what I mean without further explanation? But you will understand, perhaps, if you'll be good enough to listen to me a few minutes? For if it can be said at all, it can be said quickly.—

"I should tell you that I grew up in a very small town in the house of a clergyman, within whose excessively pure walls an air of old-fashioned, pathetic, scholarly optimism prevailed. One breathed there the peculiar atmosphere that recalls pulpit rhetoric—all those fine words about good and evil, about the beautiful and the ugly, that I hate so bitterly, because they, perhaps, are to blame, they alone, for my sorrows.

"Life was made up for me wholly of fine words, for I knew nothing about it but the monstrous, vague presentiments that these words aroused in me. Of people I expected either the divincly good or the diabolically evil; of life I expected the enchantingly beautiful or horrible, and I was filled with a great longing for all this—a deep, anxious longing for some spacious reality, for experience, of whatever sort, for happiness that should be intoxicatingly glorious and for ineffably, unimaginably terrible grief.

"I remember, sir, with melancholy distinctness the first great disappointment of my life, and I beg you to note that it did not consist merely in the dashing of a high hope but in the coming of a disaster. I was still almost a child when a fire broke out one night in my father's house. It had gained headway so quietly and so treacherously that one whole little storey was on fire, up to the very door of my bedroom; and the stairway, too, was about to go up in flames. I was the first to discover it, and I know that I rushed through the house shouting again and again: 'Now we're on fire! Now we're on fire!' I recall these words with the greatest distinctness, and I understand the feelings that prompted them, though I was probably scarcely conscious of them at the time. This, I felt, is a conflagration; now I'm experiencing it! Isn't it worse than this? Is this all there is to it?—

"Yet it was not a trifle, heaven knows. The whole house burned down, and we were saved with difficulty from the utmost peril. I myself suffered very severe injuries. It would be wrong, too, to say that it was just my fancy that had run ahead of the events and had painted the destruction of our house by fire as something more terrible. But I had always had a vague presentiment, a shadowy conception of something far more dreadful, and, compared with it, the reality seemed flat. This conflagration was my first great experience; a fearful hope was disappointed by it.

"You need not be afraid that I'm going to keep on recounting my disappointments to you, one by one. It is enough to say that with disastrous eagerness I fed my magnificent expectations of life on a thousand books, on the works of great writers. Oh, how I have learned to hate them—these poets who write their fine words on every wall, who would paint them on the roof of heaven with a brush dipped in Vesuvian fire—while I cannot but feel that every fine word is a mockery or a lie!

"Ecstatic poets have wailed to me that language is poor, alas, so poor! But no, sir, it is quite the contrary! Language, it seems to me, is rich, extravagantly rich compared with the meanness and limitation of life. Even pain has its limits—physical pain, in unconsciousness; spiritual pain, in apathy. And it is not otherwise with happiness! But the human need for communicating joy and sorrow has invented sounds that transcend these limits, by lying.

"Is all this because I am as I am? Am I different from others in feeling so? Am I the only one on whom the effect of certain words is so thrilling that they awaken in me anticipations of experiences that do not exist at all?

"I started out in this famous life of ours full of a passionate desire for one experience, if only one, that would come up to my great anticipations. But, God help me, it has never been granted! I have roamed about the world visiting the most celebrated places on earth, standing before works of art before which mankind dances—which it honors with its finest words. I have stood before each of them and said to myself: 'Yes, it is beautiful. And yet—is it no more beautiful?—Is this all?'

"I have no sense of actuality; perhaps that tells the whole story. Once I was somewhere in the mountains, standing beside a narrow, deep ravine. The steep cliffs were bare and perpendicular, and below, the water rushed along over boulders. I looked down and thought: What if I plunged down now? But I had come to know enough about myself to reply: If this were to happen, I should say to myself as I fell, 'Now you're plunging down, now it's happening! But what does it really amount to?'

"Will you credit me with having seen enough of life to be allowed a word further on the subject? Years ago I loved a girl—a delicate, charming creature. I should have liked to take her by the hand and lead her away under my protection; but she did not love me. That was not strange, and another became her protector. Could there be a more torturing experience? Is there anything more painful in life than that sharp misery cruelly mingled with voluptuousness? I have lain awake over it many a night with my eyes open—and sadder, more tormenting than anything else about it was always the thought: This is my great sorrow! Now I'm experiencing it! But what does it really amount to?

"Need I tell you about my happiness? For I have experienced happiness, too, and happiness, too, has disappointed me.—I won't go into this, for all I could give you would be clumsy examples. They wouldn't make it clear to you that it is life in general, the whole of life in its mediocre, uninteresting, dull course, that has brought me disillusion, disillusion, disillusion.

"What is man, so lauded as a demigod? young Werther writes somewhere in 'The Sorrows of Werther.' Do his powers not fail him just when he needs them most? When he soars aloft in joy or sinks down in sorrow, is he not always stopped and called back again to dull, cold consciousness at the very moment when he longs to lose himself in the fulness of the infinite?

"I often think of the day when I saw the ocean for the first time. The ocean is mighty, the ocean is wide; and my glance roved far out from the shore, in search of freedom. But there was the horizon. Why must I have a horizon? I expected the infinite of life.

"Perhaps my horizon is narrower than other people's! I've said before that I have no sense of actuality—or is it, perhaps, that I have too much sense of it? Do I come to the end of my powers too soon? Have I done with things too quickly? Do I know happiness and grief only in their lowest gradations, only in a rarefied form?

"I do not believe it; and I do not believe what people say, I believe those least who, as they come face to face with life, chime in with the fine words of the writers—it is all cowardice and sham! Have you noticed, by the way, that there are people so vain and so greedy for the respect and the secret envy of others that they pretend they have experienced only the fine words of happiness—and not those of sorrow?

"It has grown very dark—and you're scarcely listening to me; so I will confess to myself, again to-day, that I, too, once tried to lie, as other people do—tried to make myself appear happy before myself and others. But it was many years ago that this particular vanity collapsed, and I have become lonely, unhappy, and a bit queer. I don't deny it.

"Now it is my favorite occupation to watch the starry heavens at night, for that is the best way of looking away from the earth and from life, isn't it? And perhaps I may be pardoned for trying at least in this way to preserve my anticipations? To dream of a life free from limitations, in which reality will rise to my great anticipations without the torturing residue of disillusion? Of a life in which there will no longer be a horizon?

"So I dream of this, and I wait for death. Oh, I know death so well already, Death, the ultimate disillusion! This is Death, I shall say to myself at the last moment. Now I'm experiencing it!—And what does it really amount to?

"But it has grown cold in the square, sir. I'm capable of feeling that, at any rate, you see!—I must go now. Good-bye."

COUNTRY FULL OF SWEDES

By ERSKINE CALDWELL

THERE I was, standing in the middle of the chamber, trembling like I was coming down with the flu, and still not knowing what god-awful something had happened. In all my days in the Back Kingdom, I never heard such noises so early in the forenoon.

It was about half an hour after sunrise, and a gun went off like a cofferdam breaking up under ice at twenty below, and I'd swear it sounded like it wasn't any further away than my feet are from my head. That gun shot off, pitching me six-seven inches off the bed, and, before I could come down out of the air, there was another roar like somebody coughing through a megaphone, with a two weeks' cold, right in my ear. God helping, I hope I never get waked up like that again until I can get myself home to the Back Kingdom where I rightfully belong to stay.

I must have stood there I don't know how long, shivering in my nightshirt, my heart pounding inside of me like a ramrod working on a plugged-up bore, and listening for that gun again, if it was going to shoot some more. A man never knows what's going to happen in the State of Maine. That's why I wish sometimes I'd never left the Back Kingdom to begin with. I was making sixty a month, with the best of bed and board, back there in the intervale; but like a damn fool I had to jerk loose and come down here near the Bay. I'm going back where I came from, God helping; I've never had a purely calm and peaceful day since I got here three-four years ago. This is the worst country for the unexpected raising of all kinds of unlooked for hell a man is apt to run across in a lifetime. If a man's born and raised in the Back Kingdom, he ought to stay there where he belongs; that's what I'd done if I'd had the sense to stay out of this down-country near the Bay, where you don't ever know, God helping, what's going to happen next, where or when.

But there I was, standing in the middle of the upstairs chamber, shaking like a ragweed in an August windstorm, and not knowing what minute, maybe right at me, that gun was going off again, for all I knew. Just then, though, I heard Jim and Mrs. Frost trip-trapping around downstairs in their bare feet. Even if I didn't know what god-awful something had happened, I knew things around the place weren't calm and peaceful, like they generally were of a Sunday morning in May, because it took a stiff mixture of heaven and hell to get Jim and Mrs. Frost up and out of a warm bed before six of a forenoon, any day of the week.

I ran to the window and stuck my head as far out as I could get it, to hear what the trouble was. Everything out there then was as quiet and peaceful as midnight on a back road in dead of winter. But I knew something was up, because Jim and Mrs. Frost didn't make a practice of getting up and out of a warm bed that time of forenoon in the chillish Maytime.

There wasn't any sense in standing there in the cold air shivering in my nightshirt; so I put on my clothes, whistling all the time through my teeth to drive away the chill, and trying to figure out what damn fool was around so early shooting off a gun of a Sunday morning. Just then I heard the downstairs door open, and up the steps, two at a time, came Jim in his breeches and his shirttail flying out behind him.

He wasn't long in coming up the stairs, for a man sixty-seven, but before he reached the door to my room, that gun went off again: BOOM! Just like that! And the echo came rolling back through the open window from the hills: *Boom! Boom!* Like fireworks going off with your eyes shut. Jim had busted through the door already, but when he heard that *Boom!* sound he sort of spun around, like a cockeyed weather vane, five-six times, and ran out the door again like he had been shot in the hind parts with a moose gun. That *Boom!* so early in the forenoon was enough to scare the daylights out of any man, and Jim wasn't any different from me or anybody else in the town of East Joloppi. He just turned around and jumped through the door to the first tread on the stairway like his mind was made up to go somewhere else in a hurry, and no fooling around at the start.

I'd been hired to Jim and Mrs. Frost for all of three-four years, and I was near about as much of a Frost, excepting name, as Jim himself was. Jim and me got along fine together, doing chores and haying and farm work in general, because neither one of us was ever trying to make the other do more of the work. We were hitched to make a fine team, and I never had a kick coming, and Jim said he didn't either.

The echo of that gunshot was still rolling around in the hills and coming in through the window, when all at once that god-awful cough-like whoop through a megaphone sounded again right there in the room and everywhere else, like it might have been, in the whole town of East Joloppi. The man or beast or whatever animal he was who hollered like that had ought to be locked up to keep from scaring all the women and children to death, and it wasn't any stomach-comforting sound for a grown man who's used to the peaceful calm of the Back Kingdom all his life to hear so early of a Sunday forenoon, either.

I jumped to the door where Jim, just the minute before, leaped through. He didn't stop till he got clear to the bottom of the stairs. He stood there, sticking his frazzled head around the corner of the door, looking up at me like a wild-eyed cow moose surprised in the sheriff's corn field.

"Who fired that shot, Jim?" I yelled at him, leaping down the stairs quicker than a man of my years ought to let himself do.

"Good God!" Jim said, his voice hoarse and falling all to pieces like a stump of punk-wood, "The Swedes! The Swedes are shooting!"

"What Swedes, Jim—those Swedes who own the farm and buildings across the road?" I said, trying to find the buttonholes in my shirt. "Have they come back to live on that farm?"

"Yes!" he said, his voice croaking deep down in his throat, like he had swallowed too much water. "The Swedes are all over the place. They're everywhere you can see, there's that many of them."

"What's their name, Jim?" I asked him. "You and Mrs. Frost never told me what their name is."

"I don't know. I never heard them called anything but Swedes, and that's what it is, I guess."

I ran across the hall to look out a window, but it was the wrong side of the house. Mrs. Frost was stepping around in the downstairs chamber, locking things up in the drawers and closets and forgetting where she was hiding the keys. I could see her through the open door, and she was more scared looking than Jim was. She was so scared of the Swedes she didn't know what she was doing, none of the time.

"What made the Swedes come back for, Jim?" I said to him. "I thought you said they were gone for good, this time."

"Good God, Stan," he said, "I don't know what they came back here for. I guess hard times are bringing everybody back to the land, and the Swedes are always in the front rush of everything. I don't know what brought them back, but they're all over the place, shooting and yelling and raising hell. There are thirty-forty of them, looks like to me, counting everything with heads."

"What they doing now, Jim, except yelling and shooting?"

"Good God," Jim said, looking behind him to see what Mrs. Frost was doing with his things in the downstairs chamber, "I don't know what they're not doing. But I can hear them, Stan! You hurry and lock up all the tools in the barn and bring in the cows and tie them up in the stalls. I got to hurry out now and pull up and bring in all of those new cedar fence posts across the front of the yard before they start taking them off. Good God, Stan, the Swedes are everywhere you look outdoors! We have got to make haste, Stan!"

Jim ran to the side door and out to the back of the house, but I took my time about going. I wasn't scared of the Swedes, like Jim and Mrs. Frost were, and I didn't aim to have Jim putting me to doing tasks and chores, or anything else, before breakfast and the proper time. I wasn't any more scared of the Swedes than I was of the Finns and Portuguese, anyway. It's a pure shame for Americans to let Swedes and Finns and the Portuguese scare the daylights out of them. God helping, they are no different than us, and you never see a Finn or a Swede scared of an American.

But there wasn't any sense in trying to argue with Jim and Mrs. Frost right then, when the Swedes, like a fired nest of yellow-headed bumblebees, were swarming all over the place as far as the eye could see, and when Mrs. Frost was scared to death that they were coming into the house to carry out all her furniture and household goods. So while Mrs. Frost was tying hers and Jim's shoes in pillowcases and putting them out of sight in the closets, I went to the kitchen window and looked out to see what was going on around the tall yellow house across the road.

Jim and Mrs. Frost both were right about there being Swedes all over the place. God helping, there were Swedes all over the country, near about all over the whole town of East Joloppi, for what I could see out the window. They were as thick around the barn and pump and the woodpile as if they had been a nest of yellow-headed bumblebees buzzing all over the country. There were Swedes everywhere a man could see, and the ones that couldn't be seen, could be heard yelling their heads off inside the yellow clapboarded house across the road. There wasn't any mistake about their being Swedes there, either; because I've never yet seen a man who mistakes a Swede or a Finn for an American. Once you see a Finn or a Swede you know, God helping, that he is a Swede or a Finn, and not a Portuguese or an American.

There was a Swede everywhere a man could look. Some of them were little Swedes, and women Swedes; but when you come right down to it, there's no sense in counting out the little Swedes and the women Swedes.

Out in the road in front of their house were seven-eight autos and trucks loaded down with furniture and household goods. All around, everything was Swede. The Swedes were yelling and shouting at one another, the little Swedes and the women Swedes just as loud as the big Swedes, and it looked like none of them knew what all the shouting and yelling was for, and when they found out, they didn't give a damn about it. That was because all of them were Swedes. It didn't make any difference what a Swede was yelling about; just as long as he had leave to open his mouth, he was tickled to death about it.

I have never seen the like of so much yelling and shouting anywhere else before; but down here in the State of Maine there's no sense in being taken back at the sights to be seen, because any-thing on God's green earth is likely and liable to happen between day and night, and the other way around, too.

Now you take the Finns; there's any number of them around in the woods. When a Finn crew breaks a woods camp, it looks like there's a Finn behind every tree in the whole State, but you don't see them go making the noise that Swedes do, with all their yelling and shouting and shooting off guns. Finns are quiet about their hell-raising. The Portuguese are quiet, too; you see them tramping around, minding their own business, and working hard on a river dam or something, but you never hear them shouting and yelling and shooting off guns at five-six of a Sunday morn-ing. There's no known likeness to the noise that a houseful of Swedes can make when they get to yelling and shouting at one another early in the forenoon.

I was standing there all that time, looking out the window at the Swedes across the road, when Jim came into the kitchen with an armful of wood and threw it into the woodbox behind the range. "Stan," he said, "the Swedes are everywhere you can look outdoors. They're not going to get that armful of wood, anyway, though."

Mrs. Frost came to the door and stood looking like she didn't know it was her business to cook breakfast for Jim and me. I made a fire in the range and put on a pan of water to boil for the coffee. Jim kept running to the window to look out, and there wasn't much use in expecting Mrs. Frost to start cooking unless some-body set her to it, in the shape she was in, with all the Swedes around the place. She was so upset, it was a pity to look at her. But Jim and me had to eat, and I went and took her by the arm and brought her to the range and left her standing there so close she would get burned if she didn't stir around and cook break-fast.

"Good God, Stan," Jim said, "those Swedes are into every-thing. They're in the barn, and in the pasture running the cows, and I don't know what else they've been into since I looked last. They'll take the tools and the horses and cows, and the cedar posts, too, if we don't get out there and put everything under lock and key."

"Now, hold on, Jim," I said, looking out the window. "Them you see are little Swedes out there, and they're not going to make off with anything of yours and Mrs. Frost's. The big Swedes are busy carrying in the furniture and household goods. Those Swedes aren't going to tamper with anything of yours. They're people just like us. They don't go around stealing everything in sight. Let's just sit here by the window and watch them while Mrs. Frost gets breakfast ready."

"They're Swedes, though, Stan," Jim said, "and they're moving into the house across the road. I've got to put everything under lock and key before they—"

"Hold on, Jim," I told him, "it's their house they're moving into. God helping, they're not moving into your and Jim's house, are they, Mrs. Frost?"

"Jim," Mrs. Frost said, shaking her finger at him and looking at me wild-eyed and sort of flustered-like, "don't you sit there and let Stanley stop you from saving the stock and tools. Stanley came down here from the Back Kingdom, and he doesn't know anything about Swedes."

Mrs. Frost was partly right, because I've never seen the things in my whole life that I've seen down here near the Bay; but there wasn't any sense in Americans like Jim and Mrs. Frost being scared of Swedes. I've seen enough Finns and Portuguese in my time in the Back Kingdom, up in the intervale, to know that Americans are no different from the others.

"Now, you hold on a while, Jim," I said. "Swedes are no different than Finns. Finns don't go around stealing another man's stock and tools. Up in the Back Kingdom the Finns are the finest kind of neighbors."

"That may be so in the Back Kingdom, Stan," Jim said, "but Swedes down here near the Bay are nothing like anything you've ever seen before. Those Swedes over there work in a paper mill over to Waterville three-four years, and when they've saved up enough money, or when they lose all they've got, as the case may be, they all move back here to East Joloppi on this farm of theirs for two-three years at a time. That's what they do. And they've been doing that for the past thirty-forty years, ever since I can remember, and they haven't changed none in all that time.

I can remember the first time they came to East Joloppi; they built that house across the road then, and if you've ever seen a sight like Swedes building a house in a hurry, you haven't got much else to live for. Why, Stan, those Swedes built that house in four-five days—just like that! I've never seen the equal to it. Of course, now, Stan, it's the worst looking house a man ever saw, because it's not a farm house, and it's not a city house, and it's no kind of a house an American would erect. Why, those Swedes threw that house together in four-five days—just like that! But whoever saw a house like that before, with three storeys to it, and only six rooms in the whole building? And painted yellow, too. Good God, Stan, white is the only color to paint a house, and those Swedes went and painted it yellow. Then on top of that, they went and painted the barn red. And of all of them shouting and yelling, at all times of the day and night, a man never saw or heard before. Those Swedes acted like they were purely crazy for the whole of four-five days, and they were, and they still are. But what gets me is the painting of it yellow, and the making of it three storeys high, with only six rooms in the whole building. Nobody but Swedes would go and do a thing like that; an American would have built a farm house, resting square on the ground, with one storey, maybe a storey and a half, and then painted it white. Good God, Stan, those fool Swedes had to put up three storeys, to hold six rooms, and then paint the building yellow."

"Swedes are a little queer, sometimes," I said. "But Finns and Portuguese are, too. And Americans sometimes—"

"A little queer!" Jim said. "Why, Stan, the Swedes are the queerest people on the earth. You don't know Swedes. This is the first time you've ever seen those Swedes across the road, and that's why you don't know what they're like after being shut up in a paper mill over to Waterville for four-five years. They're purely wild, I tell you, Stan. They don't stop at anything they set their heads on. If you were to walk out there now and tell them to move their autos and trucks out of the road so that towns-people could get past without so much trouble, they'd tear you apart, they're that wild after being shut up in the paper mills these three-four, maybe five, years."

"Finns get that way, too," I tried to tell Jim. "After Finns have been shut up in a woods camp all winter, they make a lot of noise when they get out. Everybody who has to stay close to the job for four-five years likes to act free when he gets out from under the job. Now, Jim, you take the Portuguese—"

"Don't you sit there and let Stanley keep you from putting the tools away, Jim," Mrs. Frost said. "Stanley doesn't know the Swedes like we do. He's lived up in the Back Kingdom most of his life, and he's never seen Swedes—"

"Good God, Stan," Jim said, standing up, he was that nervous and upset, "the Swedes are overrunning the whole country. I'll bet there are more Swedes in the town of East Joloppi than there are in the whole Union. Everybody knows there's more Swedes in the State of Maine than there are in the old country. They take to this State like potato bugs take to—"

"Don't you sit there and let Stanley keep you back, Jim," Mrs. Frost put in again. "Stanley doesn't know the Swedes like—"

Just then one of the big Swedes started yelling at some of the little Swedes and women Swedes. I'll swear, those big Swedes sounded like a pasture full of hoarse bulls, near the end of May, mad about the black flies. God helping, they yelled like they were fixing to kill all the little Swedes and women Swedes they could get their hands on. It didn't amount to anything though, because the little Swedes and women Swedes yelled right back at them just like they were big Swedes, too. The little Swedes and women Swedes couldn't yell hoarse bull bass, but it was close enough to it to make a man who's lived most of his life in the intervale in the Back Kingdom think that the whole town of East Joloppi was full of big Swedes.

Jim was all for getting out after the tools and stock right away, but I pulled him back to the table. I wasn't going to let Jim and Mrs. Frost start me doing tasks and chores before breakfast and the regular time. Forty dollars a month isn't much to pay a man for ten-eleven hours' work a day, including Sundays, and I set myself that I wasn't going to work twelve-thirteen hours for them, even if I was practically one of the Frosts myself, except in name, by that time.

"Hold on, Jim," I said, "let's just sit here by the window and watch them carry their furniture and household goods inside while Mrs. Frost's getting the cooking ready to eat. If they start taking off any of you and Mrs. Frost's things, we can see them just as good from here by the window as we could out there in the yard and road."

"Now, Jim, I'm telling you," Mrs. Frost said, shaking all over, and not even trying to cook the breakfast, "don't you sit there and let Stanley keep you from saving the stock and tools. He doesn't know the Swedes like we do."

Jim wasn't for staying in the house when all of his tools were lying around in the yard, and while his cows were in the pasture unprotected, but he saw how it would be better to wait where we could hurry up Mrs. Frost with the cooking, if we were ever going to eat breakfast that forenoon. She was so excited and nervous about the Swedes moving back to East Joloppi from Waterville that she hadn't got the beans and brown bread fully heated from the night before, and we had to sit and eat them cold.

We were sitting there by the window eating the cold beans and brown bread, and watching the Swedes, when two of the little Swedes started running across Jim and Mrs. Frost's lawn. They were chasing one of their big yellow tomcats they had brought with them from Waterville. The tom was as large as a six-months collie pup, and he ran like he was on fire. His great big bushy tail stuck straight up in the air behind him, like a flag, and he was leaping over the lawn like a devilish calf, new born. Jim and Mrs. Frost saw the little Swedes and the big yellow tom at the same time I did.

"Good God," Jim said, raising himself part of the way out of his chair, "here they come now!"

"Hold on, Jim," I said, pulling him back to the table. "They're only chasing one of their tomcats. They're not after anything that belongs to you and Mrs. Frost. Let's just sit here and finish eating the beans, and watch them out the window."

"My crown in heaven!" Mrs. Frost cried out, running to the window and looking through. "Those Swedes are going to kill every plant on the place. They'll dig up all the bulbs and pull up all the vines in the flower bed."

"Now, you just sit and calm yourself, Mrs. Frost," I told her. "Those little Swedes are just chasing a tomcat. They're not after doing hurt to your flowers."

The big Swedes were unloading the autos and trucks and carrying the furniture and household goods into their three-storey, yellow-clapboarded house. None of them were paying any attention to the little Swedes chasing the yellow tom over Jim and Mrs. Frost's lawn.

Just then the kitchen door burst open, and the two little Swedes stood there looking at us, panting and blowing their heads off.

Mrs. Frost took one look at them, and then she let out a yell, but the kids didn't notice her at all.

"Hey," one of them shouted, "come out here and help us get the cat! He climbed up in one of your trees."

By that time, Mrs. Frost was all for slamming the door in their faces, but I pushed in front of her and went out into the yard with them. Jim came right behind me, after he had finished calming Mrs. Frost, and telling her we wouldn't let the Swedes come and carry out her furniture and household goods.

The yellow tomcat was all the way up one of Jim's young maple shade trees. The maple wasn't strong enough to support even the smallest of the little Swedes, if he should take it into his head to climb to the top after the tom, and neither Jim nor me was hurting ourselves trying to think of a way to get the feline down. We were all for letting the cat stay where he was, but the little Swedes couldn't wait for anything. They wanted the cat right then and there, and no wasting of time in getting him.

"You boys go home and wait for the tom to come down," Jim told them. "There's no way to take him down now, until he gets ready to come down of his own free will."

But no, those two boys were little Swedes. They weren't thinking of going back home till they got the yellow tomcat down from the maple. One of them ran to the tree, before Jim or me could head him off, and started shinnying up it like a pop-eyed squirrel. In no time, it seemed to me like, he was up among the limbs, jumping around up there from one limb to another like he lived in it.

"Good God, Stan," Jim said, "can't you keep them out of the trees?"

There was no answer for that, and Jim knew there wasn't. There's no way of stopping a Swede from doing what he's set his head on doing.

The boy got almost to the top, where the yellow tom was clinging, when the tree began to bend towards the house. I knew what was coming, if something wasn't done about it pretty quick, and so did Jim. Jim saw his young shade tree begin to bend, and he almost had a fit looking at it. He ran to the lumber pile and came back dragging two pieces of two-by-fours. He got them up against the tree before it had time to do any splitting, and then we stood there shoring up the tree and yelling at the little Swede to come down out of there before we broke his neck for being up in it.

The big Swedes across the road heard the fuss we were making, and they came running out of that three-storey, six-room house like it had been on fire inside.

"Good God, Stan," Jim shouted at me, "here comes the Swedes!"

"Don't turn and run off, Jim," I cautioned him, yanking him back by his coattail. "They're not wild beasts; we're not scared of them. Hold on where you are, Jim!"

I could see Mrs. Frost's head almost breaking through the window glass in the kitchen. She was all for coming out and driving the Swedes off her lawn and out of her flowers, but she was too scared to unlock the kitchen door and open it.

Jim was getting ready to run again, when he saw the Swedes coming towards us like a nest of yellow-headed bumblebees, but I wasn't scared of them and I held Jim's coattail and told him I wasn't. Jim and me were supporting the young maple, and I knew if one of us let go, the whole tree would bend to the ground and split wide open. There was no sense in ruining a young maple shade tree like that, and I told Jim there wasn't.

"Hey," one of the big Swedes shouted at the little Swede up in the top of the maple, "come down out of that tree and go home to your mother."

"Aw, to hell with the old lady," the little Swede shouted down. "I'm getting the cat by the tail."

The big Swede looked at Jim and me. Jim was almost ready to run again, by that time, but I wasn't, and I held him and told him I wasn't. There was no sense in letting the Swede scare the daylights out of us.

"What in hell can you do with kids when they get that age?" he asked Jim and me.

Jim was all for telling him to make the boy come down out of the maple before it bent over and split wide open, but I knew there was no sense in trying to make him come down out of there until he got good and ready, or else got the yellow tom by the tail.

Just then another big Swede came running out, holding a double-bladed ax out in front of him, and yelling for all he was worth at the other Swedes.

"Good God, Stan," Jim said, "don't let those Swedes cut down my young maple!"

I had lots better sense than to try to make the Swedes stop doing what they had set their heads on doing. A man would be purely a fool to try to stop it from raining from above when it got ready to, even if he was trying to get his corn planted.

I looked around again, and there was Mrs. Frost all but popping through the window glass. I could see what she was thinking, but I couldn't hear a word she was saying. It was good and plenty though, whatever it was.

"Come down out of that tree!" the Swede yelled at the boy in Jim's maple.

Instead of starting to climb down, the little Swede reached up for the big yellow tomcat's tail. The cat reached out a big fat paw and harried the boy five-six times, just like that, quicker than the eye could follow. The kid let out a yell and a shout that must have been heard all the way to the other side of town, sounding like a whole houseful of Swedes up in the maple.

The big Swede covered the distance to the tree in one stride, pushing everything behind him.

"Good God, Stan," Jim shouted at me, "we've got to do something!"

There wasn't anything a man could do, unless he was a man

of prayer. Americans like Jim and me had no business getting in a Swede's way, especially when he was swinging a big double-bladed ax, and he just out of a paper mill after being shut up making paper four-five years.

The big Swede grabbed the ax and let go at the trunk of the maple with it. There was no stopping him then, because he had the ax going, and it was swinging like a cow's tail in a swarm of barn flies. The little maple shook all over every time the ax blade struck it, like wind blowing a cornstalk, and then it began to bend on the other side from Jim and me where we were shoring it up with the two-by-fours. Chips as big as dinner plates were flying across the lawn and peltering the house like a gang of boys stoning telephone insulators. One of those big dinner plate chips crashed through the kitchen window where Mrs. Frost was, about that time. Both Jim and me thought at first she had fallen through the window—when we looked again, we could see that she was still on the inside, and madder than ever at the Swedes.

The two-by-fours weren't any good then, because it was too late to get to the other side of the maple in time to keep it from bending over in that direction. The Swede with the ax took one more swing, and the tree began to bend towards the ground.

The tree came down, the little Swede came down, and the big yellow tom came down on top of everything, holding for all he was worth to the top of the little Swede's head. But long before the tree and the boy struck the ground, the big yellow tom-cat had sprung what looked like thirty feet, and landed in the middle of Mrs. Frost's flowers and bulbs. The little Swede let out a yell when he hit the ground that brought out six-seven more Swedes from that three-storey, six-room house, piling out into the road like it was the first time they had ever heard a kid bawl. The women Swedes and the little Swedes and the big Swedes piled out on Jim and Mrs. Frost's front lawn like they had been dropped out of a dump truck. The big yellow tom had made one more spring when he hit the flower bed, and that leap landed him over the stone wall. Then he struck out for the woods with every Swede on the place behind him.

I thought Mrs. Frost was going to have a fit right then and there in the kitchen window. When she saw that swarm of Swedes chasing across her lawn, and the big yellow tom in her flower bed among the tender plants and bulbs, digging up the things she had planted, the Swedes with their No. 12 heels squashing the green shoots she had been nursing along—well, I guess she just sort of caved in, and fell out of sight for the time being. I didn't have the time to run to see what was wrong with her, because Jim and me had to tear out behind the tom and the Swedes to try to save as much as we could.

"Good God, Stan," Jim shouted at me, "go in the house and ring up all the neighbors on the line, and tell them to hurry over here and help us before the Swedes come back and wreck my farm and buildings. There's no telling what they'll do next. They'll be setting fire to the house and barn next thing, maybe."

But I didn't have time to waste talking to the neighbors on the telephone line. About that time, some of the other Swedes, who were still inside the house across the road, began shooting off those guns again, and Jim and me struck out for the kitchen door. Mrs. Frost held it open for us, when she saw us on our way, because she knew we were headed for the shelter of the house. There's something about a lot of guns going off in Swedes' houses that makes a man jumpy, and there was no sense in staying in the open and getting plugged with moose bullets, whether they were aimed any which-way by the Swedes, or just fired off haphazard towards us.

"Good God," Jim shouted, running around the kitchen, dancing up and down so high his knees were just about hitting his chin, "those Swedes are purely crazy now! They're shooting every which-way!"

Mrs. Frost tiptoed to the window and looked out through the broken pane where the chip came sailing through. "If I had a gun," she said, "I'd go shoot every one of those Swedes before the day is done."

"Hold on," Jim said, grabbing Mrs. Frost by her arms and holding her as tight as he could. "Don't you go doing anything to those Swedes. We don't want to make them mad."

"God helping, Jim," I said, "aren't those Swedes already mad about something or other? Weren't they mad just a little while ago, out there on the lawn, cutting down the maple and to get that yellow tom down to the ground?"

"You don't know the Swedes like we do, Stan," Jim said,

turning Mrs. Frost loose and standing by the range shivering and shaking. "You've lived most of your life up in the Back Kingdom. Those Swedes were only after getting that yellow tom. They weren't mad about anything. Nobody provoked them."

"Well, Jim," I said, "if you want me to, I'll go over there to that house across the road and raise hell with every Swede on the inside of it for cutting down your young maple and tearing up Mrs. Frost's flower bed."

"My crown in heaven," Mrs. Frost said, running to Jim and holding on to him, "Jim, don't let Stanley make the Swedes mad. This is the only place we have to live in, and they'll be here a year now this time, maybe two-three, if the hard times don't get any better soon."

"That's right, Stan," he said. "You don't know them like we do. You would have to be a Swede yourself to know what to tell them. Don't go over there doing anything like that."

"But, Jim," I said, "you and Mrs. Frost aren't scared of the Swedes, are you?"

"Good God, no," he said, his eyes popping out; "but don't go making them mad."

ON THE GREAT ROAD

By IVAN BUNIN

P ARASHKA'S father lived on the great Novosilsk road. Wishing to keep away from the gentry, Ustin had chosen a piece of land that was till then uninhabited. Seas of rye poured in billowy fields around his farmyard and merged in the vast Russian steppe. Two solitary scrub oaks stood in the rye outside the yard; shallow gullies receded from it into the distance, overgrown in summer with white flowers. Beyond the great road, one could see a small wood of oaks in the midst of the rye. Further on was the village—the ancient free village of Bayevo—but this was wholly hidden by the billowy fields of rye. Many travellers passed along the great road. The tracks they left and the ruts, crisscrossing, stretched endlessly and were lost in a fine, tangled maze.

Ustin had long been a widower—it was rumored that he had killed his wife out of jealousy. He depended for his living not on tilling the soil like a peasant but on lending money. He sowed just enough land for his own use, around the scrub oaks and above the gullies. His cows were a poor lot, but he owned fine horses. His house had been managed first by his mistress, a widow, then by a beggar-woman, later by his elder daughter, Evgenya. But he soon got rid of Evgenya, who was unlike him and distasteful to him, and replaced her with a working man, the elderly and somewhat crack-brained Volodya. Ustin absented himself a great deal, and the barefoot, taciturn Parashka was left to grow up alone.

One day—she was then in her fourteenth year, and it happened in the summer just after Evgenya had moved to Bayevo —an immense flock of sheep was being herded along the great road, a frequent occurrence: a merchant would buy one or two hundred head at one fair and have them driven to another, hiring for the purpose several tramps with an overseer in charge. The summer sunset was fading, far away behind the farmhouse. In anticipation of her father's arrival from town, Parashka sat on the threshold and gazed at the vanishing evening meadows and down the long stretch of the empty road. In a dense, dirty gray mass the sheep slowly shuffled past her, making low indeterminate sounds by their movement and breathing, and exuding an odor of fleece and fodder, steppe grass and wormwood. Behind them came the dogs with their red tongues hanging parched and dusty from the day's journey, and a tall ragged youth walking beside a ragged old man, and last of all, astride a white, hooknosed Kirghiz horse, whip in hand, a cap pushed back over the nape of his neck, rode a young merchant.

"How do you do, my beauty?" said the old man, stepping away from the sheep. "Please do a stranger a favor. Ask your father for a match."

She looked at him for a long time without answering. He wore no hat, but the shreds of one hung on his smooth staff. He pressed his shiny hands down on the staff to restrain their trembling, and breathed with difficulty. In his tattered reddish overcoat, barely covering his naked body and belted with a strip of cloth, and his worn shoes, greenish gray and shaggy, his face deathly pale with puffy eyes, he presented a fierce appearance, but in his hoarse voice there was goodness, weariness. The gray hair was visible on his chest, which betrayed the beating of the heart under it.

"Father isn't at home," Parashka replied after sharp scrutiny.

"Just as I thought, just as I thought," said the old man. "Life goes on, an' you're growing up. 'Evening's a quail, a speckled quail, that keeps calling through the long night, the dark night.' What's one to do, then, my beauty?"

The youth also came up to her, followed at a slow trot by the man on horseback, who, in the manner of riders of the steppe, pressed his feet in the stirrups under the belly of the thick-chested Kirghiz horse, which appeared hungry and heated, tossing its large head back and twisting its neck. They gave the old man a mocking glance—they knew his way of speaking—and looked more attentively at Parashka. The youth was tall and slender, with sloping shoulders, and a round feline face; he wore a convict's cap. The man on horseback was very swarthy and lean but broad-shouldered; he had gleaming eyes.

"I know her father," he said, looking down from his saddle at Parashka, at her small feet, her tanned shoulders and dirty chemise. "A rich rogue. Just go in and have a look on the oven shelf, or behind the icon," he added gruffly.

Without taking her eyes off the Kirghiz horse—a short, sturdy, yet light-footed beast, tossing its heavy head and gnaw-ing with yellow teeth at the spittle-flecked bridle—Parashka sprang up from the threshold; then she ran into the house and returned with a box of matches. Meanwhile, the merchant had dismounted from the old, dry, dirty Cossack saddle, and stretched his short legs. The youth walked away, his eyes fixed somewhere upon the fields. The merchant took the matches and, in silence, also walked away, leading his horse towards the flock of sheep, which had come to a stop with lowered heads. Parashka was to remember always his dust-covered coat, his glossy breeches thrust into broad-topped boots with narrow toes, his embroidered shirt with its dirty collar, and, above all, his face, which, as if dusted with powder, was covered with bluish-tipped pimples, and his swarthy cheeks that showed a sparse growth of stiff beard, scarcely less sparse than the stiff jet-black hairs above the corners of his mouth. As he walked away, he turned to glance at her again, and astonished her with the beauty of his hard eyes. The old man, who apparently had noticed this, said in a strange tone as he also took his leave: "Well, that's how we live.—Good-bye, and thank you, my beauty. Remember what a terrible old bare-foot man once told you. This merchant-thief has it in him to ruin you. Don't waste any looks on such as he. . . ."

And then, on the field beyond the great road, where the flock of sheep stopped to rest for the night, there flamed for a long time, in the darkening blue of the evening, a hot yellow camp-fire. It grew late, and her father had not yet come home. As she sat on the threshold, Parashka could hear the man Volodya at his milking in the shed, but she did not take her eyes off the fire. "Evening's a quail"—she remembered the old man's words—and, aware of a sweet longing they awakened, she looked into

the dark night and imagined she saw the quail, which was calling—calling in the boundless sea of rye. The fire flamed redder
and redder—and he, this dark-eyed merchant, who had it in
him to ruin her, was still there, very near. At last, the measured, comforting sound of her father's cart became audible. She
jumped up, ran inside the dark house and, lying down, pretended to sleep. Her father drove up to the door, shouted to
Volodya, then entered and hung something up on the wall. The
drowsy flies in the sieves and strainers near the stove began to
hum.

"Father," called Parashka in a low voice.

"Well, dear?" her father replied in a whisper.

"Who's this barefoot old man that comes round?"

"If you took your shoes off, you'd be barefoot too!"

"He's not really barefoot. He's got boots on—what's left of
them."

"That means he's drunk 'imself to pieces. But where did you
see 'im?"

Parashka told of the passers-by, but she said nothing of the
old man's parting words.

"That means they were driving Balmashev's flock," he said,
without paying much attention to her story as he moved a
horse's bridle from one hook to another. "Yes, yes, I see, the
campfire's still going—"

"Why was his horse all blood?"

"Whose horse?"

"The overseer's. The horse's chest is all red scabs."

"That all comes from its being a Kirghiz horse," her father replied. "It's a mean, very fierce breed. That's the bad
blood coming out. An' did he have a brand on 'im?"

Parashka thought a while. "What may a brand be?"

"It's a kind of a stamp—like letters burnt into the leg—to
make you see it's no common horse but a Kirghiz."—"Well, go
to sleep, sleep, if you've already had supper," he added. "As
for me, I'm going into the pantry to have a bite."

And, having opened the window, he went into the other
part of the house. Through the window she could see the night
sky dotted with pale stars; and the fresh air drew in, mingled

with the smell of the dying campfire. And so, troubled by this smell that reminded her of something, and at the same time listening to her father scolding Volodya in a low voice outside the window, she fell asleep in that mood, half pain, half allurement, that unknown passing travellers awaken—a mood of enchantment at the vague thought of him who had it in him to ruin her, of the young merchant who could bear her away into the remote distance. . . .

Two years went by, and now a third had come. In some ways Parashka had changed a great deal. Gradually she took her place in the management of the house. She carried all sorts of heavy things, lifting pots and pans from the oven, straining her young body; and she milked the cows and mended her father's clothes. Yet her inner nature had changed but little.

One summer she was seized by a passion for the village. She began to adorn herself, to pay visits to her sister Evgenya, to join with other girls in the round dances, to sing and skip about with them, pretending to be a lively piece. Then she dropped it all, again felt a stranger to the village, to the girls, to Evgenya. Evgenya also visited the farmhouse. She lived the life of a soldier's wife; she had no children; she was not afraid of her widowed father-in-law. Both the girls were taciturn, but otherwise they were different in every way. No one, indeed, would have thought of taking the attractive and outwardly calm Parashka for Evgenya's sister. Evgenya was strong, broad-shouldered; she drew her eyebrows together when she looked at you, at the same time pursing her lips. To the delicate oval of Parashka's shy virginal face her sister's short aggressive face with its high cheek bones presented a startling contrast.

Only Parashka's father was close to her. Her love for him increased with each year. But it was not a simple, tranquil love.

She loved her father timidly, with that poignant feeling that daughters so often have for widowed fathers. To take her mother's place, to be his housekeeper, to look after him, to drag pots out of the oven for him—this was her greatest pride and joy. At times this joy was poisoned with pain—for she would suddenly remember some mistress who had once managed her father's house. In that terrible affair between her father and mother, of which she understood little although she had heard from Evgenya some incoherent whispers even during her childhood, she generally took her father's side. But at times she was troubled by doubts: had he really been in the right? And then it would seem to her that there had never been in this world a person better or more beautiful than her mother. Parashka saw but little of her father, and she understood him even less; she always felt shy and embarrassed in talking with him. And he did not have the reputation of being a simple or easy-going man. With his clean-cut, regular features, his spare form, and his small bronze beard and keen green eyes, he reminded old servants in the big country houses of a mounted Circassian guard who had once lived with the gentry. Yet there was also something of the peasant in his cautious manners and his clumsy boots, in his thick curls, which he brushed to one side, in the coarse shirt and rough sleeveless peasant's coat which he wore. He was shrewd and courteous, even good in a fashion, but everyone was a little afraid of him. He was exceedingly judicious. People came to him from the hamlets and villages for assistance, which he never refused. He listened attentively, shook his head, constantly pushing back the bronze locks from his forehead. He looked searchingly at visitors but not sternly, nodding assent, never interrupting them with so much as a whisper. He charged only a moderate rate of interest. But, after all, he lived by lending money, and such people always arouse a measure of fear.

Parashka had grown thin. In her face there appeared an elusive likeness to her father, such as one may sometimes come to see in daughters who love their fathers, even where at first glance no likeness is apparent. They had in common the faculty of concealing much, of withholding themselves, of receiving similar impressions. For example, they were both considerably disturbed by the sight of an immense gypsy caravan going down the great road in the autumn towards the valleys of the south.

"When I was a youngster I once ran away to follow the gypsies," Ustin said one day, with a grin.

"Well, what happened? Did you change your mind?" Parashka asked.

"Yes, I changed my mind. It's the proper thing to do, daughter," he said, no longer smiling. "One shouldn't do things in a hurry—"

"An' why not?"

"Well, never mind"—he did not answer at once and evaded her glance. "The fact is, the blood sometimes comes into your eyes, and makes trouble—"

She understood him, shrank back, and was silent.

There were other things around her that affected Parashka besides her father's mysteriousness—his past, his journeys, and his cares, about which he never confided in anyone. In the autumn and the winter she slept a great deal. In the summer sometimes she did not sleep for three nights together. Her favorite spot was the threshold, where she would stand by the hour, her head turned to one side. Somewhere into the distance, towards some happy land, went the passing travellers. An itinerant beggar in skull-cap and cassock strode along with rapid step, swinging his tall staff, looking boldly and eagerly ahead of him, his sun-streaked, tangled hair brushing his shoulders. She followed him with her steady gaze, although she was afraid of tramps, afraid when they turned in towards the house to ask for alms. At a jog trot, the three horses stumbling and snorting, a country gentleman's jaded *troika* passed down the middle of the road. The much-travelled look of the dust-covered carriage, the sound of the creaking springs, awakened a longing in her—indefinable desires. When she saw a flock of sheep go by, she fixed her eyes avidly on the drivers, and remembered the evil foretold. But it was at the endless seas of rye that billowed away beyond the great road, towards the southeast, into the tormenting distances of the steppe, that she gazed most often.

As for love—to her it was no simple word. She had learned it early, and even while she was still a child it disturbed her. Once in the heat of a summer noon she saw sitting on the stones by her father's storehouse a poor drunken woman from Bayevo. She was on her way to the fair—to sell her sick bony nag standing near by. She had spread before her some matches with a tin of cheap tobacco; she smoked and smiled at Parashka, who was playing in the dust. "W-well, hasn't your father driven out his *love-bird* yet?" she asked in a secretive hoarse whisper. And Parashka always remembered this particular word and intuitively sensed its mysterious meaning. After that, whenever she happened to run into the house and see a woman on her father's knee, a sweet terror and shame overcame her. Later, from her sister and from the girls of the village she learned songs—all with a single theme—love. And she sang them, and inwardly they stirred her, especially one very old song: "And he fell asleep, asleep, my dear one, on a girl's arm, a muslin sleeve. . . ." All her companions were getting ready for one thing—for married life, for intimacy with their husbands. She too had begun early to be disturbed by a presentiment of this intimacy. Her sister would often say simply: "Father's a loose man, he's living with some woman again. If it costs me a hundred rubles, I'll find her out!" But not for a hundred rubles would Parashka have tried to find out about her father's mistress, although she thought about her day and night.

One day shortly after her husband was called up for his army service, Evgenya came to the farmhouse. "Is father at home?" she shouted hoarsely, appearing at the frozen window. Then she entered and, seating herself on the bench, began to munch bread, and went on saying that she had just come in for a minute, all the while glancing at the tall lean peasant Volodya, who repeatedly came and went through the room. Fussing over some ropes and reins lying on the bench, he mumbled to Evgenya in a thick voice: "Why don't you take your coat off?" Parashka's sister slowly drew back her head, covered by a hempen kerchief: "I've just dropped in for a minute—" She wore bast shoes, and had on a red skirt of coarse wool and a rough bodice tightly fitted over her full breasts. A strong odor emanated from her—the odor of a robust healthy woman, of the smoke in a peasant's hut and of the rye bread which she was slowly munching. "Oh, why do I go on sitting here?" she exclaimed. And suddenly she rose and went resolutely out. But she did not turn her steps homeward; instead she went in the direction of the shed, where Volodya had gone. Parashka rushed up to the door of the shed and stood there stock-still, her ear pressed to the keyhole. Several minutes passed—and still there was no sound. But to Parashka it seemed that she heard everything, saw everything. . . .

As she took her mother's place in the house and became its mistress, she began to feel grown up, and at times carried on real conversations with her father. One summer evening he was sitting close to the small lamp, sorting the various smudged scraps of paper piled on the table, and taking others out of his bosom and the pocket of his peasant's coat. He was intent upon something and kept moving his lips. Then, with a stump of a pencil he began writing, leaning his chest against the table and pushing back his hair with his sleeve; he fidgeted a long time with the papers before setting down a figure. Parashka, sitting near the stove, worked at the spinning wheel; with her left hand she twisted the thread, while with the right she adroitly managed the spindle. She was good to look upon in her many-colored print dress, her head uncovered, her eyelids lowered; she herself became aware of this from the strange, affectionate glances which her father, raising his eyes from his work, from time to time cast at her. She seemed to sit calmly, lightly on the bench, her rounded knees slightly parted, gently pressing the pedal of the spinning wheel with the tip of the left foot and making it hum. "Father," she said suddenly, "were you always so handsome?"

"Eh, what?" he asked in a whisper, as was his habit. "Always. But why?"

"Why, then, didn't mother love you?"

"Who told you that?"

"Oh, I know," she said enigmatically.

He was silent. Then he began to hide the papers in his bosom and to fasten the hooks of his coat; he tossed his head, brushing the locks of hair back from his brow.

"There are some things you'd better not 'ave heard," he said in a low voice.

"They say—you killed her.—Why? For another woman?"

"And you needn't go into that either," he said quietly and simply. "Now, I don't pry into your affairs, do I?"

She reflected. "Why should you pry into my affairs? I'm all on the outside."

"Go on arguing!" he said. "You're just like her."

She flushed. "No, I'm like you—I'll never betray you for anyone in the world!"

"You will, daughter, you will—"

She recalled the merchant who had come with the sheep, the summer evening, which seemed so remote now and so lovely, the old yellow-toothed fiery Kirghiz horse, his powerful chest with the stripes of dried blood. Then her father said in an even voice, as if he were reading from a book: "I'll never give you up until the proper time comes. It's for you, daughter, for you alone, that I work from morning till night. I'll wait until a good, handsome man turns up—"

"But you have a love-bird," she whispered.

"That's all nonsense, all nonsense," he answered warmly, without raising his voice. "All that needn't concern you. It's shameful to gossip with one's father about such things—"

She began to cry. He went up to her, put an arm around her head and kissed her hair. His thin skin flushed suddenly red, his green eyes burned brightly and tenderly. She managed to get a glimpse of them just as he turned and went out of doors, and she wept from a kind of incomprehensible joy, and even more incomprehensible sorrow. *Akh,* how could anyone be better and handsomer than her father!

She was low-spirited. But her arms and legs grew rounder, her small breasts rose higher, her hair became thicker and glossier. When she bathed, she began to feel ashamed of her nakedness. Her sixteenth spring! Soon, soon she would be betrothed; matchmakers would arrive to interview her father; her right to love and to choose would be established—though, of course, she would never marry anyone. Her sister became franker with her—this gratified her vanity. She revealed the mysteries of love to Parashka, and said how eagerly she awaited the return of her soldier husband, how impatient she was growing. Parashka, too, felt a desire to talk about herself, her thoughts, her weariness. She also wanted to hint that she knew about Volodya.

Going with her sister to the door, she would stand a long time at the threshold. The cocks sang out—she heard them, shutting her eyes. The shadowy March mist drowsed above the gray snow of the fields—it seemed to her that she already heard in the mist the cawing of the first rooks. The muddy winter road ran off into the mist, and disappeared—it lured one on, drew one towards distant depths. There were tricklings of water; the hens stood under them and also drowsed—then suddenly grew restless and began to cackle through their heaviness. An excited panting dog, chained near the storehouse, played about gaily, with a simulated fierceness. Startled and trembling, Parashka would rush indoors again.

Only Volodya shared her solitude in the warm house. It was his fifth year with Ustin. Now he awakened only horror and repulsion in her—she had felt this way from the evening when Evgenya had gone into the shed to him. Yet she often stayed alone with him. She knew that he would never dare touch her—her father would have killed him—yet she thought about it. And the sweet agony of her secret thoughts became all the more intense because of the horror and repulsion. At a glance he was not bad-looking; he was no longer young, but he was well-built and lithe, like a young man of twenty. Sometimes she tried to talk with him about something which had no connection with the household—about the village, about girls, about young men. That would set him pondering. Sitting on a bunk, he would throw aside the rope he was twining, and keep turning the cheap cigar between his fingers. His grayish lean face bent forward so that a lock of gray hair fell across his low forehead, he seemed attractive. But he no sooner opened his mouth than he was transformed into a fool. No matter what subject she began the conversation with, he always brought it back to such questions as who lived where among the workmen and, above all, what wages each man was getting.

"He gets big money—" he would mutter, and as he muttered, his mustache would become slobbered.

When the south wind blew in spring, consuming the thaw-
ing snow, and she grew even more disturbed, he saw it and
felt it. He would enter the house as if to attend to something,
would hang up or take down a bridle and, deliberately linger-
ing, would begin with some jest: "It's time to put the bit in
order and bridle you, to lead you to the stallion." Whereupon
she would laugh with a strange loudness. Or he would walk
past her and give her an appraising scrutiny. She would meet
his eyes with wide eyes, full of expectation. Another minute,
it seemed, and she would be completely in his power. But no
sooner had he stretched out his arms than her eyebrows trembled violently, her face became distorted with fear and flushed
with anger. She would jump up and, with that sudden harshness with which girls so often stupefy men, would scream
loudly, seizing anything which came to hand: "Just touch me!
And I'll batter in your snout! I'll tell father as soon as he
comes home! And there won't be the ghost of you left here,
you devil!"

Spring came. The winds and the mists had consumed the
gray snow; a softness hovered over the wet fields. Passion
week ended, Easter eve followed. It was a dismal evening.
Parashka and her father drove in a cart to the village church.
The bare limbs of the trees on the edge of the village made a
comfortless sound, while behind them in the treacherous twilight showed blue-white clouds, threatening rain and snow and
giving the horizon a dour look. But in the icy wind which blew
from under the clouds there was freshness, the aroma of spring.
Parashka's face burned—from the wind and from her rouge
and from an inward agitation—also from having washed and
dressed herself up in clean clothes for the occasion, and from
the excitement of riding in a new cart by the side of her rich
and handsome father as he drove his well-fed horse along the
road.

The broad village street was slushy; ice lay about in huge
humps. In the village the evening seemed still more desolate,
in the unfamiliar street along which the lights already shone
from the poor but snug little houses. But even in these early
lights, and in the flakes of snow which the wind suddenly swept

the length of the street, strangely whitening its filth and its
dark roofs—in all this, the spring holiday was evident. Half
closing their eyes against the snow, Parashka and Ustin turned
away with bowed heads. Now and then, Parashka glanced up
furtively, and her heart grew faint with an incomprehensible
joy at the sight of her father's dear face, his thin skin, grown
more youthful looking in the wind, his shining snow-flecked
beard and wet eyelashes.

Suddenly someone shouted loudly at them: "Gone blind,
have you? Drive a little more to the right, please!"

And on opening her eyes Parashka saw a tall horse and a
carriage, high in front, and in the carriage—the raised collar
of an overcoat, and the merchant, his face also turned away
from the snow and the wind. He glanced at her—and instantly
she recognized him.

"What makes you shout so?" Ustin replied with gaiety in
his voice. "And to-morrow's Easter!"

"Sorry, Ustin Prokofitch," the merchant replied. "One can't
see a thing—"

And the two vehicles parted company.

After a long silence, Parashka asked calmly, "Do you know
him?"

"An' who doesn't know the rogue?" said Ustin. "He lived
at Balmashev's farm. Now he's hatching a business of his own.
He's hopping about like a thief, an' he wants to open up a shop
in the village—"

Parashka put her dress in order, drew the shawl across her
face, held her breath. Her heart thumped, her face grew serious. She accepted this chance meeting as something that had
to happen; it did not even surprise her. What did surprise her
was the lightness with which fate had so unexpectedly taken a
turn.

During Easter week the merchant paid Ustin a friendly call.
In the three years since Parashka had first seen him, he had not
changed in the least; only his fiery eyes had become more restless. Even his clothes were the same, but this time the collar of
his shirt was clean. She learned that his name was Nikanor;
from his talk with her father she gathered that he was still un-

certain of his future. Should he, or should he not, go to Rostov, where somebody was ready to hire him? He drank tea and vodka with his host. She did not try to grasp the meaning of his words, but merely listened to the sound of his clear voice. She did not raise her eyes. Dressed all in white and rouged, she sat in the corner and chewed sunflower seeds, pretending not to notice the visitor. For his part, he also avoided noticing her, or appeared not to notice. But when he took his leave, he stretched out a hand to her. She was not used to touching the hands of strangers, and reached out hers rather awkwardly— and grew pale. This handclasp gave her a strange pleasure, then made her flush with shame as if it were the beginning of their secret coming together.

After this he did not appear for a long time. For days on end she stood at the threshold, and impatiently awaited him with the persistent and unreasoning hope of adolescents. It seemed to her that he was under a compulsion, that he must at all costs come back and continue what he had begun, though she knew very well that he had begun nothing.

Let him but arrive—she thought—and I'll turn my back on him and go away. I'll show him that I have no need of him—

Almost an entire month had passed. May brought cold and rain—and still there was no sign of him. On the eve of St. Nicholas' day she looked for him especially, she knew not why; she was tormented by such a desire to see him that it seemed to her impossible it could go unfulfilled. That evening she went to bed early and wept so angrily and so bitterly as to drench the pillow, yet so silently that her father, who slept but a few feet away, did not even suspect her tears. He only heard her tossing and turning over, and from time to time asked her in a strange, agitated voice what troubled her and kept her from sleep.

The next morning her father went away somewhere. She looked at the windowpanes with rivulets of rain running down them; and suddenly she felt that she was no longer waiting for anything, no longer wanted anything, that it was a pleasant thing merely to rise, to clean the house, to build a fire in the stove, to attend to everyday matters. Towards evening she rigged herself out, stuck two dry cornflowers into her braid wound round her head, and thought of setting the samovar going.

The rain ceased. Everything was wet—the green of the road and the green of the rye fields, beyond which were moist blue walls of clouds casting their shadows upon everything. The samovar was boiling; its grating flamed red in the dark passageway. She stepped out of the house, with the smoke-blackened teapot in her hand, singing, "It is fearful to face the Judgment Seat, to receive the golden crown—" and coming in again waited for the samovar to boil harder. Just then Volodya came from the farmyard and crossed the threshold, bringing in a fresh smell of rain and musty wet cloth. He was about to approach her, aware of her yielding mood, when close to the door frame there appeared the head of a tall horse someone had driven up. Volodya walked straight on through the house, opened the door leading to the shed and disappeared, while Parashka, without raising her eyes, again went faint.

"How do you do?" said the merchant boldly from the threshold. "Seems I've come at the right time, just as you're about to have tea."

And, laughing, he took off his cap and shook it. His black peasant's coat was sleek from the rain. His swarthy face, with its look of being sprinkled with powder, was wet.

He did not speak now at all in the tone in which he had addressed her in her father's presence. She made no answer, and flushed. He was also silent for a moment—the cooing of the pigeons in a dark corner under the roof became clearly audible—then he walked up to her and, glancing at the samovar, asked, "Isn't your father at home?"

"No," she answered in a low voice as she bowed her head, upon which the cornflowers showed very blue.

"A pity," he said and struck his whip across his bootleg. "So you're alone and making the best of it?"

"Yes, making the best of it," she replied, with a faint smile.

"Well, never mind. I'll run in again another time," he said. "Good thing I've got an excuse. Really, I don't feel a bit like myself. I've been dying to see you."

"You don't believe me?" he said, cautiously embracing her. "Well, I'm telling the truth. I fell in love with you the first time I saw you, the day I was driving the sheep. And then when I saw you in the village, I was so blinded I nearly drove the horse down into the ravine. I just felt that there must be a romance between us or I'd go to the devil!"

"I've heard such tales before," she answered with difficulty. "Let me go," she said coldly, pushing his arm away with her elbow.

But he did not release her. He knew that she had not yet heard such tales. He tightened his embrace and now spoke with genuine warmth: "May God cause me to die without absolution, if I lie! May He deny me the sight of my own father and mother—"

She was silent. It seemed to her as if she were on the verge of falling. He glanced furtively around him, then bent over her, found her lips and pressed her face back. The long, stolen kiss left them both breathless. Then, with a pretense of despair, he waved his arms and walked to the threshold.

"Now I'm done for!" he said, seating himself in his cart. "My peace is gone forever—"

And swiftly he drove his tall horse across the bright green grass; it loomed against the cloud whose shadow was already merging with the twilight.

Soon he had vanished from sight. Everything suddenly grew quiet, and it seemed to her as if, at first but a few steps away, a struggle was going on between two quail who kept calling to each other as they flew farther and farther off into the remote rye fields, beyond the little wood now barely visible. . . .

He came twice more, both times unseasonably. Ustin was at home. And she pretended not to notice him, while he talked with her father in a business-like fashion. Frustrated in her desire to see him face to face, if only for a moment, she moved about like one drunken. . . .

Evgenya's soldier husband returned. With his wife, his father, and his stepmother, he arrived on St. Peter's day at Ustin's house, driving a short light-bay horse, harnessed to a new cart, the wheels smeared with fresh brown tar. The sol-

dier's father, a short-legged peasant with a black beard turning gray near the mouth, and a peculiarly jovial manner, had
just wed for the third time; his wife was lame, she had insolent
eyes and pointed youthful breasts. Everyone felt embarrassed
on his account, but he himself was cheerful and garrulous, probably to conceal his own embarrassment. Ill at ease, they drank
too much at lunch. They also ate too much, and kept pressing
one another to take more of the various dishes. They talked
nonsense, and again, with hits at the newly wed old man, in
riddles and proverbs, each in turn interrupting the others. During the entire meal Parashka feared that at any moment a quar-
rel might break out, and she felt faint, as if overcome by fumes.

After lunch they drank tea and vodka just outside the house,
on the green grass in the shade. All sense of shame lost, the
soldier's drunken father went to their cart and returned reel-
ing, with an accordion, which he thrust into his son's hands de-
manding that he play a dance tune. The soldier, with smutty
face and uniform undone, sat on the bench near the table and
rolled from side to side, every instant on the verge of falling.
For a long time he could not grasp what his father wanted.
Finally, he understood and abruptly, savagely began to play,
"If only the hen would give birth to a bull—" The thrice-wed
man thrust his hands under his black peasant's coat behind his
back, and danced in a squatting posture, bending his knees
low and beating a rhythm upon the ground with his boots.
Clapping the palms of her hands together, his lame wife came
forward and joined in, her goat-like breasts shaking up and
down. Evgenya's face became rigid with sluggish spite. Ustin
leaned his head upon an elbow propped on the table, his thin
fingers thrust into his bronze locks, his teeth tightly set. An
ill-natured smile had congealed in the corners of his lips. His
eyes sparkled with a kind of morose joy.

"Daughter! Come here!" he shouted rather sternly, moving
his eyebrows in such a way as to belie his tone. "Come here and
kiss me!"

"You are drunk," Parashka answered. "I am ashamed to
look at you!"

Her lips trembled. She turned on her heels and went off, out of sight of the house. There the sun, now low on the horizon, dazzled her. Two young doves, their wings flashing, flew down from the oaks and dropped amid the rye, into the shallow hollows overgrown with flowers. How quiet it was here after the din of the drunkards! The vast stretch of the rye fields in the light of the sunset was golden and serene, lovely to look upon. Parashka sat down by a hedge and gave full vent to her tears.

After she had wept a long time, she dried her tears and decided to return to the house and there, with her sister's help, to put an end to the indecency—to separate the drunkards, to remove the vodka and the samovar. Night had already come, strange and radiant. High up in the heavens, immense dull clouds appeared in ponderous piles—the heavens seemed vaster and more majestic than ever, and the moon shining in them seemed larger and more mirror-like. On the wide road, over the rye fields, shadows moved in great patches. The poles of the cart, which stood near the house, and the straw in it gleamed silvery. The soldier's father sprawled in the cart, wrangling with his drunken wife. An overturned bench lay near the table. A streak of light shone on the copper of the samovar where it stood to one side; a pool of spilt water shone dimly on the table, for someone had removed the samovar tap. Under the projecting eaves of the storehouse the panting dog on his chain was playing pranks, as if excited by the moon, now shining, now hidden. Parashka went into the house. Close to the lamp the soldier sat at the table, both elbows resting on it, holding up his stupefied head in his hands. He was muttering something. Drowsily and sullenly the flies buzzed in the sieves and strainers which hung on the wall near the stove. As for the soldier, he was talking to someone, boasting that as a man of importance he would be "assigned" to the service of some sort of *barin*, some man of standing like Yakov Ivanovitch. . . .

But where was her father? Where was Evgenya? Parashka turned, walked out into the passageway, and paused on the threshold. Now the high warm moon shone brightly amid the dull cloud masses. Just across the threshold, holding the reins in one hand and a whip in the other, stood the merchant, his tall horse, saddled, behind him. The moonlight gave his face a changed expression.

"Your dad's in fine shape—and full, oh my!" he said, with a smile, to Parashka, who was stunned with fright. "I just met him in the rye. Drunk?—well, you could squeeze the vodka out of him! He was saying, 'I'm off to the village!' and Evgenya was pulling him back."

Parashka was silent. The merchant dropped the reins, took her icy hand in his own strong hot one, and pushed her into the passageway. She moved back, leaning on him. She was dimly aware, over his shoulder, of the smoky-green strip of moonlight which fell through a hole in the roof into the darkness, as he pressed her against the cold stone of the wall and began kissing her face, whispering ardently between kisses: "Just wait, for God's sake, just wait—'Where, alas the day, when like an arrow we flew, when they burnt us with love, when they scorched us with flame.'—I've lost my senses over you! I'll take you away to Rostov. I'll marry you there. We'll settle on the steppe, in the Caucasus. We'll make thousands out of horses. You'll go finer than any dressmaker!"

She recalled him as he was when she first saw him—with the sheep and dogs, on his branded Kirghiz horse—and she put one arm around his neck, trembling from head to foot with happiness and tenderness, and hid her face against his breast. Then, abruptly and resolutely, with both arms she embraced him. . . .

When she came to herself, she remained sitting for a long time in a corner on the straw. The merchant tried to kiss her, to say something impetuously. She pushed him away, and violently shook her head, to show that she was not listening. He glanced furtively out through the passageway, and said rapidly that he would come again the next night, that she must meet him under the two oaks beyond the house, that he had something important to discuss with her.

"I'll come, I'll come," she replied.

"See that you don't fool me," he said, in a forced tone, as if he understood that she would not come.

She could hear the clink of the stirrup as he vaulted into the saddle, and the stamp of the horse's hooves impatient to start. She looked at the strip of moonlight, then lowered her eyes.

When the merchant, turning, said again to her, "See that you don't fool me," she suddenly saw framed in the little window of the door leading to the shed the cap and face of Volodya. There was as much horror in his eyes as if death herself had looked in. "And now it's all the same!" she thought. Her heart thumped so hard that breathing was difficult; her breast rose and fell, and she pressed her hands against it. This did not prevent her from thinking clearly. What she thought was very simple: she was lost! And it was all so terrible, and so unexpected, as such things are in a dream!

Several days after the feast day, Ustin still went about frowning. He was ashamed of his drunkenness. As for Parashka, she was weary from weakness: she felt broken and wanted to lie in bed from morning till night. But it was necessary to be up, to seem cheerful and calm, even to joke at dinner with her father and Volodya. From morning till night she thought of one and the same thing.

Ustin kept going off and coming back again. It seemed to her that if he had stayed at home and had not hurried away, if he had not upset her with his comings and goings, she could have got hold of herself and devised some way out, some means of saving herself. It was terrible to think that if he lingered at home and watched her closely, he might guess everything. But at times she desired, ardently desired, to have him understand; then somehow the whole thing would find some natural way of settling itself. It seemed to her that if only the days were rainy, gloomy, she could bear it all more easily. But they were bright now, sultry, and endless. The busy time in the fields was approaching; the heavy, dryish rye was ripening, yellowing—and there was no place to hide from the glare and the heat. After that strange feast day, which had destroyed the workaday routine of the farmhouse, the place had become, as it were, even more silent than usual; and a strained hush hovered over the house and over the bright yellow fields.

Day after day, she sat on the bench near the table in the hot empty house, observing the numberless flies with the tiny new ones on the hot dusty windowpanes. Volodya said nothing, but as always seemed preoccupied; he found all manner of trifling things to do out of doors and rarely came into the house. When he did enter, he acted as if nothing had happened; only he made no more amorous advances. What did it mean? It must be that he was waiting for some propitious moment and was hoping that this time he would not fail. Parashka smiled bitterly. The fool! It would be better if he told her father everything he had seen!

One day at noon, when a soft luminous haze hovered over the rye fields and the hot dusty road, and the high dazzling clouds were but faintly visible, a team of horses stopped before the storehouse. In the carriage sat a lady who, as Parashka knew, owed Ustin a great deal. She looked fatigued and worried; there was dust on her gray face. In a pensive tone, she began saying over and over the same thing—what a pity it was that she had not found Ustin at home. She lingered for an incredibly long time, looking about her. Then, screwing up her eyes, she began to examine Parashka's emaciated face, her transparent green eyes. "Are you well?" she suddenly asked.

Parashka answered simply and firmly that she was well, but after the lady had taken her departure she spent an hour looking in the mirror as she sat on the bench by the window; she was shocked by her likeness to her father, and her heart grew faint with horror. She had changed a great deal—a child could see that—how had her father failed to observe it? But he would soon see it too; then he would grasp everything, all that had happened—and what then?

In her mind's eye she reviewed her whole short life. And she saw for the first time that she had never before even suspected the kind of enchantment she lived under, how much her thoughts centered around one thing, how many confused and captivating pictures of some remote happy city, of remote steppes and roads, her imagination held, how tenderly in her dreams she loved someone.—She now felt that by his terrible deed Nikanor killed both her and himself. Suddenly she saw this short-legged thief as he really was—and he became hateful to her. She could not love him—she had never really loved him. Now it was impossible to think of the man without feeling shame, aversion, despair. The prophecy of the terrible barefoot old man had come true. She felt herself infected, as it were, with some shameful incurable disease, and forever separated from her father by a bottomless chasm.

As she went on musing, crying quietly, taking the kerchief off her head and smoothing it, her heart overflowed while her thoughts grew more and more vague. She remembered how she had loved, awaited someone—and how this love had been returned—and nowhere could she find relief from anguish over the past, from pity for herself, from tenderness for him whom she had dreamed so long of loving. She thought of her father to whom she had once said, "I'm all on the outside," and she was ready to cry out, to run to his room, to fling herself at his feet, that he might stamp upon her, crush her under his boots, if only that would assuage her torment at the thought of the old days irretrievably lost. "For you, daughter, for you alone," —she recalled his tender words and she wept, growing faint with passionate sorrow and tears.

One evening Ustin and Volodya left for the village together to have their hair cut. The evening was clear and peaceful; the flat expanse of ripe rye beyond the great road appeared rose-yellow in the luminous twilight; black arrow-like swallows, their tiny ruddy breasts glowing, flew past the open window at which Parashka sat. Suddenly, on the horizon, up from the rye field, rose the short figure of Nikanor; apparently he had been hiding there. He hurried towards the house across the field and dry wheel-ruts.

"Hello," he said in a low voice, pausing near the threshold. "No one at home?"

"No one," Parashka answered, her pale lips scarcely moving.

"We have some business to do. Let's go behind the house, under the oaks."

He spoke as a husband speaks, as an intimate endowed with some power, as a man with whom she already had an indissoluble and secret bond. She understood that it was not for business alone that he had called her. And suddenly, with a sweet agony, her heart sank again at the stark power of his command, at the presentiment that what had seemed so terrible to her the first time would happen again. And silently she rose and followed him.

Then all the while glancing around, he told her firmly, abruptly, why he had come. She must help him take two mares from her father's stable and run away with him to Rostov. She did not appear surprised and answered calmly, without lifting her eyes, "Very well."

The sun was sinking below the bearded ears of rye, where they sat by a hedge, and poured upon them a golden dust. From the great road, from the southeast, there blew the faint breeze of approaching July, the harvest time, when the deep dull blues of the sky are unchanging, and the droning insects with harsh wings descend on the rye and rock on its wind-blown ears.

Nikanor went on to say that within a week Ustin would leave one night for the Tikhvinsk fair. He would take Volodya with him and would not return until late the next night. Nikanor was sure of this, for he had promised Ustin that he also would be at the fair to help him sell a stallion. This meant that during dinner time, when not a soul was likely to be about in the fields, it would be possible to take the mares, and hitching them to the cart, drive them quickly away in the direction of Lebedyani, keeping to the by-roads, which were generally untravelled until the busy harvest season arrived. At night they would find shelter in secret places—amid the grain, where the devil himself wouldn't think of looking for them. With daylight they would proceed farther. In Lebedyani he had a loyal crony with a heart of gold, who would dispose of the mares for him for three or four hundred rubles. They would then have over five hundred rubles, which would enable them to reach Rostov, where they would begin a business he had had long in mind.

"What sort of business?" Parashka asked.

"You are curious, aren't you?" said Nikanor with a smile.

"It had better be done by night," she said earnestly.

"What's come over you?" said Nikanor scornfully, rolling a cigarette with a piece of newspaper. He sighed. "No, my girl, that wouldn't work out. You'd better follow my plan."

"Isn't it possible to do it sooner?" Parashka asked, her eyes on her small bare feet.

"Act in haste, repent at leisure."

She made no reply, but in her heart hatred flamed up against him. To wait a whole week! Didn't he have enough feeling to understand her torments? Wouldn't it be better to hang herself at once on this oak?—she thought, but without putting her thought into so many words; and she began to bite her lips hard, to keep her face muscles from trembling. But she could not control herself and burst into tears.

"What's the matter with you?" Nikanor asked in astonishment.

She made no reply, and only wept the more bitterly.

"I spoke to you, didn't I?" he shouted gruffly.

"Let me alone!" She shouted back with such hatred and ferocity that Nikanor actually moved away from her.

"All right—enough, enough," he said, puzzled. "But it would be much better if we discussed this business—"

And she stopped crying, and sat like one stupefied. . . .

For a whole week, until the time for the Tikhvinsk fair, Ustin, as if out of spite, stayed at home. Evgenya came—to complain of her soldier husband, who after his term of military service now turned out to be a complete fool and drunkard, and of her lame mother-in-law, who was evil and dissolute, and had her father-in-law completely under her thumb. But even Evgenya did not disconcert Parashka, who no longer thought, no longer felt. In her stupefaction, a sense of fateful sin overcame her, endued her with a shameless calm. She slept a great deal during the week, both day and night. Every time she awoke, she would jump up, dumfounded by the thought of what was almost immediately ahead of her.

At last the final night came.

It was singularly like the night when she had watched the campfire flaring beyond the great road. Now, as then, as she lay in the dark room, she saw through the window the noc-

turnal sky all studded with pale stars. And now, as then, her
father was saying something in a passionate voice outside the
window. Suddenly the door of the house was noiselessly pushed
open.

"Daughter, are you asleep?" he asked in a low tone, as he
paused near the threshold.

"No—" she murmured with difficulty.

Not noticing her strange tone, he moved towards the plank
bed upon which she lay. He found her in the darkness, sat down
near her, and laid a hand on her half-naked shoulder. His hand
trembled.

"Daughter, what's the matter with you?" he asked quietly
and solemnly, bending towards her face. She felt the touch of
his beard, the warmth of his pleasant breath, and the pleasant
rye odor of vodka. "Now don't hide anything from me," he
said, embracing her, the coarse cloth of his peasant's coat scratching her shoulder. "You're young, warm-blooded—"

Her heart fluttered. "Father!" she wanted to cry out in a
voice full of tears—and in the single cry to put all her anguish
and helplessness. "Father—" she wanted to say—"he's ruined
me, he's shamed me! I don't love him, I don't know whom I
love! I wouldn't leave you for anyone in the world—" He
drew still closer to her and suddenly whispered in quite a different tone, ingratiatingly, caressingly: "Would you like to
have a little present? A new dress, maybe? I'm going to town
now, to the fair—what would you like to have me buy you?
Eh? Be quick now, don't be afraid—"

And his trembling hand passed down her back. Dumfounded, she struggled away from him, so that he almost fell
from the bench on which he sat. She jumped to her feet and
retreated to a corner, holding up her arms to ward him off. He
stepped back, murmuring, "What's got into you? What is it?
Why do you act like this?"

"Go away—" she spoke barely audibly, conscious that her
lips were stiff. And, in a daze of joy, in a paroxysm of rapture,
despair, she thought, "A-ah! So that's how it is!"

He stood there for a few moments, and then went out. She
heard his voice outside, unnaturally loud, above the creaking

of the cart, the neighing of the shying stallion tied to the cart, and then she heard her father and Volodya climb into the cart and set off. With feline keenness of sight she peered into the darkness of the house, that had become, as it were, transparent, and at the pale stars in the heavenly dome visible through the open window. For a long time she stood upon the plank bed, in the dead silence of night in the steppe that surrounded her. Then she lay down cautiously and at once fell asleep.

She awoke to a heavy, scorching, dazzling day; in the sultriness the shining horizon looked hazy and whitish. When she opened her eyes, it was already almost lunch time. The sun beat down upon the dim fly-specked windows, filled the house with heat and light. Scarcely awake, without stopping to wash, her head heavy with stupor, she ran barefoot to the threshold and stood in the sun. It was already high in the heavens, and the stark heat poured over her from head to foot. The sea of ripe grain, with its thick, dimly gleaming dust, seemed to have moved closer, erecting a solider barrier against the farmyard and the road. And in the dense hot air this dust color of the rye, its heavy ears bowed low and stiff in the silence, gave the impression of terrible, suffocating heat.

As in a daze, she glanced round her and tried hard to remember. What was she to do now? Last night, after her father's departure, it had seemed as if all of a sudden everything had become clear, simple, decided. Yet now, despite all her efforts, she could not remember just what it was that had been decided or in what way. That someone would shortly come to get her, and that it would be necessary to leave as soon as possible when this happened, and that she would have to hide, all this she recalled. But how had it happened that she had not bidden her father good-bye, had not said to him what she had thought of in the night, and what it was necessary to say? True, after what had happened yesterday, she might go without saying good-bye, without a word; but how came it that she had given no thought to what she ought to take with her? She had not gathered her things together, nor had she taken the trouble to wash or dress. Confused and stupefied, she remained standing in the sultry heat with uncovered head; she pressed her hands under her armpits and felt the heat on her naked shoulders, while her bare feet touched the hot stone of the threshold. The white dog was lying, with his tongue hanging out, in the short shadow of the storehouse. Frightened she glanced now at him, now at the rye, now at the by-road. . . .

Then suddenly, above the rye, against the dim, silvery horizon, appeared the shaft-bow of a cart, framing the head of a tall lean horse. Nikanor sat high at the front of his cart, his cap pushed back over the nape of his neck, and pulled at the taut reins. Urging his horse to a trot, and raising the dust, he turned sharply in, and the rattling cart rolled up to the very threshold. His eyes were dilated, his dark sunburnt face was all in a sweat, his face had a strange expression—as if of astonishment.

"Well, you?" he said in a rapid whisper, as he jumped down from the cart, without noticing that Parashka was barefoot and almost naked. "Everything ready? Have they left?"

Without answering, she glared savagely at him, sprang away from the threshold and with flashing bare feet went towards the farmyard gates, in the direction of the stalls. Pressing her hot shoulder heavily against the gates, she pushed them open creaking before her. She walked across the deep dried manure, up to the dark stalls of the mares. Nikanor followed her, leading his horse to the gates and muttering, "But why haven't you put your clothes on?" On the door to the stalls hung a large padlock. Parashka turned round.

"I haven't got a key," she said, staring at Nikanor with large, motionless, transparently green eyes.

Nikanor glanced round him and caught sight of the stone upon which the axes were sharpened. Snatching it up in both hands, he struck with it at the padlock. The lock flew off together with the hinge—and Parashka caught it in the air and held it tight in her small sunburned hand. Nikanor pushed his cap still further back on the nape of his neck and, wet with sweat, with a bridle in one hand, he entered the stalls; lowering his head he peered into the darkness, where, pressing against the wall with lowered head, stood a bay mare, a beauty with lilac-colored eyes. Parashka took a long step and, awkwardly but with her whole strength, struck Nikanor across the temple with the lock. He stumbled sharply and fell, his head striking the manure. Parashka jumped away, and flew like an arrow out of the enclosure back through the gates. As she passed, Nikanor's horse took fright and dashed beside her into the road. The dust rose, the cart rattled, and the horse took the road towards town, towards the whitish shining distance beyond the crest of a hill. Parashka turned in another direction, across the road, through the rye. As she ran she glanced behind her and suddenly paused, for there was Nikanor, capless, his face and shirt red with blood, rushing out through the gates. Stumbling, he started off after the frightened horse. Parashka gave a piercing scream and then plunged into the dense suffocating rye. . . .

The peasants who drove their carts that day along the by-roads saw her running rapidly here and there in the pathless depths of the rye. Now she crouched down to rest, and peered out—and again she ran on, her head uncovered and her white chemise flashing in the sun.

It was five days before they caught her. As she tried to fight off her pursuers she seemed endowed with terrific strength, and savagely bit three peasants who twisted her arms in the effort to bind her with a new rein.

THE PORTABLE PHONOGRAPH

By WALTER VAN TILBURG CLARK

THE red sunset, with narrow, black cloud strips like threats across it, lay on the curved horizon of the prairie. The air was still and cold, and in it settled the mute darkness and greater cold of night. High in the air there was wind, for through the veil of the dusk the clouds could be seen gliding rapidly south and changing shapes. A queer sensation of torment, of two-sided, unpredictable nature, arose from the stillness of the earth air beneath the violence of the upper air. Out of the sunset, through the dead, matted grass and isolated weed stalks of the prairie, crept the narrow and deeply rutted remains of a road. In the road, in places, there were crusts of shallow, brittle ice. There were little islands of an old oiled pavement in the road too, but most of it was mud, now frozen rigid. The frozen mud still bore the toothed impress of great tanks, and a wanderer on the neighboring undulations might have stumbled, in this light, into large, partially filled-in and weed-grown cavities, their banks channelled and beginning to spread into badlands. These pits were such as might have been made by falling meteors, but they were not. They were the scars of gigantic bombs, their rawness already made a little natural by rain, seed, and time. Along the road, there were rakish remnants of fence. There was also, just visible, one portion of tangled and multiple barbed wire still erect, behind which was a shelving ditch with small caves, now very quiet and empty, at intervals in its back wall. Otherwise there was no structure or remnant of a structure visible over the dome of the darkling earth, but only, in sheltered hollows, the darker shadows of young trees trying again.

Under the wuthering arch of the high wind a V of wild geese

fled south. The rush of their pinions sounded briefly, and the faint, plaintive notes of their expeditionary talk. Then they left a still greater vacancy. There was the smell and expectation of snow, as there is likely to be when the wild geese fly south. From the remote distance, towards the red sky, came faintly the protracted howl and quick yap-yap of a prairie wolf.

North of the road perhaps a hundred yards, lay the parallel and deeply intrenched course of a small creek, lined with leafless alders and willows. The creek was already silent under ice. Into the bank above it was dug a sort of cell, with a single opening, like the mouth of a mine tunnel. Within the cell there was a little red of fire, which showed dully through the opening, like a reflection or a deception of the imagination. The light came from the chary burning of four blocks of poorly aged peat, which gave off a petty warmth and much acrid smoke. But the precious remnants of wood, old fence posts and timbers from the long-deserted dugouts, had to be saved for the real cold, for the time when a man's breath blew white, the moisture in his nostrils stiffened at once when he stepped out, and the expansive blizzards paraded for days over the vast open, swirling and settling and thickening, till the dawn of the cleared day when the sky was thin blue-green and the terrible cold, in which a man could not live for three hours unwarmed, lay over the uniformly drifted swell of the plain.

Around the smoldering peat, four men were seated cross-legged. Behind them, traversed by their shadows, was the earth bench, with two old and dirty army blankets, where the owner of the cell slept. In a niche in the opposite wall were a few tin utensils which caught the glint of the coals. The host was re-wrapping in a piece of daubed burlap four fine, leather-bound books. He worked slowly and very carefully, and at last tied the bundle securely with a piece of grass-woven cord. The other three looked intently upon the process, as if a great significance lay in it. As the host tied the cord, he spoke. He was an old man, his long, matted beard and hair gray to nearly white. The shadows made his brows and cheekbones appear gnarled, his eyes and cheeks deeply sunken. His big hands, rough with frost and swollen by rheumatism, were awkward but gentle at their task. He was like a prehistoric priest performing a fateful ceremonial rite. Also his voice had in it a suitable quality of deep, reverent despair, yet perhaps at the moment, a sharpness of selfish satisfaction.

"When I perceived what was happening," he said, "I told myself, 'It is the end. I cannot take much; I will take these.'"

"Perhaps I was impractical," he continued. "But for myself, I do not regret, and what do we know of those who will come after us? We are the doddering remnant of a race of mechanical fools. I have saved what I love; the soul of what was good in us is here; perhaps the new ones will make a strong enough beginning not to fall behind when they become clever."

He rose with slow pain and placed the wrapped volumes in the niche with his utensils. The others watched him with the same ritualistic gaze.

"Shakespeare, the Bible, 'Moby Dick,' the 'Divine Comedy,'" one of them said softly. "You might have done worse, much worse."

"You will have a little soul left until you die," said another harshly. "That is more than is true of us. My brain becomes thick, like my hands." He held the big, battered hands, with their black nails, in the glow to be seen.

"I want paper to write on," he said. "And there is none."

The fourth man said nothing. He sat in the shadow farthest from the fire, and sometimes his body jerked in its rags from the cold. Although he was still young, he was sick and coughed often. Writing implied a greater future than he now felt able to consider.

The old man seated himself laboriously, and reached out, groaning at the movement, to put another block of peat on the fire. With bowed heads and averted eyes, his three guests acknowledged his magnanimity.

"We thank you, Dr. Jenkins, for the reading," said the man who had named the books.

They seemed then to be waiting for something. Dr. Jenkins understood, but was loath to comply. In an ordinary moment he would have said nothing. But the words of "The Tempest" which he had been reading, and the religious attention of the three, made this an unusual occasion.

"You wish to hear the phonograph," he said grudgingly.

The two middle-aged men stared into the fire, unable to formulate and expose the enormity of their desire.

The young man, however, said anxiously, between suppressed coughs, "Oh, please," like an excited child.

The old man rose again in his difficult way, and went to the back of the cell. He returned and placed tenderly upon the packed floor, where the firelight might fall upon it, an old portable phonograph in a black case. He smoothed the top with his hand, and then opened it. The lovely green-felt-covered disk became visible.

"I have been using thorns as needles," he said. "But to-night, because we have a musician among us," he bent his head to the young man, almost invisible in the shadow, "I will use a steel needle. There are only three left."

The two middle-aged men stared at him in speechless adoration. The one with the big hands, who wanted to write, moved his lips, but the whisper was not audible.

"Oh, don't!" cried the young man, as if he were hurt. "The thorns will do beautifully."

"No," the old man said. "I have become accustomed to the thorns, but they are not really good. For you, my young friend, we will have good music to-night."

"After all," he added generously, and beginning to wind the phonograph, which creaked, "they can't last forever."

"No, nor we," the man who needed to write said harshly. "The needle, by all means."

"Oh, thanks," said the young man. "Thanks," he said again in a low, excited voice, and then stifled his coughing with a bowed head.

"The records, though," said the old man when he had finished winding, "are a different matter. Already they are very worn. I do not play them more than once a week. One, once a week, that is what I allow myself."

"More than a week I cannot stand it; not to hear them," he apologized.

"No, how could you?" cried the young man. "And with them here like this."

"A man can stand anything," said the man who wanted to write, in his harsh, antagonistic voice.

"Please, the music," said the young man.

"Only the one," said the old man. "In the long run, we will remember more that way."

He had a dozen records with luxuriant gold and red seals. Even in that light the others could see that the threads of the records were becoming worn. Slowly he read out the titles, and the tremendous, dead names of the composers and the artists and the orchestras. The three worked upon the names in their minds, carefully. It was difficult to select from such a wealth what they would at once most like to remember. Finally, the man who wanted to write named Gershwin's "New York."

"Oh, no!" cried the sick young man, and then could say nothing more because he had to cough. The others understood him, and the harsh man withdrew his selection and waited for the musician to choose.

The musician begged Dr. Jenkins to read the titles again, very slowly, so that he could remember the sounds. While they were read, he lay back against the wall, his eyes closed, his thin, horny hand pulling at his light beard, and listened to the voices and the orchestras and the single instruments in his mind.

When the reading was done he spoke despairingly. "I have forgotten," he complained; "I cannot hear them clearly."

"There are things missing," he explained.

"I know," said Dr. Jenkins. "I thought that I knew all of Shelley by heart. I should have brought Shelley."

"That's more soul than we can use," said the harsh man. " 'Moby Dick' is better."

"By God, we can understand that," he emphasized.

The Doctor nodded.

"Still," said the man who had admired the books, "we need the absolute if we are to keep a grasp on anything."

"Anything but these sticks and peat clods and rabbit snares," he said bitterly.

"Shelley desired an ultimate absolute," said the harsh man. "It's too much," he said. "It's no good; no earthly good."

The musician selected a Debussy nocturne. The others considered and approved. They rose to their knees to watch the Doctor prepare for the playing, so that they appeared to be actually in an attitude of worship. The peat glow showed the thinness of their bearded faces, and the deep lines in them, and revealed the condition of their garments. The other two continued to kneel as the old man carefully lowered the needle onto the spinning disk, but the musician suddenly drew back against the wall again, with his knees up, and buried his face in his hands.

At the first notes of the piano the listeners were startled. They stared at each other. Even the musician lifted his head in amazement, but then quickly bowed it again, strainingly, as if he were suffering from a pain he might not be able to endure. They were all listening deeply, without movement. The wet, blue-green notes tinkled forth from the old machine, and were individual, delectable presences in the cell. The individual, delectable presences swept into a sudden tide of unbearably beautiful dissonance, and then continued fully the swelling and ebbing of that tide, the dissonant inpourings, and the resolutions, and the diminishments, and the little, quiet wavelets of interlude lapping between. Every sound was piercing and singularly sweet. In all the men except the musician, there occurred rapid sequences of tragically heightened recollection. He heard nothing but what was there. At the final, whispering disappearance, but moving quietly so that the others would not hear him and look at him, he let his head fall back in agony, as if it were drawn there by the hair, and clenched the fingers of one hand over his teeth. He sat that way while the others were silent, and until they began to breathe again normally. His drawn-up legs were trembling violently.

Quickly Dr. Jenkins lifted the needle off, to save it and not to spoil the recollection with scraping. When he had stopped the whirling of the sacred disk, he courteously left the phonograph open and by the fire, in sight.

The others, however, understood. The musician rose last, but then abruptly, and went quickly out at the door without saying anything. The others stopped at the door and gave their thanks in low voices. The Doctor nodded magnificently.

"Come again," he invited, "in a week. We will have the 'New York.' "

When the two had gone together, out towards the rimed

road, he stood in the entrance, peering and listening. At first, there was only the resonant boom of the wind overhead, and then far over the dome of the dead, dark plain, the wolf cry lamenting. In the rifts of clouds the Doctor saw four stars flying. It impressed the Doctor that one of them had just been obscured by the beginning of a flying cloud at the very moment he heard what he had been listening for, a sound of suppressed coughing. It was not near-by, however. He believed that down against the pale alders he could see the moving shadow.

With nervous hands he lowered the piece of canvas which served as his door, and pegged it at the bottom. Then quickly and quietly, looking at the piece of canvas frequently, he slipped the records into the case, snapped the lid shut, and carried the phonograph to his couch. There, pausing often to stare at the canvas and listen, he dug earth from the wall and disclosed a piece of board. Behind this there was a deep hole in the wall, into which he put the phonograph. After a moment's consideration, he went over and reached down his bundle of books and inserted it also. Then, guardedly, he once more sealed up the hole with the board and the earth. He also changed his blankets, and the grass-stuffed sack which served as a pillow, so that he could lie facing the entrance. After carefully placing two more blocks of peat upon the fire, he stood for a long time watching the stretched canvas, but it seemed to billow naturally with the first gusts of a lowering wind. At last he prayed, and got in under his blankets, and closed his smoke-smarting eyes. On the inside of the bed, next the wall, he could feel with his hand the comfortable piece of lead pipe.

QUEENS OF FRANCE
By THORNTON WILDER

A lawyer's office in New Orleans, 1869.
The door to the street is hung with a reed curtain, through which one obtains a glimpse of a public park in sunshine.
A small bell tinkles. After a pause it rings again.
Marie-Sidonie Cressaux pushes the reeds apart and peers in. She is an attractive young woman equal to any situation in life except a summons to a lawyer's office.
M'su Cahusac, a dry little man with sharp black eyes, enters from an inner room.

Marie-Sidonie (*indicating a letter in her hand*). You . . . you have asked me to come and see you.
M. Cahusac (*severe and brief*). Your name, Madame?
Marie-Sidonie. Mamselle Marie-Sidonie Cressaux, M'su.
M. Cahusac (*after a pause*). Yes. Kindly be seated, Mamselle.

He goes to his desk and opens a great many drawers, collecting documents from each. Presently having assembled a large bundle he returns to the centre of the room and says abruptly:

Mamselle, this interview is to be regarded by you as strictly confidential.
Marie-Sidonie. Yes, M'su.
M. Cahusac (*after looking at her sternly a moment*). May I ask if Mamselle is able to bear the shock of surprise, of good or bad news?
Marie-Sidonie. Why . . . yes, M'su.
M. Cahusac. Then if you are Mamselle Marie-Sidonie Cressaux, the daughter of Baptiste-Anténor Cressaux, it is my duty to inform you that you are in danger.
Marie-Sidonie. I am in danger, M'su?

He returns to his desk, opens further drawers and returns with more papers. She follows him with bewildered eyes.

M. Cahusac. Mamselle, in addition to my duties as a lawyer in this city, I am the representative here of an Historical Society in Paris. Will you please try and follow me, Mamselle? This Historical Society has been engaged in tracing the descendants of the true heir to the French throne. As you know, at the time of the Revolution, in Seventeen Ninety-five, to be exact, Mamselle, the true, lawful, and legitimate heir to the French throne disappeared. It was rumored that this boy, who was then ten years old, came to America and lived for some time in New Orleans. We now know that the rumor was true. We now know that he here begot legitimate issue, that this legitimate issue in turn begot legitimate issue, and that—(*Marie-Sidonie suddenly starts searching for something in her shopping bag.*) Mamselle, may I have the honor of your attention a little longer?

Marie-Sidonie (choking). My fan—my, my fan, M'su. (*She finds it and at once begins to fan herself wildly. Suddenly she cries out*): M'su, what danger am I in?

M. Cahusac (sternly). If Mamselle will exercise a moment's —one moment's—patience, she will know all. . . . That legitimate issue here begot legitimate issue, and the royal line of France has been traced to a certain (*he consults his documents*) Baptiste-Anténor Cressaux.

Marie-Sidonie (Her fan stops and she stares at him). Ba't— ba'tiste . . . !

M. Cahusac (leaning forward with menacing emphasis). Mamselle, can you *prove* that you are the daughter of Baptiste-Anténor Cressaux?

Marie-Sidonie. Why . . . why . . .

M. Cahusac. Mamselle, have you a certificate of your parents' marriage?

Marie-Sidonie. Yes, M'su.

M. Cahusac. If it turns out to be valid, and if it is true that you have no true lawful and legitimate brothers—

Marie-Sidonie. No, M'su.

M. Cahusac. Then, Mamselle, I have nothing further to do

than to announce to you that you are the true and long-lost
heir to the throne of France.

> He draws himself up, approaches her with great dignity and
> kisses her hand.
> Marie-Sidonie begins to cry.
> He goes to the desk, pours out a glass of water and murmur-
> ing, "Your Royal Highness," offers it to her.

Marie-Sidonie. M'su Cahusac, I am very sorry. . . . But there
must be some mistake. My father was a poor sailor . . . a
. . . a poor sailor.

M. Cahusac (reading from his papers). . . . A distinguished
and esteemed navigator.

Marie-Sidonie. . . . A poor sailor . . .

M. Cahusac (firmly). . . . Navigator . . .

> Pause. She looks about, stricken.

Marie-Sidonie (as before, suddenly and loudly). M'su, what
danger am I in?

M. Cahusac (approaching her and lowering his voice). As Your
Royal Highness knows there are several families in New
Orleans that claim, without documents (*he rattles the vel-
lum and seals in his hand*), without proof—that pretend to
the blood royal. The danger from them, however, is not
great. The real danger is from France. From the impassioned
Republicans.

Marie-Sidonie. Impass . . .

M. Cahusac. But Your Royal Highness has only to put Herself
into my hands.

Marie-Sidonie (crying again). Please do not call me "Your
Royal Highness."

M. Cahusac. You . . . give me permission to call you Madame
de Cressaux?

Marie-Sidonie. Yes, M'su. Mamselle Cressaux. I am Marie-
Sidonie Cressaux.

M. Cahusac. Am I mistaken . . . hmm . . . in saying that
you have children?

Marie-Sidonie (faintly). Yes, M'su. I have three children.

M. Cahusac looks at her thoughtfully a moment and returns to his desk.

M. Cahusac. Madame, from now on thousands of eyes will be fixed upon you, the eyes of the whole world, Madame. I cannot urge you too strongly to be very discreet, to be very circumspect.

Marie-Sidonie (*rising, abruptly, nervously*). M'su Cahusac, I do not wish to have anything to do with this. There is a mistake somewhere. I thank you very much, but there is a mistake somewhere. I do not know where. I must go now.

M. Cahusac (*darts forward*). But, Madame, you do not know what you are doing. Your rank cannot be dismissed as easily as that. Do you not know that in a month or two, all the newspapers in the world, including the New Orleans "Times-Picayune," will publish your name? The first nobles of France will cross the ocean to call upon you. The Bishop of Louisiana will call upon you . . . the Mayor . . .

Marie-Sidonie. No, no.

M. Cahusac. You will be given a great deal of money—and several palaces.

Marie-Sidonie. No, no.

M. Cahusac. And a guard of soldiers to protect you.

Marie-Sidonie. No, no.

M. Cahusac. You will be made president of Le Petit Salon and Queen of the Mardi Gras. . . . Another sip of water, Your Royal Highness.

Marie-Sidonie. Oh, M'su, what shall I do? . . . Oh, M'su, save me!—I do not want the Bishop or the Mayor.

M. Cahusac. You ask me what you shall do?

Marie-Sidonie. Oh yes, oh, my God!

M. Cahusac. For the present, return to your home and lie down. A little rest and a little reflection will tell you what you have to do. Then come and see me Thursday morning.

Marie-Sidonie. I think there must be a mistake somewhere.

M. Cahusac. May I be permitted to ask Madame de Cressaux a question: Could I have the privilege of presenting Her—until the great announcement takes place—with a small gift of . . . money?

Marie-Sidonie. No, no.

M. Cahusac. The Historical Society is not rich. The Historical Society has difficulty in pursuing the search for the last documents that will confirm Madame's exalted rank, but they would be very happy to advance a certain sum to Madame, subscribed by her devoted subjects.

Marie-Sidonie. Please no. I do not wish any. I must go now.

M. Cahusac. Let me beg Madame not to be alarmed. For the present a little rest and reflection. . . .

> The bell rings.
> He again bends over her hand, murmuring . . . "obedient servant and devoted subject."

Marie-Sidonie (in confusion). Goodbye, good morning, M. Cahusac. (*She lingers at the door a moment, then returns and says in great earnestness*): Oh, M. Cahusac, do not let the Bishop come and see me. The Mayor, yes—but not the Bishop.

> Enter Madame Pugeot, a plump little bourgeoise in black.
> Exit Marie-Sidonie.
> M. Cahusac kisses the graciously extended hand of Madame Pugeot.

Mme. Pugeot. Good morning, M. Cahusac.

M. Cahusac. Your Royal Highness.

Mme. Pugeot. What business can you possibly be having with that dreadful Marie Cressaux! Do you not know that she is an abandoned woman?

M. Cahusac. Alas, we are in the world, Your Royal Highness. For the present I must earn a living as best I can. Mamselle Cressaux is arranging about the purchase of a house and garden.

Mme. Pugeot. Purchase, M. Cahusac, phi! You know very well that she has half a dozen houses and gardens already. She persuades every one of her lovers to give her a little house and garden. She is beginning to own the whole quarter of Saint-Magloire.

M. Cahusac. Will Your Royal Highness condescend to sit down? (*She does.*) And how is the royal family this morning?

Mme. Pugeot. Only so-so, M'su Cahusac.

M. Cahusac. The Archduchess of Tuscany?

Mme. Pugeot (*fanning herself with a turkey's wing*). A cold. One of her colds. I sometimes think the dear child will never live to see her pearls.

M. Cahusac. And the Dauphin, Your Royal Highness?

Mme. Pugeot. Still, still amusing himself in the city, as young men will. Wine, gambling, bad company. At least it keeps him out of harm.

M. Cahusac. And the Duke of Burgundy?

Mme. Pugeot. Imagine! The poor child has a sty in his eye!

M. Cahusac. Tchk-tchk! (*with solicitude*) In which eye, Madame?

Mme. Pugeot. In the left!

M. Cahusac. Tchk-tchk! And the Prince of Lorraine and the Duke of Berry?

Mme. Pugeot. They are fairly well, but they seem to mope in their cradle. Their first teeth, my dear chamberlain.

M. Cahusac. And your husband, Madame?

Mme. Pugeot (*rises, walks back and forth a moment, then stands still*). From now on we are never to mention him again— while we are discussing these matters. It is to be understood that he is my husband in a manner of speaking only. He has no part in my true life. He has chosen to scoff at my birth and my rank, but he will see what he will see. . . . Naturally I have not told him about the proofs that you and I have collected. I have not the heart to let him see how unimportant he will become.

M. Cahusac. Unimportant, indeed!

Mme. Pugeot. So remember, we do not mention him in the same breath *with these matters!*

M. Cahusac. You must trust me, Madame. (*softly, with significance*) And *your* health, Your Royal Highness?

Mme. Pugeot. Oh, very well, thank you. Excellent. I used to do quite poorly, as you remember, but since this wonderful news I have been more than well, God be praised.

M. Cahusac (*as before, with lifted eyebrows*). I beg of you to do nothing unwise. I beg of you. . . . The little new life we are all anticipating . . .

Mme. Pugeot. Have no fear, my dear chamberlain. What is dear to France is dear to me.

M. Cahusac. When I think, Madame, of how soon we shall be able to announce your rank—when I think that this time next year you will be enjoying all the honors and privileges that are your due, I am filled with a pious joy.

Mme. Pugeot. God's will be done, God's will be done.

M. Cahusac. At all events, I am particularly happy to see that Your Royal Highness is in the best of health, for I have had a piece of disappointing news.

Mme. Pugeot. Chamberlain, you are not going to tell me that Germany has at last declared war upon my country?

M. Cahusac. No, Madame.

Mme. Pugeot. You greatly frightened me last week. I could scarcely sleep. Such burdens as I have! My husband tells me that I cried out in my sleep the words: *Paris, I come!*

M. Cahusac. Sublime, Madame!

Mme. Pugeot. Paris, I come, like that. I cried out twice in my sleep: *Paris, I come.* Oh, these are anxious times; I am on my way to the Cathedral now. This Bismarck does not understand me. We must avoid a war at all costs, M. Cahusac. . . . Then what is your news?

M. Cahusac. My anxiety at present is more personal. The Historical Society in Paris is now confirming the last proofs of your claim. They have secretaries at work in all the archives: Madrid, Vienna, Constantinople . . .

Mme. Pugeot. Constantinople!

M. Cahusac. All this requires a good deal of money and the Society is not rich. We have been driven to a painful decision. The Society must sell one of the royal jewels or one of the royal furnitures which I am guarding upstairs. The Historical Society has written me, Madame, ordering me to send them at once—the royal christening robe.

Mme. Pugeot. Never!

M. Cahusac. The very robe under which Charlemagne was christened, the Charles, the Henris, the Louis, to lie under a glass in the Louvre. (*softly*) And this is particularly painful to me because I had hoped—it was, in fact, the dream of my life—to see at least one of your children christened under all those fleurs-de-lis.

Mme. Pugeot. It shall not go to the Louvre. I forbid it.

M. Cahusac. But what can I do? I offered them the sceptre. I offered them the orb. I even offered them the mug which Your Royal Highness has already purchased. But no! the christening robe it must be.

Mme. Pugeot. It shall not leave America! (*clutching her handbag*) How much are they asking for it?

M. Cahusac. Oh, Madame, since it is the Ministry of Museums and Monuments they are asking a great many thousands of francs.

Mme. Pugeot. And how much would they ask their Queen?

M. Cahusac (*sadly*). Madame, Madame, I cannot see you purchasing those things which are rightly yours.

Mme. Pugeot. I will purchase it. I shall sell the house on the Chaussée Sainte-Anne.

M. Cahusac (*softly*). If Your Majesty will give five hundred dollars of Her money I shall add five hundred of my own.

Mme. Pugeot (*shaken*). Five hundred. Five hundred. . . . Well, you will be repaid many times, my dear chamberlain, when I am restored to my position. (*She thinks a moment.*) To-morrow at three, I shall bring you the papers for the sale of the house. You will do everything quietly. My husband will be told about it in due time.

M. Cahusac. I understand. I shall be very discreet.

> The bell rings. M. Cahusac turns to the door as Mamselle Pointevin starts to enter.

I shall be free to see you in a few moments, Mamselle. Madame Pugeot has still some details to discuss with me.

Mlle. Pointevin. I cannot wait long, M'su Cahusac.

M. Cahusac. A few minutes in the Park, thank you, Mamselle.

> Exit Mamselle Pointevin.

Mme. Pugeot. Has that poor girl business with a lawyer, M. Cahusac? A poor school-teacher like that?

M. Cahusac (*softly*). Mamselle Pointevin has taken it into her head to make her will.

Mme. Pugeot (*laughs superiorly*). Three chairs and a broken plate. (*rising*) Well, to-morrow at three. . . . I am now going to the Cathedral. I do not forget the great responsibilities for which I must prepare myself—the army, the navy, the treasury, the appointment of bishops. When I am dead, my dear chamberlain—

M. Cahusac. Madame!

Mme. Pugeot. No, no!—even I must die some day. . . . When I am dead, when I am laid with my ancestors, let it never be said of me . . . By the way, where shall I be laid?

M. Cahusac. In the church of St. Denis, Your Royal Highness?

Mme. Pugeot. Not in Notre-Dame?

M. Cahusac. No, Madame.

Mme. Pugeot (*meditatively*). Not in Notre-Dame. Well (*brightening*) we will cross these bridges when we get to them. (*extending her hand*) Good morning and all my thanks, my dear chamberlain.

M. Cahusac. . . . Highness' most obedient servant and devoted subject.

Mme. Pugeot (*beautifully, filling the doorway*). Pray for us.

> Exit Madame Pugeot.
> M. Cahusac goes to the door and bows to Mamselle Pointevin in the street.

M. Cahusac. Now Mamselle, if you will have the goodness to enter.

> Enter Mamselle Pointevin, a tall and indignant spinster.

Mlle. Pointevin. M'su Cahusac, it is something new for you to keep me waiting in the public square while you carry on your wretched little business with a vulgar woman like Madame Pugeot. When I condescend to call upon you, my good man, you will have the goodness to receive me at once. Either I am, or I am not, Henriette, Queen of France, Queen of Navarre and Aquitaine. It is not fitting that we cool our heels on a public bench among the nursemaids of remote New Orleans. It is hard enough to me to *hide myself* as a schoolmistress in this city, without having to suffer further humiliations at your hands. Is there no respect due to the blood of Charlemagne?

M. Cahusac. Madame . . .

Mlle. Pointevin. Or, Sir, are you bored and overfed on the company of queens?

M. Cahusac. Madame . . .

Mlle. Pointevin. You are busy with the law. Good! Know, then, *La loi—c'est moi.* (*sitting down and smoothing out her skirts*) Now what is it you have to say?

M. Cahusac (*pauses a moment, then approaches her with tightly pressed lips and narrowed eyes*). Your Royal Highness, I have received a letter from France. There is some discouraging news.

Mlle. Pointevin. No! I cannot afford to buy another thing. I possess the sceptre and the orb. Sell the rest to the Louvre, if you must. I can buy them back when my rank is announced.

M. Cahusac. Alas!

Mlle. Pointevin. What do you mean—"alas"?

M. Cahusac. Will Your Royal Highness condescend to read the letter I have received from France?

Mlle. Pointevin (*unfurls the letter, but continues looking, before her, splendidly*). Have they no bread? Give them cake. (*She starts to read, is shaken, suddenly returns it to him.*) It is too long. . . . What does it say?

M. Cahusac. It is from the Secretary of the Historical Society. The Society remains convinced that you are the true and long-sought heir to the throne of France.

Mlle. Pointevin. Convinced? Convinced? I should hope so.

M. Cahusac. But to make this conviction public, Madame, to announce it throughout the newspapers of the world, including the New Orleans "Times-Picayune" . . .

Mlle. Pointevin. Yes, go on!

M. Cahusac. To establish your claim among all your rivals. To establish your claim beyond any possible ridicule . . .

Mlle. Pointevin. Ridicule!

M. Cahusac. All they lack is one little document. One little but important document. They had hoped to find it in the archives of Madrid. Madame, it is not there.

Mlle. Pointevin. It is not there? Then where is it?

M. Cahusac. We do not know, Your Royal Highness. We are in despair.

Mlle. Pointevin. Ridicule, M. Cahusac!

She stares at him, her hand on her mouth.

M. Cahusac. It may be in Constantinople. It may be in Vienna. Naturally we shall continue to search for it. We shall continue to search for generations, for centuries, if need be. But I must confess this is a very discouraging blow.

Mlle. Pointevin. Generations! Centuries! But I am not a young girl, M'su Cahusac. Their letter says over and over again that I am the heir to the throne. (*She begins to cry.*)

M. Cahusac discreetly proffers her a glass of water.

Mlle. Pointevin. Thank you.

M. Cahusac (suddenly changing his tone, with firmness). Madame, you should know that the Society suspects the lost document to be in your possession. The Society feels sure that the document has been handed down from generation to generation in your family.

Mlle. Pointevin. In my possession!

M. Cahusac (firmly). Madame, are you concealing something from us?

Mlle. Pointevin. Why . . . no.

M. Cahusac. Are you playing with us, as a cat plays with a mouse?

Mlle. Pointevin. No, indeed I'm not.

M. Cahusac. Why is that paper not in Madrid, or in Constantinople or in Vienna? *Because it is in your house.* You live in what was once your father's house, do you not?

Mlle. Pointevin. Yes, I do.

M. Cahusac. Go back to it. Look through every old trunk . . .

Mlle. Pointevin. Every old trunk!

M. Cahusac. Examine especially the linings. Look through all the tables and desks. Pry into the joints. You will find perhaps a secret drawer, a secret panel.

Mlle. Pointevin. M'su Cahusac!

M. Cahusac. Examine the walls. Examine the boards of the floor. It may be hidden beneath them.

Mlle. Pointevin. I will. I'll go now.

M. Cahusac. Have you any old clothes of your father?

Mlle. Pointevin. Yes, I have.

M. Cahusac. It may be sewn into the lining.

Mlle. Pointevin. I'll look.

M. Cahusac. Madame, in what suit of clothes was your father buried?

Mlle. Pointevin. In his best, M'su.

> She gives a sudden scream under her hand as this thought strikes home. They stare at one another significantly.

M. Cahusac. Take particular pains to look under all steps. These kinds of document are frequently found under steps. You will find it. If it is not in Madrid, it is there.

Mlle. Pointevin. But if I can't find it! (*She sits down, suddenly spent.*) No one will ever know that I am the Queen of France. (*pause*) I am very much afraid, M'su Cahusac, that I shall never find that document in my four rooms. I know every inch of them. But I shall look. (*She draws her hand across her forehead, as though awaking from a dream.*) It is all very strange. You know, M'su Cahusac, I think there may have been a mistake somewhere. It was so beautiful while it lasted. It made even school-teaching a pleasure, M'su. . . . And my memoirs. I have just written my memoirs up to the moment when your wonderful announcement came to me—the account of my childhood incognito, the little girl in Louisiana who did not guess the great things before her. But before I go, may I ask something of you? Will you have the Historical Society write me a letter saying that they seriously think I may be . . . the person . . . the person they are looking for? I wish to keep the letter in the trunk with the orb and . . .

with the sceptre. You know . . . the more I think of it, the more I think there must have been a mistake somewhere.

M. Cahusac. The very letter you have in mind is here, Madame.

> He gives it to her.

Mlle. Pointevin. Thank you. And M'su Cahusac, may I ask another favor of you?

M. Cahusac. Certainly, Madame.

Mlle. Pointevin. Please, never mention this . . . this whole affair to anyone in New Orleans.

M. Cahusac. Madame, not unless you wish it.

Mlle. Pointevin. Good morning—good morning, and thank you.

> Her handkerchief to one eye she goes out.
> M. Cahusac goes to his desk.
> The bell rings.
> The reed curtain is parted, and a Negro boy pushes in a wheelchair containing a woman of some hundred years of age. She is wrapped in shawls, like a mummy, and wears a scarf about her head, and green spectacles on her nose. The mummy extends a hand which M. Cahusac kisses devotedly, murmuring, "Your Royal Highness."

The curtain falls

THE WHISTLE

By HUGH WALPOLE

MRS. PENWIN gave one of her nervous little screams when she saw the dog.

"Oh Charlie!" she cried. "You surely haven't bought it!" And her little nose, that she tried so fiercely to keep smooth, wrinkled into its customary little guttering of wrinkles.

The dog, taking an instant dislike to her, slunk, his head between his shoulders. He was an Alsatian.

"Well—" said Charlie, smiling nervously. He knew that his impulsiveness had led him once more astray. "Only the other evening you were saying that you'd like another dog."

"Yes, but *not* an Alsatian! You *know* what Alsatians are. We read about them in the paper every day. They are simply *not* to be trusted. I'm sure he looks as vicious as anything. And what about Mopsa?"

"Oh, Mopsa—" Charlie hesitated. "He'll be all right. You see, Sibyl, it was charity really. The Sillons are going to London as you know. They simply can't take him—it wouldn't be fair. They've found it difficult enough in Edinburgh as it is."

"I'm sure they are simply getting rid of him because he's vicious."

"No. Maude Sillon assured me he's like a lamb—"

"Oh, Maude! She'd say anything!"

"You know that you've been wanting a companion for Mopsa—"

"A companion for Mopsa! That's good!" Sibyl laughed her shrill little laugh that was always just out of tune.

"Well, we'll try him. We can easily get rid of him. And Blake shall look after him."

"Blake?" she was scornful. She detested Blake, but he was too good a chauffeur to lose.

"And he's most awfully handsome. You can't deny it."

She looked. Yes, he was most awfully handsome. He had laid down his head on his paws, staring in front of him, quite motionless. He seemed to be waiting scornfully until he should be given his next command. The power in those muscles, moulded under the skin, must be terrific. His long wolf ears lay flat. His color was lovely, here silver gray, there faintly amber. Yes, he was a magnificent dog. A little like Blake in his strength, silence, sulkiness.

She turned again to the note that she was writing.

"We'll try him if you like. Anyway there are no children about. It's Blake's responsibility—and the moment he's tiresome he goes."

Charlie was relieved. It hadn't been so hard after all.

"Oh, Blake says he doesn't mind. In fact he seemed to take to the dog at once. I'll call him."

He went to the double windows that opened into the garden and called: "Blake!" "Blake!" Blake came. He was still in his chauffeur's uniform, having just driven his master and the dog in from Keswick. He was a very large man, very fair in coloring, plainly of great strength. His expression was absolutely English in its complete absence of curiosity, its certainty that it knew the best about everything, its suspicion, its determination not to be taken in by anybody, and its latent kindliness. He had very blue eyes and was clean-shaven; his cap was in his hand and his hair, which was fair almost to whiteness, lay roughly across his forehead. He was not especially neat but of a quite shining cleanliness.

The dog got up and moved towards him. Both the Penwins were short and slight; they looked now rather absurdly small beside the man and the dog.

"Look here, Blake," said Charlie Penwin, speaking with much authority, "Mrs. Penwin is nervous about the dog. He's your responsibility, mind, and if there's the slightest bit of trouble, he goes. You understand that?"

"Yes, sir," said Blake, looking at the dog, "but there won't be no trouble."

"That's a ridiculous thing to say," remarked Mrs. Penwin

sharply, looking up from her note. "How can you be sure, Blake? You know how uncertain Alsatians are. I don't know what Mr. Penwin was thinking about."

Blake said nothing. Once again, and for the hundred-thousandth time, both the Penwins wished that they could pierce him with needles. It was quite terrible the way that Blake didn't speak when expected to, but then he was so wonderful a chauffeur, so good a driver, so excellent a mechanic, so honest—and Clara, his wife, was an admirable cook.

"You'd better take the dog with you now, Blake. What's its name?"

"Adam," said Charlie.

"Adam! What a foolish name for a dog! Now don't disturb Clara with him, Blake. Clara hates to have her kitchen messed up."

Blake, without a word, turned and went, the dog following closely at his heels.

Yes, Clara hated to have her kitchen messed up. She was standing now, her sleeves rolled back, her plump hands and wrists covered with dough. Mopsa, the Sealyham, sat at her side, his eyes, glistening with greed, raised to those doughy arms. But at sight of the Alsatian he turned and flew at his throat. He was a dog who prided himself on fighting instantly every other dog. With human beings he was mild and indifferently amiable. Children could do what they would with him. He was exceedingly conceited, and cared for no one but himself.

He was clever, however, and hid this indifference from many sentimental human beings.

Blake, with difficulty, separated the two dogs. The Alsatian behaved quite admirably, merely noticing the Sealyham and looking up at Blake to say, "I won't let myself go here although I should like to. I know that you would rather I didn't." The Sealyham, muttering deeply, bore the Alsatian no grudge. He was simply determined that he should have no foothold here.

Torrents of words passed from Clara. She had always as much to say as her husband had little. She said the same thing many times over as though she had an idiot to deal with. She knew that her husband was not an idiot—very far from it—but she had for many years been trying to make some impression on him. Defeated beyond hope, all she could now do was to resort to old and familiar tactics. What was this great savage dog? Where had he come from? Surely the Mistress didn't approve, and she wouldn't have her kitchen messed up, not for anybody, and as Harry (Blake) very well knew, nothing upset her like a dog fight, and if they were going to be perpetual, which, knowing Mopsa's character, they probably would be, she must just go to Mrs. Penwin and tell her that, sorry though she was after being with her all these years, she just couldn't stand it and would have to go, for if there was one thing more than another that really upset her it was a dog fight, and as Harry knew having the kitchen messed up was a thing that she couldn't stand. She paused and began vehemently to roll her dough. She was short and plump with fair hair and blue eyes like her husband's.

When she was excited, little glistening beads of sweat appeared on her forehead. No one in this world knew whether Blake was fond of her or no, Clara Blake least of all. She wondered perpetually; this uncertainty and her cooking were her principal interests in life. There were times when Blake seemed very fond of her indeed, others when he appeared not to be aware that she existed.

All he said now was, "The dog won't be no trouble," and went out, the dog at his heels. The Sealyham thought for a moment that he would follow him, then, with a little sniff of greed, settled himself down again at Clara Blake's feet.

The two went out into the thin, misty autumn sunshine, down through the garden into the garage. The Alsatian walked very closely beside Blake as though some invisible cord held them together. All his life, now two years in length, it had been always his constant principle to attach himself to somebody. For, in this curious world where he was, not his natural world at all, every breath, every movement, rustle of wind, sound of voices, patter of rain, ringing of bells, filled him with nervous alarm. He went always on guard, keeping his secret soul to himself, surrendering nothing, a captive in the country of the enemy. There might exist a human being to whom he would surrender himself. Although he had been attached to several people, he had not in his two years yet found one to whom he could give himself. Now as he trod softly over the amber and rosy leaves he was not sure that this man, beside whom he walked, might not be the one.

In the garage Blake took off his coat, put on his blue overalls and began to work. The dog stretched himself out on the stone floor, his head on his paws, and waited. Once and again he started, his pointed ears pricked, at some unexpected sound. A breeze blew the brown leaves up and down in the sun, and the white road beyond the garage pierced like a shining bone the cloudless sky.

Blake's thoughts ran, as they always did, with slow assurance. This was a fine dog. He'd known the first moment that he set eyes on him that this was the dog for him. At that first glance something in his heart had been satisfied, something that had for years been unfulfilled. For they had had no children, he and Clara, and a motor car was fine to drive and look after, but after all it couldn't give you everything, and he wasn't one to make friends (too damned cautious), and the people he worked for were all right but nothing extra, and he really didn't know whether he cared for Clara or no. It was so difficult after so many years married to tell. There were lots of times when he couldn't sort of see her at all.

He began to take out the spark plugs to clean them. That was the worst of these Daimlers, fine cars, as good as any going, but you had to be forever cleaning the spark plugs. Yes, that dog was a beauty. He was going to take to that dog.

The dog looked at him, stared at him as though he were saying something. Blake looked at the dog. Then, with a deep sigh, as though some matter, for long uncertain, was at last completely settled, the dog rested again his head on his paws, staring in front of him, and so fell asleep. Blake, softly whistling, continued his work.

A very small factor, in itself quite unimportant, can bring into serious conflict urgent forces. So it was now when this dog, Adam, came into the life of the Penwins.

Mrs. Penwin, like so many English wives and unlike all American wives, had never known so much domestic power as she descried. Her husband was, of course, devoted to her, but he was forever just escaping her, escaping her into that world of men that is so important in England, that is, even in these very modern days, still a world in the main apart from women.

Charlie Penwin had not very many opportunities to escape from his wife, and he was glad that he had not, for when they came he took them. His ideal was the ideal of most English married men (and of very few American married men), namely, that he should be a perfect companion to his wife. He fulfilled this ideal; they were excellent companions, the two of them, so excellent that it was all the more interesting and invigorating when he could go away for a time and be a companion to someone else, to Willie Shaftoe, for instance, with whom he sometimes stayed in his place near Carlisle, or even for a few days' golf with the Reverend Thomas Bird, rector of a church in Keswick.

Mrs. Penwin in fact had nerves quite in spite of his profound devotion to her, never entirely captured the whole of her husband—a small fragment eternally escaped her, and this escape was a very real grievance to her. Like a wise woman she did not make scenes—no English husband can endure scenes—but she was always attempting to stop up this one little avenue of escape. But most provoking! So soon as one avenue was closed another would appear.

She realized very quickly (for she was not at all a fool) that this Alsatian was assisting her husband to escape from her because his presence in their household was bringing him into closer contact with Blake. Both the Penwins feared Blake and admired him; to friends and strangers they spoke of him with intense pride. "What we should do without Blake I can't think!" "But aren't we lucky in *these* days to have a chauffeur whom we can completely trust?"

Nevertheless, behind these sentiments there was this great difference, that Mrs. Penwin disliked Blake extremely (whenever he looked at her he made her feel a weak, helpless, and idiotic woman) while Charlie Penwin, although he was afraid of him, in his heart liked him very much indeed.

If Blake only were human, little Charlie Penwin, who was a sentimentalist, used to think—and now suddenly Blake *was* human. He had gone "dotty" about this dog, and the dog followed him like a shadow. So close were they the one to the other that you could almost imagine that they held conversations together.

Then Blake came into his master's room one day to ask whether Adam could sleep in his room. He had a small room next to Mrs. Blake's because he was often out late with the car at night or must rise very early in the morning. Clara Blake liked to have her sleep undisturbed.

"You see, sir," he said, "he won't sort of settle down in the outhouse. He's restless. I know he is."

"How do you know he is?" asked Charlie Penwin.

"I can sort of feel it, sir. He won't be no sort of trouble in my room, and he'll be a fine guard to the house at night."

The two men looked at one another and were in that moment friends. They both smiled.

"Very well, Blake. I don't think there's anything against it."

Of course, there *were* things against it. Mrs. Penwin hated the idea of the dog sleeping in the house. She did not really hate it; what she hated was that Blake and her husband should settle this thing without a word to her. Nor, when she protested, would her husband falter. Blake wanted it. It would be a good protection for the house.

Blake developed a very odd whistle with which he called the dog. Putting his fingers into his mouth he called forth this strange melancholy note that seemed to penetrate into endless distance and that had in it something mysterious, melancholy, and dangerous. It was musical and inhuman; friends of the Penwins, comfortably at tea, would hear this thin whistling cry, coming, it seemed, from far away beyond the fells, having in it some part of the lake and the distant sea trembling on Drigg sands and of the lonely places in Eskdale and Ennerdale.

"What's that?" they would say, looking up.

"Oh it's Blake calling the dog."

"What a strange whistle!"

"Yes, it's the only one the dog hears."

The dog did hear it, at any distance, in any place. When Blake went with the car the Alsatian would lie on the upper lawn whence he could see the road and wait for his return.

He would both see and hear the car's return, but he would not stir until Blake, released from his official duties, could whistle to him—then with one bound he would be up, down the garden, and with his front paws up against Blake's chest would show him his joy.

To all the rest of the world he was indifferent. But he was not hostile. He showed indeed an immense patience, and especially with regard to the Sealyham.

The dog Mopsa attempted twice at least every day to kill the Alsatian. He succeeded in biting him severely but so long as Blake was there he showed an infinite control, letting Blake part them although every instinct in him was stirred to battle.

But after a time, Blake became clever at keeping the two dogs separate; moreover, the Sealyham became afraid of Blake. He was clever enough to realize that when he fought the Alsatian he fought Blake as well—and Blake was too much for him.

Very soon, however, Blake was at war not only with the Sealyham but with his wife and Mrs. Penwin too. You might think that the words "at war" were too strong when nothing was to be seen on the surface. Mrs. Blake said nothing, Mrs. Penwin said nothing, Blake himself said nothing.

Save for the fights with the Sealyham, there was no charge whatever to bring against the Alsatian. He was never in anyone's way, he brought no dirt in the house; whenever Charlie Penwin took him in the car he sat motionless on the back seat, his wolf ears pricked up, his large and beautiful eyes sternly regarding the outside world, but his consciousness fixed only upon Blake's back, broad and masterly above the wheel.

No charge could be brought against him except that the devotion between the man and the dog was in this little house of ordered emotions, routine habits, quiet sterility, almost terrible. Mrs. Blake, as her husband left her one night to return to his own room, broke out: "If you'd loved me as you love that dog I'd have had a different life."

Blake patted her shoulder, moist beneath her nightdress. "I love you all right, my girl," he said.

And Mrs. Penwin found that here she could not move her

husband. Again and again she said: "Charlie, that dog's got to go."

"Why?"

"It's dangerous."

"I don't see it."

"Somebody will be bitten one day, and then you *will* see it."

"There's a terrible lot of nonsense talked about Alsatians—"

And then, when everyone was comfortable, Mrs. Blake reading her "Home Chat," Mrs. Penwin her novel, Mrs. Fern (Mrs. Penwin's best friend) doing a "cross-word," over the misty, dank garden, carried it seemed by the muffled clouds that floated above the fell, would sound that strange melancholy whistle, so distant and yet so near, Blake calling his dog.

For Blake himself life was suddenly, and for the first time, complete. He had not known, all this while, what it was that he missed although he had known that he missed something. Had Mrs. Blake given him a child he would have realized completion. Mrs. Blake alone had not been enough for his heart. In this dog he found fulfilment because here were all the things that he admired—loyalty, strength, courage, self-reliance, fidelity, comradeship, and, above all, sobriety of speech and behavior. Beyond these there was something more—love. He did not, even to himself, admit the significance of this yet deeper contact. And he analyzed nothing.

For the dog, life in this dangerous menacing country of the enemy was at last secure and simple. He had only one thing to do, only one person to consider.

But, of course, life is not so simple as this for anybody. A battle was being waged, and it must have an issue.

The Penwins were not in Cumberland during the winter. They went to their little place in Sussex, very close to London and to all their London friends. Mrs. Penwin would not take the Alsatian to Sussex. "But why not?" asked Charlie. She hated it, Mrs. Blake hated it. That, Charlie objected, was not reason enough.

"Do you realize," said Mrs. Penwin theatrically, "that this dog is dividing us?"

"Nonsense," said Charlie.

"It is not nonsense. I believe you care more for Blake than you do for me." She cried. She cried very seldom. Charlie Penwin was uncomfortable but some deep male obstinacy was roused in him. This had become an affair of the sexes. Men must stand together and protect themselves or they would be swept away in this feminine flood.

Blake knew, Mrs. Blake knew, Mrs. Penwin knew that the dog would go with them to Sussex unless some definite catastrophe gave Mrs. Penwin the victory.

Lying on his bed at night, seeing the gray wolf-like shadow of the dog stretched on the floor, Blake's soul for the first time in its history trembled, at the thought of the slight movement, incident, spoken word, sound that might rouse the dog beyond his endurance and precipitate the catastrophe. The dog was behaving magnificently, but he was surrounded by his enemies. Did he know what hung upon his restraint?

Whether he knew or no, the catastrophe arrived and arrived with the utmost, most violent publicity. On a sun-gleaming, russet October afternoon, on the lawn while Charlie was giving Blake instructions about the car and Mrs. Penwin put in also her word, Mopsa attacked the Alsatian. Blake ran to separate them, and the Alsatian, sharply bitten, bewildered, humiliated, snapped and caught Blake's leg between his teeth. A moment later he and Blake knew, both of them, what he had done. Blake would have hidden it, but blood was flowing. In the Alsatian's heart remorse, terror, love, and a sense of disaster—a confirmation of all that, since his birth, knowing the traps that his enemies would lay for him, he had suspected—leapt to life together.

Disregarding all else, he looked up at Blake.

"And that settles it!" cried Mrs. Penwin, triumphantly. "He goes!"

Blake's leg was badly bitten in three places; there would be scars for life. And it was settled. Before the week was out the dog would be returned to his first owners, who did not want him—who would give him to someone else who also, in turn, through fear or shyness of neighbors, would not want him.

Two days after this catastrophe, Mrs. Blake went herself to Mrs. Penwin.

"My husband's that upset—I wouldn't care if the dog stays, Mum."

"Why, Clara, you hate the dog."

"Oh well, Mum, Blake's a good husband to me. I don't like to see him—"

"Why, what has he said?"

"He hasn't said *anything*, Mum."

But Mrs. Penwin shook her head. "No, Clara, it's ridiculous. The dog's dangerous."

And Blake went to Charlie Penwin. The two men faced one another and were closer together, fonder of one another, man caring for man, than they had ever been before.

"But Blake, if the dog bites *you* whom he cares for—I mean, don't you see? he really *is* dangerous—"

"He wasn't after biting me," said Blake slowly. "And if he *had* to bite somebody, being aggravated and nervous, he'd not find anyone better to bite than me who understands him and knows he don't mean nothing by it."

Charlie Penwin felt in himself a terrible disloyalty to his wife. She could go to — Why should not Blake have his dog? Was he forever to be dominated by women? For a brief rocking, threatening moment his whole ordered world trembled. He knew that if he said the dog was to remain the dog would remain and that something would have broken between his wife and himself that could never be mended.

He looked at Blake, who with his blue serious eyes stared steadily in front of him. He hesitated. He shook his head.

"No, Blake, it won't do. Mrs. Penwin will never be easy now while the dog is here."

Later in the day Blake did an amazing thing. He went to Mrs. Penwin.

During all these years he had never voluntarily, himself, gone to Mrs. Penwin. He had never gone unless he was sent for. She looked at him and felt, as she always did, dislike, admiration, and herself a bit of a fool.

"Well, Blake?"

"If the dog stays I'll make myself responsible. He shan't bite nobody again."

"But how can you tell? You said he wouldn't bite anyone before and he did."

"He won't again."

"No, Blake, he's got to go. I shan't have a moment's peace while he's here."

"He's a wonderful dog. I'll have him trained so he won't hurt a fly. He's like a child with me."

"I'm sure he is. Irresponsible like a child. That's why he bit you."

"I don't make nothing of his biting me."

"You may not, but next time it will be someone else. There's something in the paper about them every day."

"He's like a child with me."

"I'm very sorry, Blake. I can't give way about it. You'll see I'm right in the end. My husband ought never to have accepted the dog at all."

After Blake had gone she did not know why, but she felt uneasy, as though she had robbed a blind man, or stolen another woman's lover. Ridiculous! There could be no question but that she was right.

Blake admitted that to himself. She was right. He did not criticise her, but he did not know what to do. He had never felt like this in all his life before as though part of himself were being torn from him.

On the day before the dog was to go back to his original owners Blake was sent into Keswick to make some purchases. It was a soft blooming day, one of those North English autumn days when there is a scent of spices in the sharp air and a rosy light hangs about the trees. Blake had taken the dog with him, and driving back along the lake, seeing how it lay, a sheet of silver glass upon whose surface the islands were painted in flat colors of auburn and smoky gray, a sudden madness seized him. It was the stillness, the silence, the breathless pause—

Instead of turning to the right over the Grange bridge, he drove the car straight on into Borrowdale. It was yet early in the afternoon—all the lovely valley lay in gold leaf at the feet of the russet hills, and no cloud moved in the sky. He took the car to Seatoller and climbed with the dog the steep path towards Honister.

And the dog thought that at last what he had longed for was to come to pass. He and Blake were at length free, they would go on and on, leaving all the stupid, nerve-jumping world behind them, never to return to it.

With a wild, fierce happiness such as he had never yet shown he bounded forward, drinking in the cold streams, feeling the strong turf beneath his feet, running back to Blake to assure him of his comradeship. At last he was free, and life was noble as it ought to be.

At the turn of the road Blake sat down and looked back. All around him were hills. Nothing moved; only the stream close to him slipped murmuring between the boulders. The hills ran ranging from horizon to horizon, and between gray clouds a silver strip of sky, lit by an invisible sun, ran like a river into mist. Blake called the dog to him and laid his hand upon his head. He knew that the dog thought that they both had escaped forever now from the world. Well, why not? They could walk on, on to the foot of the hill on whose skyline the mining hut stood like a listening ear, down the Pass to Buttermere, past the lake, past Crummock Water to Cockermouth. There would be a train. It would not be difficult for him to get work. His knowledge of cars (he had a genius for them) would serve him anywhere. And Clara? She was almost invisible, a tiny white blot on the horizon. She would find someone else. His hand tightened about the dog's head.

For a long while he sat there, the dog never moving, the silver river spreading in the sky, the hills gathering closer about him.

Suddenly he shook his head. No, he could not. He would be running away, a poor kind of cowardice. He pulled Adam's sharp ears; he buried his face in Adam's fur. He stood up, and Adam also stood up, placed his paws on Blake's chest, licked his cheeks. In his eyes there shone great happiness because they two were going away alone together.

But Blake turned back down the path, and the dog realizing that there was to be no freedom, walked close behind him, brushing with his body sometimes the stuff of Blake's trousers.

Next day Blake took the dog back to the place whence he had come.

Two days later, the dog, knowing that he was not wanted, sat watching a little girl who played some foolish game near him. She had plump bare legs; he watched them angrily. He was unhappy, lonely, nervous, once more in the land of the enemy, and now with no friend.

Through the air, mingling with the silly laughter of the child and other dangerous sounds came, he thought, a whistle. His heart hammered. His ears were up. With all his strength he bounded towards the sound. But he was chained. To-morrow he was to be given to a Cumberland farmer.

Mrs. Penwin was entertaining two ladies at tea. This was the last day before the journey south. Across the dank lawns came that irritating, melancholy whistle disturbing her, reproaching her—and for what?

Why, for her sudden suspicion that everything in life was just ajar—one little push and all would be in its place—but would she be married to Charlie, would Mrs. Plang then be jealous of her pretty daughter, would Miss Tennyson, nibbling now at her pink pieces of icing, be nursing her aged and intemperate father? She looked up crossly.

"Really, Charlie, that must be Blake whistling. I can't think why now the dog's gone. To let us know what he thinks about it, I suppose." She turned to her friends, "Our chauffeur—a splendid man—we *are* so fortunate. Charlie, do tell him. It's such a hideous whistle anyway—and now the dog is gone—"

THE EGG TREE

By JAMES STILL

THE hail of early June shredded the growing blades of corn, and a windstorm breaking over Little Angus Creek in July flattened the sloping fields; but the hardy stalks rose in the hot sun, and the fat ears fruited and ripened. With the mines closed at Blackjack all winter and spring, Father had rented a farm on the hills rising from the mouth of Flaxpatch on Little Angus. We moved there during a March freeze, and the baby died that week of croup. When the sap lifted in sassafras and sourwood, Father sprouted the bush-grown patches, and ploughed deep. With corn breaking through the furrows, and the garden seeded, he left us to tend the crop, going over in Breathitt County to split rock in Brack Hogan's quarry.

There was good seasoning in the ground. Shucks bulged on heavy corn ears. Garden furrows were cracked where potatoes pushed the earth outward in their growing. Weeds plagued the corn, and Mother took us to the fields. We were there at daylight, chopping at horsemint and crab grass with blunt hoes. Sister Euly could trash us all with a corn row. She was a beanpole, thin and quick like Mother. Fletch had grown during the summer, and his face was round as a butter ball. He dug too deep, often missing the weeds and cutting the corn. Mother let him take the short rows. He slept during hot afternoons at the field's edge, deep in a patch of tansy with bees worrying the dusty blossoms over his head.

"It's a sight to have such a passel o' victuals after livin' tight as a tow-wad," Mother said. We picked a barrel of firm corn ears. Tomatoes ripened faster than they could be canned. The old apple trees in the bottom were burdened. We peeled and sulphured three bushels of McIntoshes. Fall beans were strung and hung with peppers and onions on the porch. The cushaws were a wonder to see, bloated with yellow flesh. The crooked-neck gourds on the lot fence grew too large for water dippers. They were just right for martin poles.

"If we stay on here I'm goin' to have me a mess o' martins livin' in them gourds," I told Mother.

"If your Poppy is a-mind to, we'll jist settle down awhile," Mother said. "It's a sight the rations we've got."

With the crops laid by, we cleaned up a patch of ground on the Point around the baby's grave. Mother took up a bucket of white sand from the Flaxpatch sand bar, patting it on the mound with her hands. "We're goin' to have a funeralizin' for the baby in September," she said. "Your Poppy will be agin it, but we're goin' to, whether or no. I've already spoke for Brother Sim Manley. He's comin' all the way from Troublesome Creek. I reckon we've got plenty to feed everbody."

There was nothing more to do in the garden and the fields, and during this first rest since spring, Mother began to grieve over the baby. Euly told us that she cried in the night, and slept with its gown under her pillow. We spoke quietly, and there was no noise in the house. The jarflies on the windows and the katy-dids outside sang above our words. With Mother suddenly on edge, and likely to cry at a word, we played all day on the hills. Euly ran the coves like a young fox, coming in before supper with a poke of chestnuts and chinquapins. She often made her dinner of pawpaws, smelling sickly sweet of them. I found her playhouse once in a haw patch. There were eight poppets made from corncobs sitting on rock chairs, eating giblets of cress from mud dishes. I skittered away, Euly never knowing I had been there.

Fletch followed me everywhere. Sometimes I hid, wanting to play by myself, and talk things out loud, but he would call until his voice hoarsened and trembled. Then I was ashamed not to answer, and I'd pretend I had just come into hollering dis-tance. He would come running, dodging through the weeds like a puppy. There was no getting away from Fletch.

One day me and Fletch came in from the buckeye patch with our pockets loaded. Mother and Euly were working around a dead willow in the yard, stringing the twigless branches with eggshells Mother had been saving. The eggs had been broken carefully at each end, letting the whites and yolks run out. The little tree was about five feet high, and the lean branches were already nearly covered with shells.

"I allus did want me an egg tree," Mother said. "I hear tell it's healthy to have one growin' in the yard. And I figger it'll be right brightenin' to the house with all the folks that's comin' to the funeralizin'. My dommers ought to lay nigh enough to kiver the last branch afore the time comes. Eggshells hain't a grain o' good except to prettify with." . . .

August lay heavy on the fields when Father came home for three days. Blooming whitetop covered the pasture before the house, and spindling stickweeds shook out their purple bonnets. Father came just before dark, and the pretty-by-nights were open and pert by the doorsill. He trudged into the yard without seeing the egg tree, or the blossoms beside the steps. He walked up on the porch, and we saw his nose was red, and his eyes watery. Mother caught him by the arm.

"It's this damned hay fever," Father said. "Ever' bloom on the face o' the earth is givin' off dust. Sometimes hit nigh chokes me black in the face."

He sniffled, blew his nose, and went inside with Mother. His angry voice suddenly filled the house. Mother brought out an armload of yellowrods, stickweed blooms, and farewell-to-summer that Euly had stuck around in fruit jars.

Father's face darkened when Mother told him about the funeralizing for the baby. "I've already sent on word to Preacher Sim Manley," she said.

Father groaned. "It's onreckonin' what a woman'll think about with her man off tryin' to make a livin'," he said. "Little Green wasn't nigh eight months old, and thar hain't any use of a big funeral."

"We've got plenty to feed everbody," Mother said. "I ain't ashamed o' what we got. We've done right proud this year. I'm jist gittin' one preacher, and it's goin' to be a one-day funeral."

"Thar hain't no use askin' anybody except our kin," Father said. "It'll look like we're tryin' to put on the dog."

"Everbody that's a-mind to come is asked," Mother said. "I hain't tryin' to put a peck measure over the word o' God."

Father got up and lighted the lamp on the mantel. "We'll feed right good down at Blackjack this winter," he said. "I hear tell the mines is goin' to open the middle o' October. I'm goin' back to Brack Hogan's quarry for another two weeks and then I'm quittin'. I'm longin' to git me a pick and stick it in a coal vein. I can't draw a good clean breath o' air outside a mine this time o' year. It's like a horse tryin' to breathe with his nose in a meal poke."

"I was jist reckonin' we'd stay on here another crap," Mother said. "The mines is everly openin' and closin'. The baby is buried here, too. And I never favored bringin' up children in a coal camp. They've got enough meanness in their blood without humorin' it. We done right good crapin' this year. We raised a passel o' victuals."

"Thar's goin' to be good times agin in Blackjack," Father said. "I hear they're goin' to pay nigh fifty cents a ton for coal loadin'. And they're goin' to build some new company houses, and I got my word in for one."

Mother's face was pale in the lamplight. "I reckon it's my egg tree I'm hatin' to leave," she said. "I allus did want me one."

"It's fresh news to me you got one," Father said. "I hain't seed one since afore I married and was traipsin' round on Buckhorn Creek. I wisht all the timber was egg trees. They don't give off a grain o' dust. This Little Angus hollow is dusty as a pea threshin'. It nigh makes a fellow sneeze his lungs out."

"I'm a-mind to stay on here," Mother said, her voice chilled and tight. "It's the nighest heaven I've been on this earth." . . .

Fall came in the almanac, and the sourwood bushes were like fire on the mountains. Leaves hung bright and jaundiced on the maples. Red foxes came down the hills, prowling around our chicken house, and then hens squalled in the night. Quin Adams's hounds hunted the ridges, their bellies thin as saw blades. Their voices came bellowing down to us in the dark hours. Once, waking suddenly, I heard a fox bark in defeat somewhere in the cove beyond Flaxpatch.

Mother had set the funeralizing for the last Sunday in Sep-

tember. Father came on the Wednesday before, bringing a head-
stone he had cut out of Brack Hogan's quarry, chipped from
solid limerock. The baby's name was carved on one side with a
chisel. We took it up on the Point, standing it at the head of the
mound. Father built an arbor there out of split poplar logs. We
thatched the roof with branches of linn.

"It's big enough for Preacher Sim to swing his arms in without
hittin' anybody," Father said.

Mother came up the hill to see it. "I wisht to God I'd had a
picture tuk o' the baby so it could be sot in the arbor durin' the
meetin'. I wisht to God I'd had it tuk."

Father cut down some locusts, laying the trunks in front of the
arbor for seats, and Mother took a pair of mule shears, cutting
the weeds and grass evenly.

Grandma and Uncle Jolly came Thursday morning, Grandma
riding sidesaddle on a horse-mule, and Uncle Jolly astraddle a
pony not more than a dozen hands high. His feet nearly dragged
dirt. He came singing at the top of his voice:

> Polish my boots
> And set 'em on the bench,
> Goin' down to Jellico
> To see Jim Shanks.
> Holler-ding, baby, holler-ding.
>
> Ole gray goose went to the river
> If'n I'd been a gander
> I'd went thar with 'er.
> Holler-ding, baby, holler-ding.

When they turned out of the Little Angus sand bar, Uncle
Jolly crossed his legs in the saddle, and came riding up the yard
path, right onto the porch, and would have gone pony and all into
the house if Mother hadn't been standing in the door. Father
laughed, saying, "Jolly allus was a damned fool," and Uncle
Jolly got so tickled he reeled on the porch, holding his stomach,
and he fell off into the pretty-by-night bed.

Grandma hitched the horse-mule at the fence, looking at the
egg tree as she crossed the yard. "Hit's a sight," she said, pulling
off her bonnet. "I hain't seen one in twenty year."

Aunt Rilla came in time for dinner, walking up from the creek-bed road with Lala, Crilla, Lue, and Foan strung out behind. Uncle Luce and Toll came in the night. Aunt Shridy was there by daylight next morning, and we all set to work getting ready for Sunday. The floors were scrubbed twice over with a shuck mop, and the smoky walls washed down. Jimson weeds were cut out of the backyard, and the woodpile straightened. Mother cut the heads off of fifteen dommers. The stove stayed hot all day Friday, baking and frying. Cushaw pies covered the kitchen table.

"I reckon we got enough shucky beans biled to feed creation," Grandma said. "Lonic, you hain't never been in such a good fix since you tuk a man. You'd be puore foolish movin' to Blackjack agin."

"Since I married I've been driv' from one coal mine to another," Mother said, taking her hands out of bread dough. "And I've lived hard as nails. I've lived at Blue Diamond. I've lived at Chavies, Elkhorn, and Lacky. We moved up to Hardburley twicet, and to Blackjack beyond countin'. I reckon I've lived everwhere on God's green earth. Now I want to set me down and rest. The baby is buried here, and I reckon I've got a breathin' spell comin'. We done right well this crap. We got plenty."

Grandma kept us children shooed out of the kitchen. We hung around Uncle Jolly until he put a lizard up Fletch's britches leg, and threw a bucket of water on the rest of us. "Sometimes I fair think Jolly is a witty," Aunt Rilla said.

Father met Preacher Sim Manley at the mouth of Flaxpatch Saturday morning, taking Uncle Jolly's nag for him to ride on up the creek. But they both came back walking, being ashamed to ride the sorry mount. Father said he didn't know the pony had a saddle boil until he had started with her.

Preacher Sim slept on the feather bed that night. Father took the men out to the barn to sleep on the hay. Grandma and Aunt Lemma took Mother's bed, the rest of us stretching out on pallets spread on the floor.

The moon was full, and big and shiny as a brass pot. It was day-white outside. I couldn't sleep, feeling the strangeness of so many people in the house, and the unfamiliar breathing. Before day I went out to the corncrib and got a nap until the rooster crowed, not minding the mice rustling the shucks in the feed basket.

Mother climbed up to the Point before breakfast to spread a white sheet over the baby's grave. When she came down the Adamses were there, Quin looking pale with his first shave of the fall, and Mrs. Adams flushed and hot, not wanting to sit down and wrinkle her starched dress. Cleve Horn and his family were not far behind.

Before nine o'clock the yard and porch were crowded. Neighbors came up quietly, greeting Mother, and the women held handkerchiefs in their hands, crying a little. Then we knew again that there had been death in our house. All who went inside spoke in whispers, their voices having more words than sound. The clock was stopped, its hands pointing to the hour and minute the baby died; and those who passed through the rooms knew the bed, for it was spread with a white counterpane and a bundle of fall roses rested upon it.

At ten o'clock Brother Sim opened his Bible in the arbor on the Point. "O my good brethren," he said. "We was borned in sin, and saved by grace." He spat upon the ground, and lifted his hands towards the withered linn thatching. "We have come together to ask the blessed Saviour one thing pint-blank. Can a leetle child enter the Kingdom of Heaven?" . . .

The leaves came down. October's frost stiffened the brittle grass, and spiderwebs were threads of ice in the morning sun. We gathered our corn during the cool days, sledding it down the snaky trail from field to barn. The pigs came down out of the hills from their mast hunting, and rooted up the bare potatoes with damp snouts. Father went over to Blackjack and stayed a week. When he returned there was coal dust ground into the flesh of his hands. He had worked four days in the mines, and now there was a company house waiting for us.

"I promised to git moved over in three days," Father said. "We got a sealed house with two windows in ever' room waitin' for us."

"I'm a-longin' to stay on here," Mother said. Her voice was small and hoping. "I'll be stayin' here with the children, and you can go along till spring. Movin' hain't nothin' but leavin' things behind."

Father cracked his shoes together in anger. "That's clear foolishness you're sayin'," he said, reddening. "I ain't aimin' to be a widow-man this year."

"I'm sot agin movin'," Mother said, "but I reckon I'm bound to go where you go."

"We ought to be movin' afore Thursday," Father said.

"Nigh we git our roots planted, we keep pullin' 'em up and plantin' 'em in furren ground," Mother complained. "Movin' is an abomination. Thar's a sight o' things I hate to leave here. I hate to leave my egg tree I sot so much time and patience on. Reckon it's my egg tree holdin' me."

"I never heered tell of such foolishness," Father said. "Pity thar hain't a seed so hit can be planted agin."

Cold rains came over the Angus hills, softening the roads and deepening the wheel tracks. There could be no moving for a spell, though Father was anxious to be loading the wagon. Mother sat before the fire, making no effort to pack, while the rains fell through the long, slow days.

"Rain hain't never lost a day for a miner," Father said, walking the floor restlessly.

"You ought to be nailin' up a little gravehouse for the baby then," Mother said. Father fetched some walnut planks down from the loft and built the gravehouse under the barn shed. It was five feet square with a chestnut shingle roof. During the first lull in the weather, we took it up to the Point.

When the rain stopped, fog hung in the coves, and the hills were dark and weather-gray. Cornstalks stood awkwardly unbalanced in the fields. The trees looked sodden and dead, and taller than when in leaf. Father took our stove down one night. The next morning our mare was hitched to the wagon, and the hind gate let down before the back door. Mother gave us a cold baked potato for breakfast, then began to pack the dishes. We were on the road up Flaxpatch by eight o'clock, Mother sitting on the seat beside Father, and looking back towards the Point, where the gravehouse stood among the bare locusts.

We reached Blackjack in middle afternoon. The slag pile towering over the camp burned with an acre of oily flames, and a sooty mist hung along the creek bottom. Our house sat close against a bare hill. It was cold and gloomy, smelling sourly of paint, but there were glass windows, and Euly, Fletch, and I ran into every room to look out. Old neighbors came in to shake our hands, but there was no warmth in their words or fingers.

Father started back after the last load as soon as the wagon bed was empty, leaving us to set the beds up. He came back in the night, none of us hearing him drive in the gate.

At daybreak we were up, feeling the nakedness of living in a house with many windows. We went out on the porch and looked up the rutted street. Men went by through the mud with carbide lamps burning on their caps. Mother came out presently into the yard. There was the egg tree. Its roots were buried shallowly in damp earth near the fence corner. Some of the shells were cracked, and others had fallen off, exposing the brown willow branches. Mother turned and went back into the house. "It takes a man-person to be a puore fool," she said.

BROOMSTICKS

By WALTER DE LA MARE

MISS CHAUNCEY'S cat, Sam, had been with her many years before she noticed anything unusual, anything *disturbing*, in his conduct. Like most cats who live under the same roof with but one or two humans, he had always been more sagacious than cats of a common household. He had learned Miss Chauncey's ways. He acted, that is, as nearly like a small mortal dressed up in a hairy coat as one could expect a cat to act. He was what is called an "intelligent" cat.

But though Sam had learned much from Miss Chauncey, I am bound to say that Miss Chauncey had learned very little from Sam. She was a kind indulgent mistress; she could sew, and cook, and crochet, and make a bed, and read and write and cipher a little. And when she was a girl she used to sing "Kathleen Mavourneen" to the piano. Sam, of course, could do nothing of this kind.

But then, Miss Chauncey could no more have caught and killed a mouse or a blackbird with her five naked fingers than she could have been Pope of Rome. Nor could she run up a six-foot brick wall, or leap clean from the hearth-mat in her parlor on to the shelf of her chimney-piece without disturbing a single ornament, or even tinkling one crystal glass-drop against another. Unlike Sam, she could not find her way in the dark, or by her sense of smell; or keep in good health by merely nibbling grass in the garden. If, moreover, as a little girl she had been held up by her feet and hands two or three feet above the ground and then dropped, she would have at once fallen plump on her back, whereas when Sam was only a three-months-old, he could have managed to twist clean about in the air in twelve inches and come down on his four feet as firm as a table.

While Sam, then, had learned a good deal from Miss Chauncey, she had learned nothing from him. And even if she had been willing to be taught, it is doubtful if she would ever have proved even a promising pupil. What is more, she knew much less about Sam than he knew about his mistress—until, at least, that afternoon when she was doing her hair in the glass. And then she could hardly believe her own eyes. It was a moment that completely changed her views about Sam—and nothing after that experience was ever quite the same again.

Sam had always been a fine upstanding creature, his fur jet-black and silky, his eyes a lambent green, even in sunshine, and at night a-glow like green topazes. He was now full seven years of age, and had an unusually powerful miaou. Living as he did quite alone with Miss Chauncey at Post Houses, it was natural that he should become her constant companion. For Post Houses was a singularly solitary house, standing almost in the middle of Haggurdsdon Moor, just where two wandering byeways cross each other like the half-closed blades of a pair of shears or scissors.

It was a mile and a half from its nearest neighbor, Mr. Cullings, the carrier; and yet another quarter of a mile from the village of Haggurdsdon. Its roads were extremely ancient. They had been sheep-tracks long before the Romans came to England and had cut *their* roads from shore to shore. But for many years past few travellers or carts or even sheep with their shepherd came Miss Chauncey's way. You could have gazed from her windows for hours together, even on a summer's day, without seeing so much as a tinker's barrow or a gipsy's van.

Post Houses, too, was perhaps the ugliest house there ever was. Its four corners stood straight up on the moor like a house of nursery bricks. From its flat roof on a clear day the eye could see for miles and miles across the moor, Mr. Cullings's cottage being out of sight in a shallow hollow. It had belonged to Miss Chauncey's ancestors for numbers of generations. Many people in Haggurdsdon indeed called it Chauncey's. And though in a great wind it was almost as full of noises as an organ, though it was a cold barn in winter, and though another branch of the family had as far back as the 'seventies gone to live in the Isle of

Wight, Miss Chauncey still remained faithful to its four walls. In fact she loved the ugly old place, for she had lived in it ever since she was a little girl with knickerbockers showing under her skirts and pale-blue ribbon shoulder knots.

This fact alone made Sam's conduct the more reprehensible, for never cat had kinder mistress. Miss Chauncey herself was now about sixty years of age—fifty-three years older than Sam. She was five foot ten-and-a-half inches in height. On week-days she wore black alpaca, and on Sundays a watered silk. Her large round steel spectacles straddling across her high nose gave her a look of being keen as well as cold. But truly she was neither. For even so stupid a man as Mr. Cullings could take her in over the cartage charge of a parcel—just by looking tired or sighing as he glanced at his rough-haired, knock-kneed mare. And there was the warmest of hearts under her stiff bodice.

Being so far from the village, milk and cream were a little difficult, of course. But Miss Chauncey could deny Sam nothing—in reason. She paid a whole sixpence a week to a little girl called Susan Ard who brought these dainties from the nearest farm. They were dainties indeed, for though the grasses on Haggurdsdon Moor were of dark sour green, the cows that grazed on it gave an uncommonly rich milk, and Sam flourished on it. Mr. Cullings called once a week on his round, and had a standing order to bring with him a few sprats or fresh herrings, or any other toothsome fish that was in season. Miss Chauncey would not even withhold her purse from expensive whitebait, if no other cheaper fish were procurable. And Mr. Cullings would eye Sam fawning about his cart-wheel, or gloating up at his dish, and say, " 'Ee be a queer animal, shure enough; 'ee be a wunnerful queer animal, 'ee be."

As for Miss Chauncey herself, she was a niggardly eater, though much attached to her tea. She made her own bread and cookies. On Saturday a butcher-boy drove up in a striped apron. Besides which she was a wonderful manager. Her cupboards were full of home-made jams and bottled fruits and dried herbs— everything of that kind, for Post Houses had a nice long strip of garden behind it, surrounded by a high old yellow brick wall.

Quite early in life Sam, of course, had learned to know his

meal-time—though how he "told" it was known only to himself, for he never appeared even to glance at the face of the grandfather's clock on the staircase. He was punctual, particular in his toilet, and a prodigious sleeper. He had learned to pull down the latch of the back door, if, in the months when an open window was not to be found, he wished to go out. Indeed at last he preferred the latch. He never slept on Miss Chauncey's patchwork quilt, unless his own had been placed over it. He was particular almost to a foppish degree in his habits, and he was no thief. He had a mew on one note to show when he wanted something to eat; a mew a semitone or two higher if he wanted drink (that is, cold water, for which he had a great taste); and yet another mew—gentle and sustained—when he wished, so to speak, to converse with his mistress.

Not, of course, that the creature talked *English*, but he liked to sit up on one chair by the fireside, especially in the kitchen— for he was no born parlor-cat—and to look up at the glinting glasses of Miss Chauncey's spectacles, and then down awhile at the fire-flames (drawing his claws in and out as he did so, and purring the while), almost as if he might be preaching a sermon, or reciting a poem.

But this was in the happy days when all seemed well. This was in the days when Miss Chauncey's mind was innocent of all doubts and suspicions. Like others of his kind, too, Sam delighted to lie in the window and idly watch the birds in the apple-trees— tits and bullfinches and dunnocks—or to crouch over a mousehole for hours together. Such were his amusements (for he never ate his mice) while Miss Chauncey with cap and broom, duster and dishclout, went about her housework. But he also had a way of examining things in which cats are not generally interested. He as good as told Miss Chauncey one afternoon that a hole was coming in her parlor carpet. For he walked to and fro and back and forth with his tail up, until she attended to him. And he certainly warned her, with a yelp like an Amazonian monkey, when a red-hot coal had set her kitchen mat on fire.

He would lie or sit with his whiskers to the North before noonday, and due South afterwards. In general his manners were perfection. But occasionally when she called him, his face would appear to knot itself into a frown—at any rate to assume a low sullen look, as if he expostulated "Why must you be interrupting me, Madam, while I am thinking of something else?" And now and then, Miss Chauncey fancied he would deliberately secrete himself or steal out and in of Post Houses unbeknown.

Miss Chauncey, too, would sometimes find him trotting from room to room as if on a visit of inspection. On his fifth birthday he had brought an immense mouse and laid it beside the patent toe-cap of her boot, as she sat knitting by the fire. She smiled and nodded merrily at him, as usual, but on this occasion he looked at her intently, and then deliberately shook his head. After that, he never paid the smallest attention to mouse or mouse-hole or mousery, and Miss Chauncey was obliged to purchase a cheese-bait trap, else she would have been overrun.

Almost any domestic cat may do things of this nature, and of course all this was solely on Sam's domestic side. For he shared house with Miss Chauncey and, like any two beings that live together, he was bound to keep up certain appearances. He met her half-way, as the saying goes. When, however, he was "on his own," he was no longer Miss Chauncey's Sam, he was no longer merely the cat at Post Houses, but just *himself*. He went back, that is, to his own free independent life; to his own private habits.

Then the moor on which he roved was his own country, and the humans and their houses on it were no more to him in his wild, privy existence than molehills or badgers' earths, or rabbits' mounds are to us. Of this side of his life his mistress knew practically nothing. She did not consider it. She supposed that Sam behaved like other cats, though it was evident that at times he went far abroad, for he now and again brought home a Cochin China chick, and the nearest Cochin China fowls were at the vicarage, a good four miles off. Sometimes of an evening, too, when Miss Chauncey was taking a little walk herself, she would see him—a swiftly-moving black speck—far along the road, hastening home. And there was more purpose expressed in his gait and appearance than ever Mr. Cullings showed!

It was pleasant to observe, too, when he came within miaouing distance how his manner changed. He turned at once from being a Cat into being a Domestic Cat. He was instantaneously no longer the Feline Adventurer, the Nocturnal Marauder and Haunter of Haggurdsdon Moor (though Miss Chauncey would not have so expressed it), but simply his mistress's spoiled pet, Sam. She loved him dearly. But, as again with human beings who are accustomed to live together, she did not *think* very much about him. It could not but be a shock then that latish afternoon, when without the slightest warning Miss Chauncey discovered that Sam was deliberately deceiving her!

She was brushing her thin brown front hair before her looking-glass. At this moment it hung down over her face like a fine loose veil. And as she always mused of other things when she was brushing her hair, she was somewhat absent-minded the while. Then suddenly on raising her eyes behind this mesh of hair, she perceived not only that Sam's reflection was in sight in the looking-glass, but that something a little mysterious was happening. Sam was sitting up as if to beg. There was nothing in that. It had been a customary feat of his since he was six months old. Still, for what might he be begging, no one by?

Now the window to the right of the chintz-valanced dressing-table was open at the top. Without, it was beginning to grow dark. All Haggurdsdon Moor lay hushed and still in the evening's coming gloom. And apart from begging when there was nothing to beg for, Sam seemed, so to speak, to be gesticulating with his paws. He appeared, that is, to be making signs, just as if there were someone or something looking in at the window at him from out of the air—which was quite impossible. And there was a look upon his face that certainly Miss Chauncey had never seen before.

She stayed a moment with hair-brush uplifted, her long lean arm at an angle with her head. On seeing this, Sam had instantly desisted from these motions. He had dropped to his fours again, and was now apparently composing himself for another nap. No; this too was a pretense, for presently as she watched, he turned restlessly about so that his whiskers were once again due South. His backward parts towards the window, he was now gazing straight in front of him out of a far from friendly face. Far indeed from friendly for a creature that has lived with you ever since he opened the eyes of his first kittenhood.

As if he had read her thoughts, Sam at that moment lifted his head to look at his mistress; she withdrew her eyes to the glass only in the nick of time and when she turned from her toilet there sat he—so serene in appearance, so puss-like, so ordinary once more that Miss Chauncey could scarcely believe anything whatever had been amiss. Had her eyes deluded her—her glass? Was that peculiar motion of Sam's fore-paws (almost as if he were knitting), was that wide excited stare due only to the fact that he was catching what was, to her, an invisible fly?

Miss Chauncey having now neatly arranged her "window-curtains"—the sleek loops of hair she wore on either side her high forehead—glanced yet again at the window. Nothing there but the silence of the moor; nothing there but the faint pricking of a star as the evening darkened.

Sam's cream was waiting on the hearthrug in the parlor as usual at five o'clock. The lamp was lit. The red blinds were drawn. The fire crackled in the grate. There they sat, these two; the walls of the four-cornered house beside the crossroads rising up above them like a huge oblong box under the immense starry sky that saucered in the wide darkness of the moor.

And while she so sat—with Sam there, seemingly fast asleep —Miss Chauncey was thinking. What had occurred in the bed-room that early evening had reminded her of other odd little bygone happenings. Trifles she had scarcely noticed but which now returned clearly to memory. How often in the past, for example, Sam at this hour would be sitting as if fast asleep (as now) his paws tucked neatly in, looking much like a stout alderman after a high dinner. And then suddenly, without warning, as if a distant voice had called him, he would leap to his feet and run straight out of the room. And somewhere in the house—door ajar or window agape, he would find his egress and be up and away into the night. This had been a common thing to happen.

Once, too, Miss Chauncey had found him squatting on his hind-quarters on the window-ledge of a little room that had been entirely disused since her fair little Cousin Milly had stayed at Post Houses when Miss Chauncey was a child of eight. She had cried out at sight of him, "You foolish Sam, you! Come in, sir. You will be tumbling out of the window next!" And she remembered as if it were yesterday that though at this he had stepped gingerly in at once from his dizzy perch, he had not looked at her. He had passed her without a sign.

On moonlight evenings, too—why, you could never be sure where he was. You could never be sure from what errand he had *returned*. Was she sure indeed where he was on *any* night? The longer she reflected, the deeper grew her doubts and misgivings. This night, at any rate, Miss Chauncey determined to keep watch. But she was not happy in doing so. She hated all manner of spying. They were old companions, Sam and she; and she, without him, in bleak Post Houses, would be sadly desolate. She loved Sam dearly. None the less, the spectacle of that afternoon haunted her, and it would be wiser to know all that there was to be known, even if for Sam's sake only.

Now Miss Chauncey always slept with her bedroom door ajar. She had slept so ever since her nursery days. Being a rather timid little girl, she liked in those far-away times to hear the grown-up voices downstairs and the spoons and forks clinking. As for Sam, he always slept in his basket beside her fireplace. Every morning there he would be, though on some mornings Miss Chauncey's eyes would open gently to find herself gazing steadily into his pale-green ones as he stood on his hind-paws, resting his front ones on her bed-side, and looking into her face. "Time for your milk, Sam?" his mistress would murmur. And Sam would mew, as distantly almost as a sea-gull in the height of the sky.

To-night, however, Miss Chauncey only pretended to fall asleep. It was difficult, however, to keep wholly awake, and she was all but drowsing off when there came a faint squeak from the hinge of her door, and she realized that Sam was gone out. After waiting a moment or two, she struck a match. Yes, there was his empty basket in the dark silent room, and presently from far away—from the steeple at Haggurdsdon Village—came the knolling of midnight.

Miss Chauncey placed the dead end of the match in the saucer of her candlestick, and at that moment fancied she heard a faint *whssh* at her window, as of a sudden gust or scurry of wind, or the wings of a fast-flying bird—of a wild goose. It even reminded Miss Chauncey of half-forgotten Guy Fawkes Days and the sound the stick of a rocket makes as it sweeps down through the air while its green and ruby lights die out in the immense heavens above. Miss Chauncey gathered up her long legs in the bed, drew on the flannel dressing-gown that always hung on her bed-rail, and lifting back the blind an inch or two, looked out of the window.

It was a high starry night, and a brightening in the sky above the roof seemed to betoken there must be a moon over the backward parts of the house. Even as she watched, a streak of pale silver descended swiftly out of the far spaces of the heavens where a few larger stars were gathered as if in the shape of a sickle. It was a meteorite; and at that very instant Miss Chauncey fancied she heard a faint remote dwindling *whssh* in the air. Was *that* a meteor too? Could she have been deceived? Was she being deceived in everything? She drew back.

And then, as if in deliberate and defiant answer, out of the distance, from what appeared to be the extreme end of her long garden, where grew a tangle of sloe-bushes, there followed a prolonged and as if half-secret caterwaul: very low—contralto, one might say—*Meearou-rou-rou-rou-rou.*

Heaven forbid. Was *that* Sam's tongue? The caterwauling ceased. Yet still Miss Chauncey could not suppress a shudder. She knew Sam's voice of old. But surely not that! Surely not that!

Strange and immodest, too, though it was to hear herself in that solitary place calling out in the dead of night, she none the less at once opened the window and summoned Sam by name. There was no response. The trees and bushes of the garden stood motionless; their faint shadows on the ground revealing how small a moon was actually in the sky, and how low it hung towards its setting. The vague undulations of the moor stretched into the distance. Not a light to be seen except those of the firmament. Again, and yet again, Miss Chauncey cried "Sam, Sam! Come away in! Come away in, sir, you bad creature!" Not a sound. Not the least stir of leaf or blade of grass.

When, after so broken a night, Miss Chauncey awoke a little late the next morning, the first thing her eyes beheld when she sat up in bed was Sam—couched as usual in his basket. It was a mystery, and an uneasy one. After supping up his morning bowl, he slept steadily on until noonday. This happened to be the day of the week when Miss Chauncey made bread. On and on she steadily kneaded the dough with her knuckled hands, glancing ever and again towards the motionless creature. With fingers clotted from the great earthenware bowl, she stood over him at last for a few moments, and looked at him closely.

He was lying curled round with his whiskered face to one side towards the fire. And it seemed to Miss Chauncey that she had never noticed before that faint peculiar grin on his face. "Sam!" she cried sharply. An eye instantly opened, fiercely green as if a mouse had squeaked. He stared at her for an instant; then the lid narrowed. The gaze slunk away a little, but Sam began to purr.

The truth of it is, all this was making Miss Chauncey exceedingly unhappy. Mr. Cullings called that afternoon, with a basket of some fine comely young sprats. "Them'll wake his Royal Highness up," he said. "They'm fresh as daisies. Lor, m'm, what a Nero that beast be!"

"Cats *are* strange creatures, Mr. Cullings," replied Miss Chauncey reflectively, complacently, supposing that Mr. Cullings had misplaced an *h* and had meant to say *an hero*. And Sam himself, with uplifted tail, and as if of the same opinion, was rubbing his head gently against her boot.

Mr. Cullings eyed her closely. "Why, yes, they be," he said. "What I says is, is that as soon as they're out of your sight, you are out of their mind. There's no more gratitood nor affection in a cat than in a pump. Though so far as the pump is concerned, the gratitood should be on our side. I knew a Family of Cats once what fairly druv their mistress out of house and home."

"But you wouldn't have a cat *only* a pet?" said Miss Chauncey faintly; afraid to ask for further particulars of the peculiar occurrence.

"Why no, m'm," said the carrier. "As the Lord made 'em, so they be. But I'll be bound they could tell some knotty stories if they had a human tongue in their heads!"

Sam had ceased caressing his mistress's foot, and was looking steadily at Mr. Cullings, his hair roughed a little about the neck and shoulders. And the carrier looked back.

"No, m'm. We wouldn't keep 'em," he said at last, "if they was *four* times that size. Or, not for long!"

Having watched Mr. Cullings's little cart bowl away into the distance, Miss Chauncey returned into the house, more disturbed than ever. Nor did her uneasiness abate when Sam refused even to sniff at his sprats. Instead, he crawled in under a low table in the kitchen, behind the old seaman's chest in which Miss Chauncey kept her kindling-wood. She fancied she heard his claws working in the wood now and again; once he seemed to be expressing his natural feelings in what vulgar people with little sympathy for animals describe as "swearing."

Her caressing "Sams," at any rate, were all in vain. His only reply was a kind of sneeze which uncomfortably resembled "spitting." Miss Chauncey's feelings had already been hurt. It was now her mind that suffered. Something the carrier had said, or the way he had said it, or the peculiar look she had noticed on his face when he was returning Sam's stare in the porch, haunted her thoughts. She was no longer young; was she becoming fanciful? Or must she indeed conclude that for weeks past Sam had been steadily deceiving her, or at any rate concealing his wanderings and his interests? What nonsense! Worse still:—Was she now so credulous as to believe that Sam had in actual fact been making signals—and secretly, behind her back—to some confederate that must either have been up in the sky, or in the moon!

Whether or not, Miss Chauncey determined to keep a sharper eye on him, if for his own sake only. She would at least make sure that he did not leave the house that night. But then: why not? she asked herself. Why shouldn't the creature choose his own hour and season? Cats, like owls, *see* best in the dark. They go best a-mousing in the dark, and may prefer the dark for their private, social, and even public affairs. Post Houses, after all, was only rather more than two miles from Haggurdsdon Village, and there were cats there in plenty. Poor fellow, her own dumb human company must sometimes be dull enough!

Such were Miss Chauncey's reflections; and as if to reassure her, Sam himself at that moment serenely entered the room and leapt up on to the empty chair beside her tea-table. As if, too, to prove that he had thought better of his evil temper, or to insinuate that there had been nothing amiss between himself and Mr. Cullings, he was licking his chops, and there was no mistaking the odor of fish which he brought in with him from his saucer.

"So you have thought better of it, my boy?" thought Miss Chauncey, though she did not utter the words aloud. And yet as she returned his steady feline gaze, she realized how difficult it was to read the intelligence behind those eyes. You might say that, Sam being only a cat, there was no meaning in them at all. But Miss Chauncey knew she couldn't have said it if such eyes had looked out of a *human* shape at her! She would have been acutely alarmed.

Unfortunately, and almost as if Sam had overheard his mistress's speculations regarding possible cat friends in the Village, there came at that moment a faint wambling mew beneath the open window. In a flash Sam was out of his chair and over the window-ledge, and Miss Chauncey rose only just in time to see him in infuriated pursuit of a slim sleek tortoise-shell creature that had evidently come to Post Houses in hope of a friendlier reception, and was now fleeing in positive fear of its life.

Sam returned from his chase as fresh as paint, and Miss Chauncey was horrified to detect—caught up between the claws of his right foot—a tuft or two of tortoise-shell fur, which, having composed himself by the fire, he promptly removed by licking.

Still pondering on these disquieting events, Miss Chauncey took her usual evening walk in the garden. Candytuft and virginia stock were blossoming along the shell-lined path, and roses were already beginning to blow on the high brick wall which shut off her narrow strip of land from the vast lap of the moor. Having come to the end of the path, Miss Chauncey pushed on a little further than usual, to where the grasses grew more rampant, and where wild headlong weeds raised their heads beneath her few lichenous apple trees. Still further down—for hers was a long, though narrow, garden—there grew straggling bushes of sloe, spiny white-thorn. These had blossomed there indeed in the moor's bleak springs long before Post Houses had raised its chimney-pots into the sky. Here, too, flourished a dense drift of dead nettles—their sour odor haunting the air.

And it was in this forlorn spot that—like Robinson Crusoe before her—Miss Chauncey was suddenly brought to a standstill by the sight of what appeared to be nothing else than a strange footprint in the mould. Nearby the footprint, moreover, showed what might be the impression of a walking-cane or possibly of something stouter and heavier—a crutch. Could she again be deceived? The footprint, it was true, was unlike most human footprints, the heel sunk low, the toe square. Might it be accidental? *Was* it a footprint?

Miss Chauncey glanced up across the bushes towards the house. It loomed gaunt and forbidding in the moorland dusk. And she fancied she could see, though the evening light might be deceiving her, the cowering shape of Sam looking out at her from the kitchen-window. To be watched! To be herself spied upon—and watched!

But then, of course, Sam was always watching her. What oddity was there in that? Where else would his sprats come from, his cream, his saucer of milk, his bowl of fresh well-water? Nevertheless Miss Chauncey returned to her parlor gravely discomposed.

It was an uncommonly still evening, and as she went from room to room locking the windows, she noticed there was already a moon in the sky. She eyed it with misgiving. And at last bedtime came, and when Sam, as usual, after a lick or two had composed himself in his basket, Miss Chauncey, holding the key almost challengingly within view, deliberately locked her bedroom door.

When she awoke next morning Sam was asleep in his basket as usual, and during the day-time he kept pretty closely to the house. So, too, on the Wednesday and the Thursday. It was not until the following Friday that having occasion to go into an upper bedroom that had no fireplace, and being followed as usual by Sam, Miss Chauncey detected the faint rank smell of soot in the room. No chimney, and a smell of soot! She turned rapidly on her companion; he had already left the room.

And when that afternoon she discovered a black sooty smear upon her own patchwork quilt, she realized not only that her suspicions had been justified, but that for the first time in his life Sam had deliberately laid himself down there in her absence. At this act of sheer defiance, she was no longer so much hurt as exceedingly angry. There was no doubt now. Sam was deliberately defying her. No two companions could share a house on such terms as these. He must be taught a lesson.

That evening, in full sight of the creature, having locked her bedroom door, she stuffed a large piece of mattress ticking into the mouth of her chimney and pulled down the register. Having watched these proceedings, Sam rose from his basket, and with an easy spring, leapt up on to the dressing-table. Beyond the window, the moor lay almost as bright as day. Ignoring Miss Chauncey, the creature squatted there steadily and openly staring into the empty skies, for a whole stretch of them was visible from where he sat.

Miss Chauncey proceeded to make her toilet for the night, trying in vain to pretend that she was entirely uninterested in what the animal was at. Faint sounds—not exactly mewings or growlings—but a kind of low inward caterwauling, hardly audible, was proceeding from his throat. But whatever these sounds might mean, Sam himself can have been the only listener. There was not a sign or movement at the window or in the world without. And then Miss Chauncey promptly drew down the blind. At this Sam at once raised his paw for all the world as if he were about to protest, and then, apparently thinking better of it, he pretended instead that the action had been only for the purpose of commencing his nightly wash.

Long after her candle had been extinguished, Miss Chauncey lay listening. Every stir and movement in the quiet darkness could be clearly followed. First there came a furtive footing and tapping at the register of the fireplace, so closely showing what was happening that Miss Chauncey could positively see in her imagination Sam on the hearth-stone, erecting himself there upon his hind-legs, vainly attempting to push the obstacle back.

This being in vain, he appeared to have dropped back on to his fours. Then came a pause. Had he given up his intention? No;

now he was at the door, pawing, gently scratching. Then a leap, even, towards the handle: but one only—the door was locked. Retiring from the door, he now sprang lightly again on to the dressing-table. What now was he at? By covertly raising her head a little from her pillow, Miss Chauncey could see him with paw thrust out, gently drawing back the blind from the moon-flooded window-pane. And even while she listened and watched, she heard yet again—and yet again—the faint *whssh* as of a wild swan cleaving the air; and then what might have been the cry of a bird, but which to Miss Chauncey's ears resembled a shrill cackle of laughter. At this Sam hastily turned from the window and without the least attempt at concealment pounced clean from the dressing-table on to the lower rail of her bed.

This unmannerly conduct could be ignored no longer. Poor Miss Chauncey raised herself in her sheets, pulled her night-cap a little closer down over her ears, and thrusting out her hand towards the chair beside the bed, struck a match and relit her candle. It was with a real effort that she then slowly turned her head and faced her night-companion. His hair was bristling about his body as if he had had an electric shock. His whiskers stood out at stiff angles with his jaws. He looked at least twice his usual size, and his eyes blazed in his head, as averting his face from her regard he gave vent to a low sustained *Miariou-rou-rou!*

"I say you shall *not*," cried Miss Chauncey at the creature. At the sound of her words, he turned slowly and confronted her. And it seemed that until that moment Miss Chauncey had never actually seen Sam's countenance as in actual fact it really was. It was not so much the grinning tigerish look it wore, but the sullen assurance upon it of what he wanted and that he meant to get it.

All thought of sleep was now out of the question. Miss Chauncey could be obstinate too. The creature seemed to shed an influence on the very air which she could hardly resist. She rose from her bed and thrusting on her slippers made her way to the window. Once more a peculiar inward cry broke out from the bed-rail. She raised the blind and the light of the moon from over the moor swept in upon her little apartment. And when she turned to remonstrate with her pet at his ingratitude; and at all this unseemliness and the deceit of his ways, there was something so menacing and pitiless in his aspect that Miss Chauncey hesitated no more.

"Well, mark me!" she cried in a trembling voice, "go out of the *door* you shan't. But if you enjoy soot, soot it shall be."

With that she thrust back the register with the poker, and drew down the bundle of ticking with the tongs. And before the fit of coughing caused by the consequent smotheration that followed had ceased, the lithe black shape had sprung from the bed-rail, and with a scramble was into the hearth, over the fire-bars, up the chimney, and away.

Trembling from head to foot, Miss Chauncey sat down on a cane rocking-chair that stood nearby to reflect what next she must be doing. *Wh-ssh! Wh-ssh!* Again at the window came that mysterious rushing sound, but now the flurrying murmur as of a rocket shooting up with its fiery train of sparks thinning into space, rather than the sound of its descending stick. And then in the hush that followed, there sounded yet again, like a voice from the foot of the garden—a caterwauling piercing and sonorous enough to arouse the sleeping cocks in the Haggurdsdon hen-roosts and for miles around. Out of the distance their chanticleering broke shrill on the night air; to be followed a moment afterwards by the tardy clang of midnight from the church steeple. Then once more, silence; utter quiet. Miss Chauncey returned to her bed, but that night she slept no more.

Her mind overflowed with unhappy thoughts. Her faith in Sam was gone. Far worse she had lost faith even in her affection for him. To have wasted that!—all the sprats, all the whitebait in the wide seas were as nothing by comparison. That Sam had wearied of her company was at least beyond question. It shamed her to think how much this meant to her—a mere animal! But she knew what was gone; knew how dull and spiritless in future the day's round would seem—the rising, the housework, the meals, a clean linen collar—the long, slow afternoon, forsaken and companionless! The solitary tea, her candle, prayers, bed—on and on. In what wild company was her cat Sam now? At her own refusal to face this horrid question it was as if she had heard the hollow clanging slam of an immense iron door.

Next morning—still ruminating on these strange events,

grieved to the heart at this dreadful rift between herself and one who had been her honest companion of so many years; ashamed, too, that Sam should have had his way with her when she had determined not to allow him to go out during the night—the next morning Miss Chauncey, as if merely to take a little exercise, once again ventured down to the foot of her garden. A faint, blurred mark (such as she had seen on the previous evening) in the black mould of what *might* be a footprint is nothing very much.

But now—in the neglected patch beyond the bushes of whitethorn and bramble—there was no doubt in the world appeared the marks of many. And surely no cats' paw-prints these! Of what use, too, to a cat could a crutch or a staff be? A staff or crutch which—to judge from the impression it had left in the mould—must have been at least as thick as a broomstick.

More disquieted and alarmed than ever over this fresh mystery, Miss Chauncey glanced up and back towards the chimney-pots of the house, clearly and sharply fretted against the morning light of the eastern skies. And she realized what perils even so sure-footed a creature as Sam had faced when he skirred up out of the chimney in his wild effort to merge into the night. Having thus astonishingly reached the rim of the chimney-pot—the burning stars above and the wilderness of the moor spread out far beneath and around him—he must have leaped from the top of the pot to a narrow brick ledge not three inches wide. Thence on to the peak of the roof and thence down a steep slippery slope of slates to a leaden gutter.

And how then? The thick tod of ivy matting the walls of the house reached hardly more than half-way up. Could Sam actually have plunged from gutter to tod? The very thought of such a peril drew Miss Chauncey's steps towards the house again, in the sharpest anxiety to assure herself that he was still in the land of the living.

And lo and behold, when she was but half-way on her journey, she heard a succession of frenzied cries and catcalls in the air from over the moor. Hastily placing a flower-pot by the wall, she stood on tiptoe and peered over. And even now, at this very moment, in full sight across the nearer slope of the moor she descried her

Sam, not now in chase of a foolishly trustful visitor, but hotly pursued by what appeared to be the complete rabblement of Haggurdsdon's cats. Sore spent though he showed himself to be, Sam was keeping his distance. Only a few lank tabby gibs, and what appeared to be a gray-ginger Manx (unless he was an ordinary cat with his tail chopped off) were close behind.

"Sam! Sam!" Miss Chauncey cried, and yet again, "Sam!" but in her excitement and anxiety her foot slipped on the flowerpot and in an instant the feline chase had fallen out of sight. Gathering herself together again, she clutched a long besom or garden broom that was leaning against the wall, and rushed down to the point at which she judged Sam would make his entrance into the garden. She was not mistaken, nor an instant too soon. With a bound he was up and over, and in three seconds the rabble had followed in frenzied pursuit.

What came after Miss Chauncey could never very clearly recall. She could but remember plying her besom with might and main amid this rabble and mellay of animals, while Sam, no longer a fugitive, turned on his enemies and fought them cat for cat. None the less, it was by no means an easy victory. And had not the over-fatted cur from the butcher's in Haggurdsdon— which had long since started in pursuit of this congregation of his enemies—had he not at last managed to overtake them, the contest might very well have had a tragic ending. But at sound of his baying and at sight of the cur's teeth snapping at them as he vainly attempted to surmount the wall, Sam's enemies turned and fled in all directions. And faint and panting, Miss Chauncey was able to fling down her besom and to lean for a brief respite against the trunk of a tree.

At last she opened her eyes again. "Well, Sam," she managed to mutter at last, "we got the best of them, then?"

But to her amazement she found herself uttering these friendly words into a complete vacancy. The creature was nowhere to be seen. His cream disappeared during the day, however, and by an occasional rasping sound Miss Chauncey knew that he once more lay hidden in his dingy resort behind the kindling-wood box. And there she did not disturb him.

Not until tea-time of the following day did Sam reappear.

And then—after attending to his hurts—it was merely to sit with face towards the fire, sluggish and sullen and dumb as a dog. It was not Miss Chauncey's "place" to make advances, she thought. She took no notice of the beast except to rub in a little hog's fat on the raw places of his wounds. She was rejoiced to find, however, that he kept steadily to Post Houses for the next few days, though her dismay was reawakened at hearing on the third night a more dismal wailing and wauling than ever from the sloe-bushes, even while Sam himself sat motionless beside the fire. His ears twitched, his fur seemed to bristle; he sneezed or spat, but remained otherwise motionless.

When Mr. Cullings called again, Sam at once hid himself in the coal-cellar, but gradually his manners towards Miss Chauncey began to recover their usual suavity. And within a fortnight after the full-moon, the two of them had almost returned to their old friendly companionship. He was healed, sleek, confident and punctual. No intruder of his species had appeared from Haggurdsdon. The night noises had ceased; Post Houses to all appearance—apart from its strange ugliness—was as peaceful and calm as any other solitary domicile in the United Kingdom.

But alas and alas. With the very first peeping of the crescent moon, Sam's mood and habits began to change again. He mouched about with a sly and furtive eye. And when he fawned on her, purring and clawing, the whole look of him was full of deceit. If Miss Chauncey chanced softly to enter the room wherein he sat, he would at once leap down from the window at which he had been perched as if in the attempt to prove that he had *not* been looking out of it. And once, towards evening, though she was no spy, she could not but pause at the parlor door. She had peeped through its crack as it stood ajar. And there on the hard sharp back of an old prie-Dieu chair that had belonged to her pious great-aunt Jemima, there sat Sam on his hind-quarters. And without the least doubt in the world he was vigorously signalling to some observer outside with his fore-paws. Miss Chauncey turned away sick at heart.

From that hour on Sam more and more steadily ignored and flouted his mistress, was openly insolent, shockingly audacious. Mr. Cullings gave her small help indeed. "If I had a cat, m'm, what had manners like that, after all your kindness, fresh fish and all every week, and cream, as I understand, not skim, I'd— I'd give him away."

"To whom?" said Miss Chauncey shortly.

"Well," said the carrier, "I don't know as how I'd much mind to who. Just a home, m'm."

"He seems to have no friends in the Village," said Miss Chauncey in as light a tone as she could manage.

"When they're as black as that, with them saucer eyes, you can never tell," said Mr. Cullings. "There's that old trollimog what lives in Hogges Bottom. She's got a cat that might be your Sam's twin."

"Indeed no, he has the mange," said Miss Chauncey, loyal to the end. The carrier shrugged his shoulders, climbed into his cart, and bowled away off over the moor. And Miss Chauncey returning into the house, laid the platter of silvery sprats on the table, sat down and burst into tears.

It was, then, in most ways a fortunate thing that the very next morning—three complete days, that is, before the next full-moontide—she received a letter from her sister-in-law in Shanklin, in the Isle of Wight, entreating her to pay them a long visit.

"My dear Emma, you must sometimes be feeling very lonely (it ran), shut up in that great house so far from any neighbors. We often think of you, and particularly these last few days. It's nice to have that Sam of yours for company, but after all, as George says, a pet is only a pet. And we do all think it's high time you took a little holiday with us. I am looking out of my window at this moment. The sea is as calm as a mill-pond, a solemn beautiful blue. The fishing boats are coming in with their brown sails. This is the best time of the year with us, because as it's not yet holyday-time there are few of those horrid visitors to be seen, and no crowds. George says you *must* come. He joins with me in his love as would Maria if she weren't out shopping, and will meet you at the station in the trap. Emmie is now free of her cough, only whooping when the memory takes her and never sick. And we shall all be looking forward to seeing you in a few days."

At this kindness, and with all her anxieties, Miss Chauncey all but broke down. When the butcher drove up in his cart an hour or two afterwards, he took a telegram for her back to the Village, and on the Monday her box was packed and all that remained was to put Sam in his basket in preparation for the journey. But I am bound to say it took more than the persuasions of his old protectress to accomplish this. Indeed Mr. Cullings had actually to hold the creature with his gloved hands and none too gently, while Miss Chauncey pressed down the lid and pushed the skewer in to hold it close.

"What's done's dumned done!" said the carrier, as he rubbed a pinch of earth into his scratches. "But what I say is, better done forever. Mark my words, m'm!"

Miss Chauncey took a shilling out of her large leather purse; but made no reply.

Indeed all this trouble proved at last in vain. Thirty miles distant from Haggurdsdon, at Blackmoor Junction, Miss Chauncey had to change trains. Her box and Sam's basket were placed together on the station platform beside half-a-dozen empty milk-cans and some fowls in a crate, and Miss Chauncey went to enquire of the station-master to make sure of her platform.

It was the furious panic-stricken cackling of these fowls that brought her hastily back to her belongings, only to find that by hook or by crook Sam had managed to push the skewer of the basket out of its cane loops. The wicker lid yawned open—the basket was empty. Indeed one poor gaping hen, its life fluttering away from its helpless body, was proof enough not only of Sam's prowess but of his cowardly ferocity.

A few days afterwards, as Miss Chauncey sat in the very room to which her sister-in-law had referred in her invitation, looking over the placid surface of the English Channel, the sun gently shining in the sky, there came a letter from Mr. Cullings. It was in pencil and written upon the back of a baker's bag:

"Dear Madam, i take the libberty of riteing you in referense to the Animall as how i helped put in is bawskit which has cum back returned empty agenn by rail me having okashun to cart sum hoppowles from Haggurdsdon late at nite ov Sunday. I seez him squattin at the parlor windy grimasin out at me fit to curdle your blood in your vanes and lights at the upper windies and a yowling and screetching such as i never hopes to hear agen in a Christian lokalety. And that ole wumman from Hogges Botom sitting in the porch mi own vew being that there is no good in the place and the Animall be bewhitched. Mr. Flint the fyshmunger agrees with me as how now only last mesures is of any use and as i have said afore i am wiling to take over the house the rent if so be being low and moddrate considering of the bad name it as in these parts around Haggurdsdon. I remain dear madam waitin your orders and oblidge yours truely William Cullings."

To look at Miss Chauncey you might have supposed she was a strong-minded woman. You might have supposed that this uncivil reference to the bad name her family house had won for itself would have mortified her beyond words. Whether or not, she neither showed this letter to her sister-in-law nor for many days together did she even answer it. Sitting on the Esplanade, and looking out to sea, she brooded on and on in the warm, salt, yet balmy air. It was a distressing problem. But "No, he must go his own way," she sighed to herself at last; "I have done my best for him."

What is more, Miss Chauncey never returned to Post Houses. She sold it at last, house and garden and for a pitiful sum, to the carrier, Mr. Cullings. By that time Sam had vanished, had been never seen again.

Not that Miss Chauncey was faithless of memory. Whenever the faint swish of a sea-gull's wing sounded in the air above her head; or the crackling of an ascending rocket for the amusement of visitors broke the silence of the nearer heavens over the sea; whenever even she became conscious of the rustling frou-frou of her Sunday watered-silk gown as she sallied out to church from the neat little villa she now rented on the Shanklin Esplanade— she never noticed such things without being instantly transported back in imagination to her bedroom at Post Houses, to see again that strange deluded animal, once her Sam, squatting there on her patchwork counterpane, and as it were knitting with his fore-paws the while he stood erect upon his hind.

THE PEACH STONE

By PAUL HORGAN

A S they all knew, the drive would take them about four hours, all the way to Weed, where *she* came from. They knew the way from travelling it so often, first in the old car, and now in the new one; new to them, that is, for they'd bought it second hand, last year, when they were down in Roswell to celebrate their tenth wedding anniversary. They still thought of themselves as a young couple, and *he* certainly did crazy things now and then, and always laughed her out of it when she was cross at the money going where it did, instead of where it ought to go. But there was so much droll orneriness in him when he did things like that that she couldn't stay mad, hadn't the heart; and the harder up they got, the more she loved him, and the little ranch he'd taken her to in the rolling plains just below the mountains.

This was a day in spring, rather hot, and the mountain was that melting blue that reminded you of something you could touch, like a china bowl. Over the sandy brown of the earth there was coming a green shadow. The air struck cool and deep in their breasts. *He* came from Texas, as a boy, and had lived here in New Mexico ever since. The word *home* always gave *her* a picture of unpainted, mouse-brown wooden houses in a little cluster by the rocky edge of the last mountain-step—the town of Weed, where Jodey Powers met and married her ten years ago.

They were heading back that way today.

Jodey was driving, squinting at the light. It never seemed so bright as now, before noon, as they went up the valley. He had a rangy look at the wheel of the light blue Chevvie—a bony man, but still fuzzed over with some look of a cub about him, perhaps the way he moved his limbs, a slight appealing clumsiness, that drew on thoughtless strength. On a rough road, he flopped and swayed at the wheel as if he were on a bony horse that galloped a little sidewise. His skin was red-brown from the sun. He had pale blue eyes, edged with dark lashes. *She* used to say he "turned them on" her, as if they were lights. He was wearing his suit, brown-striped, and a fresh blue shirt, too big at the neck. But he looked well-dressed. But he would have looked that way naked, too, for he communicated his physical essence through any covering. It was what spoke out from him to anyone who encountered him. Until Cleotha married him, it had given him a time, all right, he used to reflect.

Next to him in the front seat of the sedan was Buddy, their nine-year-old boy, who turned his head to stare at them both, his father and mother.

She was in back.

On the seat beside her was a wooden box, sandpapered, but not painted. Over it lay a baby's coverlet of pale yellow flannel with cross-stitched flowers down the middle in a band of bright colors. The mother didn't touch the box except when the car lurched or the tires danced over corrugated places in the gravel highway. Then she steadied it, and kept it from creeping on the seat cushions. In the box was coffined the body of their dead child, a two-year-old girl. They were on their way to Weed to bury it there.

In the other corner of the back seat sat Miss Latcher, the teacher. They rode in silence, and Miss Latcher breathed deeply of the spring day, as they all did, and she kept summoning to her aid the fruits of her learning. She felt this was a time to be intelligent, and not to give way to feelings.

The child was burned to death yesterday, playing behind the adobe chicken house at the edge of the arroyo out back, where the fence always caught the tumbleweeds. Yesterday, in a twist of wind, a few sparks from the kitchen chimney fell in the dry tumbleweeds and set them ablaze. Jodey had always meant to clear the weeds out; never seemed to get to it; told Cleotha he'd get to it next Saturday morning, before going down to Roswell; but Saturdays went by, and the wind and the sand drove the weeds into a barrier at the fence, and they would look at it every day without noticing, so habitual had the sight become. And so for many a spring morning, the little girl had played out there, behind the gray stucco house, whose adobe bricks showed through in one or two places.

The car had something loose; they believed it was the left rear fender; it chattered and wrangled over the gravel road.

Last night Cleotha stopped her weeping.

Today something happened; it came over her as they started out of the ranch lane, which curved up towards the highway. She looked as if she were trying to make the car go by leaning forward; or trying to see something beyond the edge of Jodey's head and past the windshield.

Of course, she had sight in her eyes; she could not refuse to look at the world. As the car drove up the valley that morning, she saw in two ways—one, as she remembered the familiar sights of this region where she lived; the other, as if for the first time she were really seeing, and not simply looking. Her heart began to beat faster as they drove. It seemed to knock at her breast as if to come forth and hurry ahead of her along the sunlighted lanes of the life after today. She remembered thinking that her head might be a little giddy, what with the sorrow in her eyes so bright and slowly shining. But it didn't matter what did it. Ready never to look at anyone or anything again, she kept still; and through the window, which had a meandering crack in it like a river on a map, all that she looked upon seemed dear to her. . . .

Jodey could only drive. He watched the road as if he expected it to rise up and smite them all over into the canyon, where the trees twinkled and flashed with bright drops of light on their new varnished leaves. Jodey watched the road and said to himself that if it thought it could turn him over or make him scrape the rocks along the near side of the hill they were going around, if it thought for one minute that he was not master of this car, this road, this journey, why, it was just crazy. The wheels spraying the gravel across the surface of the road travelled on outward from his legs; his muscles were tight and felt tired as if he were running instead of riding. He tried to *think*, but he could not; that is, nothing came about that he would speak to her of, and he believed that she sat there, leaning forward, waiting for him to say something to her.

But this he could not do, and he speeded up a little, and his jaw made hard knots where he bit on his own rage; and he saw a lump of something coming in the road, and it aroused a positive passion in him. He aimed directly for it, and charged it fast, and hit it. The car shuddered and skidded, jolting them. Miss Latcher took a sharp breath inward, and put out her hand to touch someone, but did not reach anyone. Jodey looked for a second into the rear-view mirror above him, expecting something; but his wife was looking out of the window beside her, and if he could believe his eyes, she was smiling, holding her mouth with her fingers pinched up in a little claw.

The blood came up from under his shirt, he turned dark, and a sting came across his eyes.

He couldn't explain why he had done a thing like that to her, as if it were she he was enraged with, instead of himself.

He wanted to stop the car and get out and go around to the back door on the other side, and open it, and take her hands, bring her out to stand before him in the road, and hang his arms around her until she would be locked upon him. This made a picture that he indulged like a dream, while the car ran on, and he made no change, but drove as before. . . .

The little boy, Buddy, regarded their faces, again, and again, as if to see in their eyes what had happened to them.

He felt the separateness of the three.

He was frightened by their appearance of indifference to each other. His father had a hot and drowsy look, as if he had just come out of bed. There was something in his father's face which made it impossible for Buddy to say anything. He turned around and looked at his mother, but she was gazing out the window, and did not see him; and until she should see him, he had no way of speaking to her, if not with his words, then with his eyes, but if she should happen to look at him, why, he would wait to see what she looked *like*, and if she *did*, why, then he would smile at her, because he loved her, but he would have to know first if she was still his mother, and if everything was all right, and things weren't blown to smithereens—*bla-a-a-sh! wh-o-o-m!*— the way the dynamite did when the highway came past their ranch house, and the men worked out there for months, and whole hillsides came down at a time. All summer long, that was, always something to see. The world, the family, he, between his father and mother, was safe.

He silently begged her to face towards him. There was no security until she should do so.

"Mumma?"

But he said it to himself, and she did not hear him this time, and it seemed intelligent to him to turn around, make a game of it (the way things often were worked out), and face the front, watch the road, delay as long as he possibly could bear to, and *then* turn around again, and *this* time, why, she would probably be looking at him all the time, and it would *be:* it would simply *be*.

So he obediently watched the road, the white gravel ribbon passing under their wheels as steadily as time.

He was a sturdy little boy, and there was a silver nap of child's dust on his face, over his plum-red cheeks. He smelled something like a raw potato that has just been pared. The sun crowned him with a ring of light on his dark hair. . . .

What Cleotha was afraid to do was break the spell by saying anything or looking at any of them. This was *vision,* it was all she could think; never had anything looked so in all her life; everything made her heart lift, when she had believed this morning, after the night, that it would never lift again. There wasn't anything to compare her grief to. She couldn't think of anything to answer the death of her tiny child with. In her first hours of hardly believing what had happened, she had felt her own flesh and tried to imagine how it would have been if she could have borne the fire instead of the child. But all she got out of that was a longing avowal to herself of how gladly she would have borne it. Jodey had lain beside her, and she clung to his hand until she heard how he breathed off to sleep. Then she had let him go, and had wept at what seemed faithless in him. She had wanted his mind beside her then. It seemed to her that the last degree of her grief was the compassion she had had to bestow upon him while he slept.

But she had found this resource within her, and from that time on, her weeping had stopped.

It was like a wedding of pride and duty within her. There was nothing she could not find within herself, if she had to, now, she believed.

And so this morning, getting on towards noon, as they rode up the valley, climbing all the way, until they would find the road to turn off on, which would take them higher and higher before they dropped down towards Weed on the other side, she welcomed the sights of that dusty trip. Even if she had spoken her vision aloud, it would not have made sense to the others.

Look at that orchard of peach trees, she thought. I never saw such color as this year; the trees are like lamps, with the light coming from within. It must be the sunlight shining from the other side, and, of course, the petals are very thin, like the love-liest silk; so any light that shines upon them will pierce right through them and glow on this side. But they are so bright! When I was a girl at home, up to Weed, I remember we had an orchard of peach trees, but the blossoms were always a deeper pink than down here in the valley.

My! I used to catch them up by the handful, and I believed when I was a girl that if I crushed them and tied them in a hand-kerchief and carried the handkerchief in my bosom that I would come to smell like peach blossoms and have the same high pink in my face, and the girls I knew said that if I took the peach *stone* and held it *long enough* in my hand, it would *sprout;* and I dreamed of this one time, though, of course, I knew it was nonsense; but that was how children thought and talked in those days—we all used to pretend that *nothing* was impossible, if you simply did it hard enough and long enough.

But nobody wanted to hold a peach stone in their hand until it *sprouted,* to find out, and we used to laugh about it, but I think we believed it. I think I believed it.

It seemed to me, in between my *sensible* thoughts, a thing that any woman could probably do. It seemed to me like a parable in the Bible. I could preach you a sermon about it this day.

I believe I see a tree down there in that next orchard which is dead; it has old black sprigs, and it looks twisted by rheumatism. There is one little shoot of leaves up on the top branch, and that is all. No, it is not dead, it is aged, it can no longer put forth blossoms in a swarm like pink butterflies; but there is that one little swarm of green leaves—it is just about the prettiest thing I've seen all day, and I thank God for it, for if there's anything I love, it is to see something growing. . . .

Miss Latcher had on her cloth gloves now, which she had taken from her blue cloth bag a little while back. The little winds that tracked through the moving car sought her out and chilled her nose, and the tips of her ears, and her long fingers, about which she had several times gone to visit various doctors. They had always told her not to worry, if her fingers seemed cold, and her hands moist. It was just a nervous condition, nothing to take very seriously; a good hand lotion might help the sensation, and in any case, some kind of digital exercise was a good thing—did she perhaps play the piano. It always seemed to her that doctors never *paid any attention* to her.

Her first name was Arleen, and she always considered this a very pretty name, prettier than Cleotha; and she believed that there was such a thing as an *Arleen look*, and if you wanted to know what it was, simply look at her. She had a long face, and pale hair; her skin was white, and her eyes were light blue. She was wonderfully clean, and used no cosmetics. She was a girl from "around here," but she had gone away to college, to study for her career, and what she had known as a child was displaced by what she had heard in classrooms. And she had to admit it: people *here* and *away* were not much alike. The men were different. She couldn't imagine marrying a rancher and "sacrificing" everything she had learned in college.

This poor little thing in the other corner of the car, for instance: she seemed dazed by what had happened to her—all she could do evidently was sit and stare out the window. And that man in front, simply driving, without a word. What did they have? What was their life like? They hardly had good clothes to drive to Roswell in, when they had to go to the doctor, or on some social errand.

But I must not think uncharitably, she reflected, and sat in an attitude of sustained sympathy, with her face composed in Arleenish interest and tact. The assumption of a proper aspect of grief and feeling produced the most curious effect within her, and by her attitude of concern she was suddenly reminded of the thing that always made her feel like weeping, though, of course, she never did, but when she stopped and *thought*—

Like that painting at college, in the long hallway leading from the Physical Education lecture hall to the stairway down to the girls' gym: an enormous picture depicting the Agony of the Christian Martyrs, in ancient Rome. There were some days when she simply couldn't look at it; and there were others when she would pause and see those maidens with their tearful faces raised in calm prowess, and in them, she would find herself— they were all Arleens; and after she would leave the picture she would proceed in her imagination to the arena, and there she would know with exquisite sorrow and pain the ordeals of two thousand years ago, instead of those of her own lifetime. She thought of the picture now, and traded its remote sorrows for those of today until she had sincerely forgotten the mother and the father and the little brother of the dead child with whom she was riding up the spring-turning valley, where noon was warming the dust that arose from the gravelled highway. It was white dust, and it settled over them in an enriching film, ever so finely. . . .

Jodey Powers had a fantastic scheme that he used to think about for taking and baling tumbleweed and making a salable fuel out of it. First, you'd compress it—probably down at the cotton compress in Roswell—where a loose bale was wheeled in under the great power-drop, and when the nigger at the handle gave her a yank, down came the weight, and packed the bale into a little thing, and then they let the steam exhaust go, and the press sighed once or twice, and just seemed to *lie* there, while the men ran wires through the gratings of the press and tied them tight. Then up came the weight, and out came the bale.

If he did that to enough bales of tumbleweed, he believed he'd get rich. Burn? It burned like a house afire. It had oil in it, somehow, and the thing to do was get it in shape for use as a fuel. Imagine all the tumbleweed that blew around the State of New Mexico in the fall, and sometimes all winter. In the winter, the weeds were black and brittle. They cracked when they blew against fence posts, and if one lodged there, then another one caught at its thorny lace; and next time it blew, and the sand came trailing, and the tumbleweeds rolled, they'd pile up at the same fence, and build out, locked together against the wires. The wind drew through them, and the sand dropped around them. Soon there was a solid-looking but airy bank of tumbleweeds built right to the top of the fence, in a long windward slope; and the next time the wind blew, and the weeds came, they would roll up the little hill of brittle twigs and leap off the other side of the fence, for all the world like horses taking a jump, and go galloping ahead of the wind across the next pasture on the plains, a black and witchy procession.

If there was an arroyo, they gathered there. They backed up in the miniature canyons of dirt-walled watercourses, which were dry except when it rained hard up in the hills. Out behind the house, the arroyo had filled up with tumbleweeds; and in November, when it blew so hard and so cold, but without bringing any snow, some of the tumbleweeds had climbed out and scattered, and a few had tangled at the back fence, looking like rusted barbed wire. Then there came a few more; all winter the bank grew. Many times he'd planned to get out back there and clear them away, just e-e-ease them off away from the fence posts, so's not to catch the wood up, and then set a match to the whole thing, and in five minutes, have it all cleared off. If he did like one thing, it was a neat place.

How Cleotha laughed at him sometimes when he said that, because she knew that as likely as not he would forget to clear the weeds away. And if he'd said it once he'd said it a thousand times, that he was going to gather up that pile of scrap iron from the front yard, and haul it to Roswell, and sell it—old car parts, and the fenders off a truck that had turned over up on the highway, which he'd salvaged with the aid of the driver.

But the rusting iron was still there, and he had actually come to have a feeling of fondness for it. If someone were to appear one night and silently make off with it, he'd be aroused the next day, and demand to know who had robbed him; for it was dear junk, just through lying around and belonging to him. What was his was part of him, even that heap of fenders that rubbed off on your clothes with a rusty powder, like caterpillar fur.

But even by thinking hard about all such matters, treading upon the fringe of what had happened yesterday, he was unable to make it all seem long ago, and a matter of custom and even of indifference. There was no getting away from it—if anybody was to blame for the terrible moments of yesterday afternoon, when the wind scattered a few sparks from the chimney of the kitchen stove, why he was.

Jodey Powers never claimed to himself or anybody else that he was any *better* man than another. But everything he knew and hoped for, every reassurance his body had had from other people, and the children he had begotten, had been knowledge to him that he was *as good* a man as any.

And of this knowledge he was now bereft.

If he had been alone in his barrenness, he could have solaced himself with heroic stupidities. He could have produced out of himself abominations, with the amplitude of biblical despair. But he wasn't alone; there they sat; there was Buddy beside him, and Clee in back, even the teacher, Arleen—even to her he owed some return of courage.

All he could do was drive the damned car, and keep *thinking* about it.

He wished he could think of something to say, or else that Clee would.

But they continued in silence, and he believed that it was one of his making. . . .

The reverie of Arleen Latcher made her almost ill, from the sad, sweet experiences she had entered into with those people so long ago. How wonderful it was to have such a rich life, just looking up things!—And the most wonderful thing of all was that even if they were beautiful, and wore semi-transparent garments that fell to the ground in graceful folds, the maidens were all pure. It made her eyes swim to think how innocent they went to their death. Could anything be more beautiful, and reassuring, than this? Far, far better. Far better those hungry lions, than the touch of lustful men. Her breath left her for a moment, and she closed her eyes, and what threatened her with real feeling— the presence of the Powers family in the faded blue sedan climbing through the valley sunlight towards the turn-off that led to the mountain road—was gone. Life's breath on her cheek was not so close. Oh, others had suffered. She could suffer.

"All that pass by clap their hands at thee: they hiss and wag their heads at the daughter of Jerusalem—"

This image made her wince, as if she herself had been hissed and wagged at. Everything she knew made it possible for her to see herself as a proud and threatened virgin of Bible times, which were more real to her than many of the years she had lived through. Yet must not Jerusalem have sat in country like this with its sandy hills, the frosty stars that were so bright at night, the simple Mexicans riding their burros as if to the Holy Gates? We often do not see our very selves, she would reflect, gazing ardently at the unreal creature which the name Arleen brought to life in her mind.

On her cheeks there had appeared two islands of color, as if she had a fever. What she strove to save by her anguished retreats into the memories of the last days of the Roman empire was surely crumbling away from her. She said to herself that she must not give way to it, and that she was just wrought up; the fact was she really *didn't* feel anything—in fact, it was a pity that she *couldn't* take that little Mrs. Powers in her arms, and comfort her, just *let* her go ahead and cry, and see if it wouldn't probably help some. But Miss Latcher was aware that she felt nothing that related to the Powers family and their trouble.

Anxiously she searched her heart again, and wooed back the sacrifice of the tribe of heavenly Arleens marching so certainly towards the lions. But they did not answer her call to mind, and she folded her cloth-gloved hands and pressed them together, and begged of herself that she might think of some way to comfort Mrs. Powers; for if she could do that, it might fill her own empty heart until it became a cup that would run over. . . .

Cleotha knew Buddy wanted her to see him; but though her heart turned towards him, as it always must, no matter what he asked of her, she was this time afraid to do it because if she ever lost the serenity of her sight now she might never recover it this day; and the heaviest trouble was still before her.

So she contented herself with Buddy's look as it reached her from the side of her eye. She glimpsed his head and neck, like a young cat's, the wide bones behind the ears, and the smooth but visible cords of his nape, a sight of him that always made her want to laugh because it was so pathetic. When she caressed him she often fondled those strenuous hollows behind his ears. Heaven only knew, she would think, what went on within the shell of that topknot! She would pray between her words and feelings that those unseen thoughts in the boy's head were ones that would never trouble him. She was often amazed at things in him which she recognized as being like herself; and at those of Buddy's qualities which came from some alien source, she suffered pangs of doubt and fear. He was so young to be a stranger to her!

The car went around the curve that hugged the rocky fall of a hill; and on the other side of it, a green quilt of alfalfa lay sparkling darkly in the light. Beyond that, to the right of the road, the land levelled out, and on a sort of platform of swept earth stood a two-room hut of adobe. It had a few stones cemented against the near corner, to give it strength. Clee had seen it a hundred times—the place where that old man Melendez lived, and where his wife had died a few years ago. He was said to be simple-minded, and claimed he was a hundred years old. In the past, riding by here, she had more or less delicately made a point of looking the other way. It often distressed her to think of such a helpless old man, too feeble to do anything but crawl out when the sun was bright and the wall was warm, and sit there, with his milky gaze resting on the hills he had known since he was born, and had never left. Somebody came to feed him once a day, and see if he was clean enough to keep his health. As long as she could remember, there'd been some kind of dog at the house. The old man had sons and grandsons and great grandsons—you might say a whole orchard of them, sprung from this one tree that was dying, but that still held a handful of green days in its ancient veins.

Before the car had quite gone by, she had seen him. The sun *was* bright, and the wall must have been warm, warm enough to give his shoulders and back a reflection of the heat which was all he could feel. He sat there on his weathered board bench, his hands on his branch of apple tree that was smooth and shiny from use as a cane. His house door was open, and a deep tunnel of shade lay within the sagged box of the opening. Cleotha leaned forward to see him, as if to look at him were one of her duties today. She saw his jaw moving up and down, not chewing, but just opening and closing. In the wind and flash of the car going by, she could not hear him; but from his closed eyes, and his moving mouth, and the way his head was raised, she wouldn't have been surprised if she had heard him singing. He was singing, some thread of song, and it made her smile to imagine what kind of noise it made, a wisp of voice.

She was perplexed by a feeling of joyful fulness in her breast, at the sight of the very same old witless sire from whom in the past she had turned away her eyes out of delicacy and disgust.

The last thing she saw as they went by was his dog, who came around the corner of the house with a caracole. He was a mongrel puppy, partly hound—a comedian by nature. He came prancing outrageously up to the old man's knees, and invited his response, which he did not get. But as if his master were as great a wag as he, he hurled himself backward, pretending to throw himself recklessly into pieces. Everything on him flopped and was flung by his idiotic energy. It was easy to imagine, watching the puppy-fool, that the sunlight had entered him as it had entered the old man. Cleotha was reached by the hilarity of the hound, and when he tripped over himself and plowed the ground with his flapping jowls, she wanted to laugh out loud.

But they were past the place, and she winked back the merriment in her eyes, and she knew that it was something she could never have told the others about. What it stood for, in her, they would come to know in other ways, as she loved them. . . .

Jodey was glad of one thing. He had telephoned from Hondo last night, and everything was to be ready at Weed. They would drive right up the hill to the family burial ground. They wouldn't have to wait for anything. He was glad, too, that the wind wasn't blowing. It always made his heart sink when the wind rose on the plains and began to change the sky with the color of dust.

Yesterday: it was all he could see, however hard he was *thinking* about everything else.

He'd been on his horse, coming back down the pasture that rose up behind the house across the arroyo, nothing particular in mind—except to make a joke with himself about how far along the peaches would get before the frost killed them all, *snap*, in a single night, like that—when he saw the column of smoke rising from the tumbleweeds by the fence. Now who could've lighted them, he reflected, following the black smoke up on its billows into the sky. There was just enough wind idling across the long front of the hill to bend the smoke and trail it away at an angle, towards the blue.

The hillside, the fire, the wind, the column of smoke.

Oh by God! And the next minute he was tearing down the hill as fast as his horse could take him, and the fire—he could see the flames now—the fire was like a bank of yellow rags blowing violently and torn in the air, rag after rag tearing up from the ground. Cleotha was there, and in a moment, so was he, but they were too late. The baby was unconscious. They took her up and hurried to the house, the back way where the screen door was standing open with its spring trailing on the ground. When they got inside where it seemed so dark and cool, they held the child between them, fearing to lay her down. They called for Buddy, but he was still at school up the road, and would not be home until the orange school bus stopped by their mailbox out front at the highway after four o'clock. The fire poured in cracking tumult through the weeds. In ten minutes there were only little airy lifts of ash off the ground. Everything was black. There were three fence posts still afire; the wires were hot. The child was dead. They let her down on their large bed.

He could remember every word Clee had said to him. They were not many, and they shamed him, in his heart, because he couldn't say a thing. He comforted her, and held her while she wept. But if he had spoken then, or now, riding in the car, all he could have talked about was the image of the blowing rags of yellow fire, and blue, blue, plaster blue behind and above, sky and mountains. But he believed that she knew why he seemed so short with her. He hoped earnestly that she knew. He might just be wrong. She might be blaming him, and keeping so still because it was more proper, now, to *be* still than full of reproaches.

But of the future, he was entirely uncertain; and he drove, and came to the turn-off, and they started winding in back among the sandhills that lifted them towards the rocky slopes of the mountains. Up and up they went; the air was so clear and thin that they felt transported, and across the valleys that dropped between the grand shoulders of the pine-haired slopes, the air looked as if it were blue breath from the trees. . . .

Cleotha was blinded by a dazzling light in the distance, ahead of them, on the road.

It was a ball of diamond-brilliant light.

It danced, and shook, and quivered above the road far, far ahead. It seemed to be travelling between the pine trees on either side of the road, and somewhat above the road, and it was like nothing she had ever seen before. It was the most magic and exquisite thing she had ever seen, and wildly, even hopefully as a child is hopeful when there is a chance and a need for something miraculous to happen, she tried to explain it to herself. It could be a star in daytime, shaking and quivering and travelling ahead of them, as if to lead them. It was their guide. It was shaped like a small cloud, but it was made of shine, and dazzle, and quiver. She held her breath for fear it should vanish, but it did not, and she wondered if the others in the car were smitten with the glory of it as she was.

It was brighter than the sun, whiter; it challenged the daytime, and obscured everything near it by its blaze of flashing and dancing light.

It was almost as if she had approached perfect innocence through her misery, and were enabled to receive portents that might not be visible to anyone else. She closed her eyes for a moment.

But the road curved, and everything travelling on it took the curve too, and the trembling pool of diamond-light ahead lost its liquid splendor, and turned into the tin signs on the back of a huge oil truck which was toiling over the mountain, trailing its links of chain behind.

When Clee looked again, the star above the road was gone. The road and the angle of the sun to the mountaintop and the two cars climbing upward had lost their harmony to produce the miracle. She saw the red oil truck, and simply saw it, and said to herself that the sun might have reflected off the big tin signs on the back of it. But she didn't believe it, for she was not thinking, but rather dreaming; fearful of awakening. . . .

The high climb up this drive always made Miss Latcher's ears pop, and she had discovered once that to swallow often prevented the disagreeable sensation. So she swallowed. Nothing happened to her ears. But she continued to swallow, and feel her ears with her cloth-covered fingers, but what really troubled her now would not be downed, and it came into her mouth as a taste; she felt giddy—that was the altitude, of course—when they got down the other side, she would be all right.

What it was was perfectly clear to her, for that was part of having an education and a trained mind—the processes of thought often went right on once you started them going.

Below the facts of this small family, in the worst trouble it had ever known, lay the fact of envy in Arleen's breast.

It made her head swim to realize this. But she envied them their entanglement with one another, and the dues they paid each other in the humility of the duty they were performing on this ride, to the family burial ground at Weed. Here she sat riding with them, to come along and be of help to them, and she was no help. She was unable to swallow the lump of desire that rose in her throat, for life's uses, even such bitter ones as that of the Powers family today. It had been filling her gradually, all the way over on the trip, this feeling of jealousy and degradation.

Now it choked her, and she knew she had tried too hard to put from her the thing that threatened her, which was the touch of life through anybody else. She said to herself that she must keep control of herself.

But Buddy turned around again, just then, slowly, as if he were a young male cat who just happened to be turning around to see what he could see, and he looked at his mother with his large eyes, so like his father's: pale petal-blue, with drops of light like the centres of cat's eyes, and dark lashes. He had a solemn look, when he saw his mother's face, and he prayed her silently to acknowledge him. If she didn't, why, he was still alone. He would never again feel safe about running off to the highway to watch the scrapers work, or the huge diesel oil tankers go by, or the cars with strange license plates—of which he had already counted thirty-two different kinds, his collection, as he called it. So if she didn't see him, why, what might he find when he came back home at times like those, when he went off for a little while just to play?

They were climbing down the other side of the ridge now. In a very few minutes they would be riding into Weed. The sights as they approached were like images of awakening to Cleotha. Her heart began to hurt when she saw them. She recognized the tall iron smokestack of the sawmill. It showed above the trees down on the slope ahead of them. There was a stone house which had been abandoned even when she was a girl at home here, and its windows and doors standing open always seemed to her to depict a face with an expression of dismay. The car dropped farther down—they were making that last long curve of the road to the left—and now the town stood visible, with the sunlight resting on so many of the unpainted houses and turning their weathered gray to a dark silver. Surely they must be ready for them, these houses; all had been talked over by now. They could all mention that they knew Cleotha as a little girl.

She lifted her head.

There were claims upon her.

Buddy was looking at her soberly, trying to predict to himself how she would *be*. He was ready to echo with his own small face whatever her face would show him.

Miss Latcher was watching the two of them. Her heart was racing in her breast.

The car slowed up. Now Cleotha could not look out the windows at the wandering earthen street, and the places alongside it. They would have to drive right through town, to the hillside on the other side.

"Mumma?" asked the boy softly.

Cleotha winked both her eyes at him, and smiled, and leaned towards him a trifle.

And then he blushed, his eyes swam with happiness, and he smiled back at her, and his face poured forth such radiance that Miss Latcher took one look at him, and with a choke, burst into tears.

She wept into her hands, her gloves were moistened, her square shoulders rose to her ears, and she was overwhelmed by what the mother had been able to do for the boy. She shook her head and made long gasping sobs. Her sense of betrayal was not lessened by the awareness that she was weeping for herself.

Cleotha leaned across to her, and took her hand, and murmured to her. She comforted her, gently.

"Hush, honey, you'll be all right. Don't you cry, now. Don't you think about us. We're almost there, and it'll soon be over. God knows you were mighty sweet to come along and be with us. Hush, now, Arleen, you'll have Buddy crying, too."

But the boy was simply watching the teacher, in whom the person he knew so well every day in school had broken up, leaving an unfamiliar likeness. It was like seeing a reflection in a pond, and then throwing a stone in. The reflection disappeared in ripples of something else.

Arleen could not stop.

The sound of her 'hooping made Jodey furious. He looked into the rear-view mirror and saw his wife patting her and comforting her. Cleotha looked so white and strained that he was frightened, and he said out, without turning around: "Arleen, you cut that out, you shut up, now. I won't have you wearin' down Clee, God damn it, you quit it!"

But this rage, which arose from a sense of justice, made Arleen feel guiltier than ever; and she laid her head against the car window, and her sobs drummed her brow bitterly on the glass.

"Hush," whispered Cleotha, but she could do no more, for they were arriving at the hillside, and the car was coming to a stop. They must awaken from this journey, and come out onto the ground, and begin to toil their way up the yellow hill, where the people were waiting. Over the ground grew yellow grass that was turning to green. It was like velvet, showing dark or light, according to the breeze and the golden afternoon sunlight. It was a generous hill, curving easily and grandly as it arose. Beyond it was only the sky, for the mountains faced it from behind the road. It was called Schoolhouse Hill, and at one time, the whole thing had belonged to Cleotha's father; and before there was any schoolhouse crowning its noble swell of earth, the departed members of his family had been buried halfway up the gentle climb.

Jodey helped her out of the car, and he tried to talk to her with his holding fingers. He felt her trembling, and she shook her head at him. Then she began to walk up there, slowly. He leaned into the car and took the covered box in his arms, and followed her. Miss Latcher was out of the car on her side, hiding from them, her back turned, while she used her handkerchief and positively clenched herself back into control of her thoughts and sobs. When she saw that they weren't waiting for her, she hurried, and in humility, reached for Buddy's hand to hold it for him as they walked. He let her have it, and he marched, watching his father, whose hair was blowing in the wind and sunshine. From behind, Jodey looked like just a kid. . . .

And now for Cleotha, her visions on the journey appeared to have some value, and for a little while longer, when she needed it most, the sense of being in blind communion with life was granted her, at the little graveside where all those kind friends were gathered, on the slow slope up of the hill on the summit of which was the schoolhouse of her girlhood.

It was afternoon, and they were all kneeling towards the upward rise, and Judge Crittenden was reading the prayer book.

Everything left them but a sense of their worship, in the present.

And a boy, a late scholar, is coming down the hill from the school, the sunlight edging him; and his wonder at what the people kneeling there are doing is, to Cleotha, the most memorable thing she is to look upon today; for she has resumed the life of her infant daughter, whom they are burying, and on whose behalf, something rejoices in life anyway, as if to ask the mother whether love itself is not ever-living. And she watches the boy come discreetly down the hill, trying to keep away from them, but large-eyed with a hunger *to know* which claims all acts of life, for him, and for those who will be with him later; and his respectful curiosity about those kneeling mourners, the edge of sunlight along him as he walks away from the sun and down the hill, is of all those things she saw and rejoiced in, the most beautiful; and at that, her breast is full, with the heaviness of a baby at it, and not for grief alone, but for praise.

"I believe, I believe!" her heart cries out in her, as if she were holding the peach stone of her eager girlhood in her woman's hand.

She puts her face into her hands, and weeps, and they all move closer to her. Familiar as it is, the spirit has had a new discovery. . . .

Jodey then felt that she had returned to them all; and he stopped seeing, and just remembered, what happened yesterday; and his love for his wife was confirmed as something he would never be able to measure for himself or prove to her in words.